200 kilometres around
BRISBANE

**Your essential guide to Brisbane,
South-east Queensland and
Northern New South Wales**

J & C Cunnington, M Lynch

1st edition

Published in Australia by Gregory's Publishing Company
(A division of Universal Press Pty Ltd)
ACN 000 087 132

Marketed and distributed by Universal Press Pty Ltd
New South Wales: 1 Waterloo Road,
Macquarie Park 2113
Ph: (02) 9857 3700 Fax: (02) 9888 9850
Queensland: 1 Manning Street, South Brisbane 4101
Ph: (07) 3844 1051 Fax: (07) 3844 4637
South Australia: Freecall: 1800 021 987

Victoria: 585 Burwood Road,
Hawthorn 3122
Ph: (03) 9818 4455 Fax: (03) 9818 6123
Western Australia: 38a Walters Drive,
Osborne Park 6017
Ph: (08) 9244 2488 Fax: (08) 9244 2554
International distribution
Ph: (02) 9857 3700 Fax: (02) 9888 9850

The Publisher would be pleased to receive additional or updated material, or suggestions for future editions. Please address these to the Publishing Manager, Maps and Guides at Universal Press Pty Ltd.
If you would like to use any of the maps in this book please contact the CMS Manager at Universal Press Pty Ltd.

National Library of Australia Cataloguing-in-Publication data

ISSN 1443-119X
Gregory's 200 kilometres around Brisbane: your essential guide to
Brisbane, South-east Queensland and Northern New South Wales.

1st ed.
Includes index.
ISBN 0 7319 1147 4.

1. Brisbane (Qld) – Guidebooks. 2. Brisbane (Qld) – Tours. 3.
Queensland – Guidebooks. 4. Queensland – Tours. I. Title: Two
hundred kilometres around Brisbane. II. Title: 200 kilometres
around Brisbane.

Publishing Manager: Greg Reid
Production Manager: Harold Yates
Production Editor: Kim Ross
Book Design: Jason Gemenis
Typesetting: Kerry Klinner
Proof Reader: Joy McCarthy
Cartographic Design: Laurie Whiddon, Map Illustrations
Cartography: Laurie Whiddon, Map Illustrations

Photographic Research: Kathleen Gandy, Col Cunnington
Cover photographs: front, Brisbane CBD, Gold Coast,
Breaka Beach, Southbank, Spring Bluff Railway Station,
Toowoomba, back, Brisbane CBD, Noosa River,
sunflowers, Toowoomba, mountain country, Southern
Downs (Tourism Queensland), Byron Bay beach (Tourism
New South Wales).
Printed by Australian Print Group, Maryborough, Victoria

Disclaimer
The authors and publisher disclaim any responsibility to any person for loss or damage suffered from any use of this guide for any purpose. While considerable care has been taken by the authors and the publisher in researching and compiling the guide, the authors and the publisher accept no responsibility for errors or omissions. No person should rely upon this guide for the purpose of making any business, investment or real estate decision.

The representation of any maps of any road or track is not necessarily evidence of public right of way. Third parties who have provided information to the authors and publisher concerning the roads and other matters did not warrant to the authors and publisher that the information was complete, accurate or current or that any of the proposals of any body will eventuate and, accordingly, the authors and publisher provide no such warranty.

Contents

Acknowledgments

The Publisher would like to gratefully acknowledge the following organisations and individuals for their generosity in supplying photographs and images, and for their permission to reproduce photographic material used in this book.

Tourism House
55 Harrington Street
The Rocks NSW 2000
Ph: 61 2 9931 1111
Fax: 61 2 9931 1490
www.tourism.nsw.gov.au

PO Box 1399
Ballina NSW 2478
Ph: 61 2 6686 8282
Fax: 61 2 6686 9090

PO Box 1107
Tamworth NSW 2340
Ph: 61 2 6766 8484
Fax: 61 2 6766 5332

Beaudesert Shire Council: p.234;
Blue Tongue Helicopters: p.66 top left;
Boonah Shire Council: p.231;
Boondooma Homestead: p.157 bottom right;
Brisbane City Council: p.31;
Brisbane Tourism: p.17 bottom; p.21;
Caboolture Shire Council: p.42 bottom left, bottom right; p.44; p.48 bottom left; p.137 top right, bottom right; p.138; p.140 top right;
Cooloola Regional Tourism Development Bureau: p.74 bottom right; p.75; p.83; p.85; p.113 top; p.114; p.115 bottom left, bottom right; p.117 top right; p.127 bottom right;
Crystal Castle: p.272 top right;
Elvis Parsley's Grapelands: p.140 bottom right;
Fiona Parsons: p.175 top right;
Fraser Coast and South Burnett Regional Tourism Board Ltd: p. 95 top left; p.98 bottom right; p.104 top left;
Gatton Potato Festival: p.215;
Gold Coast Tourism Bureau Ltd: p.55; p.218 top left; p.226 bottom left; p.228; p.233 top right, bottom right; p.257 bottom; p.261 top left; p.275 bottom left; p.248 bottom left; p.249 top left; p.253 bottom right;
Hillview Crafts and Garden: p.155 bottom right;
Kilcoy Shire Council: p.124 bottom left; p.136

Kilkivan Great Horse Ride: p.113 bottom right;
Kingaroy Wines: p.163;
Kingston Park Raceway: p.35;
Marek Coowatch: p.28;
Maroochy Shire Council: p.78 top left;
Melaleuca Station: p.272 bottom;
New South Wales National Parks and Wildlife Service: p.47, bottom right; p.74 top left; p.200 bottom right; p.257 top right; p.271 top left;
Pink Poodle Motel: p.250;
Pioneer Plantation: p.273 top left;
Redlands Tourism: p.19; p.38; p.58 top right, bottom right; p.61 bottom right;
Robyn South: p.235;
South Stradbroke Island Resort: p.54 bottom left;
Southern Downs Tourist Association: p.192; p.193 bottom; p.196; p.197 bottom right; p.199 top right;
Superbee Honey Factory: p.82;
Tenterfield and District Visitors Centre: p.258;
Toowoomba & Golden West Regional Tourist Association: p.174; p.179 bottom right; p.180 top left;
Tourism New South Wales: p.254; p.255; p.259 top right, bottom right; p.261 bottom right; p.262; p.263 top right, bottom left; p.267; p.268; p.269; p.270; p.271 bottom right; p.275 top left, bottom right; p.276 bottom;

Tourism Queensland: p.8; p.9; p.11 top right, bottom left; p.12 top right, bottom left; p.13 top right, bottom; p.14; p.15 top left, top right, bottom; p.16; p.17 top right; p.18 top left, bottom right; p.25 top left, bottom; p.25 top right, bottom left; p.26 top right, bottom; p.27; p.29 top left, bottom left; p.30; p.32 top left, bottom right; p.34; p.39; p.41; p.43; p.45; p.46; p.47 bottom left; p.48 top right; p.49; p.50; p.51 bottom left, bottom right; p.52; p.53; p.54; p.56; p.57 top right; p.59; p.61 top right; p.62; p.63; p.65 top left, bottom right; p.66 bottom right; p.67 top left, bottom right; p.68; p.69; p.70; p.71; p.73; p.76 top left, bottom right; p.77; p.78 bottom right; p.79; p.80; p.81; p.86 top right, bottom left; p.86; p.87; p.88; p.89; p.91; p.92; p.93 top left, bottom left; p.94 top left, bottom right; p.95 bottom right; p.96 bottom left, bottom right; p.97 top right, bottom; p.98 bottom right; p.99 top right, bottom; p.100 bottom left, bottom right; p.101; p.102 top; bottom left; p.103 top right, bottom; p.104 top right, bottom right; p.105; p.106; p.107; p.108; p.111; p.112; p.115 top left; p.117 top left, bottom right; p.118; p.119; p.120; p.121 top right, bottom left; p.122; p.123; p.124 bottom right; p.125; p.126 top, bottom left; p.127 top left; p.128; p.129; p.130; p.131; p.133; p.134 bottom left, bottom right; p.135 top, bottom right; p.138 bottom; p.139; p.141; p.143 top right, bottom; p.144; p.145; p.148; p.149; p.151; p.152;

p.153; p.154; p.155 bottom left; p.156 top, bottom left; p.157 top right, bottom left; p.158; p.159; p.160; p.161; p.162; p.164 top, bottom right; p.165 top left, top right, bottom right; p.167; p.168; p.169; p.171; p.172 top left, bottom left; p.173 top right, bottom right; p.175 top left, bottom left; p.176; p.178; p.179 top left; p.180 bottom left; p.181; p.182 top, bottom left; p.183; p.185; p.186; p.189; p.189 top right, bottom left; p.190; p.191; p.193 top right; p.194 bottom left, bottom right; p.197 top right; p.198; p.199 bottom; p.200 bottom right; p.201; p.202 top left, bottom right; p.203; p.205 top left, top right, bottom left; p.206; p.207; p.208; p.209; p.211; p.212; p.361; p.214; p.216; p.217; p.218 bottom; p.220; p.222; p.223; p.224; p.225; p.226 top left, bottom right; p.227 bottom left, bottom right; p.229; p.236; p.237; p.239; p.240 top left, bottom left; p.241 top left, bottom right; p.242; p.243; p.245; p.246; p.247 bottom left, bottom right; p.248 top left, bottom right; p.249 bottom right; p.251 top left, bottom right; p.252; p.273 bottom right;

Tourism Sunshine Coast: p.109;
Tweed River Houseboats: p.274;
Viewfinder Australia Photo Library: p.20;
Wintersun Rock and Roll Nostalgia Festival: p.260

For further travel information contact

BRISBANE TOURISM
Ground Floor, City Hall
King George Square
Brisbane Qld 4000
PO Box 12260 Elizabeth St
Brisbane QLD 4002
Phone: (07) 3221 8411
Fax: (07) 3229 5126
Email: enquiries@brisbanetourism.com.au
Website: brisbanetourism.com.au

GOLD COAST TOURISM BUREAU
2nd Floor
64 Ferny Avenue
Surfers Paradise Qld 4217
PO Box 7091
Gold Coast Mail Centre Qld 9726
Phone: (07) 5592 2699
Fax: (07) 5570 3144

TOURISM SUNSHINE COAST
The Wharf Complex
Cnr River Esplanade & Parkyn Parade
Mooloolaba Qld 4557
Phone: (07) 5477 7311
Fax: (07) 5477 7322
Email: tourism@sunzine.net

**FRASER COAST SOUTH BURNETT
REGIONAL TOURISM BOARD**
388 Kent Street
Maryborough Qld 4650
PO Box 446
Maryborough Qld 4650
Phone: (07) 4122 3444
Fax: (07) 4122 3426
Email: info@frasercoast.org
Website: www.frasercoast.org

**TOOWOOMBA & GOLDEN WEST
REGIONAL TOURIST ASSOCIATION**
Downs Business Cente
4 Little Street
Toowoomba Qld 4350
PO Box 3090
Toowoomba Qld 4350
Phone: (07) 4632 1988
Fax: (07) 4632 4404
Email: tgwrta@iqnetlink.com.au

**SOUTHERN DOWNS
TOURIST ASSOCIATION**
Warwick Tourist Information Centre
49 Albion Street
Warwick Qld 4370
PO Box 900
Warwick Qld 4370
Email: sdta@flexi.net.au
Website: www.qldsoutherndowns.org.au

WHERE ELSE BUT
200KM AROUND
BRISBANE

Brisbane®
City of Sun Days

THE *ever* CHANGING
ALWAYS
amazing GOLD COAST

SUNSHINE COAST

Just north of Brisbane. Just perfect.

Queensland's
Fraser Coast
Perfect by Nature

South East Queensland
COUNTRY
WAKE UP TO THE BEAUTY OF IT.

TOURISM
QUEENSLAND

Gregory's 200 kilometres around

BRISBANE

Your essential guide to Brisbane, South-east Queensland & Northern New South Wales

Tour Regions

- Brisbane
- Moreton Bay Islands
- The Sunshine Coast
- The Fraser Coast
- Gympie, Mary Valley and the Blackall Range
- The Brisbane Valley, Caboolture and Pine Rivers
- Kingaroy, the Bunya Mountains and the South Burnett
- Toowoomba, the Eastern Downs and Steele Rudd Country
- Warwick, Stanthorpe and the Southern Downs
- Ipswich, Lockyer Valley and the Scenic Rim
- Gold Coast
- Northern New South Wales

SCALE 1:2,100,000

0   20   40   60   80   100

Kilometres

COPYRIGHT © UNIVERSAL PRESS PTY LTD (PUBLISHER) 2000

Region Maps

.... Dual Carriageway
.... Through Route
.... Major Road
.... Minor Road
.... Railway

Tour/District Maps

.... Dual Carriageway
.... Through Route
.... Major Road
.... Minor Road
.... Railway
.... Walking Track

Street Maps

RIVERSIDE EXPWY .... Dual Carriageway
VULTURE ST .... Through Route
GEORGE RD .... Major Road
MARY ST .... Minor Road
.... Railway
.... Walking Track

Explanation of Map Symbols

.... Airport/Airfield
.... Boat Ramp
.... Camping Ground
.... Caravan Park
.... Cave
.... Cycleway
.... Ferry
.... Golf Course
.... Hospital
.... Lighthouse
.... Lookout 360°, 180°
.... Metroad Route Marker
.... Monument
.... Museum
.... National Route Marker
.... One Way Traffic
.... Parking
.... Patrolled Beach
.... Picnic Area
.... Point of Interest
.... State Route Marker
.... Toilets
.... Tourist Information
.... Mall/Plaza
.... National Park, State Forest, Park, Reserve

Brisbane
city of Sun Days ™

Left: **City skyline, Brisbane**
Right: **Botanical Gardens: City**

Brisbane

Take a morning stroll through the heady scent of frangipani flowers, splash about at inner-city Breaka Beach, glide down the Brisbane River on a cruise boat or dance the night away at one of the many clubs around town. This is Brisbane, the 'most livable city in Australia', the capital city of Qld, and a place that seduces locals and visitors alike.

The 3rd largest city on the continent and still growing, Brisbane has a temperate climate, an easygoing pace and great physical charm. Its picturesque wooden houses are set among lush green subtropical foliage, including giant Moreton Bay Fig trees, and the songs of native birds such as the kookaburra fill the air. Brisbane is also a thriving metropolis, with all the delights of city life. Giving impetus to this is its position as the gateway to the internationally famous attractions of the Gold Coast (p.237), Far North Qld and the tropical islands that dot the coastline from Cape York Peninsula to Tweed Heads.

Whether you prefer sipping a glass of wine on a latticed verandah or having a spin of the wheel at the Treasury Casino, there is something for everyone in this pretty place, with its appealing mixture of the casual and the cultivated, the flamboyant and the homespun.

ℹ Tourist information

Brisbane City Council Call Centre
Ph: (07) 3403 8888
www.brisbane.qld.gov.au

Brisbane Tourism Information Centres
Queen St Mall, Brisbane 4000
Ph: (07) 3229 5918
City Hall, King George Sq, Brisbane 4000
Ph: (07) 3221 8411 and then dial 1
www.visitbrisbane.com.au

Naturally Queensland Information Centre (EPA)
(info on national parks)
Ground floor, 160 Ann St, Brisbane 4000
Ph: (07) 3227 8187
www.env.qld.gov.au

Queensland Government Travel Centre
243 Edward St, Brisbane 4000
Ph: (07) 3874 2800
www.Qld-travel-centre.com.au

Trans Info
(public transport info hotline)
Ph: (07) 131 230

Must see, must do

★ **Boondall Wetlands** (p.30)
★ **Brisbane River cruise** (p.14)
★ **Brisbane Botanical Gardens: City** (p.31)
★ **Cleveland Pt** (p.18)
★ **Mt Coot-tha Lookout** (p.30)

Radio stations

4QR ABC: AM 612
Radio Bay: FM 100.3 (Bayside)
Radio Logan: FM 101 (Southside)
4-MMM: FM 104.5
4-ZZZ: FM 102.2 (Community Radio)
Radio B: FM 105.3

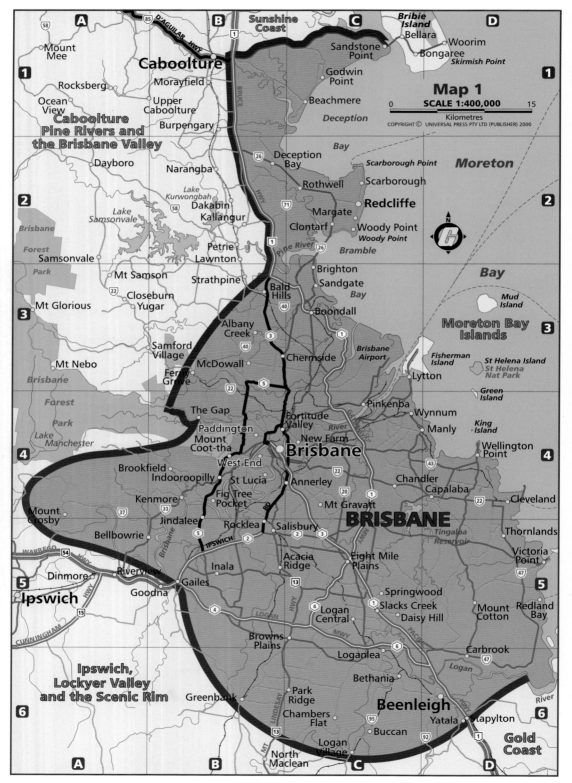

Natural features

Dominating the landscape of Brisbane is the Brisbane River, a fresh-water river which curves its way from the Conondale Ra, east of Kingaroy, to Moreton Bay. The river's sweep through the heart of the city breaks Brisbane into pockets of distinctive local cultures, and the water gives an extra sparkle to the sunshine typical of this SE corner of Qld. The city centre itself is flat, bounded by 11 hills and, further out, the Glass House Mts to the north and the D'Aguilar Ra — including Mt Glorious and Mt Nebo — and Mt Coot-tha to the west. Ridges carved into the steep rockface mark major road routes, especially in the inner suburbs. The metropolis stretches north towards the Sunshine Coast and south towards the Gold Coast. Westwards lies the Darling Downs region, and to the east the Pacific Ocean.

Brisbane's subtropical location means that it experiences high humidity in the summer months (Dec–Mar). For the remainder of the year, the average temperature is a mild 25°C, with dry winters. Blooms such as frangipani and poinciana add colour and spice to the scenery in summer, and mangoes grow within reach of the casual passerby. The flowering of the city's many jacarandas gives the city a lavishly lilac look in Oct–Nov. All year round, butterflies, birds and bats are in evidence, and umbrella trees, banana palms and a variety of ferns grow in abundance. Small wonder that Brisbane is now officially called the 'City of Sun Days'!

History

The large expanse of land making up present-day Brisbane was once the dwelling place of several Aboriginal peoples who belonged to the Yugarabul language group. These peoples were defined by their relationship to the river, with 2 distinct economies. One was in the coastal region, where fishing was the main source of food; the other was in the sub-coastal region, where game such as kangaroos was hunted. Firestick farming — the burning of grasslands to produce further growth — also provided food for this latter group.

Like several other major cities in Australia, Brisbane's white settlement began in the form of a penal colony. In 1823 John Oxley, Surveyor-General of the Colony of NSW, was sent northwards to investigate sites for a remote settlement removed from the distractions of free settlers. He charted the Brisbane River and the Moreton Bay area. One year later, the Moreton Bay penal settlement was established at Redcliffe, north of the present-day CBD. The convicts and their guards were moved in 1825 to what is now the centre of Brisbane in response to inadequate fresh water supplies, indigenous unrest and the failure of introduced plant species on the Redcliffe Peninsula.

'See you round the ridges'
This local expression refers both to Brisbane's hilly geography and its effect on social life. The steeply ridged land around the inner suburbs can make face-to-face communication a complicated business.

Flowering jacarandas

What's in a name?
In an affectionate reference to Brisbane's occasionally glitzy style, locals refer to the city as 'Brisvegas'. An alternative is 'Brissie', an example of the Australian custom of abbreviating names.

Over the following years Brisbane grew into a town, with the Brisbane River as its lifeline to the outside world. There was a building boom between the 1860s and the 1880s, the evidence of which may be seen in the grand public edifices still standing today. In the 20th century, Brisbane became a city. This status was consolidated by the 1984 Commonwealth Games and the 1988 World Expo, 2 events with a long-lasting influence on local cuisine, culture and architecture.

While Qld is the only Australian state in which more of the population live outside the metropolis than otherwise, Brisbane holds its own, helped along by a healthy economy and a diverse cultural life. Brisbane currently has a population of 1.6 million, made up of people from all over the world.

Brisbane River

Getting there

By air

Brisbane Airport (with separate domestic and international terminals) is located approximately 21km from the CBD. Regional airlines such as **Flight West** and **Eastern Australia** also use the airport to link rural centres and tourist spots to Brisbane. Taxis offer a quick 20min ride into town. A coach shuttle, **Skytrans**, operates daily. It leaves every 30min,

taking the same amount of time to reach the city, and terminates at the Brisbane Transit Centre, Roma St, which is 0.5km from the CBD. Ph: (07) 3236 1000

By road

The Bruce Hwy, commencing in Fortitude Valley, takes travellers northwards towards the Sunshine Coast, while the Gold Coast Hwy heads south from the Riverside Expressway. The Expressway runs

Brisbane on the WWW

Brisbane Stories is a website dedicated to local cultural life and history. The areas covered are:

★ **Art Circuit** — a virtual tour of Brisbane's galleries;

★ **The Gabba** — info about the historic inner-city suburb of Woolloongabba;

★ **Boondall Wetlands** — a narrative about the establishment and survival of this large community-managed wetlands park in the city's north;

★ **Deck to Deck** — documentation tracing the waves of migration to Brisbane since white settlement;

★ **Maggil's Country** — an exploration of Moggill Creek by Maggil, a fictional eastern water dragon;

★ **Literary Trail** — an electronic tour down Albert St by Qld writers.

There are also links to related sites.

brisbanestories.powerup.com.au/core/home/stories_home.htm

Qld Performing Arts Complex

southwards along the Brisbane River from the CBD, giving a spectacular view of the river, and includes the Captain Cook Bridge, 1 of 5 bridges in the city reach. The Western Hwy, west of the CBD, takes travellers to Ipswich and the Darling Downs region. To the east, via various routes, lie the Bayside suburbs.

Buses between Brisbane and other centres, both intrastate and interstate, depart daily. Brisbane Transit Centre is the terminus for all bus lines, which include **Greyhound/Pioneer, Kirklands Bus Line** and **McCafferty's**.

For info at a glance regarding city bus transport, a pamphlet outlining a variety of services is available from City Hall (p.14). These services include **Cityxpress** (express buses into the city), **City Precincts Express** and **Rockets** (peak-hour services) and **Citybus** (an all-stops service in the inner suburbs). **Great Circle Line** buses connect major shopping centres in a ring of outlying suburbs. Buses pass through every 30min on weekdays and Sats. A special service in New Farm and West End, **Hail and Ride**, has local bus circuits every 15min, 7am–7pm. Some of the bus services terminate earlier on weekends.

Also available at City Hall is a colour-coded map to inner-city bus travel. Of special interest here is the **City Circle** bus, which offers a cheap and easy option for travel within the CBD.

Another handy option is a multiple-use travel pass. A **South-East Explorer** gives unlimited travel at any time on buses, trains and catamarans except City Sights buses (p.14).

Details about transport options can be obtained from Trans Info and tourist info centres (p.9).

Taxi services include **Yellow Cab** Ph: (07) 131 924, **Black and White Cabs** Ph: (07) 131 008 and **Brisbane Cabs** Ph: (07) 3360 0000.

By rail

Trains travel between Brisbane and Sydney daily. The major intrastate rail route is between Brisbane and Cairns in Far North Qld. Other lines offer access from less remote regional areas. All long-distance routes terminate at the Brisbane Transit Centre. For info on long-distance rail travel, Ph: (07) 132 235.

Qld Rail has a network of suburban lines. Stations in the inner-city area include Central Stn, cnr Ann and Edward Sts; Roma St Stn, in the Brisbane Transit Centre; and Vulture St Stn, just across the river in the South Bank Parklands recreational area, South Brisbane. A **Citytrain Day Rover** pass offers unlimited train travel after 9am, Mon–Fri, and all day Sat, Sun and public holidays. Call Trans Info for route details and where to obtain timetables and maps (p.9).

Story Bridge
The Story Bridge, erected in 1940, spans the Brisbane River between the city and Kangaroo Pt, giving a spectacular view of the CBD. In its early years locals would promenade along the bridge as entertainment on Saturday nights.

Captain Cook Bridge

By ferry

CityCats (catamarans) travel as far as St Lucia to the west and Hamilton to the east every 30min or less, 7 days a week, 6am–10.30pm. Passengers can disembark at any stop along the way, including South Bank or the Riverside Centre, Eagle St Pier. Small ferries make shorter trips across the river in the inner-city area.

Disabled access

Most modes of public transport attempt to accommodate disabled passengers. Brochures about train services are available from Qld Rail (Ph: (07) 3255 5555), and for buses, ferries and CityCats from Brisbane City Council Call Centre. Alternatively, contact Trans Info (p.9). There are also disabled parking bays in the CBD. Note: While ferries and CityCats are wheelchair accessible, pontoon access varies.

Getting around
Cruises

To see Brisbane from the river, there is a variety of cruises and boat rides on offer, most of which provide a commentary as well as plenty of pampering.

For a leisurely pace, try the **Mirimar Cruise**, a 12km ride upstream from the CBD. The ride takes sightseers past a rare inner-city colony of fruit bats and through

River cruise

some of Brisbane's most salubrious suburbs, and ends at Lone Pine Koala Sanctuary (p.30). Trips depart daily at 10am (Ph: (07) 3221 0300). Other river rides include the **Synergy Cruise**, on board a 24m launch (Ph: (07) 3300 9930); *Kookaburra Queen* cruises, offering a range of trips on a paddlewheeler (Ph: (07) 3221 1300); the *Lady Brisbane* trips to St Helena Island (p.59) by night or day (Ph: (07) 3262 7422); and *Brisbane Star* cruises, 4hr tours every Sun (Ph: 018 190604).

Tours and guided walks

For history lovers, the **City Sites** bus offers a run through Brisbane's past. This open-air vehicle travels through a range of contemporary and historical CBD sites, such as the smartly casual Eagle St Pier (p.20), a precinct of shops and cafes, and Chinatown's duck-lined windows in the neighbouring suburb of Fortitude Valley (p.23). No booking is required for the 80min tour, and passengers can embark or disembark at any of the 19 stops along the way. The service is offered daily every 40min, 9am–12.20pm and 1.40pm–4.20pm. Tickets give unlimited travel on Brisbane's buses, ferries and CityCats for the day of purchase, and can be bought at any Council Customer Service Centre or newsagency.

At night Brisbane assumes a different look, and another bus tour, **City Nights**, tracks down the sights under the lights. Tours depart at 6pm daily from the City Hall City Sights Bus Stop 2, cnr Adelaide and Albert Sts, and include a complimentary drink at Mt Coot-tha Lookout, 7km from the city centre (p.30). The tour runs for 2.5hr. For info on both these tours, contact a tourist info centre.

City Heights is a 2hr bus tour of the Mt Coot-tha Lookout and Botanical Gardens (p.32). Tours depart daily at 2pm from the City Hall City Sights Bus Stop 2, cnr Adelaide and Albert Sts. Ph: (07) 131 230

The **Heritage Trail: Brisbane City Centre** is a self-guiding walk through the centre of town. Beginning at King George Sq, set between Adelaide and Ann Sts

City Hall

The **Albert St Literary Trail** has a series of bronze plaques featuring quotes about Brisbane from Australian literature. Ph: (07) 3403 6096

Festivals and events
Australia Day celebrations
On Australia Day, 26 Jan, fireworks light up the sky over the city and crowds stand on the river banks to watch the spectacle and the free concert at **South Bank Parklands**. Various events around town, such as folkdancing and community picnics, add to the sense of collective celebration – and there are now special ceremonies, devised in collaboration with local Murris (the regional word for Aboriginals) to commemorate the area's original inhabitants.

Family fun

Streets of Brisbane
A festival of street theatre and perform-ance, which includes stilt-walkers, mime artists and face-painters, is held during Mar–Apr at **South Bank Parklands**, with free entertainment for all ages.

Brisbane–Gladstone Yacht Race
This 50-year-old Easter yacht race travels from Brisbane north to the regional city of Gladstone in Apr. The first race, in

and facing City Hall, the tour takes in such sights as the majestic City Hall itself; the Shrine of Remembrance, erected to commemorate the soldiers of WWI; the 3-storey People's Palace, once the headquarters of the Salvation Army and now a backpacker hostel; and Parliament House, the seat of State government. Guides are available from the City Council tourist info desk, inside the front doors of City Hall.

There is a variety of such **Heritage Trail walks**, covering the CBD and several suburbs, with pamphlets including a map and descriptions of historical sites available at City Hall and related locations. The walks cover such sights as McWhirters, a former department store in Fortitude Valley with a lavish Art Deco facade; the Woolstores in New Farm, where sheep wool was stored until sold; and Princess Theatre, Brisbane's oldest surviving theatre – complete with resident ghost – in South Brisbane.

Step into the Past runs guided walking tours of the history of the CBD, including morning tea, every weekday, commencing at 9.30am. **Bread or Blood**, beginning at 1.30pm, Sun–Fri, traces colonial life in all its blood and grime. Both tours start from the tourist info centre in the Queen St Mall. Ph: (07) 3272 4662

Street theatre

1949, attracted only 7 participants. Nowadays, there are between 60 and 70 entrants. Ph: (07) 3869 2311

Queensland Jazz Carnival

Held in early May, the Jazz Carnival features a wide array of jazz styles and showcases Qld jazz musicians in an inner-city venue that changes from year to year. Ph: (07) 3391 2006

Brisbane River Fun Run

Also held in May, this 5km or 10km race or walk begins and ends at Suncorp Stadium, **Milton**. Entrants of all shapes and sizes are encouraged, and the emphasis is on fun and fitness rather than competition. Ph: (07) 3349 1459

Caxton St Seafood and Wine Festival

In the suburb of **Paddington**, on the edge of the CBD, the Caxton St Seafood and Wine Festival takes place over one weekend in May. The 'seafood quarter' is blocked off for the festival, with a bright array of stalls and entertainers — and plenty of BBQ seafood. Ph: (07) 3369 5544

Seafood fiesta

Paniyiri Greek Festival

Another May event, this outdoor celebration of Greek culture and cuisine in Australia is timed to coincide with the end of winter in Greece. The festival is traditionally held in Musgrave Park, **West End**, home to many Greek-Australians. Ph: (07) 3844 3669

Queensland Winter Racing Carnival

Punters will enjoy this combination of carnival and horse racing in May–Jun. As well as racing, the season includes balls, fashion parades and parties. **Eagle Farm** and **Ascot** are at the hub of things, but many events take place citywide — especially among Brisbane's high society and racing fraternity. Ph: (07) 3221 1003

Queensland Day

Held on 6 Jun, a public holiday, this day is a celebration of the proclamation of the Colony of Qld in 1859. Celebrations continue over the course of a week and include such events as a Youth Day and a Senior Citizens Day. Ph: (07) 3244 2111

Brisbane Medieval Fayre

A more unusual public event is held in Jun at Musgrave Park, **West End**. Wandering minstrels, jugglers, jesters and acrobats feature among the many who re-enact medieval life in dress and play. Ph: (07) 3221 7332

Stage X Festival

A biennial festival held in various inner-city locations in mid-Jul, this multi-arts event caters for young people between the ages of 12 and 25. Over 10 days of music, drama, dance, visual art, new technologies and talk offer the opportunity to celebrate youth cultures in all their diversity. Ph: (07) 3255 0344

Brisbane International Film Festival

This festival, held in Aug–Sept, includes local, national and international feature, short, animated and documentary films. The main location is the magnificent Regent Centre, in **Queen St Mall**. Ph: (07) 3220 0444

Downtown
Weekly street publications and the local daily supply details of what's on around town. **West End**, **Paddington**, **New Farm** and the **Valley** are the best sources of entertainment info.

Royal Brisbane Show

'The Ekka' (Exhibition), as the show is also known, is a display of agricultural produce and stock which takes place over 10 days in Aug at the RNA Exhibition Grounds, **Fortitude Valley**. Exhibitions of traditional rural skills such as wood-chopping and a carnival atmosphere make this a perennial favourite with locals. At its opening day in 1876, it drew a crowd of 12 000 out of a city population of 22 000. Ph: (07) 3852 1831

Spring Hill Fair

This fair was conceived by the 'Duchess of Spring Hill', Celia McNally, who lived in the area from the 1950s to the 1990s and frequently stoushed with authorities who tried to change the event's style. Ms McNally's legacy is a gathering every Sept in Water St, **Spring Hill** and includes food, stalls, donkey rides and street entertainment. Ph: (07) 3229 5918 or 3221 8411

Brisbane Festival

A multi-arts biennial event, the Brisbane Festival is staged in a variety of inner-city venues over 2 weeks in Sept.

Out of the Box

Also occurring every 2 years in Sept, at the Qld Performing Arts Complex,
South Bank, this arts festival is unique in its audience focus on young children between 3 and 8 yrs. Ph: (07) 3840 7584

September Moon Festival

Brisbane's large Chinese-Australian population celebrates this traditional festival in Chinatown, in colourful inner-city **Fortitude Valley**. Lion dances, moon cakes and fireworks are all part of the fun. Other locations with a large Chinese-Australian population, such as the southern suburb of **Sunnybank**, also hold festivities.

Brisbane River Festival

This 10-day celebration takes place in riverside venues in late Sept, opening at **Newstead Park**, and includes Brisbane Day celebrations. Events such as an International Dragon Boat Regatta and a river bonfire and fireworks display make this a fun time for all ages. Ph: (07) 3268 5693

Brisbane Writers' Festival

In mid-Oct this festival is held at the Qld Cultural Centre, **South Bank** and brings together writers of local, national and international reputation in a mixture of panels, symposiums, launches and readings. Ph: (07) 3840 7088

Agricultural display

September Moon Festival

Koalas in the Wild

Goodwill Games

In Sep–Oct 2001 this 12-day, 12-sport event will be staged in Brisbane. The Games, brainchild of CNN chief Ted Turner, have never been held outside the US and Russia, and will be the biggest sporting event anywhere in the world for that year.

Main localities

For ease of reference, areas have been listed alphabetically in 6 sections: bayside, city centre, inner suburbs, northside, southside and westside.

Bayside

A quiet spot for fishing or paddling, fun and games on the Manly Marina, a meeting place for clubs, or a trip back in time, Brisbane's bayside suburbs offer old-fashioned hospitality and modern service in a place only 20km from the CBD. This charming area is made up of old timber houses and wide, shaded streets, and borders onto Moreton Bay (p.39).

Cleveland *Map 2*

Cleveland, part of the **Redlands Region** historical precinct and only 30min from the CBD, is one of Qld's earliest European settlements as well as the site of its oldest banyan tree. It is also a great place for fishing. From **Cleveland Pt**, an area rich in local history, North

Stradbroke and Moreton Islands can be glimpsed across the water. Late afternoon gives a particularly beautiful cast to the view. Ferries depart from Cleveland for North Stradbroke Island on a daily basis (p.49).

The *Cleveland Heritage Trail* traces white settlement by its constructions. These include the **Lighthouse**, erected in 1847, and the **Courthouse**, built in 1853 and now a restaurant but with the cells still clearly identifiable. Ph: (07) 38221 3210

Nearby is **Ormiston House** (Wellington St, Ormiston), built in 1862. The house and gardens are open to the public and Devonshire teas are available. Wheelchair accessible. Open Sun, 1.30pm–4pm; coaches: weekdays by appt. Ph: (07) 3286 1425

Also within easy driving distance of Cleveland Pt is the **Redland Museum**, at the Cleveland Showgrounds (Smith St), which has a wide range of antique machinery and dolls as well as examples of 19th-century architecture and a chapel. Most of what is on display is local to the area. Wheelchair accessible. Open Fri–Sat, 1pm–3pm; Sun, 11am–4pm. Ph: (07) 3286 3494

Koalas in the Wild (Redland Bay Rd, Pt Halloran Reserve), a nature reserve near Cleveland, has one of the largest colonies of wild koalas in Australia. It is also home to a rare species of butterfly.

Bayside parklands
A series of linked Bayside parks comprising mangroves, open forest and foreshore offer walking and bike tracks as well as picnic facilities. Access is from Wynnum, Manly, Lota or Gumdale.

Lighthouse, Cleveland

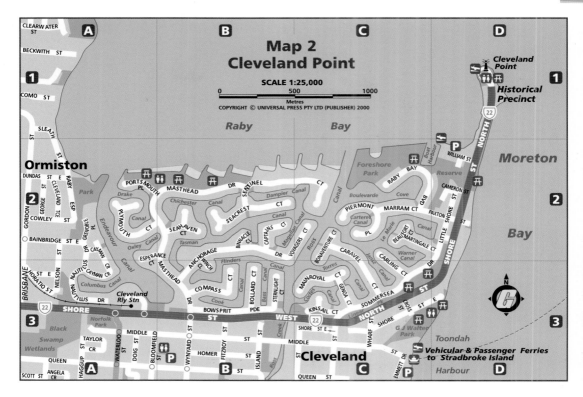

A tour is available, which includes lunch at the **Grand View Hotel**, built in 1851 and overlooking Moreton Bay. Wheelchair accessible. Open daily: group bookings only. Ph: (07) 3821 3210

Like St Helena Island (p.59), **Wellington Pt**, a little to the north, was named in the early days of settlement, when Napoleon's defeat and place of exile were part of recent history. The site is in the Redland Shire area, which has rich red volcanic soil and was once called the 'salad bowl of Brisbane' because of its many market gardens. Ocean views make this another great place to look out on the neighbouring islands.

Grand View Hotel, Cleveland

Manly Marina

Royal yachties
The **Royal Qld Yacht Squadron Club** (at Manly Marina) was given its title by King Edward VII in 1902.

Manly *Map 1 D4*

A peaceful place with a flat foreshore, Manly is ideal for 'Sunday promenades' any day of the week. The **Manly Harbour Village** (Cambridge Pde) is one of Brisbane's few remaining waterfront villages. The **Wynnum–Manly Yacht Club** (Royal Esp) offers inexpensive breakfasts, and there is an abundance of electric BBQs, picnic tables and playgrounds along the shoreline. Wheelchair accessible.

Manly Marina is one of the largest marinas in the southern hemisphere and berths 410 craft. It was built for the Royal Qld Yacht Squadron, which was established in 1885.

Wynnum *Map 1 D4*

Further north is Wynnum. Here, visitors can step back into Brisbane's recent past among quiet streets and quaint corner shops. A *Heritage Trail* pamphlet outlines the features of the area. These include the **Wynnum Wading Pool**, a sportsground-sized seawater pool, the **Wynnum Jetty** and the **Wynnum Mangrove Boardwalk** (open 7am–5pm). All are located on or near the coastal Bay Terrace. From the shoreline, St Helena Island, once a penitentiary for those felons regarded as 'irredeemable', can be seen. Island tours depart regularly (p.18).

A sealed pathway, shared by both pedestrians and cyclists, runs along the Wynnum beachfront. Pelicans and other sea birds are visible in the area, especially around the **Wynnum Fish Markets** (18 Fox St). Here, fresh fish, raw or cooked, can be bought virtually straight off the boat. Wheelchair accessible.

A city oasis
Giant Moreton Bay fig trees at the intersection of Elizabeth and Eagle Sts mark the spot where a creek once flowed through the CBD and into the river.

City centre
City Hall and King George Sq
Map 3 C4

The sandstone City Hall, erected in the 1920s and distinguished by its Ionic columns, faces onto King George Sq (Ann and Adelaide Sts). Here, tourists, amateur preachers, shoppers and schoolchildren mingle in the shadow of the City Hall clock tower, for many years the highest man-made point in Brisbane. A variety of tours of City Hall are available, from a 1hr guided tour to an 'armchair' video screening which is followed by morning or afternoon tea. Wheelchair accessible. Ph: (07) 3225 4890

Customs House *Map 3 C3*

Customs House (399 Queen St), to the east of the city, lies in a riverside precinct that was once Brisbane's major port. Recently restored to its former glory, the building now offers cultural and educational events such as music recitals and lectures by visiting artists, as well as an art gallery and a licensed brasserie. Wheelchair accessible. Open daily, Sun-Mon, 10am–5.30pm; Tue-Sat, 10am–10pm. Ph: (07) 3365 8999

Eagle St Pier and Riverside Markets *Map 3 C4*

Nearby is Eagle St Pier (1 Eagle St), a popular spot for food and people-watching. Both casual and formal dining are available, with most venues offering a view of the water and the Story Bridge. The pier is also the site of the Riverside Pure Crafts Markets, an open-air marketplace filled with stalls selling

Parliament House

architecture. Wheelchair accessible.
Ph: (07) 3221 1999

Parliament House *Map 3 C5*

At the south end of George St, this
Victorian building, constructed in 1868,
is a monument to the prosperity of the
day, featuring French Renaissance-
style architecture and gold-leafed
ceilings. Free public tours are available
Mon–Fri. Wheelchair accessible.
Ph: (07) 3406 7562

Queen St Mall *Map 3 C4*

At the heart of the city, this mall is *the*
place for people to saunter, shop or
simply sit and watch the world go by.
It is a casual yet defined space, made up
of a strip of retail outlets and arcades
bordering a paved streetscape. Years ago
a tram line ran here, between verandah-
fronted shops. Nowadays, singers,
didgeridoo players and local groups
celebrating special events can be seen
at any hour of the day or night.

Queensland Sciencentre *Map 3 C5*

Just down the road from the mall is
Brisbane's science museum, at
110 George St. There are interactive
displays for adults and children.
Wheelchair accessible. Open daily,
10am–5pm. Ph: (07) 3220 0166

everything from body piercings to baby
booties. Wheelchair accessible. Open
every Sun, 7am–5pm.

Heritage Hotel *Map 3 C4*

This exclusive hotel (39 Edward St), at
the south end of the CBD, looks out on
the river and towards the City Botanical
Gardens. Casual visitors are welcome to
wander through the grand surrounds,
have breakfast or afternoon tea on the
terrace or move inside to one of the bars
or dining venues that form this excellent
example of 19th-century colonial

**One House of
Parliament**
Qld is unique among
Australian states
in only having 1 House
of Parliament.
In the 1920s,
parliamentarians
voted to remove the
Legislative Council.

Wining and dining

All budgets are catered for at inner-city eateries. At the Story Bridge end of
Adelaide St, **Jameson's Restaurant and Bar** (475 Adelaide St; Ph: (07) 3831 7633)
and **e'cco bistro** (100 Boundary St; Ph: (07) 3831 8344) offer sophisticated wining
and dining. **e'cco**, located in a former tea warehouse, won the 1997 Remy Martin
Cognac/*Australian Gourmet Traveller* award for the best restaurant in Australia. At
the other end of the scale, the **Red Cross Cafe** under City Hall, King George Sq,
offers simple fare as well as good toilet and changeroom facilities. (Access by lift
or stairs.) Ph: (07) 3403 4557. Or try the **Shingle Inn** (254 Edward St), a Brisbane
institution and still a popular choice for country visitors.

Info on what's what in Brisbane cuisine is available from tourist info centres or
from the quarterly free *Dining Out* guide.

A twist of fate
A pedestrian mall was
part of Brisbane's
original 1839 town
plan. **Queen St Mall**
was constructed, 143
years later, in
preparation for the
1982 Commonwealth
Games. It was
extended for the 1988
World Expo.

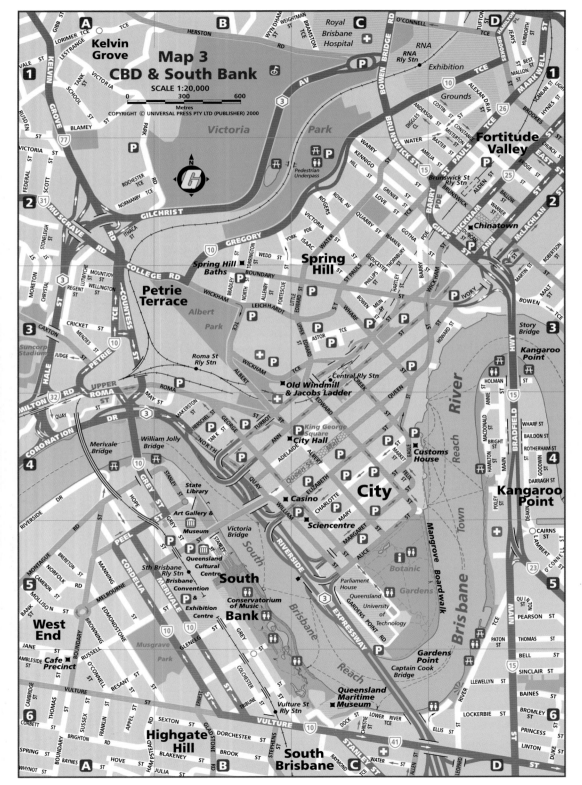

Map 3
CBD & South Bank

SCALE 1:20,000

St John's Anglican Cathedral
Map 3 C3

At 410 Ann St, this Gothic-style cathedral, located at the east end of town, has taken over 100 years to build, using traditional artisan tools and methods. Wheelchair accessible. Guided tours available daily, 10am–4pm, or by appt. Ph: (07) 3835 2231

Treasury Casino *Map 3 C4*

At the George St end of Queen St Mall, the Conrad International Treasury Casino is housed, ironically, in what was once the 'vault of government'. The heritage-listed sandstone building contains over 100 gaming tables and over 1000 gaming machines as well as bars, restaurants and cafes, and free live entertainment nightly. Wheelchair accessible; non-smoking areas. Open 24 hours daily. Ph: (07) 3306 8888

Inner suburbs

The inner suburbs make up a hilly ring of workers' cottages and colonial mansions wedged tightly up against each other. Formerly, the area was the site of shipping, farming, industry and commerce. Now it is a popular place for coffee, nightclubbing and inner-city living.

Fortitude Valley *Map 3 D2*

Once the wild side of town, 'the Valley' has a wide range of cafes and restaurants, including outdoor seating, as well as clubs, shops and a shopping mall. There is a strong and visible youth culture here but the area has something for everyone. Line dancers of all ages, for example, dance in **Brunswick St Mall** – a popular place for a rendezvous – every Sun afternoon. The Valley was originally named after a ship that brought European settlers to the new and growing town of Brisbane.

Chinatown Mall lies at the heart of a Chinese-Australian precinct made up of groceries, cafes, restaurants and other retail outlets. Bounded by Wickham and Ann Sts, it was officially opened in 1987 but the area has long been a marketplace for the Asian-Australian population of Brisbane. The **Sept Moon Festival** (p.17) attracts the crowds, but the mall and its surrounds are always popular places for yum cha and entertainment year-round.

Kangaroo Pt *Map 3 D4*

Kangaroo Pt, a small land mass abutting the Brisbane River, has an unusual attraction for the adventurous. **Abseiling** at Kangaroo Pt cliffs, bordering the South Bank Parklands (p.26), is permitted, and climbers can be seen attempting to scale the heights most days of the week. As well as climbing, hardy souls and companions can enjoy a BBQ at one of the picnic areas below. A boardwalk,

Valley living

The **Cosmopolitan Cafe**, commonly known as Cosmo's, is a Brisbane landmark. Generations of people have sat and sipped the home-ground coffee under its umbrellas in Brunswick St Mall. A cluster of second-hand, retro or specialist shops, such as **Kleptomania** (713 Ann St) and **Red Books** (350a Brunswick St), attract a young, funky clientele.

Popular clubs and bars include Dooley's Irish Pub, Ric's Bar and the Wickham Hotel. **Dooley's** (394 Brunswick St) celebrates, as might be expected, St Patrick's Day (on Mar 17) in high style with games, contests and green beer. **Ric's** (Brunswick St Mall) presents local contemporary musicians most nights of the week and offers occasional performances or launches in its upstairs space. The **Wickham** (308 Wickham St) is a lively gay venue.

Little China

The Chinese first came to Brisbane in the 1860s, after gold was found in Gympie, with many migrants setting up businesses in **Fortitude Valley**. Since then, there have always been Chinese-Australians living or working in the Valley.

A head for heights?

Qualified instructors from the **Outdoor Pursuits Group** teach the basics of abseiling at Kangaroo Pt. Classes take place every second Sun, 1pm–5pm. Rockclimbing is also available from 8.30am on the same day. Ph: (07) 3257 0433

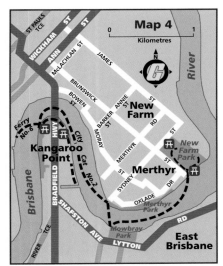

colourful outdoor sculptures and playground equipment make this a family-friendly place. On the clifftops are more tables and a magnificent view of the Brisbane River and the CBD. The cliffs are floodlit at night, creating a spectacular view. Rock from here was used by convicts to build retaining walls along the riverbank last century.

Another popular activity is walking along the riverbank from South Bank, under the Story Bridge, to **Dockside**, a cafe-hotel precinct on the eastern side of

Kangaroo Pt. Ferries and catamarans stop at the point at regular intervals, and picnic tables and coin-operated BBQs make this area a popular location.

While in the area, take a walk from **Dockside around Kangaroo Pt** (see map 4) and then a ferry across the Brisbane River to New Farm Park. The 2km round trip takes about 1hr.

Milton and Rosalie *Map 5*

Smart cars line Park Rd, **Milton**, Brisbane's fashionable 'Little Italy', a street with many cafes and restaurants. At Park Rd's end, a plaque marks the spot where Surveyor-General John Oxley landed in 1823.

Lovers of Australia's national drink can look around Milton's **Brewery**, recognisable by its famous XXXX sign. The 45min Castlemaine Perkins tour commences at the Sports Club (Heussler Terrace) on Mon, Tue and Wed at 11.30am and 1.30pm, and at 7pm on Wed nights. There is an opportunity to sample the local product at the end of the tour. Ph: (07) 3361 7597

The small suburb of **Rosalie**, adjacent to Milton, has recently developed its own cafe precinct at the intersection of Nash St and Baroona Rd. The mood is a little more casual than Park Rd, but just as

A contented life

Jerry's Barbershop, in Baroona Rd, Rosalie, is an old-fashioned business without a telephone, bookings system or assistant. Jerry Nolan, who has been cutting hair since 1951, says, 'I'll never be a millionaire but I enjoy my job.'

Alfresco dining, Milton

lively. Between the two suburbs is **Gregory Park**, a large grassy area with tables, seating, swings and a small concrete area for ball games.

New Farm *Map 1 C4*

New Farm was originally a prison farm, supplying produce to the colony's earliest settlers. It was given its name because there was already a farm in South Brisbane. New Farm is now a distinguished suburb, full of grand houses as well as apartment blocks and workers' cottages. **New Farm Park** (at the river end of Brunswick St) is a central landmark of the area (p.32).

New Farm has parks, cafes, restaurants, a cinema, bookshops and other retail outlets and is home to many artists and art galleries. The **Art Circuit** takes the visitor on a 'gallery crawl' through more than 15 art spaces mainly located in the New Farm area. Pamphlets are available from galleries and City Hall. The Hail and Ride service, which deposits art aficionados at the door of each gallery, operates daily (p.13).

Newstead *Map 1 C4*

On the eastern side of Fortitude Valley is **Newstead House**, on Breakfast Creek Rd. This historic residence was built in 1846

and was home to the first Surveyor-General of Qld. A curiosity is the wrought-iron urinal discreetly hidden not far from the main house. Limited wheelchair accessibility. Open Mon–Fri, 10am–4pm; Sun and most public holidays, 2pm–5pm. Ph: (07) 3216 1846. Surrounding the house are lush rolling lands which stretch down to Breakfast Creek. This is **Newstead Park**, which has unlimited entry as well as picnic facilities.

Breakfast Creek was once a camping ground for local Aborigines because of its access to fresh water. These days it is again a gathering place. **Breakfast Creek Wharf**, an assortment of cafes and restaurants, is across the road from Newstead House. **Breakfast Creek Hotel**, built in 1889 and once a haunt for wharfies, still serves hand-pulled beer 'off the wood'. River cruises depart from the boardwalk. **Golden Gondola** cruises are available daily by appt. Ph: 0419 400 944

Newstead House

Paddington and Petrie Terrace *Map 1 B4 & 3 B3*

Paddington is a working-class suburb that has become gentrified over the last 20 years. Workers' cottages have been renovated into smart city residences and old 'Queenslanders' shine with new coats of paint. A *Heritage Trail* pamphlet

New Farm Park

Made of wood
The 'Queenslanders' wooden houses on stilts ('stumps') — that characterise Paddington offer a picturesque sight amid the subtropical foliage.

tracks the life of **Given and Latrobe Terraces,** the main precinct of the area, including a description of the tram line that once ran through the suburb. There are many cafes in this stretch of Paddington, along with shops selling books, retro fashion and gifts. Antique-shopping at the **Paddington Antique Centre** (167 Latrobe Terrace) is a popular weekend pastime. Wheelchair accessible.

At the city end of the suburb is a cluster of cafes and nightclubs, as well as the famous **Gambaro's** (33 and 34 Caxton St) where seafood is served with plenty of Italo–Australian hospitality. The Caxton St Seafood and Wine Festival takes place in this stretch of inner-city Brisbane every May. Nearby, for those in search of other pleasures, is **La Boite Theatre** (57 Hale St), a venue offering theatre works by contemporary Australian playwrights.

The tiny suburb of **Petrie Terrace,** also located nearby, was once a popular site of residence for well-off families. Its name comes from one such family, the illustrious Petrie clan, who helped make a town out of the pioneer settlement.

South Brisbane *Map 3 C6*

South Brisbane is one of Brisbane's oldest suburbs. Its central feature is the **South Bank Parklands**, a well-designed, informal recreational precinct of 16ha, including shops, cafes, playgrounds, picnic tables,

South Bank craft market

coin-operated BBQs and an IMAX cinema screen. South Bank was the site of the 1988 World Expo (p.12). A highlight of the parklands is **Breaka Beach**, an artificial lagoon with palm trees and sand. Swimming is permitted within prescribed hours (seasonal variations). A walking/cycling path borders the river edge, with fantastic views of the city. Entry to South Bank is free. Wheelchair accessible. Contact the Visitor Info Centre on (07) 3867 2051 (8am–8pm).

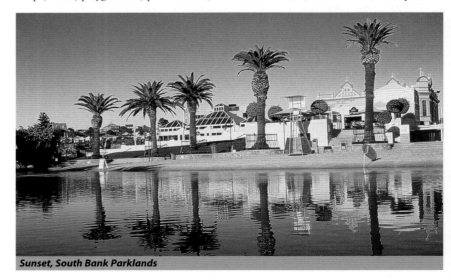

Sunset, South Bank Parklands

Qld Art Gallery

South Bank holds a **craft market** in the Stanley St Plaza. Woodwork, glassware and other hand-crafted goods are for sale in the colourful market tents. Open Fri, 5pm–10pm; Sat, 11am–5pm; Sun, 9am–5pm.

At the east end of South Bank is the **Qld Maritime Museum** (Dry Dock, Stanley St). The museum displays nautical relics from Qld's past including 2 of the 12 18-pounder guns sent out from Britain at the end of the 19th century in response to the fear of a Russian invasion. Wheelchair accessible. Open daily, 9.30am–5pm. Ph: (07) 3844 5361

The **Qld Cultural Centre** is on the Melbourne St end of South Bank. It includes the Qld Art Gallery, the Qld Museum, the Qld Theatre Company, the State Library and the Qld Performing Arts Complex. All buildings are wheelchair accessible. Phone the Entertainment Info Line at any time for info about shows Ph: (07) 3867 2020. For general info, call (07) 3840 7100 in business hours, or ring the appropriate numbers for specific inquiries.

The **Qld Art Gallery** is a handsome building set in tranquil tropical surroundings, with pools of still water. The collection includes works of national and international significance. A courtyard cafe offers light meals and snacks. Open daily, 10am–5pm, except public holidays. Ph: (07) 3840 7333

The **Qld Museum** has an extensive permanent collection of social and natural history artefacts as well as regular exhibitions. Open daily, 9.30am–5pm; Ph: (07) 3840 7555

An array of performance venues is contained within the **Qld Performing Arts Complex**. They range in size from the Cremorne Theatre, for intimate theatre productions, to the Concert Hall, a large auditorium for concerts and other musical events. A recent addition is the 800-seat Optus Playhouse. Ph: (07) 3846 4444

Just behind the complex are the undulating 'sails' (roof) of the **Brisbane Convention and Exhibition Centre** (Ph: (07) 3308 3000) and the **Conservatorium of Music** (Ph: (07) 3875 6111). The latter includes a concert hall with excellent acoustics.

Spring Hill *Map 3 C2*

This tiny, hilly place of crooked streets and quaint houses was Brisbane's first suburb. Once the province of boarding houses and brothels, the area has become gentrified over the last couple of decades. One feature is the **Spring Hill Baths** (14 Torrington St), built last century and now restored to their original elegance. Spring Hill's community spirit is manifest at the **Spring Hill Fair**, famous for its character and eccentricity (p.17).

Teneriffe *Map 5*

Teneriffe is a recently developed area to the east of New Farm and owes its increasing popularity to its proximity to the city and the river. What were once giant warehouses have been turned into retail outlets which include cafes and restaurants.

West End *Map 3 A5*

Another inner-city suburb with plenty of local colour is West End. The suburb has traditionally been a home for new immigrants and its life, architecture and food reflect an interesting cultural mix. The large and eye-catching **Greek Orthodox Church and Community Centre** (36 Browning St) is one example. **Boundary St** and **Hardgrave Rd** are the 2 major retail strips and offer good dining and cafes, as well as street theatre.

Woolloongabba *Map 5*

One of Woolloongabba's main claims to fame is that it is home to the **Brisbane Cricket Ground**, commonly called 'the Gabba'. Bounded by South and East Brisbane, the suburb is a walk through Brisbane's past. A *Heritage Trail* pamphlet, available from City Hall, takes the visitor along **Merton Rd**, a street lined with 19th-century dwellings.

For those seeking some pampering, **Hotel Diana** (12 Annerley Rd) houses **Apollo's**, Brisbane's only traditional Asian

bathhouse. It has separate facilities for men and women, including sauna, pool, gym and massage. Open Mon–Thur, 6am–9pm; Fri, 6am–8.30pm; Sat–Sun, 8am–7pm. Ph: (07) 3391 2911

Northside

Stretching up towards the Sunshine Coast, Brisbane's Northside encompasses wetlands, coastal regions, prestigious residential areas, pioneer settlements and cane farms. There are 2 main routes to Northside from the city: the Bruce Hwy or the Gateway Arterial. The highway continues up the coast whereas the arterial ends as it enters the Redcliffe Peninsula region.

Ascot and Hamilton *Map 5*

About 10km NE of the city are Ascot and Hamilton, two 'old-money' Brisbane suburbs. **Ascot** is the home of the **Eagle Farm Racecourse** (Lancaster Rd), where high society and the racing world meet annually. **Racecourse Rd** provides an array of upmarket eateries for those who tire of betting. The **Massey St Lookout**, in **Hamilton**, gives a wonderful view of the city, the river and the eastern suburbs. A **Heritage Trail** walk takes in a mini-tour of colonial times in this hilly area adjacent to the Brisbane River.

Redcliffe Peninsula *Map 1 C2*

This area was the site of the first European settlement in Qld, in 1824. Walk or drive one of the **Heritage Trail** routes to discover old hotels such as the **Belvedere**; the **memorial** to John Oxley, who organised the settlement of the area; a **weir** constructed by convicts; the **Redcliffe Jetty**; and the **First Settlement Memorial Wall**. Towns on the Peninsula include **Scarborough**, **Margate** and **Redcliffe**, which – like the Wynnum–Manly area (p.20) – give the feel of a bygone era in the architecture of the houses, the old-fashioned shopfronts and the sleepy feel of the area. The **Newport Waterways Marina** (Griffith Rd, Scarborough) offers extensive boat-mooring facilities as well as an open-air cafe right on the water.

There are good beaches for swimming and sunbathing, and an esplanade promenade for pedestrians. Picnic and

The Gabba

Fishing opportunities

Fishing is a way of life for many people, and the Brisbane area offers plenty of opportunities. Ocean lovers can try **Fisherman's Island**, at the mouth of the Brisbane River, along the **Moreton Bay** foreshores, at creek mouths or on the bay itself. Alternatively, there is good freshwater fishing in the upper reaches of the Brisbane River. Find out where fishing is permitted, as Qld fishing regulations are strict in an effort to protect the environment. For info, contact the Qld Fisheries Management Authority (Ph: (07) 3225 1848), the Dept of Environment and Heritage (Ph: (07) 3224 5612) or any office of the Boating and Fisheries Patrol. A pamphlet, *Guidelines for Recreational Fishing in Qld*, is available from tourist info centres.

playground facilities, and electric BBQs, are dotted along the foreshore. A basketball court on the foreshore at **Suttons Beach**, Redcliffe, offers stunning views of the ocean and a sea breeze to assist keen players. Parents and toddlers can rest or play at amphitheatre-style seating nearby. Further along the beach are artificial lagoons for children. Most places are wheelchair accessible.

Southside

South of Brisbane lies the Gold Coast (p.237) and the Lamington Plateau (p.209). Between the CBD and the city fringe is a great urban sprawl – Southside – dotted with hills and creeks.

Beenleigh *Map 1 C6*

The **Spirit and Brew Tour** is a trip to Australia's oldest working rum distillery, located on Pacific Hwy, Beenleigh, on the outskirts of Brisbane. The tour includes a visit to the nearby Carlton Brewhouse (also on the Pacific Hwy), where samples are offered and a brewing test is given to those who want to try their hand at mixing a drink. The trip includes lunch. Ph: (07) 3325 0322

Rocklea *Map 1 D5*

For lovers of pawpaw, lady finger bananas and mangoes, **Brisbane Markets** (Sherwood Rd, Rocklea) is the place to visit. The markets supply Brisbane's retailers with tropical fruit and colourful vegetables as well as less exotic fresh produce. Formerly in Market St, City, and then in Roma St, the markets have been located in Rocklea for over 30 years. Open to the public, Mon–Fri, from 9am; closing times vary.

Tropical fruit on display

Temple of Peace
Visit **Toowong Cemetery** to see the 'Temple of Peace', erected by Richard Ramo in memory of his 3 sons (who all perished in WWI), his adopted son, Fred (who died tragically in 1923) and the family dog ('maliciously poisoned').

Tarragindi *Map 1 C4*

A panoramic view of Brisbane is found at the **Mt Gravatt Lookout** (Toohey Rd, Tarragindi). Only 10km from the CBD, the lookout has swings, picnic tables, BBQs and a small lawn. On a neighbouring hillside, **Toohey Forest Park** marks a green oasis between suburban homes. Some wheelchair accessibility.

Westside

The western suburbs of Brisbane are characterised by leafy valleys and rolling hills. The many apartments, houses and town units scattered amid this lush landscape contain an affluent professional population along with university students, old-timers and families.

Fig Tree Pocket *Map 1 B4*

Lone Pine Koala Sanctuary (Jesmond Rd) was the first koala sanctuary in the world. Established in 1927, it houses a number of other native animals such as emus, wombats and possums. Scenic access is by river, on the Mirimar Cruise (p.14). Buses also travel to the sanctuary. A cafe is located outside the grounds with picnic tables nearby. Open daily, 8am–5pm. Wheelchair accessible. Ph: (07) 3378 1366. www.koala.net/

Mt Coot-tha *Map 5*

Dominating the city landscape is **Mt Coot-tha**, located 7km west of the city centre, with its lookout, cafe, restaurant and offstreet parking. Its name derives from the indigenous word *kuta*,

meaning 'place of native honey'. Early white settlers called the mountain One Tree Hill. Mt Coot-tha offers panoramic views of Brisbane, stretching from Moreton Bay to Flinders Peak. Around and beyond this popular spot is **Mt Coot-tha Forest**, part of **Brisbane Forest Park**, which stretches over 28 500ha.

Toowong *Map 5*

An unusual attraction of the area is the **Brisbane General Cemetery** (Frederick St). Established in 1871, the cemetery is located on a hill. Its graves offer a microcosm of the history of Brisbane, ranging from ornate Victorian mausoleums to the culturally diverse headstones of today. A pamphlet giving details of a **Heritage Trail** walk around the cemetery is available at City Hall.

Reserves and state forest parks

Boondall Wetlands *Map 1 C3*

This magnificent reserve is almost on the outskirts of Brisbane. It can be reached by turning off the Gateway Arterial about 15km from the CBD. It includes over 1000ha of tidal flats, mangroves, open forest, melaleuca swamps and salt marshes. Entry is unrestricted and can be made either from Boondall or via Nudgee Beach. Canoeing is permitted on **Nudgee Creek**, and a **Canoe Trail** has been established.

There are walking and cycling tracks, and a boardwalk along Nudgee Beach. Aboriginal sculptural signage has also

Giant tree
Fig Tree Pocket is named for an enormous Moreton Bay fig tree discovered by European settlers as they charted the Brisbane River. The first whites to see the tree wrote that 'others will recognise it when they see it'.

View from Mt Coot-tha

Boondall Wetlands

Aboriginal art trail
This trail at Slaughter Falls features contemporary indigenous art works including rock paintings and a dance pit. The walk takes 30min. Info about the artwork is on small signs at each location. Ph: (07) 3403 2533

Slaughter Falls walk
Trek along a bushland track to a pretty picnic spot beside clear creek waters. The distance is 2km (return).

been developed. Parts of the wetlands are wheelchair accessible. Phone the Visitors Centre on (07) 3865 5187, 8.30am–4.30pm, for further details.

Daisy Hill State Forest Park *Map 1 C5*
En route to the Gold Coast, this area (at Daisy Hill Rd, Daisy Hill) protects 435ha of spotted gums, ironbark and other native plant and animal life. It has picnic and BBQ facilities. The **Daisy Hill Koala Centre** (p.32) is located here.

Mt Coot-tha Forest *Map 5*
Mt Coot-tha Forest offers a variety of scenic drives, walking tracks and picnic sites only 20min from the CBD. These include **Sir Samuel Griffith Dr**, which descends from the Mt Coot-tha Lookout and does a circuit past several picnic spots. Offshoots allow alternative ways back to the CBD.

Walks include the **J C Slaughter Falls Track**, which travels from the Mt Coot-tha Lookout to a picnic area at **Slaughter Falls**. This is a pretty and tranquil spot, with BBQs (wood supplied), shelters, tables, toilets, water and a playground for children. The walk has some steep sections. Access by car from Sir Samuel Griffith Dr is clearly signposted.

Raven St Reserve *Map 1 B3*
The **Downfall Creek Bushland Centre** (815 Rode Rd, McDowall) includes the

Raven St Reserve. This 24.3ha area of heath woodland includes flora such as weeping myrtle and black she-oak, and fauna such as wallabies and scrub turkeys. Facilities include BBQs, picnic tables and shelters, walking and cycle tracks, and a playground. Wheelchair accessible. Ph: (07) 3403 5937

Tinchi Tamba Wetlands *Map 1 B3*
Part of a series of linked wetlands, Tinchi Tamba Wetlands, at Deep Water Bend, is about 20km from the CBD. Access is via Wyampa Rd, Bald Hills (not the Gateway Arterial). There is an abundance of fauna, including bearded dragons and flying foxes, and flora. Canoeing, fishing, picnicking, walking or cycling are all permitted. Basic toilet and picnic-table facilities are provided.

Parks and gardens
Brisbane Botanical Gardens: City *Map 5* ❶
Originally established as a fruit and vegetable garden in 1828, the 18.3ha City gardens are open 24 hours a day and are bordered by the Brisbane River. Highlights include the **Mangrove Boardwalk**, a 400m wooden structure along the riverbank, which is lit until midnight, and the variety of garden settings laid out in the grounds, including rainforest, palm grove and formal garden. Ph: (07) 3403 7913

Bridge apartments
Two units are built into the supports of the **Walter Taylor Bridge**, Indooroopilly. The waiting list for residency in this unusual location with its river views is very long despite the constant stream of traffic underneath.

Botanical Gardens: Mt Coot-tha

Brisbane Botanical Gardens: Mt Coot-tha *Map 5* ❹

The gardens at Mt Coot-tha were created in 1976 in response to the limited space for expansion in the City gardens and a newfound awareness of environmental issues. Mt Coot-tha's 52ha offer a sensuous display of tropical and subtropical plants including an Australian rainforest and an Aboriginal plant trail, as well as plants from around the world. Another attraction at the gardens is the **Tropical Display Dome** (open 9.30am–4.30pm), which displays a large number of plants from the tropics. Wheelchair accessible. Open daily, 8am–5.30pm (5pm, Apr–Aug); the gardens are closed to vehicles from 4.30pm and on weekends.

Also at Mt Coot-tha gardens is the **Sir Thomas Brisbane Planetarium**.

New Farm Park *Map 1 C4*

Step under the avenue of jacaranda trees at **New Farm Park**, at the very end of Brunswick St, New Farm, and enter a parkland with attractions for all ages. There are playgrounds for toddlers and children, large, grassy areas for games and sports, picnic tables and coin-operated BBQs. A feature is a row of giant Moreton Bay fig trees, linked by rope ladders and timber play equipment as well as the vines and branches of the trees themselves. A bowling club and tennis courts abut the grounds. For those in search of tranquillity, a stroll among the rose gardens or along the bank of the bordering Brisbane River is the perfect choice. Ferries, CityCats and buses stop next to the park.

Other attractions

Daisy Hill Koala Centre *Map 1 C5*

Located in **Daisy Hill State Forest** (p.31). Open daily, 10am–4pm. Wheelchair accessible. Ph: (07) 3299 1032

Jacob's Ladder and the Old Windmill *Map 3 C3*

West of King George Sq, try climbing **Jacob's Ladder**, stone steps carved out of the side of a steep hill off Turbot St which houses a tiny park. At its top is a taste of history in the **Old Windmill**, on **Wickham Terrace**, the oldest European building in

Qld. The mill was constructed by convicts in 1828 for grinding grain. Since then, it has been variously used as a telegraph signal station, a timepiece, a fire observation tower and a broadcasting station. The mill is now protected by heritage legislation. Wheelchair access via Wickham Terrace.

Sir Thomas Brisbane Planetarium *Map 5*

This observatory is in the **Mt Coot-tha section** of **Brisbane Botanical Gardens**. Of special interest is the Cosmic Skydome, a 12m dome onto which images of the night sky are projected as a commentary takes place. Wheelchair accessible. Open Wed–Sun. Bookings advisable. Ph: (07) 3403 2578 for info and session times.

Recreational activities

Action

Archerfield Speedkarts (Colebard St, Archerfield) has real racing carts in a daredevil arena. Open Mon–Fri, 9am–10pm; Sat, 8am–10pm; Sun, 8am–6pm. Ph: (07) 3274 2280. www.gokarts.net.au

Old Windmill

GolfMania (320 Manly Rd, Manly West) offers driving ranges, minigolf, a pro shop and professional clinics, as well as a children's playground and a cafe. Open Mon, 10am–10pm; Tue–Sun, 8am–10pm. Ph: (07) 3397 1222

Go hot-air ballooning with **Fly Me to the Moon** (95 Dykes St, Mt Gravatt). Takeoff is just after dawn and the balloon travels 10–15km during the trip. Ph: (07) 3849 3185

Kingston Park Raceway (20 Mudgee St) offers another opportunity for go-kart enthusiasts. Open Mon–Thur, 10am–8pm; Fri–Sat, 10am–10pm; Sun, 10am–6pm. Ph: (07) 3208 8399. www.gokarts.com.au

Milton Tenpin Bowl (Frew St) is a bowling alley complete with bar and disco lights on the lanes. Open daily, 9am–midnight. Ph: (07) 3369 2488

Teenagers can try the free skateboarding facilities at **Neal Macrossan Playground**, cnr Caxton and Caroline Sts, Paddington. The park also has playground equipment and a basketball surface. Ph: (07) 3403 8888

Art

Galleries are located throughout the city. A full listing of CBD galleries can be obtained from City Hall, which itself houses the **City Hall Art Gallery**, a space showing contemporary artists. Open daily, 10am–5pm, Ph: (07) 3221 8411. A pamphlet outlining an inner-city **Art Circuit** (p.25) is also available. For suburban galleries, try a tourist info centre for details or advice.

Cycling

A sealed bike track runs along the bank of the Brisbane River, on the southern fringe of the city centre. The track is shared with pedestrians and offers an easy, level surface for the day tripper as well as a long stretch of bikeway for the serious cyclist. A map of metropolitan bikeways, of which there are several, is available from City Hall.

The Brisbane River

The Brisbane River has played an integral role in the history of Brisbane. Local indigenous people relied on the river for food, fishing in places like present-day Gardens Point, at the end of the City Botanical Gardens. After John Oxley charted its course in 1823, the area was progressively opened up to Europeans. First sailing ships and then steamers transported people and supplies. Sand-dredging began in 1862 in an effort to make the river more suitable for passage. However, a badly situated port at Brisbane's centre was eventually transferred to Fisherman's Island after WWII. Floating bathing boxes and swimming pools were popular at the turn of the century, but floods have devastated the city more than once. During the 1974 flood, one of the most severe on record, the river was over 3km wide in some places.

In recent years the social, economic and environmental impact of dredging, uncontrolled drainage and riverside construction has been assessed and the river's importance to the original inhabitants acknowledged. Today, the Brisbane River is regaining its place as a central feature of local life with an embargo on harmful industrial activity and the development of riverside precincts, pathways and parks.

Film

Brisbane boasts a range of cinemas in both the CBD and suburbs. Pride of place goes to the **Regent Centre** in Queen St Mall. Beginning its life as a theatre, the building's ornate gold-leaf ceiling has been refurbished and there is a marble staircase to a second floor. The foyer and one of the ground-floor theatres have been restored to near-original condition – with cinematic modifications.

Another noteworthy city cinema is the **Dendy** (346 George St), which shows arthouse films. Mock-marble statues and sky-blue lighting greet ticket buyers on arrival. The **Schonell Theatre**, at the University of Qld, St Lucia, also screens alternative films. The **Classic Cinema** (963 Stanley St, East Brisbane) shows old favourites in an old-style setting. The *Courier-Mail*, Brisbane's daily newspaper, has film listings and cinema details, as do the free weekly street papers.

Literature

The keen browser will discover several good bookshops in the CBD, such as **Folio Books** (85 Albert St), **Mary Ryan's Bookshop** (Queen St Mall) and **McGills Bookstore** (201 Elizabeth St). Worth a look is the extensive children's section in the **American Book Store** (173 Elizabeth St) and the music magazines in **Rocking Horse Records**' upstairs space (101 Adelaide St). Generally, most of the inner suburbs have independent bookshops, while outer suburbs accommodate chain stores.

Music

In recent years, Brisbane has gained fame for the international success of some of its pop/rock bands, such as Savage Garden and Regurgitator. These groups are, however, only the tip of a large and eclectic music culture, reflected in the variety of venues offering live music. Jazz and blues are heard, for example, at such locations as the **Jazz-n-Blues Bar** (Centra Brisbane Hotel, Roma St) and the **Pavilion Bar** (Heritage Hotel, Edward St). The **Treasury Hotel**, cnr George and Elizabeth Sts, puts on local rock and roll bands almost every night. **Clubs** such as **City Rowers Tavern** (Eagle St) are scattered around the city centre, with several clustered in Elizabeth and Mary Sts, as well as in Fortitude Valley (p.23).

Shopping

Facing Queen St Mall are 5 major shopping areas, each with its own style. The **Myer Centre** has 4 levels of assorted shops and businesses, as well as a department store. On the top floor is an amusement centre, **Top's**, where an unusual attraction – a 'dragon coaster' (a junior version of the rollercoaster) – sweeps through the air. Open Mon–Thurs, 9am–5pm; Fri, 9am–9pm; Sat, 9am–4pm; Sun, 10.30am–4pm. Single tickets, a pack of 10 or a day pass are available. Ph: (07) 3221 9177

Wintergarden, a spacious marbled complex, houses several interstate designer outlets, while the elegant **Brisbane Arcade**, with its leadlight windows and elaborate glass roof, nurtures local talent. **Broadway**, a venue with an emphasis on the young shopper, contains an array of retailers and eateries, and the **David Jones** department store offers a wide range of stock. Grand 19th-century facades can be seen above the mall's duty-free shops,

South Bank Parklands

Kingston Park Raceway

banks, fashion stores and other solo businesses. Most CBD shops open 9am–5.30pm weekdays, and 9am–4pm weekends. Wheelchair accessible.

Many suburbs have small shopping centres, and complexes are located at Brookside, Carindale, Chermside, Garden City, Indooroopilly, Logan, Stafford, Toombul and Toowong.

Theatre

Brisbane's premier theatres are located at the **Performing Arts Complex** at South Bank (p.27). Brisbane has always had a strong amateur dramatics tradition, however, and small theatres are dotted throughout the suburbs. Other larger or CBD performance spaces include **La Boite Theatre** (p.26), the **Metro Arts Theatre** (109 Edward St), featuring contemporary performance, and the **Princess Theatre** (p.15), which offers a range of shows on a venue-for-hire basis.

On the water

Amazons (42 Amazons Pl, Jindalee) in Brisbane's SW, is an amusement park with water rides. In pride of place is a large waterslide. Open daily Sept–Mar, 10am–5pm. Ph: (07) 3279 3334

Oxley Creek Canoe Trail travels from Pamphlett Bridge, Tennyson, to Kendall, a journey along the Brisbane River of about 2.5hr with the tide.

There are several other entry points, all of which are wheelchair accessible. Ph: (07) 3225 6757. This is one of several established canoe trails on the river, creeks and other water tributaries around Brisbane. Contact a tourist info centre for info on trails and tours.

On a steamy summer day, take a cooling dip at the **Valley Swimming Pool** (Wickham St, Fortitude Valley), built in 1925 and a wonderful example of the architecture of the time. Pick up a pamphlet about public aquatic centres from City Hall.

Fun for the young

- ★ Breaka Beach, South Bank Parklands (p.26)
- ★ Brisbane River walking/cycling track (p.34)
- ★ Neal Macrossan Playground, Paddington (p.33)
- ★ New Farm Park, New Farm (p.25, 32)
- ★ Suttons Beach, Redcliffe (p.29)
- ★ Top's Amusement Centre, CBD (p.34)
- ★ Valley Swimming Pool, Fortitude Valley (p.35)
- ★ Wynnum Wading Pool, Wynnum (p.20)

Suggested tours – Map 5

Hilltop tour

Approximate distance

17km return from Brisbane CBD

About the tour

Take a journey 'round the ridges' of the Westside. The trip starts with the brashness of cafe society in Park Rd, and then slips into old-world charm as well as the beauties of nature. Government House and Brisbane General Cemetery offer a glimpse of the grand days of yesteryear while Brisbane Forest Park and the Mt Coot-tha Botanical Gardens provide a study in contrasts. The sweeping circuit of Sir Samuel Griffith Dr leads to Simpson Falls, a good place for a stretch of the legs. From there, it's only a hop, step and a jump back into Brisbane's inner-suburban life including colonial buildings on Petrie and Wickham Terraces.

Places of interest

❶ **Park Rd, Milton** (p.24)
❷ **Government House, Rosalie**
❸ **Brisbane General Cemetery, Toowong** (p.30)
❹ **Brisbane Botanical Gardens: Mt Coot-tha** (p.32)
❺ **Mt Coot-tha Lookout** (p.30)
❻ **Brisbane Forest Park** (p.141)
❼ **Simpson Falls, Mt Coot-tha Park** (p.32)
❽ **Latrobe and Given Terraces, Paddington** (p.26)
❾ **Petrie and Wickham Terraces** (p.26)
❿ **Old Windmill, Wickham Terrace** (p.32)

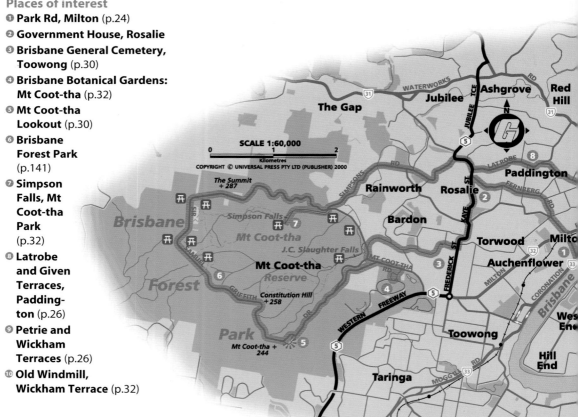

Historic tour

Approximate distance

10km round trip from Brisbane CBD

About the tour

Colonial history and contemporary life intersect in this potted version of Brisbane's heritage. Begin with a cup of tea at the City Botanical Gardens before taking a walk along Merton Rd, Woolloongabba, and on to the Gabba, Brisbane's premier cricket ground. A trip across the Story Bridge to Fortitude Valley's Chinatown offers a glimpse into Brisbane's Chinese-Australian history. NE from here is colonial Newstead House, and the antique shops of Clayfield. Driving back towards the city, a stop in Spring Hill gives the opportunity for a ramble through its laneways and a look at the Spring Hill Baths.

Places of interest

❶ **Brisbane Botanical Gardens: City** (p.31)

❷ **Merton Rd, Woolloongabba** (p.28)

❸ **Brisbane Cricket Ground, Woolloongabba** (p.28)

❹ **Story Bridge** (p.13)

❺ **Chinatown, Fortitude Valley** (p.23)

❻ **Newstead House, Newstead** (p.25)

❼ **Breakfast Creek, Newstead** (p.25)

❽ **Sandgate Rd, Clayfield**

❾ **Old Museum, Bowen Hills**

❿ **Spring Hill Baths, Spring Hill** (p.27)

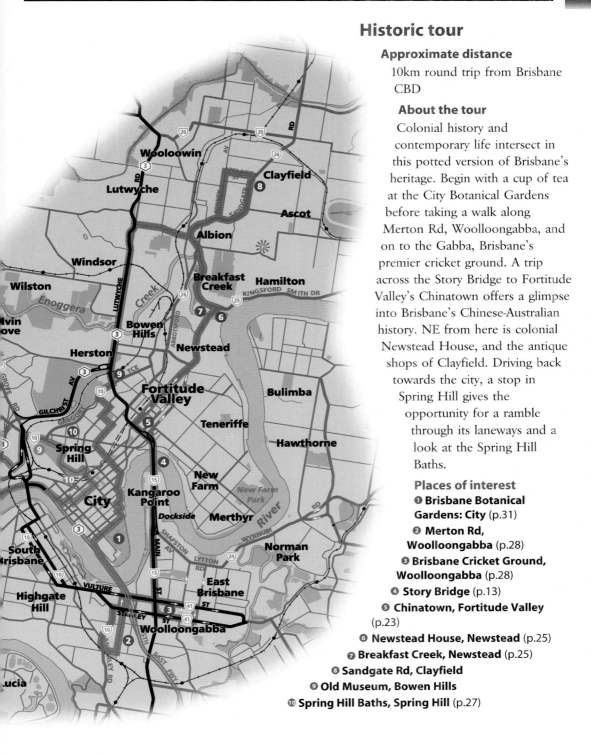

Left: **North Gorge,
Point Lookout**
Right: **Whale-
watching**

Moreton Bay Islands

'The Bay' — a 100km expanse of boat-dotted water sheltered from the open sea by a band of long sand islands. This is where city-siders go to hoist a sail, cast a line, or just to feel the sea wind in their hair.

The Pacific pounds the eastern beaches of Bribie, Moreton, North Stradbroke and South Stradbroke Islands, which shield the inner reaches. The sand masses of the outer islands taper south from outcrops of volcanic rock, rising along their spines to mountainous dunes. Mt Tempest, on Moreton, presides over richly vegetated valleys, heath-covered hills, sandblows and the long scoop of the ocean beach.

Through the passages between the islands, the swell brings blue-green ocean water deep into the Bay. It is claimed that 365 islands can be found within these sheltered waters. The islands of the central Bay appear from a distance to be little more than tricks of light, small mirages floating here and there on the wide, shimmering sweep of water. To the south they become more numerous, and more substantial, crowding together in a maze of mangrove-lined waterways.

i Tourist information

Bribie Island Tourist Information Centre
Benabrow Ave, Bellara 4507
Ph: (07) 3408 9026

Brisbane Tourism
Ground Floor, City Hall, King George Square, Brisbane 4000
Ph: (07) 3221 8411
www.visitbrisbane.com.au

Naturally Queensland Information Centre (EPA) (info on national parks)
Ground Floor, 160 Ann St, Brisbane 4000
Ph: (07) 3227 8185
www.env.qld.gov.au

Tourism Queensland
Level 36/123 Eagle St, Brisbane 4000
Ph: (07) 3406 5400
www.tq.com.au

Redlands Tourism
152 Shore St West, Cleveland 4163
Ph: (07) 3821 0057
www.redland.net.au/redlandstourism

Must see, must do

★ **Cape Moreton Lighthouse** (p.46)
★ **Day trip to Coochie** (p.56)
★ **Gorge Walk, North Stradbroke** (p.53)
★ **Island-hopping the southern Bay** (p.58)
★ **Whale-watching** (pp.49, 54)

Radio stations

4QR: AM 612 (boating, surfing and fishing reports: Sat, 7.10 am)

Bay FM: FM 100.3

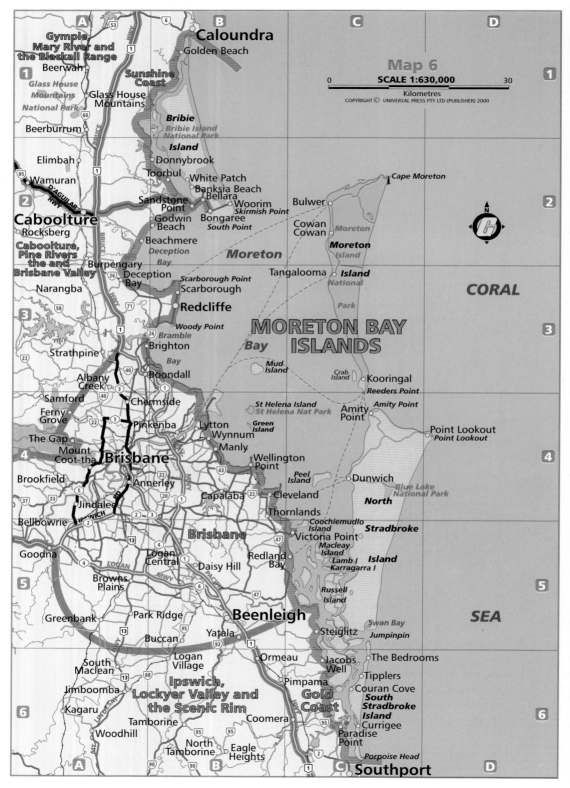

Map 6

SCALE 1:630,000

0 — 30

Kilometres

COPYRIGHT © UNIVERSAL PRESS PTY LTD (PUBLISHER) 2000

**Gympie,
Mary River and
the Blackall Range**

**Caboolture,
Pine Rivers
the and
Brisbane Valley**

**Ipswich,
Lockyer Valley and
the Scenic Rim**

Caloundra

Golden Beach

Beerwah

Glass House
Mountains
National Park

Sunshine
Coast

Glass House
Mountains

Beerburrum

*Bribie
Bribie Island
National Park*

Island

Elimbah

Donnybrook

Toorbul

White Patch

Wamuran

Banksia Beach

Bellara

Sandstone
Point

Woorim

Skirmish Point

Caboolture

Godwin
Beach

Bongaree

South Point

Rocksberg

Bulwer

Cowan
Cowan

Narangba

Burpengary

Beachmere

Deception

Bay

Moreton

*Moreton
Island*

Deception
Bay

Scarborough Point

Tangalooma

Island

National

Scarborough

Redcliffe

Park

**MORETON BAY
ISLANDS**

CORAL

Woody Point

Bramble

Strathpine

Brighton

Bay

Bay

*Mud
Island*

*Crab
Island*

Kooringal

Reeders Point

Albany
Creek

Boondall

Samford

Chermside

*St Helena Island
St Helena Nat Park*

Amity
Point

Amity Point

Ferny
Grove

Pinkenba

*Green
Island*

Point Lookout

Point Lookout

The Gap

Lytton

Wynnum

Mount
Coot-tha

Brisbane

Manly

Brookfield

Annerley

Wellington
Point

*Peel
Island*

Dunwich

*Blue Lake
National Park*

Jindalee

Capalaba

Cleveland

North

Bellbowrie

Thornlands

Stradbroke

Goodna

Brisbane

*Coochiemudlo
Island*

Victoria Point

*Macleay
Island*

Island

Logan
Central

Redland
Bay

*Lamb I
Karragarra I*

Daisy Hill

Browns
Plains

*Russell
Island*

Greenbank

Park Ridge

Beenleigh

Steiglitz

Swan Bay

Jumpinpin

SEA

Buccan

Yatala

Logan
Village

Ormeau

Jacobs
Well

The Bedrooms

South
Maclean

Pimpama

Tipplers

Jimboomba

**Ipswich,
Lockyer Valley and
the Scenic Rim**

Kagaru

Coomera

**Gold
Coast**

Couran Cove

*South
Stradbroke
Island*

Tamborine

Woodhill

North
Tamborine

Eagle
Heights

Currigee

*Paradise
Point*

Porpoise Head

Southport

Natural features

Moreton Bay is defined by large sand islands in the east, and the scalloped coast of the mainland to the west and south.

In the north the Bay is open to the ocean; to the south it narrows, closing with the mainland in a jostle of smaller islands. The prevailing south-easterlies bring good rainfall, replenishing the many freshwater lakes and allowing the islands to support a variety of plant communities, including thick woodland.

Bribie Island is a huge sandspit, forested with stands of cypress, melaleuca, banksia, box, eucalypts and exotic pine plantations.

To the east lies **Moreton Island**. At its NE tip are the cliffs of Cape Moreton, a rocky promontory anchoring the drifting sands of aeons. Its spectacular dunes culminate in Mt Tempest, 273m high, which rises almost at the midpoint of the island.

North Stradbroke Island, too, was built by the action of wind and wave, its dune systems running from the rocky outcrop at the NE tip.

South Stradbroke Island once formed the tail of its northern neighbour, but was severed at Jumpinpin during a storm in 1896.

Many of the southern Bay islands combine mainland features — red-soil hills, stately trees and melaleuca wetlands — with sandy coves and mangrove flats.

History

For many thousands of years, the islands of Moreton Bay were home to Aboriginal clans — Bribie to the Joondoburrie people, Moreton to the Ngugi, and Stradbroke to the Noonuccals and the Goenpuls.

Here, as elsewhere, traditional Aboriginal society declined with the European settlers' expropriation of their lands, forced removal to missions, introduced diseases and, at times, violent conflict with the newcomers. On Bribie, for example, the Aboriginal population was reduced from as many as 1000 in 1800 to nil in 1897.

Aboriginal people on the ocean-front islands would have seen the sails of the *Endeavour* as James Cook and his crew passed by in 1770. In 1799 Matthew Flinders and his crew entered Moreton Bay, exploring as far south as Coochiemudlo Island.

The penal settlement established on the mainland in 1824 was at first reliant on ships for its provisions, so a pilot station was set up at Amity Pt, on Stradbroke Island, to guide ships through the shoal-bedevilled South Passage. In 1827 a convict outstation was established at Dunwich, on Stradbroke's western shore, to tranship stores en route to Brisbane. It later functioned as a mission, a quarantine station, a Benevolent Institution, a lazaret (for lepers) and a base for sandmining.

Wild Guide

The ***Wild Guide to Moreton Bay***, published by the Qld Museum, is a superb full-colour guide to the Bay's habitats, plants, birds and marine life.

Cape Moreton, Moreton Island

A fishing industry was soon established in the Bay. For a while in the 19th century, dugong-hunting was a commercial enterprise, and in the period 1951–62 there was a whaling station at Tangalooma, on Moreton Island.

Since the late 1940s, sandmining companies have operated on North Stradbroke and there are still sandmining leases over large parts of the island.

Bribie Island

Bribie is the 3rd-largest, the most developed and, being linked to the mainland by a bridge, the most accessible of the Bay islands. It was named after a basket-maker/fisherman who absconded from the Moreton Bay penal settlement to live on the island with the Joondoburrie people in about 1840.

Bribie is a low sand island marking the northerly limits of the Bay. Its shores are edged with white sand beaches, with stretches of mangroves in the more sheltered spots. Beyond the built-up areas in the south are national parks, which preserve the natural landscapes of the island. Pine plantations occupy the remaining areas.

Getting there

Bribie is within an hour's drive of Brisbane. Take the Bruce Hwy to the Bribie Island exit and follow the Caboolture–Bribie road east across the bridge over Pumicestone Passage to the township of Bellara.

All the settled parts of the island are served by sealed roads, and it is easy to get around in an ordinary car. For driving in national parks and for travel on the ocean beach a 4WD is essential. A **beach permit** is required for travel in some national park areas and on the beaches. Apply at the Bongaree Caravan Park (Welsby Pde, Bongaree) or at the Caboolture Shire Council's Customer Service Centre in Hasking St, Caboolture, Ph: (07) 5420 0100. Registration papers and a current driver's licence are necessary, and a fee will be charged.

Getting around

Bribie Island 4WD Scenic Tours operates daily, taking visitors along the 30km of ocean beach and calling in at 3 lagoons and the WWII military installations. It is necessary to book in advance. Ph: (07) 3408 8300

Explore difficult-to-get-to reaches of the Pumicestone Passage Marine Park and spot dolphins, loggerhead turtles — and possibly even the elusive dugong — with **Ferryman Cruises**, Bellara, Ph: (07) 3408 7124, or **Dolphin Wild-Island Cruises**, Sandstone Pt, Ph: (07) 5497 5628.

The southern parts of Bribie are ideal for **bike rides**. Bike tracks run across the island beside First Ave and along the foreshore at Bongaree. Hire a bicycle at **Bribie Sports and Cycles** (opposite the public library in Welsby Pde, Bongaree).

Dolphin Wild-Island Cruise

Touring the beach at Bribie

Pumicestone Passage

Festivals and events

Local **hobby and craft markets** are held every 4th Sun (am) at the Community Arts Centre, Sunderland Dr, Banksia Beach, and every 3rd Sun (am) in the First Ave carpark, Bongaree.

For background on Bribie's bird life, **bird walks** are held on the 1st Sat of each month. Phone Peter on (07) 5497 5741.

Main localities

Bellara *Map 7 A2*

The gateway to Bribie is Bellara, a thriving township on Pumicestone Passage. On Marine Pde is a 'talking monument', which presents the history of Bribie Island at the touch of a button. Near the Sylvan Beach Esp are boats for hire and the departure point for cruises of the Passage. The tourist info centre in Benabrow Ave has a wealth of information on Bribie. Open Mon-Fri, 9am-4pm; Sat, 9am-3pm; Sun, 9.30am-1pm. Ph: (07) 3408 9026

Bongaree *Map 7 B2*

Bongaree grew up around its jetty where, before the days of the bridge, boats arrived with holiday-makers and day-trippers. Now people come there to fish, or to take a walk out over the clear waters of the Passage.

Woorim *Map 7 D2*

On the ocean beach is the township of Woorim, strung in relaxed fashion along streets running north and south behind the dunes. The old Blue Pacific Hotel still stands opposite the main access to the beach. Across the water lies Moreton Island, protecting Bribie from a SE swell. From the lookout at Boyd St, you can see Moreton's spectacular dunes.

National and conservation parks

Settlement is restricted to the southern part of Bribie, and almost a third of the island is given over to national park.

Bribie Island NP *Map 6 B1*

Bribie Island NP occupies the western foreshores of the island from Banksia Beach north to the Spit and down the eastern coast as far as Woorim.

There are campsites at Mission Pt, Lime Pocket, Westaways Creek, Gallagher Pt and Poverty Creek, all of which can be reached by boat. From the park entry at the end of White Patch Esp there are 4WD/walking tracks to Gallagher Pt (3km, 1-way) and Poverty Creek (7km, 1-way). Picnic tables, fireplaces and toilets are provided at Mission Pt. Visitors are asked to bring their own drinking water and firewood. **Camping permits** should be obtained from the ranger on patrol, by self-registering at Mission Pt, or by phoning the NP Ranger Office at White Patch Esp (Ph: (07) 3408 8451). No domestic animals are permitted within the park or along the beaches that adjoin it.

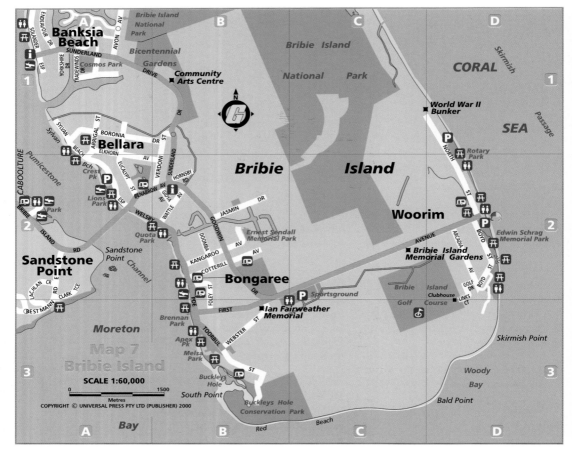

Map 7
Bribie Island
SCALE 1:60,000
0   1500
Metres
COPYRIGHT © UNIVERSAL PRESS PTY LTD (PUBLISHER) 2000

Buckley's Hole Conservation Park
Map 7 B3

This is a favourite bird-watching spot where as many as 350 species of birds have been known to gather, at times including black swans.

Parks and gardens

Most of the foreshore areas in the south are parkland, with shady trees, BBQs, drinking fountains and picnic tables. At **Brennan Park**, Bongaree, is a bandstand and children's play area.

Other attractions

Aquatic Leisure Complex

This complex in Goodwin Dr is equipped with outdoor and indoor heated swimming pools, volley-ball courts, BBQs and a coffee shop. Open daily; times vary. Ph: (07) 3410 0200

Community Arts Centre, Banksia Beach *Map 7 B1*

This centre in Sunderland Dr is set among the **Bicentennial Gardens**, an area of natural bushland with various short walks, including a guided wildflower walk with wheelchair access, and a special walk for the visually impaired. Maps are available at the centre. The gardens also feature a talking monument, which gives a brief account of the Aboriginal history of the island. Open Tue–Sun, 10am–4pm. Ph: (07) 3408 9288

Ian Fairweather memorial *Map 7 B3*

Near the junction of Goodwin Dr and First Ave a path leads to a monument that has been erected among the trees where the hut of this highly original painter once stood. He lived and worked as a recluse on Bribie Island from 1953 until his death in 1974. The walking/bike

Black swan, Buckley's Hole

track from Woorim has been named **Fairweather Track** in his honour.

Melsa Park *Map 7 B3*
At this park, on Toorbul St, **Bongaree**, there are rides on model steam trains, running every 3rd Sun of the month.

White Patch Gallery
The White Patch Gallery specialises in high-quality paintings, sculpture and pottery by Australian artists. Open Tue–Sun, 10am–5pm. Ph: (07) 3408 9000

WWII bunker *Map 7 D1*
This relic of WWII stands in the dunes at the end of North St, **Woorim**. It was a naval control station for the anti-submarine detection cables laid on the seabed between Bribie and Moreton Islands. Other military emplacements can be seen further north along the beach.

Recreational activities
Bushwalking
With its extensive national park areas and easy-walking terrain, Bribie is an ideal place for bushwalking, birdwatching and enjoying the display of wildflowers that lights up the wallum heath in winter and spring. The national park tracks and the walks in the **Bicentennial Gardens** wind through expanses of bridal bush, boronia, dillwynia, grass trees and bungwall fern.

On the water
Many people come to Bribie simply to enjoy the pleasures of the beach. Woorim Beach, protected from the SE swell by Moreton Island, usually has the gentlest of surfs, and the Pumicestone Passage beaches are good places for still-water **swimming**.

Fishing is a favourite pastime on Bribie, whether from boats, the jetty or the beaches. The summer whiting really fire at Skirmish Pt on light gear and worm bait.

Both Pumicestone Passage and the waters off Woorim Beach are ideal for **sailing** and **windsurfing**, and **waterskiing** is popular in the protected waters of the Passage.

Sailing at Bribie

Fun for the young
★ Aquatic Leisure Complex (p.44)
★ Bike-riding (p.42)
★ Model steam train rides, Bongaree (p.45)
★ Swimming (p.45)

Moreton Island
Moreton is a sand island, formed by the action of wind and tide. Most of it is wilderness, with only small pockets of settlement at Bulwer, Cowan Cowan, Tangalooma, Kooringal and the Cape Moreton Lighthouse.

Visitors to Moreton Island are asked to respect its special status: leave your pets at home, do not use local wood for fires (bring your own), and take all your rubbish with you when you leave.

Getting there
By air
An air charter service to Tangalooma Resort leaves from Eagle Farm. Ph: (07) 3268 6333

By catamaran
A high-speed catamaran runs daily to Tangalooma Resort from the Holt St terminal, Pinkenbah (a courtesy bus carries passengers from the CBD to the wharf). Ph: (07) 3268 6333

By private boat
Only experienced boat-owners should make the lengthy Bay crossing to Moreton Island. There is shelter at Days Gutter, near Kooringal, and the Tangalooma Wrecks.

By vehicular ferry
The *Combie Trader* runs daily between Scarborough and Bulwer. Ph: (07) 3203 6399

The *Moreton Venture* leaves Whytes Island, Lytton, for the Tangalooma Wrecks and occasionally Reeders Pt, near Kooringal, every day except Tue. Ph: (07) 3895 1000

Prohibited zone
All forms of fishing, crabbing and bait-collecting are prohibited in the Tripcony Bight Protection Zone in Pumicestone Passage. This is a special section of the Moreton Bay Marine Park.

Blue Lagoon, Moreton Island

The **Redland Barge Transport Services'** *Sirenia* runs Fri, Sat and Sun between Redland Bay and Reeders Pt. Ph: (07) 3829 0600

Island Transport Services has a new service running daily between Amity (on North Stradbroke) and Reeders Pt. Bookings essential. Ph: (07) 3829 0008

Getting around

There are no sealed roads on Moreton, so visitors must rely on private 4WDs, 4WD tours operated by the *Combie Trader*, bus tours run by the Tangalooma Resort, and their own legs. The beaches and the well-signposted sand tracks are the only thoroughfares, and a **vehicle permit** is required (available from barge operators). The island has many walking tracks, of varying length and difficulty.

Settlements

Bulwer *Map 6 C2*

Bulwer is the site of a 19th-century pilot station for ships entering Moreton Bay. It was established in 1848, after the treacherous South Passage was abandoned in favour of the route around Cape Moreton. The township survived the closure of the pilot station in 1909 and now has holiday houses set among the trees and a permanent population of about 30. Bulwer has a general store, a shop selling fishing supplies and a petrol bowser. Three hulks

scuttled there in the 1930s to form a small boat harbour now lie on the beach. **Comboyuro Pt**, just north of Bulwer, is a favourite fishing spot. Its eroding shore is strewn with the bleached timbers of fallen trees.

Cape Moreton *Map 6 C2*

Cape Moreton commands sweeping views south to Stradbroke Island, west across Bribie to the Glass House Mts, and north and east across the Pacific Ocean. It is the dramatic site of the **Cape Moreton Lighthouse**, Qld's 1st, which was built by civil prisoners in 1857 from local sandstone. The headland rises 100m above the sea, and the tower itself is 23m high. (The lighthouse is not open to the public.)

Cowan Cowan *Map 6 C2*

This entirely residential and holiday-rental settlement has no facilities for casual visitors. It was the site of a signal station during WWII. 4WDs are not permitted on the beach at this point, and the track bypasses the township.

Kooringal *Map 6 C3*

Kooringal nestles among cypress pines and banksias near the small-boat anchorage of Days Gutter. It has a permanent population of about 20 and a number of holiday houses. There is a general store, selling basic supplies, alcohol and petrol.

A marine gem

Flinders Reef, off Cape Moreton, has the highest number of coral species of any subtropical or temperate reef on the east coast, and is now a high-conservation zone with all forms of fishing prohibited.

Tangalooma *Map 6 C3*

This luxury resort was built on the site of the old Tangalooma whaling station, established in 1951 and closed in 1962. The beach in front of the resort is for the exclusive use of resort guests — no 4WD or pedestrian traffic is allowed. But everyone is free to visit 'The Wrecks' nearby, which provide anchorage for boats and an excellent spot to fish, snorkel and scuba-dive (p.49).

National and marine parks

Moreton Island itself is 94% national park. It is surrounded by the waters of the **Moreton Bay Marine Park.**

Other attractions

Big and Little Sandhills *Map 9*

These sandhills streak the south of the island with bands of dazzling white. The Big Sandhills reach a height of 80m.

Blue Lagoon *Map 9* ❹

Blue Lagoon is the largest freshwater lake on the island. Its limpid waters are replenished by rainwater filtered by the surrounding dunes, and a pure-white sand beach fringes its eastern shore.

The Desert *Map 9* ❺

South of Tangalooma is the Desert, a sandblow with shifting dunes as desolate as a Saharan landscape.

Honeyeater Lake *Map 9* ❻

This small lake is sunk deep in a plateau of woodland and heath. The short walk from the carpark to a lookout above the lake runs through a garden of wild-flowers. Watch for the yellow streak of a white-faced honeyeater.

Honeymoon Bay *Map 9*

This is a deep sandy cove carved into the volcanic hills near North Pt.

Mirapool Lagoon *Map 9* ❶

This lagoon at the southern end of the island is a refuge for a variety of wading birds.

Mt Tempest *Map 9* ❿

Said to be the highest permanent sandhill in the world, Mt Tempest rises above the surrounding ridges to a height of 273m. From its summit the climber is rewarded with views unsurpassed on the island.

The rough access road runs 2.5km from Middle Rd to a parking area, from which a walking track zigzags to the summit through flowering heath and stunted scribbly gums. It is a leisurely 45min climb, with a 30min descent.

Rous Battery *Map 9* ❷

Clinging to the dunes above Toompani Beach is Rous Battery, the remains of a WWII defence post. The arc of an old

Cape Moreton Lighthouse

Moreton's marsupials
Bandicoots are the largest marsupial found on Moreton — the island has no kangaroos, wallabies or koalas.

Coconut palms, Tangalooma

gun emplacement cantilevers dramatically over the eroded slope.

Tangalooma Wrecks *Map 9* ❷

The Tangalooma Wrecks are 15 hulks scuttled to provide anchorage for small craft. The oldest is the *Maryborough*, an iron-hulled bucket dredge built in 1885. This is the spot to snorkel, scuba-dive or wet a line.

White Rock *Map 9* ❸

White Rock erupts like a huge sandcastle from Gonzales Beach. It is part of a stretch of strange formations of 'coffee rock', carved from the vari-coloured cliffs that flank the beach.

Recreational activities

Much of the recreational activity on Moreton Island is nature-based, from birdwatching to scuba-diving.

Birdwatching

Birdwatchers will find much to delight them — many varieties of honeyeater, quail, kite, sea-eagle, pelican, resident waders, and, from Sept to Apr, thousands of migratory birds.

Bushwalking

The beaches are the hiker's natural highways, but they must be shared with 4WDs.

Inland, there are long walking trails along the **Telegraph Track** (8km 1-way) and the **Rous Battery Track** (9km 1-way). Shorter tracks wind up Mt Tempest (2km return), around North Pt, to the Big Sandhills, and from Tangalooma to the Desert.

Camping

Many people visit Moreton for away-from-it-all camping. There are designated campsites at **Comboyuro Pt, Ben-Ewa, Eagers Creek, Tangalooma Wrecks** and **Blue Lagoon** (see map 9). You will need a **camping permit** (available from the barge operators or by contacting the ranger before your visit).
Ph: (07) 3408 2710

Fishing

Fish the beaches and headlands for whiting, tailor, bream, dart and flathead, or the offshore reefs for game fish. Rock fishers take good hauls of bream and tailor from North Pt in winter, especially when the south-easters blow.

Watching marine life

Spotting marine life is another favourite activity for visitors. Dugongs, dolphins, manta rays and turtles abound in the waters around the island, and **Cape**

Game fishing

Fun for the young

★ Climbing the Big and Little
   Sandhills (p.47)
★ Whale-watching from Cape
   Moreton (p.48)

Moreton is the perfect vantage point from which to watch the stately progress of migrating humpback whales Jun–Nov. **Tangalooma Resort** offers a whale-watch cruise that leaves Brisbane 3 times a week from mid-Jun to end Oct. Ph: (07) 3268 6333

In the water

The wrecks near Tangalooma and at the **Curtin artificial reef** are major breeding grounds for fish, and are ideal spots for snorkelling and scuba-diving. The coral and fish at **Flinders Reef** and **Smith Rock** are special attractions for divers.

Inquisitive dolphin

North Stradbroke Island

'Straddie', or Minjerribah (generally accepted as its Aboriginal name), is the largest of the Moreton Bay islands. Its bountiful waters, variety of plant communities and comparative abundance of land animals supplied the local people with a good living long before Cook made his fateful voyage past its shores.

These days people are drawn by Straddie's relaxed island atmosphere, its forests and wildflowers, its bays and rocky points, and its long stretches of sandy beach. They come, too, for the fishing, the surfing — and for the minerals that can be extracted from its ancient dunes.

Getting there

By road

The **North Stradbroke Island Bus Service** runs from the Transit Centre in Roma St, Brisbane, to the passenger ferries (see below) at Toondah Harbour, Cleveland, 4 times a day, Mon–Fri. Ph: (07) 3211 2501

By rail

There is a frequent Citytrain service to Cleveland, and the 2 ferry companies send courtesy buses to carry passengers to Toondah Harbour (see below).

By passenger ferry

The **Stradbroke Ferries Water Taxi** makes several trips every day from Toondah Harbour, Cleveland, to Dunwich (25min). Bookings not required. Ph: (07) 3286 2666

The *Stradbroke Flyer* passenger ferry also leaves several times daily from Toondah Harbour, and deposits its passengers at the One Mile jetty at Dunwich (about 30min). Bookings are necessary in the holiday season. Ph: (07) 3286 1964

Foot passengers can leave their cars in parking lots at either passenger ferry departure point at Toondah Harbour, or take a bus or Citytrain to Cleveland.

Keen riders take their bikes on the passenger ferry and cycle across the island. (It is about 20km from Dunwich to Point Lookout.) Within the townships it is generally easy, and more pleasant, to get about on foot or by bike. Amity, being flat, is a particularly good spot to cycle.

First encounter
Matthew Flinders landed on Stradbroke in 1803 and collected fresh water from a spring at what is now called **Cylinder Beach**. This was the first recorded meeting between Stradbroke's Aborigines and Europeans.

A bus meets the Stradbroke Ferries Water Taxi at Dunwich and the *Stradbroke Flyer* at One Mile, taking passengers to Amity and Point Lookout. Ph: (07) 3409 7151

Taxis can be hired from the **Stradbroke Cab Service**, Ph: (07) 3409 9800, and the **Yellow Maxi Taxi**, Ph: 131 924.

By vehicular ferry

Many visitors bring their cars with them on the vehicular ferries. There are sealed roads running between the 3 main townships, and to the small settlement of Flinders Beach.

Islands Transport Services runs a vehicular catamaran daily from cnr Banana and Weinam Sts, Redland Bay. Bookings essential. Ph: (07) 3829 0008

Stradbroke Ferries has a vehicular ferry service running daily from Toondah Harbour, Cleveland, to Dunwich (about 1hr). Bookings essential. Ph: (07) 3286 2666

4WD vehicles are permitted along most of Flinders Beach and Main Beach providing the owner has a **beach permit**, available from: Redlands Tourism, near Cleveland Stn, open Mon–Fri, 8.30am–5pm; Sat–Sun, 9am–4pm (Ph: (07) 3821 0057); North Stradbroke Island Visitors Centre, Junner St, Dunwich, open Mon–Fri, 8.30am–4.30pm; Sat–Sun, 8.30am–3pm (Ph: (07) 3409 9555) and, after hours, from the camping ground rangers or (at Point Lookout) Bob's 727 and the BP Roadhouse.

The unsealed roads are generally unsuitable for 2WD vehicles, and many are sand tracks that vanish into the scrub. Travel to some parts is severely restricted because there is no public access to roads controlled by the sandmining company, which has leases over much of the island. As well, many fire trails have now been closed off.

Getting around

North Stradbroke Island Bus Tours has tours from the mainland (leaving from the Transit Centre, Roma St, Brisbane) with pick-ups at Cleveland and Dunwich) Mon, Wed and Fri. Bookings essential. Ph: (07) 3211 2501

4WD tours are offered by **Coastal Island Safaris**, Ph: (07) 5598 8144, **Stradbroke Island Tours**, Ph: (07) 3409 8051, and **Sunrover Expeditions Island Day Tours**, Ph: (07) 3203 4241.

Festivals and events

Point Lookout Inshore Rescue Boat Classic Carnival

Held on the last weekend in May at **Main Beach**. Ph: (07) 3821 0057

Lantern and Music Festival

This festival of song and dance, held in Jun every 2 years at the **Point Lookout oval**, welcomes the whales as they migrate north.

Straddie Fishing Classic

This fishing competition, held in Aug, is run by the Stradbroke Island Beach Hotel. Ph: (07) 3409 8188

Main Beach, Point Lookout

Amity Stock

A rock music festival held at Amity in Sept.

Straddie Assault

A surf riders' event hosted by the local club and held at **Main Beach** in Oct. Ph: (07) 3409 8334

Townships

Amity *Map 6 C4*

This is the oldest European settlement on the island, a pilot station having been established there in the early 19th century. The land on which the old buildings stood has been carried away by the swift currents of the Rainbow Channel, which sweep around the point. It continues its remorseless work today, undermining the rocks that are dumped on the shore to protect the remaining land.

Amity is a leafy, peaceful place. Wander along the shore there and you may be observed by a pod of resident dolphins, sporting in Rainbow Channel just metres from where you stand.

The settlement has a camping ground/caravan park, safe swimming area, jetty and boat ramp. Bream are caught off the rocks and jetty, whiting and flathead from the spit, and tailor and dart on nearby Flinders Beach. **Island Boat and Canoe Hire** has an office near the boat ramp. Ph: (07) 3409 7429

Dunwich *Map 6 C4*

Dunwich is the spot where most visitors first set foot on Straddie. Its spreading fig trees, green oval, tranquil Bay outlook and colonial buildings give the township an old-world atmosphere. A free **historical trail guide** (available from the Visitors Centre) identifies convict relics and colonial structures, and tells the stories behind the headstone inscriptions in **Dunwich Cemetery** at One Mile. Dunwich is also the loading terminal for the mineral sands and silica sand (for glass-making) mined on the island.

Poet and Aboriginal rights campaigner Oodgeroo Noonuccal (Kath Walker) was born on the island, and is buried at her home at Moongalba, outside Dunwich.

North Stradbroke Island Historical Museum in Welsby St (open Wed and Sat, 10am–2pm; bus tours at other times by arrangement) has a display of early photographs, shipwreck relics and other items of historical interest. Ph: (07) 3409 9699; (07) 3409 9180 for bus tours.

The **Fig Tree Art Gallery**, cnr Finnegan St and Stradbroke Pl, has a display of contemporary paintings, prints and garden sculpture. Ph: (07) 3409 9643

There are caravan parks/camping grounds at Adam's Beach, to the south, and at Bradbury's Beach, near One Mile.

The **Little Ship Club** at One Mile provides anchorage for yachts and other small craft, and facilities for their crews. It is also a popular venue for island entertainment.

Dunwich looks out past tiny Bird and Goat Islands to **Peel Island**, a former leper colony that has been declared a national park. Private boats can land on the white-sand beach at Horseshoe Bay, but elsewhere is barred to the public, and there are no ferry services to the island.

Horseshoe Bay, Peel Island

Point Lookout *Map 6 D4*

The rays of the morning sun light up Point Lookout a moment before they strike anywhere else in Qld. 'The Point' is a series of rocky promontories, bays and beaches on the NE end of Straddie, where people come to surf, fish, wander, watch the wildlife, and enjoy a quiet seaside holiday. To the south, Main Beach stretches for over 30km, taking the full force of the prevailing winds and ocean swell. If fishing this beach at dawn, look out for the grey kangaroos that visit the dunes.

Point Lookout offers ample rental, resort and hostel accommodation. It is well supplied with general stores, gift shops and a variety of eating places. There are camping grounds at Adder Rock, Thankful Rest (Home Beach) and Cylinder Beach.

Other attractions

Blue Lake *Map 9* ⑩

Blue Lake, or Karboora, in Stradbroke's only national park, is set deep in the forested hills a km or so behind Main Beach. It is a 'window' lake, formed where the water table meets the surface. Blue Lake has clear, deep water and an eerie atmosphere. There is an easy walking track, leading 2.5km in from the sealed Tazi Rd. To protect the fragile lake environment, it is suggested that visitors walk in rather than driving on the 4WD access track.

Brown Lake *Map 9* ⑪

Brown Lake, or Bumiera, is a 'perched' lake, formed above the water table. Its peaty bottom gives the shallow water a tea-coloured stain. The lake is easily reached from Dunwich in a conventional vehicle, and has picnic areas with BBQs. Jet skis and ski boats are no longer allowed on Brown Lake.

Eighteen Mile Swamp *Map 9* ❾

This wetland area behind the foreshore dunes of the ocean beach sustains a rich variety of wildlife. It stretches from north of the Causeway to the far south of the island.

Flinders Beach *Map 9*

Flinders Beach, between Adder Rock and Amity Pt, is a noted refuge for migratory birds such as the eastern curlew, which breeds in Siberia and NW China. Beach users should avoid disturbing these birds, which need all their energy for their amazing flights.

Keyhole Lakes *Map 9* ❻

A former sandmining road — now a potholed track — continues from the Fisherman's Rd to the freshwater Keyhole Lakes, which lie just behind the dunes of Main Beach. (Don't turn off the road onto the sand access tracks to the lakes without a 4WD.)

Myora Springs *Map 9* ❷

The East Coast Rd passes over Myora Springs, just beyond Dunwich. Here a freshwater stream spills into a tidal pond in the dappled green light of a patch of littoral rainforest. A shell midden is visible among the trees on the northern bank. The rare swamp orchid, *Phaius*

Follow the Goompi Trail

A local Aboriginal guide takes visitors on a walking tour of **Dunwich**, during which they learn about bush tucker, traditional hunting methods, bush medicine, fire-making, boomerangs, nullas, spears — and much more. The tour leaves at 10am, Mon–Fri (except 25 Dec–5 Jan), from the North Stradbroke Island Visitors Centre, Junner St. Bookings essential. Ph: (07) 3409 9555 or 3409 9025

Cylinder Beach

tankarvilliae, the largest of Australia's terrestrial orchids, grows nearby and blooms in early spring. Its endangered status is due to illegal collecting and the destruction of its habitat.

Recreational activities
Bushwalking
The **Blue Lake Walk** winds 2.5km through North Stradbroke Island's only national park — a natural garden of scribbly gums, bloodwoods, angophora, grass trees and wildflowers — to Blue Lake.

The **Point Lookout–Amity Walk** along Flinders Beach takes about 2½ hr.

The **Reserve Walk**, above Frenchman's and Deadman's Beaches, winds through brushbox forest. There are observation platforms from which to watch the passing humpback whales in winter.

The **Gorge Walk** (see map 8) is an easy 30min walk around the main Point Lookout cliffs, with steps in the steepest parts. There are several seats along the way, and lookout points from which to watch whales, turtles, dolphins, manta rays and sharks. Whale Rock, at the end of the headland between the gorges, is named for its dramatic blowhole.

Camping
Camping is permitted at many places along Flinders and Main Beaches, as well as the camping grounds at Dunwich,

Blue Lake, North Stradbroke Island

Amity and Point Lookout. All campsites, including foreshore camping, should be **booked before arrival**. Phone the visitors centre, (07) 3409 9555.

On and in the water
Surf fishermen take good catches of whiting, dart, flathead, bream and tailor from gutters along Flinders and Main Beaches. Those spinning with lures from the rock headlands can expect hook-ups from trevally and yellowtail kingfish. On the heavily fished grounds around Flat Rock, Boat Rock and the Group, boat fishermen bottom-bounce for snapper and sweetlip, and troll lures and bait for Spanish mackerel. Join Point Lookout fisherman Mal Starkey for an **offshore fishing trip** on the *Khiton*. Ph: (07) 3409 8353

Sheltered swimming
In a stiff south-easter, **Cylinder Beach** offers good protection. When the north-easter blows, try **South Gorge** and **Main Beach**.

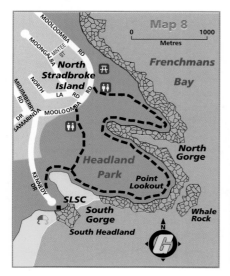

Map 8 — North Stradbroke Island, Frenchmans Bay, Headland Park, Point Lookout, North Gorge, South Gorge, South Headland, Whale Rock, SLSC

Fun for the young

★ Boogie-boarding at Cylinder Beach (p.52)

★ Jetty fishing at Amity (p.51)

★ Whale-watching from Point Lookout (p.54)

Jetty fishing, Amity

Land-based whale-watching

From Jun to Aug a stately train of humpback whales travel north past **Point Lookout** and **Cape Moreton** to calve in the warm waters of the Barrier Reef. The laggards then cross paths with those returning south from about Aug to Nov.

The headlands are box seats for views of breaching, tail-slapping and other frisky behaviour. Locals say that the show is best at dawn and dusk, and that the returning whales put on a more spectacular display.

Stradbroke Adventures organises explorations of headland features such as the Bat Cave and the Cathedral on a 3hr trip to sea in a kayak. Ph: 0417 741 963 or 0417 799 257

Dive the reefs out to Flat Rock with the **Stradbroke Island Scuba Centre**, East Coast Rd, Point Lookout. Ph: (07) 3409 8715

The **Amity Pt Holiday Village** runs organised marine adventures and educational programs. Ph: (07) 3409 7161

South Stradbroke Island

South Stradbroke is the severed tail of North Stradbroke Island, stretching 20km south from Jumpinpin to the Southport Broadwater. It forms a 2km-wide barrier between the Pacific Ocean and the tangle of islands in the south of the Bay.

The island is an Environmental Reserve, and all fauna and flora are protected — including 4 colonies of golden swamp wallabies, found only on North and South Stradbroke.

There are 4 camping grounds (run by Gold Coast Tourist Parks) and 2 resorts on the island, all on the Bay side. (It is recommended that campers bring their own drinking water.)

Getting there

By air

Seair Seaplanes flies daily from Marina Mirage to South Stradbroke Island Resort. Contact the resort for details. Ph: (07) 5577 3311

By boat

Many people travel to the island in their own boats. **Gold Coast Water Taxis** covers the 4 camping areas, with pick-ups anywhere on the Gold Coast. Ph: 018 759 789

There is a regular **Fast Cat ferry** between Runaway Bay Marina (Bayview St, Runaway Bay) and Couran Cove Resort. Ph: (07) 5529 6399

Daily cruise boats to South Stradbroke Island Resort leave from Cavill Ave, Surfers Paradise. A regular **Fast Cat ferry** service operates between Runaway Bay Marina and the resort. There is also a limited **ferry service** from the Horizon Shores Marina, Cabbage Tree Point Rd, Woongoolba. Ph: (07) 5577 3311 for all 3 services.

Getting around

There are no cars on the island. Apart from the Couran Cove **cycling** tracks and the 3-carriage electric '**People Mover**', which links the Broadwater with the ocean beach, all movement on the island itself is on foot. There are a number of

Bayside beach, South Stradbroke Island

Straddie's top eateries

★ Superb cuisine is to be found at the **Blue Water Bistro**, Point Lookout. Award-winning restaurateur Andrew Mirosch specialises in cooking his own catch. Licensed/BYO, with bookings essential. Ph: (07) 3409 8300

★ Have breakfast and coffee high above Frenchman's Beach at the **Laughing Buddha Cafe**. Ph: (07) 3409 8549

★ Enjoy a steak from the **Waves Brasserie**, at the Stradbroke Hotel, with stunning views to Shag Rock and Moreton Island beyond. Ph: (07) 3409 8188

walking tracks through and across the island. **Private boats** are the main means of travel along the western shore.

Main localities

The Bedrooms Camping Area *Map 6 C6*

This is the northernmost camping spot, frequented particularly by fishermen working the Jumpinpin area.
Ph: (07) 5577 2849

Couran Cove Resort *Map 6 C6*

Couran Cove is an eco-tourism development that prides itself on its environmental sensitivity and the aesthetic appeal of its design. Its accommodation ranges from a luxury hotel to an ocean-front campsite with 'hard-stand' tents. All accommodation is energy-efficient.

Among its array of facilities are restaurants, a 25m heated pool, gyms, a games hall, tennis courts, lawn bowls, rock-climbing and abseiling walls, a cycling track, and canoes and kayaks. Lessons in yachting, windsurfing and parasailing are available. There is also a 4ha patch of natural rainforest, which is being carefully restored to its former rich diversity of plant life.

Day-trippers are welcome at the resort, and organised day tours can be booked. Ph: (07) 5529 6399

South Currigee Camping Area

South Currigee is near the southern end of the island, close to the Broadwater.
Ph: (07) 5577 3932

North Currigee Camping Area

This campsite is about a third of the way up the island from the southern tip.
Ph: (07) 5577 2577

South Stradbroke Island Resort

This resort, on Tipplers Passage, offers luxury Fijian-style accommodation, restaurants, a pool, a range of facilities to cater for most tastes and interests, and a choice of activities from archery to scenic flights. Ph: (07) 5577 3311

Tipplers Camping Area *Map 6 C6*

Tipplers camping area is next to South Stradbroke Island Resort. Hot showers are available at the camping area 7.30am–8.30am and 5.30pm–6.30pm.
Ph: (07) 5577 2849

Couran Cove Resort

Recreational activities

Bushwalking

The absence of traffic, generally flat terrain, network of tracks and abundance of wildlife make South Stradbroke Island a perfect place for bushwalking. Both resorts have organised bushwalking expeditions.

On and in the water

The Jumpinpin area in the north is a choice spot for bream, flathead, whiting and tailor. There are good catches of tailor from the surf beach in winter.

The sheltered waters inside South Stradbroke, from Jumpinpin down to the Broadwater, are perfect for small boats, and the full range of water activities, from canoeing to yachting, is covered by the 2 resorts. For surfers, there is the stretch of ocean beach immediately to the east of Couran Cove, which is patrolled by lifeguards provided by the resort.

Southern Bay Islands

In the southern Bay is a community of islands — wooded hills with small rocky promontories, intimate crescents of coral sand and fringes of mangrove set in a web of deep green waterways and sandy shoals. To the east, North and South Stradbroke Islands stretch like a slender shield against the might of the ocean.

For a sailing tour of these and other islands, visitors can board the **Bay Dolphin** catamaran. The tour includes Bird Island and Peel Island, as well as Canaipa Passage and the islands of Macleay, Lamb, Russell and Coochiemudlo. Day tours (6hr) and twilight tours (seasonal) leave from Raby Bay, Cleveland. Ph: (07) 3207 9620. **Captain Silver Cruises** also offers sailing tours of southern Moreton Bay, leaving from Cleveland or North Stradbroke. Ph: (07) 3409 8636

Coochiemudlo Island
Map 6 C5

Coochiemudlo, or 'Coochie', is the most accessible of the southern Bay islands. Its name means 'red rock', referring to the high red-clay banks on the SW end. Before the coming of the Europeans, local Aboriginal people would visit the island to collect the clay for use as a pigment in ceremonial body-painting.

Getting there

Coochie is a short ferry ride from Victoria Pt and makes a fun day-trip from Brisbane, especially for young families. The **Coochiemudlo Island Ferry Service** offers regular passenger and vehicular ferry services from Victoria Pt, about a 45min drive from Brisbane. Bookings essential for vehicular ferry only. Ph: (07) 3820 7227

Casuarina-fringed beach, southern Bay islands

Jetty at Main Beach, Coochiemudlo

Getting around

The ferry pulls in at the coral-sand Main Beach, which runs the full length of the southern shore. Beyond the foreshore parkland is the settlement, scattered among the trees. A stroll around the island takes about 90min. It is easy walking along the treed bluffs and beaches.

It's easy cycling, too; **bikes** can be hired by the hour from the **Coochie Island Resort**, in Victoria Pde. Ph: (07) 3207 7521

Island tours with the **Coochie Bus Service** connect with every water taxi. Ph: 015 113 686

Festivals and events

In Jul the Coochie locals commemorate the 1799 visit of Matthew Flinders to Norfolk Beach with **Flinders Day**, when they don period costume to re-enact the landing. **Coochie Craft Markets** are held several times a year.

Other attractions

The calm waters of **Main Beach** are perfect for small children. Here toddlers can splash and paddle, while older siblings cycle the sea in an aqua bike (for hire from **Coochie Boat, Paddle Ski & Aqua Bike Hire**, in Mareela St. Ph: (07) 3207 8207)

Morwong Beach, on the north, looks out towards Peel Island. It is a small stretch of creamy sand, fringed by casuarinas and protected from the south-easterlies. Aboriginal stone tools have been found here.

Norfolk Beach, named after Flinders' ship, has an easterly aspect and looks towards Potts Pt, Macleay Island. The coral-strewn beach is interrupted by slabs of magenta rock, occasional twisted mangroves and the silvered skeletons of fallen gums. There is good fishing here.

Partner potters Viv and Denise display their original design ideas in clay at **Wright's Pottery**, 42 Victoria Pde. Ph: (07) 3207 6461

Fun for the young

★ Aqua-biking at Main Beach
★ Cycling around the island

Russell, Lamb, Karragarra and Macleay Islands

Getting there

The **Bay Islands Taxi Service**, Ph: (07) 3409 1145, runs water bus and water taxi services from the Weinam Creek Marina at Redland Bay, from Toondah Harbour at Cleveland and from Victoria Pt. The trip by water bus from Redland Bay directly to Russell Island takes 15min.

Canaipa Passage, from Russell Island

Those who need to take a car can use the **Bay Islander Service** from Weinam Street, Redland Bay, Ph: (07) 3829 0999, or the **Islands Transport Vehicular Ferry Service** from Cnr Banana and Weinam Sts, Redland Bay. Ph: (07) 3829 0008. Bookings essential.

Bay Island Day Tours runs an 'on-demand' guided bus tour that takes in the highlights of Russell Island. Ph: (07) 3409 1209

Getting around

On **Russell** and **Macleay** there are occasional buses, and taxis that can be hired for a guided tour of the islands' scenic spots. Contact **Russell Island Taxi Cab**, Ph: 018 785 218, or **Macleay Island Taxi Service**, Ph: 0418 734 741.

A fun way to see **Russell** is by bicycle (take one with you on the ferry). A bitumen road runs along the spine of the island from the main settlement on the northern shore right down to the southern tip — a leisurely 1hr ride each way, but longer if you explore the side roads that branch off enticingly towards the water. **Macleay** also lends itself to cycling.

On the smaller islands of **Lamb** and **Karragarra**, walking or cycling is the only means of getting about, but this is no hardship because the distances are small,

the cars few or non-existent, the trees shady and the vistas pleasing. Walking also gives nature-lovers a chance to enjoy the wildflowers and the calls of the birds that fill the trees.

The islands

Lamb and Karragarra Islands *Map 6 C5*

Both Lamb and Karragarra are tiny islands with sheltered coves, promontories of red rock, pebbly and sandy beaches and beautiful trees. They are

On the water, Russell Island

Island-hopping

Spend a day island-hopping around these 4 southern Bay islands aboard the **Bay Islands Taxi Service** at only $1 a hop!

Prison ruins, St Helena Island

mainly residential, but offer visitors peaceful spots to picnic or pull up a boat. Mangroves fringe Karragarra's southern shore. There is a kiosk near the jetty on Lamb Island, but it is closed noon–3pm weekdays. Karragarra has no shops, so bring a picnic lunch. **Noyes Homestead**, on Karragarra, is a historic house set among cypress pines.

Macleay Island *Map 6 C5*

Macleay is the 2nd-largest of the inner Bay islands and is closely settled. Its facilities are directed chiefly at its residents, but visitors can pull up their boats to picnic beside its sandy beaches, or enjoy a game of bowls at a waterfront clubhouse with a spectacular view over the Bay to Coochie.

    Potts Pt is a famous beauty spot looking out across a wide expanse of Bay towards Coochie, Peel and North Stradbroke Islands.

Russell Island *Map 6 C5*

The largest of the inner Bay islands, Russell has much to explore. It is a place of undulating hills, red soil, fruit farms, forests and melaleuca wetlands.

    On the eastern side, the deep, silent waters of Canaipa Passage slide between Russell and the steep sand ridges of North Stradbroke. To the SE the passage

opens to Jumpinpin, with a view of the Gold Coast high-rise and the muted thunder of the surf on Stradbroke's eastern shore. While at the southern tip, visit the **Russell Island Glass Gallery** in Crescent Dr.

St Helena Island *Map 6 B4*

St Helena is an outcrop of basalt rock with grassy slopes, sandy beaches and a belt of mangroves on its eastern shore, about 6km from the mouth of the Brisbane River. The island was a prison from 1867 until 1932 and today it is managed by the Dept of Environment because of its historical value. An accredited tour guide or ranger is required for access to the ruins of the old prison. Tours leave from the shelter-shed area at noon daily. Ph: (07) 3369 5113

    A B Sea Cruises offers conducted tours on the *Cat-o'-Nine-Tails*, leaving from Manly. Ph: (07) 3396 3994

    The shadowy past returns to Moreton Bay on **St Helena by Night** — night-time spotlight tours with live theatrical portrayals of prison life performed among the ruins. Cruise and dinner included. Ph: (07) 3893 1240

    Adai Cruises runs full-day guided tours from 101 Kingsford Smith Dr, Breakfast Creek. Ph: (07) 3262 7422

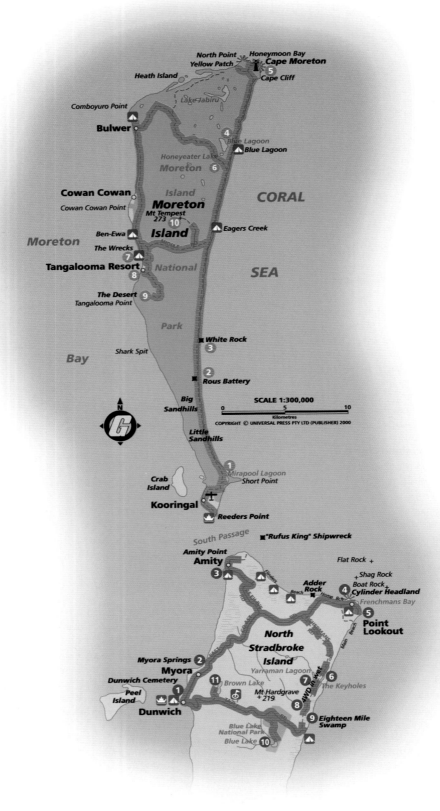

North Point
Honeymoon Bay
Yellow Patch
Cape Moreton
5
Heath Island
Cape Cliff

Comboyuro Point

Lake Jabiru

4
Blue Lagoon
Blue Lagoon

Bulwer

Honeyeater Lake

6
Moreton

Island

Cowan Cowan
Cowan Cowan Point

Moreton

CORAL

Mt Tempest
273
10

Island
Ben-Ewa
Eagers Creek
The Wrecks

Moreton

7
Tangalooma Resort
National
8

SEA

The Desert
9
Tangalooma Point

Bay
Shark Spit

Park

White Rock
3

Big
Sandhills

Rous Battery
2

SCALE 1:300,000
0   5   10
Kilometres
COPYRIGHT © UNIVERSAL PRESS PTY LTD (PUBLISHER) 2000

Little
Sandhills

1
Mirapool Lagoon
Short Point

Crab
Island

Kooringal

Reeders Point

South Passage
"Rufus King" Shipwreck

Amity Point
Amity
Flat Rock

3
Shag Rock
Boat Rock
Adder
Rock
4
Cylinder Headland
Beach
Frenchmans Bay
5

North
Point
Lookout

Stradbroke
Myora Springs
2
Island
Myora
Yarraman Lagoon
Dunwich Cemetery
11
Brown Lake
7
6
Peel
Island
1
Mt Hardgrave
+219
The Keyholes

8
Dunwich
9
Eighteen Mile
Swamp

Blue Lake
National Park
Blue Lake
10

Suggested tours – Map 9

Two-day scenic fishing tour (4WDs only)

Approximate distance

40km from Brisbane CBD to vehicular ferry at Redland Bay; round trip tour from Reeders Pt — 130km

About the tour

This flexible tour takes you past many of Moreton Island's most interesting sights while allowing you to wet a line at any one of a number of fishing spots along the way — for example, the gutters of the eastern beach, the rocks at North Pt, and the timbers at Comboyuro Pt. The order in which you complete the legs of the tour is up to you. (It will need to be modified if you are landing at Bulwer, rather than Reeders Pt.) Camp overnight at an established camping ground or a site of your own choosing, and set off in the morning on the remaining routes.

Places of interest

❶ **Mirapool Lagoon** (p.47)
❷ **Rous Battery** (p.47)
❸ **White Rock** (p.48)
❹ **Blue Lagoon** (p.47)
❺ **Cape Moreton lighthouse** (p.46)

❻ **Honeyeater Lake** (p.47)
❼ **Tangalooma Wrecks** (p.48)
❽ **Tangalooma Resort** (p.47)
❾ **The Desert** (p.47)
❿ **Mt Tempest** (p.47)

Tangalooma Wrecks

'Straddie without a 4WD' tour

Approximate distance

35km from Brisbane CBD to vehicular ferry at Cleveland; round trip tour from Dunwich — 60km (80km if Fisherman's Rd via Keyhole Lakes is unusable)

About the tour

Explore North Stradbroke's best-loved spots from Bay to sea. Most of the tour follows bitumen roads, with only 1 stretch of unsealed road, usually in good enough condition for a conventional car in dry weather. (In wet weather, or if in doubt, avoid the old mining road from the Keyhole Lakes to the Causeway.) It takes in all the island's main settlements (Dunwich, Amity and Point Lookout), skirts the Keyhole Lakes and the Eighteen Mile Swamp, visits the Blue Lake NP (there is an easy walking track to the lake itself) and Brown Lake, and returns to Dunwich.

Places of interest

❶ **Dunwich Cemetery** (p.51)
❷ **Myora Springs** (p.52)
❸ **Amity** (p.51)
❹ **Cylinder Headland and Beach** (p.52)
❺ **Whale Rock and Gorges** (p.53)
❻ **Keyhole Lakes** (p.52)

❼ **Yarraman Lagoon** (no vehicle access)
❽ **Keyholes road** (p.52)
❾ **Eighteen Mile Swamp** (p.52)
❿ **Blue Lake** (p.52)
⓫ **Brown Lake** (p.52)

Frenchman's Beach, Point Lookout

Left: **Sunset on the Noosa River**
Right: **Point Cartwright**

SUNSHINE COAST™

The Sunshine Coast

North of Moreton Bay, the glittering beaches of the Sunshine Coast scallop the Pacific shore as far as Fraser Island. Headlands and estuaries break the long sweeps of sand into coves and communities, where traditional seaside pursuits — surfing, fishing and mucking about in boats — vie with more expensive pleasures.

Along much of the coast, high-rise units and opulent resorts have replaced the holiday houses of simpler times. The shifting sandbanks of the river mouths have given way to canal estates and lavishly appointed marinas. Amusements of every type are on hand to offer distraction should the sea and sunshine lose their sparkle. But there is wilderness too — tracts of wallum heath where wildflowers bloom, and rivers sliding through the hush of forest palms. At Noosa, walking paths penetrate the depths of rainforest and skirt secluded coves. Across Laguna Bay, the high coloured-sand cliffs of Teewah sweep in a graceful arc north to Double Island Pt. Hidden in their lee is Cooloola, a place of secret waterways and forests.

On the coast or in the hinterland, the region has something for everyone — glamour, sophistication, thrills 'n' spills, and pockets of unspoilt beauty.

ℹ Tourist information

Caloundra City Tourist Information Centre
7 Caloundra Rd, Caloundra 4551
Ph: (07) 5491 0202

Maroochy Tourism Centre
Sixth Ave, Maroochydore 4558
Ph: (07) 5479 1566

Nambour Tourist Information Centre
5 Coronation Ave, Nambour 4560
Ph: (07) 5476 1933

Naturally Queensland Information Centre (EPA)
(info on national parks)
Ground Floor, 160 Ann St,
Brisbane 4000 Ph: (07) 3227 8185
www.env.qld.gov.au

Rainbow Beach Tourist Centre
8 Rainbow Beach Rd,
Rainbow Beach 4581
Ph: (07) 5486 3227

Tourism Noosa Information Centre
Hastings St Roundabout,
Noosa Heads 4567
Ph: (07) 5447 4988

Must see, must do

★ **Carlo Sandblow, Rainbow Beach** (p.74)
★ **Eumundi Markets** (p.76)
★ **Fairhill Nursery** (p.80)
★ **Noosa NP** (p.79)
★ **Tanawha Tourist Dr** (p.82)
★ **UnderWater World, Mooloolaba** (p.72)

Radio stations

ABC Radio Wide Bay: AM 156.6
4GY Gympie: AM 558
Classic Hits FM: FM 87.8 (Noosa), 88 (Mooloolaba)
ABC Coast FM: FM 90.3 (Sunshine Coast), 95.3 (Cooloola Coast)
Sea FM: FM 91.9

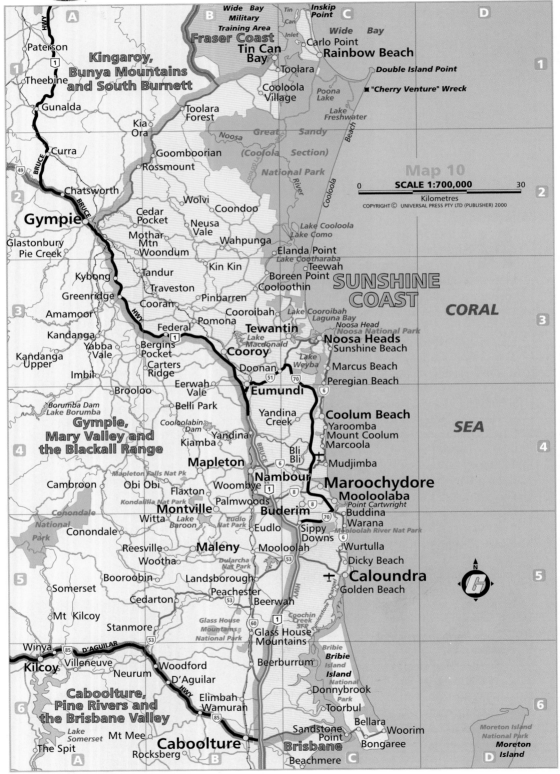

Kingaroy,
Bunya Mountains
and South Burnett

Paterson

Theebine

Gunalda

Curra

Chatsworth

Gympie

Glastonbury
Pie Creek

Kybong

Greenridge

Amamoor

Kandanga

Kandanga
Upper

Yabba
Vale

Imbil

Brooloo

Cedar
Pocket

Mothar
Mtn

Woondum

Tandur

Traveston

Cooran

Federal

Bergins
Pocket

Carters
Ridge

Eerwah
Vale

Belli Park

Kia
Ora

Toolara
Forest

Goomboorian

Rossmount

Wolvi

Coondoo

Neusa
Vale

Wahpunga

Kin Kin

Pinbarren

Cooroibah

Pomona

Tewantin

Cooroy

Doonan

Eumundi

Yandina
Creek

Yandina

Kiamba

Wide Bay
Military
Training Area

Fraser Coast

**Tin Can
Bay**

Toolara

Cooloola
Village

Elanda Point

Teewah

Boreen Point

Cooloothin

Lake
Macdonald

Lake
Weyba

Lake Cootharaba

Lake Cooroibah
Laguna Bay

Noosa Head

Tin
Can
Inlet

Carlo Point

Rainbow Beach

Double Island Point

"Cherry Venture" Wreck

Wide   Bay

Lake
Freshwater

Poona
Lake

Lake Cooloola
Lake Como

Noosa National Park

Noosa Heads

Sunshine Beach

Marcus Beach

Peregian Beach

Coolum Beach

Yaroomba

Mount Coolum

Marcoola

Mudjimba

**SUNSHINE
COAST**

CORAL

SEA

Great   Sandy

(Cooloola   Section)

National Park

Map 10

SCALE 1:700,000

0   30

Kilometres

COPYRIGHT © UNIVERSAL PRESS PTY LTD (PUBLISHER) 2000

Gympie,
Mary Valley and
the Blackall Range

Borumba Dam
Lake Borumba

Cooloolabin
Dam

Mapleton

Cambroon

Obi Obi

Flaxton

Woombye

Palmwoods

Montville

Witta

Lake
Baroon

Eudlo
Nat Park

Eudlo

Maleny

Mooloolah

Nambour

Bli
Bli

Maroochydore

Mooloolaba

Point Cartwright

Buddina

Warana

Buderim

Sippy
Downs

Mooloolah River Nat Park

Wurtulla

Mapleton Falls Nat Pk

Kondalilla Nat Park

Conondale

National
Park

Cononmale

Reesville

Wootha

Booroobin

Landsborough

Peachester

Dularcha
Nat Park

Glass House
Mountains
National Park

Dicky Beach

Caloundra

Golden Beach

Somerset

Cedarton

Mt Kilcoy

Stanmore

Beerwah

Beerburrum

Coochin
Creek SF

Brisbane

Bribie
Island

Bribie

Island

National

Donnybrook

Park

Toorbul

Sandstone
Point

Bellara

Woorim

Bongaree

Winya

Kilcoy

Villeneuve

Neurum

D'AGUILAR

Woodford

D'Aguilar

Elimbah

Wamuran

Glass House
Mountains

Caboolture,
Pine Rivers and
the Brisbane Valley

Lake
Somerset

Mt Mee

The Spit

Rocksberg

Caboolture

Beachmere

Moreton Island
National Park

**Moreton
Island**

Natural features

The Sunshine Coast has been shaped by the winds and tides of the Coral Sea, the prevailing south-easterlies sculpting the dunes and giving the vegetation a landward lean. Rocky headlands interrupt the northward sweep of sand. Where these are substantial enough to provide shelter, there still remain some pockets of littoral rainforest, notably at Noosa. The high dunes of Teewah perform the same function, protecting large areas of rainforest in the Cooloola section of the Great Sandy NP.

The Mooloolah and Maroochy Rivers snake down from the ranges in the hinterland, flowing through rich canefields and melaleuca wetland before entering the sea in meandering estuaries and, nowadays, canal developments. The Noosa River winds through the Cooloola everglades, widens into Lakes Cootharaba and Cooroibah, slides past the old and new holiday houses of Tewantin and Noosaville, and meets the ocean at Laguna Bay.

Here and there abrupt peaks, such as Dunethin Rock and Mt Cooroora, interrupt the rolling farmland of the hinterland, and nearer the coast the wallum lowlands are broken by the ancient, eroded shapes of Mt Coolum and Mt Peregian. Just behind Mooloolaba is the small plateau of Buderim, the most easterly projection of the fertile, volcanic hills that tumble down from the Blackall Ra towards the sea.

History

European settlers were slow to venture into the lands of the Kabi Kabi Aborigines along the coastal plain north of Brisbane. The despised wallum country, and the 50-mile 'prohibition zone' around the Moreton Bay penal settlement, meant that early land exploration was directed to more fertile and hospitable areas. The bush north of Brisbane became a refuge for convicts fleeing the lash, and some enterprising escapees found a place in tribal society.

In 1838 Andrew Petrie found bunya pine in the Maroochy area and red cedar on the Mooloolah River; in 1842, with a small party, he sailed further north to Noosa Head and beyond. Eventually, incursions by timbergetters led to the opening of the coastal strip to European settlement and the 'dispersal' of its Aboriginal owners, remembered in place names such as Murdering Creek.

As the forests were greedily cut out, the settlers turned to agriculture. Cattle were being grazed at Yandina in the 1850s, and cane farms sprang up on the fertile flats of the Maroochy River. Bananas and then ginger were grown at Buderim after the timber supplies were exhausted.

Until WWII, the string of small coastal settlements from Caloundra to Noosa subsisted as sleepy fishing villages and modest holiday havens. Then came the postwar development boom. While the pace of change on the Sunshine Coast was at first slower than on the Gold Coast, today it rivals it.

Coolum

Noosa from the air

Steaming north

SunSteam runs occasional steam-train rides from Brisbane to various places of interest, including the Ginger Factory at Yandina. Charters available.
Ph: (07) 3807 1296, 6pm–9pm

Getting there

By air

Qantas (Ph: 131 313) and **Ansett** (Ph: 131 300) have regular services between most of Australia's capital cities and the Sunshine Coast Airport, north of Maroochydore. **Sunstate Airlines** operates a daily service from Brisbane Airport. Ph: 131 313

By road

From the major north–south axes of the Bruce Hwy and the Sunshine Coast Mwy, numerous connecting roads run in to the main Sunshine Coast centres such as Caloundra, Mooloolaba, Maroochydore, Coolum and Tewantin/Noosaville/Noosa.

Tin Can Bay and Rainbow Beach are reached by continuing on the Bruce Hwy to Gympie and then taking Tin Can Bay Rd.

From the Roma St Transit Centre in Brisbane, **McCafferty's Express Coaches** runs a daily service calling at Caloundra, Maroochydore and Noosa (Ph: 131 499) and some **Greyhound Pioneer** services call at Maroochydore, Noosa, Nambour and Cooroy (Ph: 132 030).

Sun-Air Bus Service has frequent daily services between Brisbane and all the Sunshine Coast centres as far as Noosa/Tewantin. Ph: (07) 5478 2811 or 1800 804 340

Sunbus has frequent local 'hail and ride' services between all major points on the Sunshine Coast. Ph: 131 230

Suncoast Pacific has daily services linking the Sunshine Coast (including Tin Can Bay), Brisbane and the Gold Coast. Ph: (07) 5443 1011 (Maroochydore) or (07) 3236 1901 (Brisbane Transit Centre)

Polleys has a Cooloola Coast service from Gympie to Tin Can Bay and Rainbow Beach, Mon–Fri. Ph: (07) 5482 2700

By rail

Many of the towns in the Sunshine Coast hinterland that are now bypassed by the Bruce Hwy have a regular electric train service from Brisbane. The Nambour and Gympie trains together service all stations in this region; both stop at Palmwoods, Woombye and Nambour, and the Gympie train also stops at Yandina, Eumundi, Cooroy, Pomona, Cooran and Traveston, terminating at Gympie North. **Trainlink** is a Sunbus service connecting with Nambour station and stopping at Eumundi, Noosaville and Noosa Heads. Ph: 131 230

Getting around

Cruises

The *Mudjimba*, a classic riverboat, takes passengers on a 1hr harbour and canal cruise of the Mooloolah River. Ph: (07) 5444 7477

Also on the Mooloolah River are the **Mooloolaba by Night** dinner cruise and

Suit yourself

TransInfo sells **South East Explorer** tickets, which allow passengers to use flexible combinations of rail, bus and ferry services to places as far north as Noosa.
Ph: 131 230

Caloundra

Ettamogah Pub, Aussie World

the **Mooloolaba Party Boat** BBQ lunch cruise. Ph: (07) 5444 7590

Cruise Maroochy Eco runs 3 different cruises on the Maroochy River and its associated waterways. Ph: (07) 5476 1711

Everglades Water Bus Co (Ph: 1800 688 045), **Everglades Cruises** (Ph: (07) 5449 9177), **Noosa Sound Cruises** (Ph: (07) 5447 3466) and **Noosa River Tours** (Ph: (07) 5449 7362) all offer various cruises on the Noosa River and the Cooloola waterways. **Noosa Magic** at Harbourtown Marina, Tewantin, offers sailing tours on Laguna Bay and the Noosa River. Ph: 1800 720 071

Try **Ron and Doug's Island Cruises**, Caloundra, for a 2hr crabbing cruise or a full-day wine-and-dine cruise in Pumicestone Passage. Ph: 018 452 885

Scenic flights

Blue Tongue Helicopters, based at Sunshine Coast Airport, north of Maroochydore, takes passengers on sightseeing flights over the major Sunshine Coast sights. Ph: (07) 5448 8166

Rainbow Air, based at the Inskip Pt airfield, operates light-plane flights from Brisbane, Maroochydore and Noosa to Rainbow Beach and Fraser Island. It also offers local joyflights, and flights and instruction in hang gliding, paragliding and ultra-lights. Ph: (07) 5486 3773

Sunshine Coast Air Charter (Ph: 1800 654 463) and **Sunshine Coast Scenic Flights** (Ph: (07) 5491 1988), both based at Caloundra Airport, offer scenic joyflights over the surrounding district.

Tours

By bus

Sun-Air (Ph: (07) 5478 2811 or 1800 804 340), **Diana's Tours** (Ph: (07) 5494 5219) and **Elite Tours** (Ph: (07) 5494 5195) run trips to the main attractions of the Sunshine Coast and its hinterland, such as the Eumundi Markets, Aussie World/Ettamogah Pub and the Big Pineapple. The **Seafood Extravaganza Lunch and Courtesy Tour** runs from Noosa to Caloundra and various hinterland attractions, Ph: (07) 5494 3700. **Tropical Coast Tours** at Noosa has 7 Sunshine Coast tours to choose from, Ph: (07) 5449 0822. **Wild Dolphins Tours** runs half-day bus tours from Noosa to see the dolphins of Tin Can Bay at Norman Pt boat ramp, Ph: 014 665 183. **Kids Day Out – Tours for Kids** has a choice of 7 tours designed especially for children. Each tour visits 3 Sunshine Coast attractions. Pick-ups from Noosa to Caloundra. Ph: 0414 769 305

Tours to coloured sands of Teewah Beach

Tour the Sunshine Coast by motorbike

By 4WD

Around the Back Roads has half-day trips in a 4WD coaster bus to the coloured sands at Teewah Beach, with pick-ups from Caloundra to Maroochydore, Ph: (07) 5494 5219. **Inside Track 4WD Safaris** offers a trip to the coloured sands and dolphin-viewing at Tin Can Bay, Ph: (07) 5442 8814. **Noosa Beach Safaris** visits Teewah Beach and Rainbow Beach, Ph: (07) 5449 1400. **Off Beat Rainforest Tours** has 4WD tours of wilderness areas in the Sunshine Coast hinterland, with pick-ups from Noosa to Caloundra, Ph: (07) 5473 5135. **Rainbow Beach Adventure Centre**, 66 Rainbow Beach Rd, Rainbow Beach, has 4WDs for hire, Ph: (07) 5486 3499. **Rainbow Beach Taxi and Tour Services** also operates from Rainbow Beach, Ph: (07) 5486 3164. **Sun Safari Tours** at Rainbow Beach offers 4WD sightseeing tours of the coloured sands, Double Island Pt and Fraser Island, Ph: (07) 5486 3154.

By motorbike

Southern Cross Motorcycle Tours offers anything from short joyrides to day-long tours of the Sunshine Coast and its hinterland, Ph: (07) 5445 0022. **Viking Motorcycle Tours** at Noosa takes passengers on tours of the Sunshine Coast and its hinterland, and also has bikes for hire, Ph: (07) 5474 1050.

Festivals and events

Sydney to Mooloolaba Yacht Race
Yachts from all over Australia compete in this classic race, held in Apr each year. Ph: (07) 5444 1355

Bay to Bay Yacht Race
In this May event, over 200 trailer sailors sail for 2 days up the straits from **Tin Can Bay** to **Hervey Bay**.

Cooloola Seafood Festival
Held in **Tin Can Bay** in Jun, highlighting fresh seafood brought straight from the trawlers. Ph: (07) 5486 4394

King of the Mountain Festival
In 1958, when Bruce Samuels won a bet that he could run from **Pomona** to the top of Mt Cooroora and back in under 1hr, a tradition was born. The all-day festival, held on the 4th Sun in Jul, is an opportunity for townsfolk to get together and for competitors to win acclaim. Ph: (07) 5485 4125

Rainbow Beach Fishing Classic
This week-long event is held on the last weekend in Jul, with anglers participating from all over SE Qld. Ph: (07) 5486 3227

Nambour Sugar Festival
A street parade and family fun day mark this Aug event to celebrate a local industry.

Kin Kin Carnival and Great Horse Race
The focus of this carnival is a cross-country horse race held on the 3rd Sun of Oct each year at the Kin Kin sports ground, behind the pub.

Main localities and towns

For ease of reference, towns have been listed alphabetically in 2 sections: the coast and the hinterland.

The coast

Alexandra Headland *Map 11 A1*
The bluff at Alexandra Headland, just north of Mooloolaba, is a good spot to view Mudjimba (Old Woman Island) and the hunched mass of Mt Coolum. Alexandra Headland has a white-sand

beach, a skateboard park and plenty of holiday units.

The **Olympia Theme Park**, cnr Okinja Rd and Wirraway St, caters for families with 5 super slides, 2 junior slides, a laser game, mini-golf, a games room, food bar and BBQs. Open daily, 9am–9pm, in summer holidays (depending on weather). Ph: (07) 5443 7222

Caloundra *Map 10 C5*

Within easy reach of Brisbane, Caloundra is one of the most urbanised of the Sunshine Coast centres, with a multitude of high-rise apartments and a busy shopping district, but it has nevertheless managed to retain something of its 'old fibro beach cottage' appeal.

The Caloundra City Tourist Info Centre, 7 Caloundra Rd, is well stocked with tourist brochures on the Sunshine Coast and its hinterland. Open Mon–Fri, 8.15am–4.55pm; Sat, Sun and public holidays, 9am–5pm. Ph: (07) 5491 0202

Caloundra has many beaches: the tranquil **Golden Beach** and **Bulcock Beach** for boating, fishing and safe swimming spots in the lee of Bribie Island and the Caloundra Bar; **King's Beach**, a patrolled surfing beach with a fenced saltwater pool on the southern side of the Caloundra headland; **Shelly Beach**, a fishing beach with rock pools, BBQ facilities and walking track north of the main headland (no swimming); **Moffat Beach**, a fishing and walking beach running north from the cliffs of Moffat Head, with BBQ facilities and playground at the mouth of Tooway Creek; **Dicky Beach**, a patrolled surfing and fishing beach with BBQ and playground; and **Currimundi**, bordered on the north by Currimundi Lake (a popular fishing and picnic spot). On the northern shore of the lake is the **Currimundi Conservation Park** (p.78).

The **old lighthouse** that now stands in Woorim Park, Golden Beach, was built in 1898 and operated until 1969. A new lighthouse in Canberra Terrace now guides ships on their way to and from the Port of Brisbane. A fine vantage point for watching the large vessels that glide past close to shore is the **headland walkway** at King's Beach.

At the **Seaview Artists Gallery**, 4 Seaview Terrace, Moffat Beach, visitors can watch the resident artists at work and choose from a wide selection of paintings, sculpture and pottery. Open daily, 9am–5pm. Ph: (07) 5491 4788

The community-owned **Qld Air Museum** at 7 Pathfinder Dr, Caloundra Aerodrome, was established to honour Australia's aviation heritage. Its collection includes 18 famous aircraft, both military and civilian, aero engines and general aviation memorabilia. Open Wed, Sat, Sun and public and school holidays, 10am–4pm. Group visits by appt. Ph: (07) 5492 5930

Shipwreck memorial

In 1893 the SS *Dicky* was forced ashore at the beach that now bears its name. A memorial to the ship stands in the **Dicky Beach park**.

King's Beach, Caloundra

Aviation heritage

The Douglas DC-3 in the **Qld Air Museum** is the oldest aircraft of this type remaining in Australia and was used by General Douglas MacArthur during WWII.

To the north, beyond Currimundi Lake, the Kawana Waters residential communities continue unabated to Mooloolaba, quarantined from the golden surfing beaches of Wurtulla, Bokarina, Warana and Buddina by a continuous Esplanade Park.

Coolum *Map 10 C4*

The old fishing village of Coolum, in the northern lee of Point Perry, has become a place of high-rise units and sophisticated restaurants, but the fishing is still good around the rocks.

Point Arkwright is the most southerly of the Coolum group of cliffs and headlands. A walkway leads through a small reserve to a lookout over the sea.

The hills south of the town centre drop steeply down to a shore of rockpools, ledges and charming coves. To the north, the beach stretches through Peregian and Marcus Beach to Sunshine Beach, where the headlands of Noosa begin. The beach at Coolum is patrolled in summer, and the surf is good.

Lows Lookout on Toboggan Hill (turn off David Low Way up Scrub Rd) has views north to Mt Peregian (also known as Emu Mt), and inland over the canefields.

Maroochydore *Map 10 C4*

Maroochydore, on the southern bank of the Maroochy River estuary, has grown from a quiet fishing village to a modern holiday town with a plethora of leisure activities on offer. Tourist info is available Mon–Fri, 9am–5pm; weekends, 9am–4pm, from **Maroochy Tourism**, Sixth Ave. Ph: (07) 5479 1566

There is a patrolled surf beach on the ocean side, and on the riverbank is the old resort of **Cotton Tree**, with riverside parks and esplanade. Craft of all kinds, from dinghies to outrigger canoes, take advantage of the quiet waters of the Maroochy estuary, and dive boats head out to Mudjimba (Old Woman Island) NE of the river mouth. **Local craft markets** are held every Sun morning in Main St, Cotton Tree.

Maze Mania 4 Kids is an indoor playground for under-12s. It has slides, tunnels, a mirror maze, flying fox and other fun equipment, and is netted and padded for safety. It is on Comstar Ave, off Maud St. Open daily, 9am–5.30pm. Ph: (07) 5479 5333

On David Low Way is a two-thirds-sized replica of James Cook's barque the ***Endeavour***. Open Sun–Thurs, 9am–noon. Groups by appt. Ph: (07) 5476 8391

Sheltered cove, Coolum

Surf beach, Alexandra Headland

Mooloolaba *Map 10 C4*

Mooloolaba is a thriving tourist centre on the north shore of the river mouth ('the Spit'), with a crescent-shaped ocean beach, a safe harbour and a resident fleet of trawlers. The ocean esplanade is lined with alfresco cafes and boutiques.

The Mooloolah River enters the sea here just north of Pt Cartwright. Craft from all over the world are moored in **Mooloolah Boat Harbour,** and in Apr the yachts of the classic Sydney to Mooloolaba Race round Pt Cartwright at their journey's end. At the harbour, on Parkyn Pde, is **The Wharf,** a large complex of shops, eateries, fun parlours and rides. Most of the area is wheelchair accessible. A number of ocean and river cruises leave from here (p.66). There is a tourist info centre at the complex,

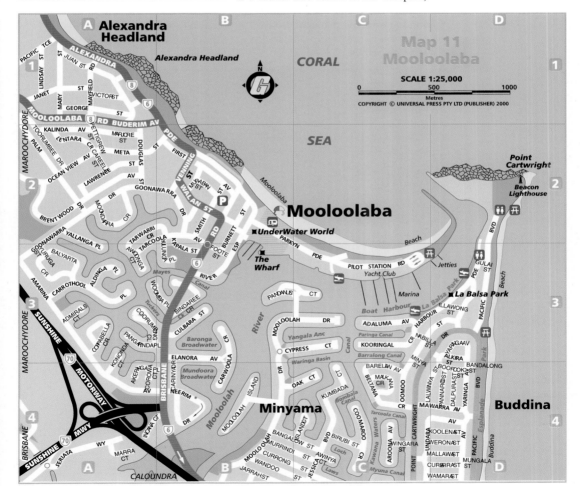

which has details about the cruises — and the other attractions that the region has to offer. Ph: (07) 5444 8488

Part of the Wharf complex is **UnderWater World**, which has a spectacular range of aquatic life, from sharks and freshwater crocs to seahorses and starfish. View grey nurses, tropical fish, gropers and stingrays from 80m of transparent underwater tunnel. There are also interactive displays, a seal show (5 sessions a day) and an underwater roller-coaster simulator ('Ride the Dive'). Open daily, 9am–6pm. Infoline: (07) 5444 2255

Noosa *Map 10 C3*

Noosa remains one of the loveliest spots on the Australian east coast, despite the excesses of wealth and commercialism. The view over Laguna Bay to the Teewah dunes still takes the breath away, and the rainforest, coves and dramatic rocky promontories of the Noosa NP are a feast for the senses.

The Noosa River's backwaters and the old mangrove flats of Hay's Island have been disciplined into the Noosa Sound development behind the fragile peninsula on which the humming centre of Noosa has grown. Stylish **Hastings St**, running down this peninsula to Noosa Woods and the man-made Spit, fairly fizzes with chic boutiques and world-class restaurants and cafes. This is where the 'beautiful people' come to see and be seen.

Up on the hill on Noosa Dr is the iconic **Noosa Reef Hotel**, with a view to Teewah Beach.

When a south-easter is blowing, Noosa Beach, Little Cove and the bays of the national park are wonderfully sheltered places to swim. As the swell builds, surfers flock to Noosa to ride the famous point breaks around the headland from Granite Bay to First Pt.

There is a Parks and Wildlife Info Centre at the entrance to **Noosa NP** (p.79).

Conserving Noosa

For in-depth info on the local environment, visit the **Noosa Parks Association Environment Centre**, Wallace Park, Eumundi Rd, Noosaville. Ph: (07) 5474 2486

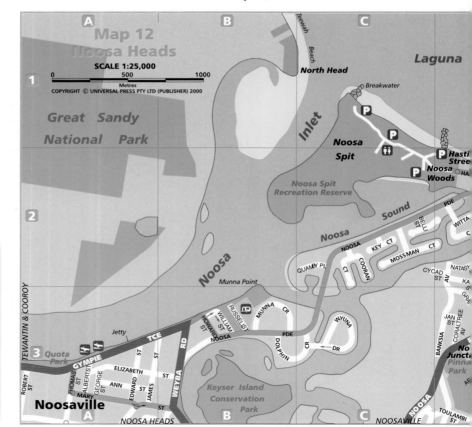

Main beach, Noosa

At Noosa's highest point is **Laguna Lookout**, on Viewland Dr, which has a commanding view over the NW hinterland and the maze of waterways at the river mouth.

Upstream past Weyba Creek and Munna Pt is **Noosaville**, where some of the original timber, fibro and tin holiday cottages can still be seen. Parks line the Noosa River along Gympie Terrace and Hilton Terrace, and its pelican-haunted waters are dotted with fishing dinghies, catamarans and houseboats.

For more details about Noosa's smorgasbord of attractions, call in at the Tourism Noosa Info Centre, at the junction of Noosa Dr and Hastings St. Open daily, 9am–5pm. Ph: (07) 5447 4988

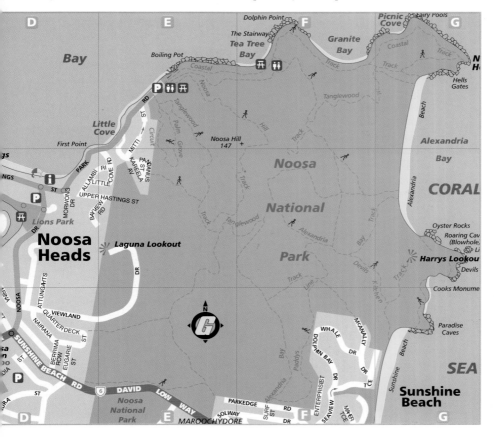

Peregian *Map 10 C3*

North of Coolum is one of the quieter Sunshine Coast beaches, beloved of those who want an unpretentious seaside holiday. Peregian has not suffered the wholesale destruction of its foredunes that has scarred many older seaside centres. Here, the holiday houses are set back from the beach in a cluster of small hills and a generous cover of native bush. To the south and west are sections of Noosa NP. Peregian has a hotel, motels, a caravan park, a pleasant shopping centre and a surf beach patrolled on weekends and holidays.

Rainbow Beach *Map 10 C1*

The young town of Rainbow Beach is just south of Inskip Pt, where the vehicular ferry leaves for Fraser Island. The township is built above the surf beach on low sand cliffs, which then rise and sweep in a majestic crescent SE to Double Island Pt.

Rainbow Beach was established in 1966 as the base for sandmining operations, turning to tourism only when mining ceased in the 1970s. Today it has something of the enterprising brashness of the Gold Coast in the late 50s. There are restaurants, shops, hire places, backpackers' accommodation, motels and units, some spectacularly sited high above the ocean. There is an unbeatable view of Fraser Island from the heights of the town.

The Dept of Environment Info Centre, on the right as you enter the township on Rainbow Beach Rd, issues **permits** for Cooloola, Fraser Island and Inskip Pt. Open daily, 7am-4pm, Ph: (07) 5486 3160. The **Tourist Centre**, 8 Rainbow Beach Rd (Ph: (07) 5486 3227), handles tour bookings for Fraser Island and the coloured sands, books accommodation and hires out 4WDs and boats. The **Rainbow Beach Adventure Centre**, 66 Rainbow Beach Rd, also provides tourist info, hires 4WDs and handles tour bookings. Ph: (07) 5486 3499

Points of interest are the dramatic **Carlo Sandblow**, high above the narrow beach just south of the Mudlo Rocks, and the **coloured sands**, which streak the

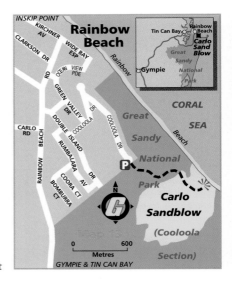

looming cliffs 2km further south. The sandblow gives a magnificent view of Double Island Pt and is a favourite launching point for hang gliders and paragliders. Access is via a leisurely walk (see map 13).

Rainbow Beach is a good spot to stay overnight for an early start to **Fraser Island** (p.92) or the **Cooloola section of Great Sandy NP** (p.78). The Cooloola Visitors Info Centre (Lake Alford, Bruce Hwy, Gympie) publishes a Cooloola Coast leaflet

Hang gliding, Carlo Sandblow

in its 'Travellin' Round' series.
This details a Rainbow Beach and
Tin Can Bay tour with a diversion to
Bymien Picnic Area in Cooloola
(p.79). Open daily, 8.30am–3.30pm.
Ph: (07) 5482 5444

Sunshine Beach *Map 10 C3*

At the far end of the long stretch of
beach that runs north from Coolum
are Sunrise and Sunshine Beaches. There
is an air of opulence here, with designer
houses arranged in tiers on the steep
hills to take in the ocean views.
From Parkedge Rd and McAnally Dr,
Sunshine Beach has privileged access to
Noosa NP (p.79).

Tin Can Bay *Map 10 B1*

Tin Can Bay, on Tin Can Inlet at
the southern end of the Great Sandy
Strait, is an old-fashioned fishing village
with a prawning fleet and processing
plants, as well as modern facilities
such as a smart boat harbour and
the up-to-the-minute Marina Restaurant.
There is a range of accommodation,
from luxury holiday units to
houseboats.

The town's main claim to fame,
however, is the custom of communing
with the local pod of the uncommon
Indo-Pacific humpback dolphins (*Sina
chinensis*). There are **dolphin-viewing
sessions** at the Norman Pt boat ramp,
principally at high tide, when the deeper
water allows the dolphins to come in to
the shoreline at the ramp. Feeding the
dolphins is now discouraged for their
protection.

The **Kate Kelly Walkway** is
a 9km environmental path which
winds through the parkland along the
foreshore – ideal for walking or cycling.
The path, which is designed for all
ages, has exercise points and is
signposted with snippets of info
about the natural and social history
of the area.

Other activities are fishing, crabbing,
canoeing, sailing, swimming and
picnicking. Keep the insect repellent
handy, as the mosquitoes and sandflies
can be fierce.

The hinterland
Boreen Pt *Map 10 B3*

Boreen Pt is a secluded settlement on the
western shore of Lake Cootharaba. It sits
on a small promontory rising out of the
surrounding melaleuca wetlands, and looks
across the lake to a sandblow streaking the
high Teewah dunes like a drift of snow.
The lake is a large expanse of shallow
water separated from the sea by these high
dunes. It is fed with fresh water at the
northern end by Kin Kin Creek and the
upper reaches of the Noosa River, and
flushed by the tide from the south. This is
a favourite place for small-craft sailing.
Around the point are small sandy beaches
washed by sepia wavelets – safe swimming
spots for children.

The stunningly sited **Jetty Restaurant**
on the lakefront tempts tourists from
Noosa, far downstream. Some disembark
from water buses or private boats; others
take the road. Open daily; morning tea
from 10.30am; lunch from noon; dinner
(Sat only) from 6.30pm. Licensed.
Ph: (07) 5485 3167

The **Sunshine Art Gallery**, 64 Laguna
St, shows works by the artist in residence,
John Robinson, as well as local pottery,
sculpture and crystal jewellery.
Open Tue–Sun, 10.30am–5.30pm.
Ph: (07) 5485 3153

Also in Laguna St, at the landward
entrance to the settlement, is the
Apollonian Hotel, an old Gympie pub
dating from the goldrush days. Among its
attractions are rainforest gardens, wide
verandahs, open fireplaces, hearty food
and wagon tours. Open daily,
10am–10pm. Ph: (07) 5485 3100

A short drive from Boreen Pt, on the
NW shore of Lake Cootharaba, is **Elanda
Point**, a setting-off place for canoe
explorations and hiking trips in Cooloola
(p.79).

Buderim *Map 10 C4*

The town is perched on the
red-soil plateau of Buderim Mt,
which overlooks Mooloolaba. Once
a rich farming area producing mainly
bananas, pineapples and ginger,
Buderim is now a residential and
retirement haven.

*Dolphin-viewing,
Tin Can Bay*

Eumundi Markets

The **old ginger factory** in the main street is now a centre for the community markets, held each Thurs. (Nowadays the ginger is processed in a gleaming new factory/tourist complex at Yandina — p.78.)

A reminder of the old Buderim is the renovated and refurnished **pioneer cottage**, at 5 Ballinger Cr. John Burnett, one of the 1st settlers on the mountain, built the cottage in about 1875. It is listed in the National Estate Register and by the National Trust. Open daily, 10am–4pm.

On Buderim's flanks are remnants of the rainforest that once clothed much of the mountain. They are protected by **Foote Sanctuary** (off Park St) and **Buderim Forest Park** (Quorn Close, off Lindsay Rd — p.80).

The best lookout spot is **Buderim Lions Club Lookout Reserve**, which looks SE over the coast, but there is also a glimpse of the sea at **White's Lookout**, to the NE.

Cooran *Map 10 B3*

The Greenridge–Pinbarren road runs west from the Pomona–Kin Kin road to the tiny hamlet of Cooran, which lies on the railway line among the hills. Just before the railway line, Tablelands Rd leads north 5km to **James M McKane Memorial Lookout**, with sweeping views across the Kin Kin Valley and Noosa plains to the huge Cooloola Sandblow and south past Noosa.

Cooroy *Map 10 B3*

Cooroy is located off the Bruce Hwy between Eumundi and Gympie. Like many other small towns in the region, it has responded to the influx of tourists from Noosa: coffee shops have sprung up in the town centre, and the streets are prettily landscaped.

The old **Cooroy Butter Factory**, at 10 Maple St, now houses an art gallery and is the venue for a range of workshops, from life drawing to mosaics. Operating times vary. Ph: (07) 5442 5055

NE of the town, 3km from Cooroy along Lake Macdonald Dr, are the **Lake Macdonald Botanical Gardens** (p.80).

Eumundi *Map 10 B3*

This old timber and railway township nestles into a tree-covered hillside amid canefields and pockets of forest.

The famous **Eumundi Markets** draw people from far and wide. They are held in the park that was once the town railway station every Sat, 6am–1pm. Ph: 0419 733 468. Indoor markets are also held every Sun, 8am–2pm, at the **Old Butter Factory**.

The town has shady parks, avenues of trees, 2 picturesque pubs, the **Historical Museum**, housed in an old church (open Mon–Wed, 10am–4pm; Sat, 9am–1pm, Ph: (07) 5442 8762), art galleries, cafes and curiosity shops. The **Eumundi Smoke House** advertises handcrafted sausages and salami, the **Imperial Hotel** sells the boutique Eumundi lager, and the **Black Snake Trading Post** and the **Hemp Hut** have craftwork, collectibles and a large stock of hemp-based products, from bed linen to beachwear.

A scenic drive leads up leafy Etheridge St to the summit of the hill, with a good view of the surrounding farmland.

Kin Kin *Map 10 B3*

The road from Pomona sweeps through bright-green hills into the tiny town of Kin Kin, on the tree-lined banks of Kin Kin Creek. The **Country Life Hotel**, a typical 2-storey timber country pub at the southern entrance to the town, has a collection of timber-getting and dairying memorabilia on display, and old local cattle brands are burnt into the front of the bar.

Nambour *Map 10 B4*

The old Cobb & Co coach stop of Nambour is the sugarcane-processing centre of the Sunshine Coast and the largest town in the district. The stacks of the sugar mill sending a plume of smoke high over the valley, the shoulder-to-shoulder shops and office buildings, the busy streets and the residential development spreading over the hills all give Nambour the industrious air of a city. But there are reminders, too, of its origins — the cane trains trundling through the town centre and the mauve

Subtropical snowflakes

Bli Bli is a major cane-growing area near Nambour, and ash falling on suburban clotheslines during the cane-firing season is known locally as 'Bli Bli snow'.

tint of remaining pineapple farms on distant slopes.

Nambour's economy is still based largely on agriculture. New crops, such as macadamia nuts and lychees, have been added to the traditional trio of sugar, pineapples and bananas.

The Moreton Central Sugar Mill, in Bury St, crushed its first cane in 1896. (The mill is no longer open to the public.)

There is a tourist info centre at 5 Coronation Ave, open Mon-Fri, 8.30am–5pm; Sat-Sun, 10am–2pm. Ph: (07) 5476 1933

Pomona *Map 10 B3*

The town of Pomona, 3km from the Bruce Hwy, clings to the lower slopes of precipitous Mt Cooroora. Once a timber and dairying centre, Pomona is now beginning to make the most of its scenery and traditions to attract the Noosa tourists.

Mt Cooroora (438m) is the focus of the King of the Mountain Festival (p.68), which began in 1958 with a bet by Bruce Samuels, a local footballer and railway porter, that he could run to the summit and back in less than 1hr. He proved the scoffers wrong, returning with 20min to spare, and collected his £100 wager. Samuels' feat, recorded on the wall of the **Railway Hotel** bar, led to challenges and the establishment of the official race.

On the other side of the tracks, in what was once the town centre, is the **Noosa Shire Museum**, 29 Factory St.

Open Thurs, noon–4pm; Sun, 1pm–4pm. Ph: (07) 5485 1080. Here also is the historic **Majestic Theatre**, which was established in 1921 and has Thurs-night and matinee screenings of silent films; special screenings for groups by appt. Ph: (07) 5485 2330.

Tewantin *Map 10 C3*

This historic township lies on a bend of the Noosa River upstream from Noosaville. The wide streets, spreading poinciana trees and old timber houses give the town a comfortable, established air.

The **Noosa Regional Gallery**, at Riverside in Pelican St, prides itself on being innovative and responsive to community needs. Among its unusual facilities are a gallery bus for to-the-door transport and a Children's Corner. Open Tue-Sun, 10am–4pm. Ph: (07) 5449 5340

The **Big Shell**, in Gympie St, has a display of coral, shells, coloured sands and other items, many of which are for sale. Open Sun-Fri, 9am–5pm. Ph: (07) 5447 1268

Nearby, at 19 Myles St, is the **House of Bottles**, built from more than 35 000 bottles and housing a collection of more than 10 000, some of which are over 2000 years old. Souvenir bottles of coloured sands are on sale. Open daily, 9am–5pm. Ph: (07) 5447 1277

A small ferry at the river end of Moorindil St carries cars across to the North Shore and the Cooloola section of Great Sandy NP. The ferry runs Sun-Thurs, 6am–10pm; Fri-Sat, 6am–midnight.

Not so silent
The Son of the Sheik, Rudolph Valentino's last film, has been running at the **Majestic** for many years now, to the accompaniment of the theatre's mighty Wurlitzer organ.

The Big Stubby

The Big Stubby
At the **House of Bottles** you can ride a slippery slide from the top of this giant beer bottle, which is 8.5m high and was built from 17 000 stubbies.

***Ginger Factory,
Yandina***

Yandina *Map 10 B4*

Yandina is on the Maroochy River, in a setting of canefields, remnant rainforest and volcanic peaks. The northern railway line passes through the town, and the Bruce Hwy runs nearby. Yandina has been quick to take advantage of its strategic location near the turnoff to Coolum by giving a home to a number of substantial tourist attractions.

The **Ginger Factory**, 50 Pioneer Rd, is a lavish establishment built around a ginger-processing plant, originally located at Buderim. Besides selling every conceivable variety of ginger confection at the Ginger Shoppe, the complex has attractions for the whole family — rides in an old cane train, the **Bunya Park Wildlife Sanctuary**, a rainforest walk and an array of Ginger Town shops, from the Dolls Cottage to Granny's Macadamia Kitchen. Open daily, 9am–5pm. Ph: (07) 5446 7096

Directly across Pioneer Rd is **NutWorks**, which combines a macadamia-nut processing factory with a cafe and tourist shop. Open daily, 9am–5pm. Ph: (07) 5472 7777

North of Yandina, along Fairhill Rd, is the **Fairhill Native Plant Nursery** (p.80).

National parks, state forests and conservation parks

Coochin Creek State Forest Park *Map 10 C5*

This picnic and camping area, about 2km north of Coochin Creek and then 5km off the Bruce Hwy along Roys Rd to the right, is set among exotic pine forest. Nearby is the old Campbellville town site, on the banks of Coochin Creek, where timber was milled in the 1880s.

Currimundi Conservation Park

This seaside conservation park at Wurtulla, north of Caloundra, encompasses 51ha of coastal heath and melaleucas bordering the north shore of Currimundi Lake. There is a profusion of wildflowers in spring.

Great Sandy NP: Cooloola section *Map 10*

Cooloola is the wildest and most extensive national park on the Sunshine Coast. This tract of wilderness, protected by the towering coloured-sand cliffs of Teewah and Rainbow Beach, is a walker's paradise, with open woodland, wallum heath, dense rainforest, fresh and salt or brackish lakes, and dark, tannin-stained waterways that reflect the tree-lined banks

Rare plant

Walk the **Boronia Trail** (1.8km 1-way) from Harry's Hut Rd (4WD only) through woodland and rainforest to Kin Kin Creek. Here, among the towering kauri pines, the rare *Boronia keysii* can be found.

Cooloola

like mirrors. The waterways are best explored by canoe or small boat. There are many short walks from the waterways, and the 46km **Cooloola Wilderness Trail**. Hikers can start this trail at Elanda Pt on **Lake Cootharaba**, where there is a private camping area, with kiosk and canoe and boat hire, Ph: (07) 5485 3165. Canoes can also be launched at Elanda Pt to explore the Everglades and the upper reaches of these waterways. North of Elanda Pt is the **Sir Thomas Hiley Info Centre**, at **Kinaba**, which is accessible by boat or walking track. The centre has displays, a bird hide and a self-guiding mangrove walk. Open daily, 9am–3pm. Ph: (07) 5449 7364

Those who are disinclined to hike or paddle will need a 4WD, as most of the tracks through the national park are unsuitable for conventional vehicles. An exception is the drive from Rainbow Beach Rd to the **Bymien Picnic Area**, a small clearing deep in the rainforest. It has toilets and picnic tables, and there is a walking track (2km 1-way) to **Poona Lake**. Take the Freshwater Rd turnoff and drive 3km into the forest.

4WD vehicles can continue along the rough track through blackbutt and scribbly-gum forest to the **Freshwater Camp and Day-use Area**, and then Teewah Beach about 5km south of the wreck of the *Cherry Venture*.

The Dept of Environment has invaluable brochures with details of campsites, beach camping restrictions, maps of walking and vehicle tracks, and useful commentary on the country they pass through. They are available from any of the Dept of Environment centres in the region, such as the info centre at Rainbow Beach, open daily, 7am–4pm. Ph: (07) 5486 3160

Inskip Peninsula Recreation Area

Camping is permitted in designated areas on this peninsula 11km north of Rainbow Beach, from which the ferry crosses to the southern end of Fraser Island. Unlike most campsites in Cooloola, this is an area where dogs are allowed and fires may be lit (bring your own wood).

Maroochy Wetlands Sanctuary

This 108ha reserve protects mangroves and melaleucas on the Maroochy River at Bli Bli. An info and education centre and a theatrette are housed in an old canecutters' barracks.

Mooloolah River NP *Map 10 C5*

Mooloolah River NP protects an extensive area of wallum heathland, which in spring becomes a garden of wildflowers, bordered in the north by open eucalypt forests. Access is by canoe or boat from the mouth of the Mooloolah River, or by car from the Bruce Hwy, turning off 400m south of the Buderim turnoff onto Mountain Creek Rd and then Military Rd.

Mt Coolum NP

This small park protects most of Mt Coolum, except for the lowest slopes. From a carpark at the cnr of Jarnahill Dr and Tanah St West there is a track to the summit, which only experienced climbers should attempt (2hr return). Sweeping views reward the effort.

Noosa NP *Map 12*

The **Noosa Heads section** of this park is one of the most frequented walking areas on the Sunshine Coast, with 6 tracks leading through littoral rainforest, open woodland and wildflower-dotted heath, and along a rocky coast of forbidding cliffs and hidden beaches. Maps of the walking tracks are available from the info centre at the park's entrance. Open Mon–Fri, 9am–3pm. Ph: (07) 5447 3243

Noosa NP

Other sections of Noosa NP continue through the coastal wallum on the inland side of the seaside settlements as far south as Peregian and west of Coolum township, preserving remnants of the wildflower-rich heath that once extended along most of the Sunshine Coast.

Parks and gardens

Ben Bennett Botanical Park, Caloundra

The natural bushland at this park in Queen St has many species of native plant, including eucalypts, waterlilies, casuarinas, melaleucas, hakeas and a rare patch of vine thicket.

Buderim Forest Park

In this park, approached along Quorn Close (off Lindsay Rd), open eucalypt forest acts as a buffer, protecting the remnant rainforest around Martin's Creek. The walking track passes through various forest types and over a bridge that spans a waterfall. The track has steps in the steeper places.

Edna Walling Memorial Garden

Near the Quorn Close entrance to Buderim Forest Park is this tribute to the vision and talent of Edna Walling (1896–1973), one of Australia's most influential gardeners. The garden consists largely of a vine-covered arbour.

Fairhill Native Plant Nursery and Botanic Gardens *Map 14* ⑫

North of Yandina on Fairhill Rd is Fairhill, the well-known native-plant nursery and botanical gardens. The centre stocks an impressive range of indigenous plants, books, posters, pottery and basketware. There is also a gallery displaying work by potters and wildlife artists, and a highly rated BYO restaurant, Picnics at Fairhill, offering lunch and morning and afternoon teas daily, 9am–4.30pm. Ph: (07) 5446 8191

Picnic tables are scattered about in shady corners of the 5ha garden, where native trees, shrubs, ferns, palms and rainforest species host a huge range of birds.
Open daily, 8.30am–5pm.
Ph: (07) 5446 7088

Lake Macdonald Botanical Gardens *Map 14* ⑩

These gardens, established by Noosa Shire on the shore of Lake Macdonald, include palms, roses and lilies, and rainforest, indigenous, exotic and tropical species, as well as an extensive system of walkways, open lawn areas, an amphitheatre, a fish hatchery and a bush chapel. A plan of the gardens is available near the entrance.

The Big Pineapple

Other attractions

Abbey Museum

This museum of art and archaeology in Old Toorbul Point Rd (off Bribie Island Rd) is one of the most highly respected private collections in Australia. It focuses on 2 main areas: the ancient and classical world, and Western Europe from prehistory to modern times. Among the priceless exhibits are a shoe that once belonged to Mary Queen of Scots and an Ancient Egyptian death mask.

The museum has wheelchair access and gardens where visitors are welcome to picnic. Open Tue–Sat, 10am–4pm; groups and tours by appt. Ph: (07) 5495 1652

Aussie World *Map 14* ❸

For those who like their amusements to be true blue, Aussie World, with its replica of the Ettamogah Pub of cartoon fame, offers a Fun Luge, Super X Simulator, Skirmish, camel and pony rides, Aboriginal cultural activities, gift shops and demonstrations of woodcraft, leathercraft and cartoon art. Located on the Bruce Hwy north of the Caloundra turnoff. Open daily from 9am. Ph: (07) 5494 5444

Australia Zoo

Giant pythons, crocodiles, koalas and otters — the Australia Zoo (formerly the Qld Reptile and Fauna Park) is home to them all. Visitors are invited to learn more about some of the creatures who share our planet by attending daily demonstrations and feedings of over 550 animals. Located on the Glass House Mts Rd, Beerwah. Open daily, 8.30am–4pm. Ph: (07) 5494 1134

Bellingham Maze *Map 14* ❺

One of the attractions on the Tanawha Tourist Dr is this large hedge maze, with aviaries, a show garden, tearoom and picnic area. Located cnr Tourist Dr and Main Creek Rd, Tanawha Valley. Open Fri–Wed, 9am–5pm, and all holidays. Ph: (07) 5445 2979

The Big Pineapple *Map 14* ❼

This theme park, based on a working pineapple and macadamia plantation in the scenic terrain just south of Nambour, is one of the Sunshine Coast's foremost tourist attractions. The Big Pineapple itself is a tower with a lookout at the top. Inside are instructive displays about pineapples and other tropical crops grown in the district. Visitors can also travel on the Plantation Train, visit the fauna sanctuary and animal nursery and take a boat ride that traces the history of horticulture. Licensed restaurants feature tropical dishes and plantation-fresh ingredients. Located on the Nambour

Bli Bli Castle

Connection Rd at Woombye, 6km south of Nambour. Open daily, 9am–5pm. Ph: (07) 5442 1333

Bli Bli Castle

Follow the David Low Way to Bli Bli to see a 'medieval' castle set in sugar-cane fields, complete with dungeon, torture chamber and a display of medieval armour. There is also a large doll museum and dioramas depicting 7 fairytales. Lunches and teas are available. Open daily, 9am–5pm. Ph: (07) 5448 5373

Forest Glen Sanctuary *Map 14* ❻

Take the Buderim exit (heading south) or the Sunshine Mwy exit (heading north) from the Bruce Hwy for the Tanawha Tourist Dr and this wildlife park, the largest on the Sunshine Coast. The park is home to hundreds of deer and many of Australia's native animals – koalas, wombats, emus, kangaroos and wallabies. There is a special habitat for nocturnal animals. Open daily, 9am–5pm. Ph: (07) 5445 1274

Nostalgia Town

Nostalgia Town is a place for the kids – a theme park with a sense of humour, poking light-hearted fun at the solemn subject of our past. Hundreds of life-like characters inhabit the park and there is a range of activities – an Enchanted Railway, a time trip through history,

Superbee Honey Factory

remote-control boats, mini-cars, and mini-golf in a not-so-serious graveyard. It can be found on the David Low Way at Pacific Paradise, 2km south of the Sunshine Coast Airport. Open daily, 9am–5pm. Ph: (07) 5448 7155

Opals Down Under *Map 14* ❷

This centre has a large collection of Australian opals, a retail showroom, a house jeweller and an educational audio-visual presentation on the opal industry. Located on the Bruce Hwy just south of the Ettamogah Pub (take the Glenview Rd exit). Open daily, 9am–5pm. Ph: (07) 5494 5400

Ski 'n' Skurf

This cable-ski park on the David Low Way at Bli Bli offers water fun by day and night, with food and drink from the fully licensed kiosk. Open Sun–Wed, 9am–5pm; Thurs–Sat, 9am–10pm (shorter hours in winter); Christmas holidays: 8am–10pm daily. Ph: (07) 5448 7555

Superbee Honey Factory *Map 14* ❹

The highlight of the Honey Factory, set in 3ha of tropical gardens on the Tanawha Tourist Dr, is the hourly Bee Show – a demonstration (behind glass) of bee-handling and honey extraction, with free honey-tasting as a sweetener.

To keep the kids entertained there are fairytale cottages, merry-go-rounds, miniature electric cars and other amuse-ments. Lunch or snack in the family restaurant, and browse through the range of souvenirs and honey products in the gift shop. Open daily, 9am–5pm. Ph: (07) 5445 3090

Thrill Hill Family Fun Park *Map 14* ❺

The waterslide is the focus of this fun park, but there are other attractions as well: rollerskating/blading, a swimming lake, bike track, skateboard bowls, tennis court, and under-5s playground equipment. Thrill Hill has 2 kiosks and BBQ facilities. Located 2km north of the Big Pineapple on the Nambour Connection Rd. Open weekends Sept–Jun, 10am–5pm (and daily during school and public holidays); night use by appt only. Ph: 0500 521 033

Wappa Falls Astronomical Observatory and Nature's Way Museum *Map 14* ◉

Visitors are invited to explore the night sky with a selection of fine telescopes at this private observatory 2km along Wappa Falls Rd south of Yandina. The museum has over 8000 specimens of marine life and a large display of rocks and minerals. There are BBQ facilities, a children's playground and botanical gardens. Open from noon most days and nights. Bookings essential. Ph: (07) 5446 7944

Zone 3

For those who like their fantasy laced with adrenalin, Zone 3, at 3 Main Dr, Warana (just off Nicklin Way), offers a laser game in a multi-level maze and a 9-hole mini-golf course with an intergalactic theme. Open daily, 10am–10pm. Ph: (07) 5493 6333

Recreational activities
Bushwalking

The national parks of the Sunshine Coast cover a rich variety of terrain, and most have bushwalking tracks. The most extensive track system is in the **Cooloola section** of **Great Sandy NP** (p.78).

Flying

For high times over the Sunshine Coast, try **Suncoast Hang Glider and Microlights**, based near Palmwoods (Ph: (07) 5445 9185), **Parasail Mooloolaba**, at the Mooloolaba Wharf Complex (Ph: (07) 5444 7477), **Paraflying Noosa**, Main Beach, Noosa Heads (Ph: (07) 5449 9630), **Rainbow Air,** for ultra-lights, hang gliders and paragliders (Ph: (07) 5486 3773), or **Rainbow Paragliding**, 66 Rainbow Beach Rd (Ph: (07) 5486 3499).

Go-kart racing

Both the **Big Fish** at 459 Pumicestone Rd, Caboolture (Ph: (07) 5495 6010) and the **Big Kart Track** on the Glass House Mts Tourist Dr (Ph: (07) 5494 1613) feature large go-kart tracks. The Big Fish also has a 9-hole golf course and putt-putt golf course, and the Big Kart Track has a kids' track, slot-kart racing, and the Bungy Bullet, a dual-seat bungy ride.

Horseriding

Several riding centres offer treks of varying duration – some as short as 1hr, others as long as 7 days. Try the **Mooloolah Valley Riding Centre** at Kings Rd, Mooloolah (Ph: (07) 5494 7109), **Clip-Clop Treks** at Eumarella Rd (off the Sunshine Mwy), Lake Weyba, Noosa (Ph: (07) 5449 1254) or **Rainbow Beach Horse Rides** at Wyvern Rd, Rainbow Beach (Ph: 0417 757 915).

A 'must' for walkers
Published by the Caloundra branch of the Wildlife Preservation Society of Qld, *Walks in Caloundra: From the Mountains to the Sea* describes and maps 15 easily accessible walks in the region.

Dromedary day trips
For those who want to ride higher, **Camel Safaris**, based at Lake Cooroibah Resort, offers explorations of the bush and beach of Noosa's North Shore. Ph: (07) 5442 4402

Horseriding, Rainbow Beach

Fishing charters

Among the numerous reef-fishing and game-fishing charters operating from the Sunshine Coast area are:

★ from Rainbow Beach: *The Spirit of Rainbow*, Ph: (07) 5486 3128;

★ from Noosa: **Noosa Blue Water Charters** (Ph: (07) 5449 9355), **Noosa Reef Fishing and Charter** (Ph: (07) 5447 4233), *Men at Work* (Ph: (07) 5474 2444);

★ from Mooloolaba: **Gemini Reef Cruises** (Ph: (07) 5444 7477); **Mooloolaba Reef and Game Charters** (Ph: (07) 5444 3735); **Sunshine Sea Charters** (Ph: (07) 5444 7477).

For guided estuary and freshwater fishing trips, contact **River Fishing Safaris** at Noosa (Ph: (07) 5447 1121) and **Beach and Bush Fishing Adventures** at Minyama (Ph: (07) 5444 6280).

On and in the water

Canoes and kayaks

The waterways and protected ocean bays of the Sunshine Coast are ideal for paddling adventures.

Canoes and equipment can be hired at many centres, such as **Bikes and Boats** at McDonald Rd, Bli Bli, on a tributary of the Maroochy River (Ph: (07) 5448 6055), and the kiosk at Elanda Pt, Lake Cootharaba (Ph: (07) 5485 3165).

Various companies offer guided trips on the waterways: **Adventures Sunshine Coast** has a 1-day 'Escape' trip on the Mooloolah River (Ph: (07) 5444 8824); **Adventure Instruction Network** leads canoe trips on the Noosa River (Ph: (07) 5444 0827); **Aussie Sea Kayak Company** conducts kayak tours on Sunshine Coast waterways from Caloundra to Noosa (Ph: (07) 5477 5335) and **Just Paddlin' Canoe Tours** offers guided canoe trips

Fishing the North Coast

At the right time of year, good catches can be taken by anglers fishing the Sunshine Coast surf beaches and estuaries from **Tin Can Bay** and **Teewah** to **Pumicestone Passage**. Whiting, dart and flathead are target species in summer, bream and tailor in winter.

Anglers fishing with lures and live bait from rocky headlands such as **Double Island Point**, **Noosa Heads**, **Coolum** and **Point Cartwright** also tangle with heavyweight species such as yellowtail kingfish, jewfish and trevally.

Those fishing offshore take snapper, pearl perch, sweetlip and red emperor from reefs such as the **Barwon Banks**. During the warmer months, pelagics such as mackerel, tuna and marlin provide plenty of action.

For the freshwater specialist, the headwaters of the **Noosa River** are famous for their wily bass, and **Lake Macdonald**, outside Cooroy, is stocked with Australian freshwater species such as golden perch.

Houseboats at Rainbow Beach

from Rainbow Beach and Tin Can Bay (Ph: (07) 5486 4417).

Houseboats

Explore the Great Sandy Strait in a houseboat from **Rainbow Beach Houseboats**, Carlo Pt (Ph: (07) 5486 3146), **Luxury Afloat Houseboats**, Tin Can Bay (Ph: (07) 5486 4864) and **Fraser Island Houseboats**, Tin Can Bay (Ph: (07) 5486 4444) or contact **Houseboat Holidays of Queensland**, Gympie Terrace, Noosaville (Ph: (07) 5447 1777) for a relaxing time on the Noosa River.

Sailing boats

Small-craft sailing is popular on the waters of Pumicestone Passage, the Maroochy, Mooloolah and Noosa Rivers, and the Noosa River lakes.

Small sailing boats and sailboards can be hired at many of the centres. Try **Golden Beach Hire** on the Esplanade, Golden Beach, Caloundra (Ph: (07) 5492 4344), **Maroochy Sail Hire** at Bradman Ave, on the Maroochy River (Ph: 0419 399 460) or **Sail Mooloolaba** at the end of Parkyn Pde, on the Spit, Mooloolaba (Ph: 018 191 613).

On the Noosa River, catamarans, runabouts, windsurfers and canoes can be hired at a number of places along Gympie Terrace, Noosaville.

For something larger, **Sandy Straits Yacht Charters** has yachts and motorsailers for charter from its base at Carlo Pt, Rainbow Beach. Ph: (07) 5486 3273

Sailboarding, Maroochydore

Scuba-diving

ScubAddict at Poinciana Ave, Tewantin (Ph: (07) 5449 8503) and **Sunreef Diving Services** at 120 Brisbane Rd, Mooloolaba (Ph: (07) 5444 5656) are 2 of the many dive services on the Sunshine Coast.

Waterskiing

The quiet waters of Pumicestone Passage and the Mooloolah, Maroochy and Noosa Rivers are popular for waterskiing, and all are well supplied with boat ramps.

Fun for the young

- ★ Australia Zoo, Beerwah (p.81)
- ★ Big Kart Track, Landsborough (p.83)
- ★ The Big Pineapple, Woombye (p.81)
- ★ Bli Bli Castle (p.82)
- ★ Dolphin-watching at Tin Can Bay (p.75)
- ★ Forest Glen Sanctuary (p.82)
- ★ Nostalgia Town, Pacific Paradise (p.82)
- ★ Maze Mania 4 Kids, Maroochydore (p.70)
- ★ Superbee Honey Factory, Tanawha (p.82)
- ★ Thrill Hill Family Fun Park, Woombye (p.82)
- ★ UnderWater World, Mooloolabah (p.72)
- ★ Zone 3, Warana (p.83)

Fishing the North Coast

Suggested tours – Map 14
'Bruce Hwy Blockbusters' tour

Approximate distance

220km return from Brisbane CBD to Yandina

About the tour

This tour makes possible an initial reconnoitre of the main tourist attractions around a section of the Bruce Hwy from the Caloundra turnoff north to Yandina. It would be impossible to do justice to more than a few of these in the course of a day trip; for example, there is so much to see and do at places such as the Big Pineapple and Forest Glen Sanctuary that visitors may want to spend 3 or more hours there.

Places of interest

❶ **Big Kart Track** (p.83)
❷ **Opals Down Under** (p.82)
❸ **Aussie World/Ettamogah Pub** (p.81)
❹ **Superbee Honey Factory** (p.82)
❺ **Bellingham Maze** (p.81)
❻ **Forest Glen Sanctuary** (p.82)
❼ **The Big Pineapple** (p.81)
❽ **Thrill Hill Family Fun Park** (p.82)
❾ **Wappa Falls Astronomical Observatory** (p.83)
❿ **Ginger Factory/Bunya Park Wildlife Sanctuary** (p.78)
⓫ **NutWorks** (p.78)
⓬ **Fairhill Native Plant Nursery** (p.80)

Plantation Train, the Big Pineapple

Map labels

5 Kinaba
i Information Centre

nda Point
ill Point

ake
tharaba O Teewah
Sandy

National

Park

SCALE 1:361,100
0   5   10
Kilometres
COPYRIGHT © UNIVERSAL PRESS PTY LTD (PUBLISHER) 2000

ooroibah
Lake
Coorbibah   Laguna Bay

The House
of Bottles

e Big 2 3
ell   O Tewantin O 1 Noosa National Park
loosaville   **Noosa Heads**
              O **Sunshine Beach**
+ Noosa Airport
Lake
Weyba   Noosa National Park

Do O nan   O **Marcus Beach**

              O **Peregian Beach**

70   6

CORAL

ndina
reek O **Coolum Beach**
              Point Arkwright
          O **Yaroomba**

O **Mount Coolum**

O **Marcoola**

+ Sunshine Coast Airport
O **Mudjimba**

SEA

i Bli

O **Maroochydore**
O **Alexandra Headland**
Mooloolaba
       Point Cartwright
O **Buddina**

est Glen
nctuary **Buderim**
6 8
Bellingham Maze 70
5 4
erbee **Sippy** Mooloolah
ney **Downs** River
ssie   Nat Pk
rld 3
als 2 O **Warana**
wn
der

O **Wurtulla**

1 Big Kart Track 6

O **Dicky Beach**
O **Moffat Beach**

Caloundra Head
Caloundra
Aerodrome + **Caloundra**

O **Golden Beach**

Noosa hinterland tour

Approximate distance
360km return from Brisbane CBD

About the tour
Approaching via Noosa, Noosaville and Tewantin, this trip visits Boreen Pt and Elanda Pt in the Cooloola section of Great Sandy NP before continuing on to explore the scenic byways of the rural areas around Kin Kin, Cooran, Pomona, Cooroy and Eumundi. For those fit enough, there is the chance to tackle the 5.7km (1-way) walking track in to the Sir Thomas Hiley Info Centre at Kinaba (remember to carry insect repellent).

Places of interest
❶ **Noosa NP** (p.79)
❷ **The Big Shell, Tewantin** (p.77)
❸ **House of Bottles, Tewantin** (p.77)
❹ **Boreen Pt** (p.75)
❺ **Kinaba Info Centre** (p.79)
❻ **James M McKane Memorial Lookout** (p.76)
❼ **Country Life Hotel, Kin Kin** (p.76)
❽ **Majestic Theatre, Pomona** (p.77)
❾ **Cooroy Butter Factory arts centre** (p.76)
❿ **Lake Macdonald Botanical Gardens** (p.80)
⓫ **Eumundi Markets** (p.76)

Cane country near Mt Coolum

Fraser Coast
Perfect by Nature

Left: **Central Station rainforest, Fraser Island**
Right: **Wharf St Precinct, Maryborough**

The Fraser Coast

A beach that goes forever, soaring sand cliffs, noble forests, limpid creeks and encounters with the mighty humpback whale – this is the romance of the Fraser Coast.

Fraser is a dynamic island. Storms, tides and ocean currents perpetually excavate and build its shore, the contours of its dunes change subtly under the influence of the wind, and immense sandblows invade the land. Yet it supports some of the finest rainforest in SE Qld, and magnificent stands of the giant satinay, or Fraser Island turpentine. With its dramatic landforms and botanical wonders, the island is a physical testament to the power and subtlety of natural forces.

Behind Fraser, in the wide waters of Hervey Bay, flotillas of boats go out to meet the humpbacks, which dawdle here each spring before heading off again on their long journey south.

On the mainland is the old port of Maryborough, city of gracious colonial homes and stately historic buildings. At its heart, in the old wharf area on the Mary River, is a heritage precinct of rare distinction, preserved at first by decline, and then by a newly awakened sense of history.

ℹ Tourist information

Cooloola Region Visitors Information Centre
Dept of Environment and Heritage Building, Lake Alford, Bruce Hwy, Gympie 4570 Ph: (07) 5482 5444
www.cooloola.org.au

Hervey Bay
Info centres at numerous tour booking offices in Urangan, Torquay, Scarness and Pialba

Maryborough Information Centre
30 Ferry St, Maryborough 4650
Ph: (07) 4121 4111

Naturally Queensland Information Centre (EPA)
(info on national parks)
Ground Floor, 160 Ann St, Brisbane 4000 Ph: (07) 3227 8185
www.env.qld.gov.au

Rainbow Beach Tourist Centre
8 Rainbow Beach Rd, Rainbow Beach 4581 Ph: (07) 5486 3227

Rainbow Beach Adventure Centre
66 Rainbow Beach Rd, Rainbow Beach 4581 Ph: (07) 5486 3499

Must see, must do

★ **The Cathedrals coloured sands, Fraser Island** (p.94)

★ **Historic Wharf St Precinct, Maryborough** (p.97)

★ **Wanggoolba Creek at Central Station, Fraser Island** (p.100)

★ **Whale-watch cruise to Platypus Bay** (p.105)

Radio stations

ABC Radio Wide Bay: AM 855

4MB Maryborough: AM 1161

CC FM (Coast and Country): FM 93.9

ABC Radio Wide Bay FM: FM 100.1

Sea FM: FM 101.9

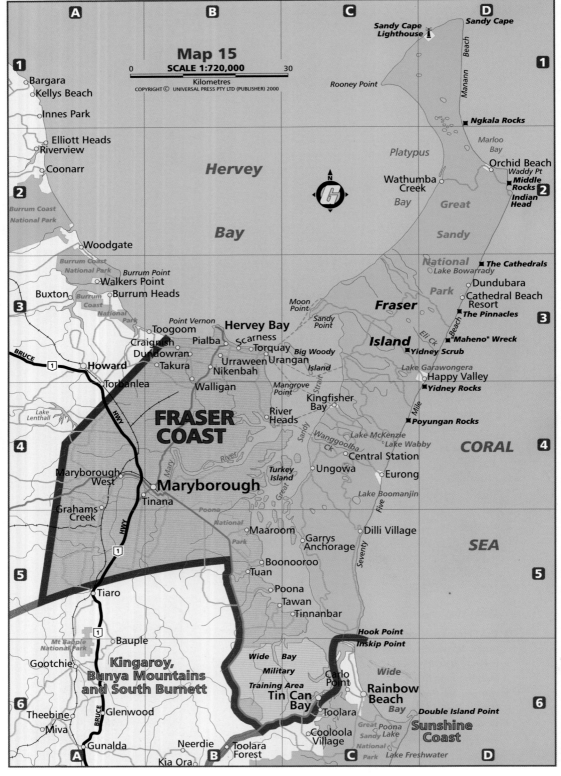

Map 15
SCALE 1:720,000
0   30
Kilometres
COPYRIGHT © UNIVERSAL PRESS PTY LTD (PUBLISHER) 2000

A | **B** | **C** | **D**

Sandy Cape
Lighthouse
Sandy Cape

Rooney Point
Manann Beach

Ngkala Rocks

Bargara
Kellys Beach

Innes Park

Hervey

Platypus
Marloo Bay

Elliott Heads
Riverview

Coonarr

Wathumba Creek
Orchid Beach
Waddy Pt
Middle Rocks

Bay
Great
Indian Head

Burrum Coast
National Park

Woodgate

Bay
Sandy

National
Lake Bowarrady
The Cathedrals

Burrum Coast
National Park
Burrum Point
Walkers Point

Buxton
Burrum Coast
National Park
Burrum Heads

Moon Point

Fraser

Dundubara
Cathedral Beach Resort
The Pinnacles

Point Vernon
Toogoom
Hervey Bay
Sandy Point

Island

Eli Ck
Beach

"Maheno" Wreck
Yidney Scrub

Craignish
Pialba
Scarness
Torquay
Big Woody Island

Dundowran
Urraween
Urangan

Lake Garawongera
Happy Valley

Takura
Nikenbah

Howard

Walligan
Mangrove Point

Yidney Rocks

Torbanlea

Strait

Kingfisher Bay

Lake
Lenthall

FRASER COAST

River Heads

Mile

Poyungan Rocks

Lake McKenzie
Lake Wabby
Sandy

Wanggoolba Ck

CORAL

Maryborough West

Mary River
Turkey Island
Ungowa
Central Station

Eurong

Grahams Creek

Maryborough
Tinana

Poona National Park

Great

Lake Boomanjin

SEA

Maaroom
Garrys Anchorage
Dilli Village

Seventy

Boonooroo
Tuan
Five

Tiaro

Poona
Tawan
Tinnanbar

Bauple
Hook Point
Inskip Point

Mt Bauple
National Park

Gootchie

Kingaroy, Bunya Mountains and South Burnett

Wide   Bay
Military
Training Area

Wide
Carlo Point

Rainbow Beach

Tin Can Bay

Bay
Double Island Point

Theebine
Glenwood

Toolara

Sunshine Coast

Miva

BRUCE

Gunalda

Neerdie
Toolara Forest

Cooloola Village

Great
Poona
Sandy Lake

National
Park
Lake Freshwater

Kia Ora

Natural features

Fraser Island, known as K'gari to the Butchulla people, is the culmination of oceanic processes that have shaped the coast of SE Qld. For millennia, the northerly drift of sand has snagged at the rocky headlands that jut out from the coastal plain into the sea, building immense dune systems, some as high as mountains, and forming the elongated arcs of the region's celebrated beaches.

At Fraser Island, these processes produce landforms of prodigious scale. Fraser is the largest sand island in the world. The ocean beach sweeps NE for 100km to the rocky promontories of Indian Head and Waddy Pt, then arcs NW, terminating in Sandy Cape. Along much of its length, it is backed by towering cliffs of coloured sand, hewn by wind and rain into fantastic shapes. In the interior are majestic forests and freshwater lakes.

Between Fraser Island and the mainland are Hervey Bay in the north, and the Great Sandy Strait in the south. Hervey Bay's mainland shore is lined with sandy beaches and a series of bayside resorts. The deep scoop of Platypus Bay, inside Fraser, is the playground of migrating humpback whales. Further south, Hervey Bay narrows to form the Great Sandy Strait. Here, at River Heads, the Mary River finally reaches the sea.

History

Indian Head, on Fraser Island, was named by James Cook for the gathering of Butchulla people ('Indians') who viewed the *Endeavour*'s passage from that vantage point.

In 1842, Andrew Petrie searched for timber in the country north of Noosa. His party discovered the Mary River, and found kauri pine growing there. Later the same year, Tiaro Stn was established. This occupation was strongly resisted by the local Aborigines, but by the 1850s many other pastoral holdings had been taken up.

In 1847, wool began to be shipped from a woolstore on the Mary River. The township that grew there – Maryborough – was relocated downriver in the 1850s. Maryborough became a centre for the region's industries – timber, sugar, dairying and heavy engineering.

By the late 1800s, the surviving Aborigines had been relocated to Fraser Island. The last Fraser Island mission closed in 1904 and most of the people were sent to other missions throughout Qld. Only a few remained to work in the timber and fishing industries.

Sandmining leases were granted on Fraser in 1949, but a conservation campaign brought mining to a halt in 1976. Logging ceased in 1991. Today, but for a few small freehold areas, Fraser Island is a World Heritage listed national park.

Shipwreck survivor
It was from this country that 'Wandi', the escaped convict David Bracefell, rescued Eliza Fraser, who had been cast ashore on Fraser Island and lived with the Aborigines there after the wreck of the *Stirling Castle* in 1836.

Indian Head and Waddy Pt, Fraser Island

Fraser's lakes
There are 2 types of lake on the island: 'perched' (on a peaty base above the water-table) and 'window' (where the water-table meets the land surface).

On the mainland, the old holiday hamlets are now hemmed in against their foreshore reserves by new residential development, forming the city of Hervey Bay, 'Whalewatch Capital of the World'.

Getting there

By air

Sunstate Airlines has daily flights to Maryborough and Hervey Bay from Brisbane (Ph: 131 313). **Flight West Airlines** also flies daily to Hervey Bay. Ph: 132 392

For access to Fraser Island, there are light aircraft services from Hervey Bay and Maryborough to designated sections of the ocean beach, and to the landing strip at Orchid Beach (p.95).

By road

To reach Hervey Bay, follow the Bruce Hwy north to Maryborough and then take the Hervey Bay road. Those travelling to Fraser Island from Inskip Pt can turn off the Bruce Hwy at Gympie onto the Tin Can Bay road and then take the road to Rainbow Beach. Access to the villages along the Great Sandy Strait is provided by the Maryborough–Tin Can Bay road.

Only 4WD-owners should consider taking their cars to Fraser Island, as the driving conditions there are quite unsuited to 2WD vehicles. Among the mainland centres that hire out 4WDs are **Aussie Trax 4x4 Hire** (Ph: 1800 062 275), **Bay 4WD Centre** (Ph: (07) 4128 2981), **Aussie Trek**

Adventure (Ph: 1800 679 479) and **Island Explorers** (Ph: (07) 4124 3770), all on Boat Harbour Dr, Hervey Bay, and **Safari 4WD Hire**, 55 Old Maryborough Rd, Hervey Bay (Ph: 1800 689 819). (See p.74 for 4WD hire from Rainbow Beach.) On the island itself, 4WD hire cars are available at most of the settlements.

Vehicle permits are required for those who wish to drive on the island. Together with **camping permits**, they are available from Dept of Environment and Heritage offices at Brisbane, Gympie, Noosa, Rainbow Beach, Maryborough and Bundaberg, as well as the Marina Kiosk at Urangan Boat Harbour (Hervey Bay), and the general store at River Heads.

McCafferty's Express Coaches (Ph: 131 499) and **Greyhound Pioneer** (Ph: 132 030) operate a number of services daily to Maryborough and Hervey Bay from the Roma St Transit Centre in Brisbane. **Suncoast Pacific** has daily services linking the Gold Coast, Brisbane and Hervey Bay via the Sunshine Coast. Ph: (07) 3236 1901

By rail

Electric trains run from Brisbane to Maryborough, connecting with buses to Hervey Bay. Ph: 132 235

By ferry and boat

One route to Fraser Island is north along the Bruce Hwy to Gympie, then to Rainbow Beach and Inskip Pt, and across

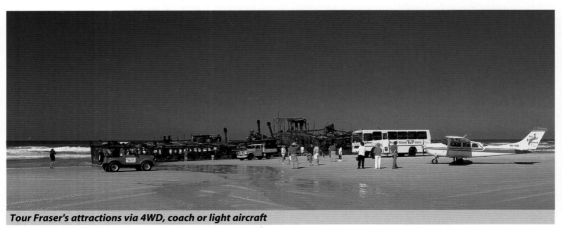

Tour Fraser's attractions via 4WD, coach or light aircraft

to Hook Pt, at the southern tip of Fraser Island, aboard the **vehicular ferry**.

Note that it is best to make the crossing around low tide for ease of passage along Fraser's ocean beach. The trip across takes about 10min, and the ferry runs on demand. Ph: (07) 5486 3227

Vehicular ferries also run to Fraser Island from:

* Urangan Boat Harbour, Hervey Bay, to Moon Pt, Ph: (07) 4125 4444 (bookings essential);
* River Heads, NE of Maryborough at the mouth of the Mary River, to Wanggoolba Creek, Ph: (07) 4125 4444 (bookings essential);
* River Heads to Kingfisher Bay Resort, Ph: (07) 4125 5511 (bookings essential).

A regular **Fast Cat** service carries passengers from Urangan Boat Harbour to Kingfisher Bay Resort, Ph: (07) 4125 5511. For private boats, there are boat ramps at many spots on the mainland shore of Hervey Bay and the Great Sandy Strait, and safe moorings at Wathumba Creek, Kingfisher Bay Resort and Garry's Anchorage, on the SW shore of the island.

Getting around

Air Fraser Island at Hervey Bay Airport operates a variety of flights, from fly-drive-camp tours, to transport to island resorts (Ph: (07) 4125 3600). **Elite Airways** also offers scenic flights from Hervey Bay Airport (Ph: (07) 4125 3111). **Marine Air Seaplanes** at Hervey Bay Airport has personalised tours to Fraser (Ph: 018 060 292).

Many cruise boats visit Fraser Island from Hervey Bay. *Stefanie* **Yacht Charters** runs overnight sailing tours of Platypus Bay, linking (if desired) with a 4WD safari tour of the island itself (Ph: 1800 650 776). *Blue Dolphin* **Sailing Cruises** lets you sail away to Fraser for a day (Ph: (07) 4125 5702). The launch *Tasman Venture II* leaves the Great Sandy Straits Marina at 9am daily for 1-day tours of Fraser Island's west coast (Ph: 1800 620 322). The **Kingfisher Bay Resort** conducts tours beginning with a Fast Cat cruise across the Great Sandy Strait (Ph: (07) 4125 5511). The yacht *Investigator III* takes passengers on

2hr cruises of the Mary River from the Mary River Marina, Maryborough (Ph: (07) 4128 9147). (See p.104 for whale-watching tours.)

(See p.104 for whale-watching tours.)

The 'roads' on Fraser Island are the ocean beach (around low tide), sand tracks and sections of 'corduroy' surfacing (wooden slats chained together and laid over the sand), none of which are suitable for conventional vehicles. Also, several tracks may be impassable at times to low-slung 4WDs.

There are numerous 4WD tours of Fraser Island on offer: **Sunrover Expeditions** offers 5-day World Heritage Nature Safaris from Brisbane (Ph: (07) 3203 4241), **Fraser Island Explorer Tours** runs 2-day adventure safaris (Ph: (07) 5447 3845) and a 3-day guided **Wilderness Adventure** leaves from Urangan Harbour, Hervey Bay, every Tue and Thurs (Ph: (07) 4120 0333).

Sunrover Expeditions leaves Brisbane on 3-day Sand Island Discovery Tours in a 4WD bus (Ph: (07) 3203 4241). **Fraser Island VIP Tours** conducts 2-day safari tours in a 4WD bus, leaving from Brisbane, with pick-up points along the way (Ph: (07) 3273 6688); these tours include overnight accommodation at Kingfisher Bay Resort. **Fraser Coast Getaway Tours** offers a Heritage Markets Tour to Maryborough and a Historical Hervey Bay Tour (Ph: (07) 4128 6214). Explore Fraser from Rainbow Beach in a 4WD coach with **Sun Safari Tours** (Ph: (07) 5486 3154). **Kingfisher Bay Resort** runs ranger-guided coach tours to Fraser Island's lakes and rainforests, and along the ocean beach (Ph: (07) 4125 5511). **Fraser Venture** (Ph: (07) 4125 4444) and **Top Tours** (Ph: (07) 4125 3933) offer 1-day and 2-day tours of Fraser from Hervey Bay.

Just Cruis'n Motorcycle Tours, based at Hervey Bay, offers tours aboard a Harley Davidson. Ph: 0412 387 828

Festivals and events
Yagubi Festival

A 3-day multicultural festival held at **Hervey Bay** in May, with music, dance, workshops, international food, a children's festival and a fire parade on the beach.

Kingfisher Bay Resort

Kingfisher Bay Fast Cat

Knowing where you're going
A map with detailed coverage of the island tracks, such as the *Fraser Island* Sunmap tourist map, is essential for 4WD touring.

Hervey Bay Family Fishing Competition

This event is conducted by the Hervey Bay Boat Club in Jun. Ph: (07) 4124 1000

Hervey Bay Whale Festival

A fun-filled fortnight in Aug celebrates the return of the humpbacks. This aquatic carnival includes an illuminated procession of floats and the Blessing of the Fleet.

Maryborough Heritage Spring Festival

Held in the 1st week of Sept. One of the features is Ebenezer's Lamplight Bazaar, with lamplit market barrows, food stalls and street entertainment.

Maryborough Masters Games

A multitude of sporting events for senior athletes from Australia and around the world. Held on the 1st weekend of Oct.

Main localities and settlements

For ease of reference, towns and settlements have been listed alphabetically in 2 sections: Fraser Island and the mainland.

Fraser Island
Cathedral Beach Resort *Map 15 D3*

North of the imposing Pinnacles is Cathedral Beach Resort, named for the dramatically eroded coloured-sand cliffs ('the Cathedrals') that line the shore along this part of the Seventy-Five Mile Beach. The settlement consists of private cabins and a camping ground set in a grove of native trees and coconut palms. Campers here need to book. Ph: (07) 4127 9177. The resort has most facilities — fuel, store, ice, gas, phone, postal service, bar and emergency helicopter landing area.

Dilli Village *Map 15 C5*

This is the 1st Fraser Island settlement encountered by travellers on the ocean beach who approach from Hook Pt. It is a private resort of prefab cabins set along a sand track behind the dunes. There is an emergency helicopter landing area here. From the village, a scenic drive (a single-lane sand track) runs inland past several lakes to Central Station (p.100).

Dundubara *Map 15 D3*

More than 75km north of Hook Pt is Dundubara, a large camping ground and ranger station set among the bloodwoods and banksias behind the dunes. The ranger station has maps and brochures with details about walking tracks and other features of the island. Basic facilities are available here, including showers, toilets, telephone, postal service, first aid, a 24hr emergency medical service and emergency helicopter landing area. However, there is no shop, ice or petrol bowser.

The Pinnacles, Fraser Island

Seventy-Five Mile Beach

Eurong *Map 15 C4*

Eurong is a comparatively large settlement on the ocean beach, about 35km north of Hook Pt. There is a ranger station with a well-equipped tourist info centre here. The centre has a highly engaging and instructive display featuring the island's natural history. The settlement supplies fuel, gas, ice and other provisions, and has a restaurant, bar and postal service. The ranger station dispenses first aid and has an emergency helicopter air strip.

Happy Valley *Map 15 D3*

Happy Valley is the main settlement on the central section of the Seventy-Five Mile Beach. A sand track leads from the beach past holiday houses to the general store and restaurant – a large inviting building with wide verandahs under shady trees. The scenic drives south past **Lake Garawongera**, and north past several other lakes, begin (or end) behind Happy Valley.

As well as accommodation, Happy Valley has a telephone, public toilets, fuel, ice, gas, a bar, a picnic area, postal facilities, an emergency helicopter landing area and, during Qld school holidays, a Qld Ambulance Service first aid station. Ph: (07) 4127 9158 for the ambulance service.

Kingfisher Bay Resort *Map 15 C4*

Set among trees on the high western shore of the island is the stylish and environmentally sensitive Kingfisher Bay Resort. It has a Day Visitor Centre, with a swimming pool, bar and bistro. The resort offers hotel or self-contained villa accommodation. Every holiday need is catered for here, from 4WD hire to high-class dining. There are **ranger-guided 4WD bus tours** to most of the island's attractions. Ph: (07) 4120 3333

Orchid Beach *Map 15 D2*

Orchid Beach is a remote but growing settlement of holiday houses set high on the dunes and connected by corduroy track. A shop in the lower part of the settlement sells all the necessities, including fuel, gas and ice. Other facilities include phone, mail service and emergency helicopter landing area. There is also an airfield nearby.

East of Orchid Beach is the Waddy Pt camping ground, a strip of sites between the beach and the high, steep dunes. From rocky Waddy Pt it is possible to see Indian Head to the south and Sandy Cape far to the north.

The mainland
Boonooroo *Map 15 B5*

Boonooroo is one of a string of small settlements on the mainland shore of the

High-fliers
Those who want to see Fraser from the air can ask at the **Eurong resort** for a joyflight over the island.
Ph: (07) 4127 9122

Great Sandy Strait. It is just south of Poona NP, 24km SE of Maryborough, on a turnoff from the Maryborough–Cooloola Rd. The township is on a point, looking NE across to Fraser Island, and south across a narrow bay to Poona Pt. All the basic facilities are available, including a picnic area, a camping and caravan park, fuel and a boat ramp.

Hervey Bay *Map 15 B3*

The old settlements that line this crescent-shaped bay between Dayman Pt and Point Vernon have fused to form the city of Hervey Bay, one of the fastest-growing cities in Australia. In earlier times, these settlements were sleepy seaside resorts for the citizens of Maryborough and the surrounding farms. Today, tourists from near and far come to watch the **humpback whales**, which sojourn in the lee of Fraser Island on their way south after their winter migration to the Great Barrier Reef (p.105). **Urangan Boat Harbour**, which is the departure point for whale-watching tours, has a tourist info centre and a secure parking area.

From east to west, the bayside centres are Urangan, Torquay, Scarness, Pialba, Point Vernon and Gatakers Bay. Most of these places have tourist info centres, where tour bookings can be made. Eateries and holiday units line the Esplanade.

Cycling is an ideal way to explore the shoreline. A bike track runs the full length of the bay through the tree-shaded foreshore reserve, and several of the tourist info centres have bikes for hire. One is the **Central Booking Office** at 341 The Esplanade, Scarness. Ph: (07) 4124 1300

Those who are interested in gemstones, crystals and jewellery may find **Crystalmania**, in the terminal building at the Urangan Boat Harbour, to their taste. Ph: (07) 4125 2811

Neptune's Reefworld, reached through Dayman Park, cnr Pulgul and Kent Sts, Urangan, features displays of living coral, sharks, stonefish, seasnakes, seal shows and 'touch tanks' with turtles

and stingrays. Wheelchair accessible. Open daily, 9.15am–4.30/5pm. Ph: (07) 4128 9828

Also at Urangan (553 The Esplanade) is Vic Hislop's **Shark Show**, which is aimed at dispelling myths and presenting the facts about sharks. The display includes movies and a frozen shark specimen. Open daily, 8.30am–6pm. Ph: (07) 4128 9137

Touch koalas and handle a snake at **Hervey Bay Natureworld**, cnr Fairway Dr and Maryborough Rd, a place for families. Natureworld offers hand-feeding of native animals and birds, a farmyard, paddle boats, a playground and BBQ facilities. Open daily, 9am–5pm. Ph: (07) 4124 1733

Also for the kids are **Golf 'n' Games Waterslide**, 4 Cypress St, Torquay (open Mon–Thurs and Sun, 10am–6pm; Fri, Sat and school holidays, 10am–9pm), Ph: (07) 4125 1166, and **M & K Model Railway and Miniature Village**, cnr Hastings St and Old Maryborough Rd (open Tue–Sat, 10am–3pm; night viewings Fri, Sat, Dec–Jan only, 6.30pm–8.30pm). Bookings essential. Ph: (07) 4124 1979

At **Village Pottery**, 65 Old Maryborough Rd, Pialba, visitors can watch pottery being made and buy pieces at factory prices. Open daily, 8.30am–5pm. Ph: (07) 4124 4987

Urangan Boat Harbour, Hervey Bay

Hervey Bay Natureworld

The **Historical Museum and Pioneer Village**, 13 Zephyr St, Scarness, is a complex of pioneer buildings graced by a large anchor and the giant 'Fighting Whiting' near the entrance. Open Fri, Sat, Sun and public holidays, 1pm–5pm. Ph: (07) 4128 1816

There are tourist info centres at Urangan, Torquay and Scarness, and at the Hervey Bay Shopping Village, cnr Ibis Blvd and Maryborough Rd.

Inskip Pt *Map 15 C6*

This is a sandy peninsula immediately to the south of Fraser Island. Its tip curves westward, like a bent finger indicating Tin Can Bay. Inskip Pt is a major access point for Fraser Island, with a vehicular barge connecting to Hook Pt. (See p.79 for details of the Inskip Peninsula Recreation Area.)

Maaroom *Map 15 B5*

The road to Maaroom passes through the coastal wallum of Poona NP and arrives at a little bayside village set among trees. Maaroom is 4km off the Maryborough–Cooloola Rd, on the northern side of the mouth of Maaroom Creek. There is a small picnic area with a shelter-shed and children's playground, and a caravan park.

Maryborough *Map 15 B4*

Maryborough, the 'Heritage City', is a substantial metropolis on the lower reaches of the Mary River. Once a major port and engineering centre, it bears the hallmarks of its earlier prosperity, with streets lined with gracious colonial homes and fine public buildings.

An info booth on the southern outskirts (near the Sun State Orchards Fruit Factory) and the main Maryborough Info Centre at 30 Ferry St (open Mon-Fri, 8.30am–5pm; Sat–Sun, 10am–4pm; Ph: (07) 4121 4111) supply handy brochures on the city. The *Walk and Drive Tours* brochure lists a host of sites of interest around the city. The *Wharf Street Precinct* brochure has comprehensive details about the early hotels, warehouses, commercial buildings, customs house and courthouse to be found at the hub of the old port. Anyone

with an interest in history or architecture will find this a richly rewarding area to explore. The **Bond Store Port of Maryborough Heritage Museum**, which is in the Wharf St Precinct, houses a range of historical displays (open Mon–Thurs, 9am–4pm; Fri, 9am–9pm; Sat–Sun, 10am–1pm; Ph: (07) 4123 1523). The Maryborough Art Society's **Old Warehouse Gallery** opposite is a venue for local and touring exhibitions. Open daily, 10am–2pm. Ph: (07) 4122 4408

Nearby, between Lennox and Sussex Sts, is **Queens Park**, a large, long-established park on the river, with grand old trees, a fernery, a Winged Victory memorial, memorial park gates, a Fairy Fountain and elaborate rotunda. On the last Sun of each month, bands play, Devonshire teas are taken and miniature steam engines haul wagonloads of passengers around the park.

At **Brennan and Geraghty's Store** at 64 Lennox St you can step into a time capsule of 100 years of merchandising. Open daily, 10am–3pm. Ph: (07) 4121 2250

The **Maryborough Heritage Markets** are held 8am–2pm every Thurs in Adelaide and Kent Sts. There is a carnival atmosphere, with entertainment, children's rides and food stalls. The Town Crier and Mary Heritage fire the 'Time Cannon' at 1pm.

City Hall, Maryborough

The 'Qld House'
Riverside streets close to Maryborough's city centre, such as **Lennox** and **Elizabeth Sts**, have many examples of elegant old iron-roofed homes with decorative timberwork and cast-iron lacework.

River of time
Explore the past on a **Maryborough Heritage River Cruise**. The tour leaves from the Mary River Marina, Wharf St. Ph: (07) 4215 3664

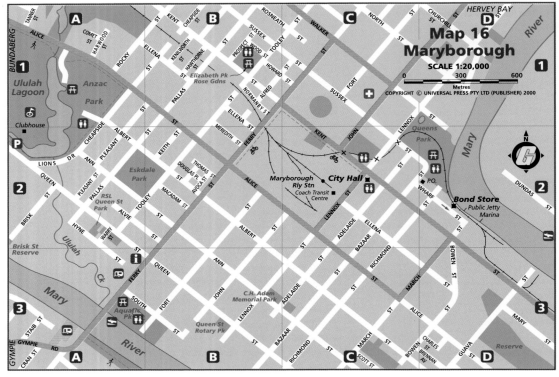

Map 16
Maryborough

SCALE 1:20,000

COPYRIGHT © UNIVERSAL PRESS PTY LTD (PUBLISHER) 2000

Upriver from the city centre, past the Granville Bridge and the Hyne and Son Sawmill, a rich molasses smell announces the presence of the **Maryborough Sugar Mill**, which crushes cane from the surrounding farms.

The **George Furber Picnic Grounds** at Baddow (reached via Aldridge St off Alice St) commemorate the 1st settlement on the original township site, about 4km from the present city centre, in 1847. On the riverbank there are small plaques to guide the visitor.

Poona *Map 15 B5*

Poona is 8km off the Maryborough–Cooloola Rd on the section of the Great Sandy Strait known as Wide Bay Harbour. Development is changing it from a small fishing village to a spreading residential and holiday centre. Like most of the other settlements on the Great Sandy Strait, Poona is set in a wooded area slightly raised above the surrounding wetlands. Poona Creek enters the bay through an inlet immediately to the south. Poona has a little sandy beach, caravan park, shop and boat ramp.

River Heads *Map 15 B4*

River Heads is at the mouth of the Mary River, looking out across the Great Sandy Strait to the dramatic sand cliffs of Fraser Island. There are boat ramps and a large carpark at the tip of the peninsula, where the vehicular ferry leaves for Fraser Island. The township has a general store where **vehicle** and **camping permits** for Fraser Island can be obtained. Ph: (07) 4125 7133

A glimpse of the past

The Ferry St Tourist Info Centre in Maryborough houses the **Croydon Foundry Office Museum**. Outside is a Disneyfied statue depicting pioneer farm, timber and industrial workers.

Great Sandy Strait

Tinnanbar *Map 15 C5*

This most southerly of the Great Sandy Strait fishing villages looks north over Shark Inlet. It is a tiny settlement, providing the basic facilities of general store, caravan park, toilets and boat ramp.

Tuan *Map 15 B5*

This small fishing settlement, on the same turnoff from the Maryborough–Cooloola Rd as Boonooroo, consists of 2 communities — Big Tuan and Little Tuan — each at the mouth of its respective creek. **Big Tuan** is a windblown settlement with a sandy beach, flocks of shore birds and a mangrove-lined creek with many boat moorings. There is a park on the foreshore, with a nearby boat ramp. At **Little Tuan** the sheltered, narrow creek is also an ideal mooring-place and the little old houses on the creek have their own jetties.

National parks

Great Sandy NP: Fraser Island section *Map 15*

Apart from a few areas of private land, Fraser Island is all national park, protecting dramatic landforms, rare forests and precious habitats. Although the island is largely sand, with only 3 outcrops of volcanic rock (Indian Head, Middle Rocks and Waddy Pt), its landscapes are strikingly rich and varied.

The shifting sands of the ocean beach are backed by coastal foredunes and, along much of the beach, coloured-sand cliffs of considerable height and dramatic form. Mixed forest grows in places that are protected from the full force of the salty onshore winds, giving way in more sheltered spots to tall eucalypt forests.

Where the dune systems rise towards the centre of the island are areas of highest rainfall and greatest protection. Here also the nutrient layers are within reach of the tree roots, so that rainforest species grow — giant kauris, satinays and hoop pines reaching above the great brush box and strangler figs, with an understorey of piccabeen palms, macrozamia and tree ferns. The central dunes are also the site of most of the famous freshwater lakes.

The older western dunes, where the nutrients have leached down beyond the reach of tree roots, are dominated by wallum shrubs and ground cover, with stunted scribbly gums, banksias and pink bloodwoods. The heathland blooms like a garden in spring, with a profusion of low-growing plants breaking into flower. Mangroves line the sheltered inlets on the western shore.

Each landscape provides a home to a different community of creatures, from the eugaries (pipis) and oystercatchers of the ocean shore, to the fairy wrens and acid frogs of the heaths and swamps.

Fraser Island turpentine

Satinay, or Fraser Island turpentine, is resistant to woodworm attack, and was in heavy demand early this century, when it was used for marine piles.

Sandblows, Fraser Island

Rare and regal

Look for the huge fronds of the rare king fern growing in the bed of **Wanggoolba Creek**. This fern uses the pressure of the creek's flow to carry water through its system and maintain its shape.

Other than Indian Head and Waddy Pt in the north, most areas of interest to tourists are in the central part of the island. Scenic drives (all 4WD sand tracks) lead past the major inland sites.

A track from Dilli Village goes past Lakes Boomanjin, Benaroon, Birrabeen and Jennings, Central Station, Pile Valley, Lakes McKenzie and Wabby, and the Hammerstone and Stonetool Sandblows, and returns to the ocean beach at a spot about 7km north of Eurong. There are also tracks connecting Eurong and Central Station that allow this drive to be truncated.

From Poyungan Valley a track runs NW past Lake Garawongera, NE to Yidney Lake and then returns to the beach at Happy Valley.

A longer track leaves from Happy Valley and runs NW through the Yidney Scrub, NE past the Boomerang Lakes, and SE past Lake Allom and the Knifeblade Sandblow, returning to the beach at The Pinnacles.

Central Station, an old forestry station in the central dunes of the southern third of the island, is set in magnificent rainforest. There is an info centre here, with a useful social- and natural-history display, and camping and picnic facilities. A short walk leads to **Wanggoolba Creek**, which threads through the rainforest gloom on a bed of pure-white sand.

Lake Boomanjin, where the film *Eliza Fraser* was made, is the largest perched lake in the world. Under a sunny sky, the clear, tea-coloured water looks dark blue. The lake has white-sand beaches and a well-equipped camping and picnic area under tall eucalypts. Further up the track is **Pile Valley**, where the soaring columns of the satinay trees, with their deeply fissured bark, have crowded out all competition. This splendid forest was saved from logging when it was declared a beauty spot in 1937.

The most visited of Fraser Island's inland sites is another perched lake, glorious **Lake McKenzie**, with its arctic colours of dazzling white and iceberg-blue. There are picnic facilities under the trees, and a nearby campsite. This is the place where visitors are most likely to encounter dingoes looking for a handout. National park signs and brochures advise visitors to keep a respectful distance from these animals and not to feed them.

To see **Lake Wabby** and the engulfing sandblow, visitors leave their cars at the parking area and walk a short distance to a dramatically sited lookout, high above its western shores.

Rainbow Gorge, in from the beach about halfway between Poyungan Rocks and Yidney Rocks, is a coloured-sand formation that can be reached on an easy 2km circuit walk (see map 17). Walkers

Feeding folly

Dingoes' ribs may show, but they are *naturally* thin. Titbits from tourists only disturb the natural balance and make the animals behave aggressively.

Lake McKenzie

Eli Creek

return through the alien sun-baked expanse of the Kirrar Sandblow.

The **Yidney Scrub**, NW of Happy Valley, is an area of tall, dense forest dominated by superb stands of satinay, brush box and kauri pine.

Eli Creek, 5km north of Happy Valley, is the largest stream on the island's east coast. Its pure, crystal-clear water and clean sandy bottom make it a favourite swimming spot. Like Lake McKenzie, it is in danger of being 'loved to death' by visitors. Its banks are protected by a boardwalk, and there are picnic facilities nearby.

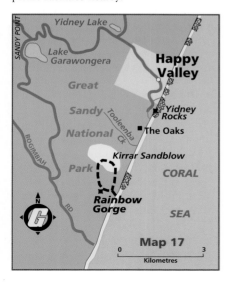

Map 17

About 10km north of Happy Valley is the rusting hulk of the *Maheno*, an old trans-Tasman liner that was stranded here by cyclonic seas in 1935 while being towed to Japan to be scrapped.

A couple of km north of the *Maheno* are the gothic forms of **the Pinnacles**, spires of red-gold 'coffee rock' carved from the cliffs by aeons of weathering.

The most easterly point of Fraser Island is **Indian Head**, a high promontory of dark volcanic rock. From the top, the view is north past Middle Rocks to Waddy Pt, and south along a beach that disappears in sea mist. This is an ideal place for spotting **whales** and **dolphins**.

The aptly named **Champagne Pools** are large rock pools carved by the sea in a shelf of rock near Middle Rocks. When the tide is right, the ocean transforms them into briny spas.

The estuary of **Wathumba Creek**, on the island's NW coast, is a haven for small boats. There is a large camping ground here, under cypress pines and Moreton Bay ash. The track to Wathumba heads SW from Orchid Beach through a variety of landscapes, from high woodland and heath to low-lying areas dominated by cabbage-tree palms.

Champagne Pools, Fraser Island

The island is criss-crossed with walking tracks of varying length. A brochure available from the 4 ranger stations on the island lists 43 short walks. Another brochure maps the 4-6-day **Forest Lakes Trail** and gives detailed info about each of its 6 sections (p.103). A touring and camping guide is also available. These and other brochures can be found at any of the Dept of Environment centres in the region, such as the info centre at Rainbow Beach, Ph: (07) 5486 3160. A kit of brochures is presented to the visitor on payment of the national park camping fee.

Poona NP *Map 15 B5*

This national park is a section of melaleuca wetland and wallum heath bordered on the west by the Maryborough–Cooloola Rd and on the east by privately owned land on the Great Sandy Strait. The park has no walking tracks, camping or day-use areas, but is bisected by the road to Maaroom.

Other attractions

Susan River Homestead Ranch Resort

Billed as providing the 'ultimate good time', this resort on the Maryborough–Hervey Bay road offers day visitors or resort guests horseriding, water-skiing and parasailing. Bookings essential. Ph: (07) 4121 6846

Cycling on the foreshore, Hervey Bay

Recreational activities

Action in the air

Skydive Hervey Bay has tandem parachute jumps with breathtaking views of Fraser Island and the Bay. Ph: (07) 4124 8248. For parasailing flights, try **Hervey High Flyer Parasailing**. Pick-ups from Torquay Beach Hire. Ph: 018 366 897

Cycling

Hervey Bay is pretty, safe and mostly flat – ideal for a little gentle bike-riding. A shady bike track runs through the reserve between the beach and the Esplanade. Visitors can hire bikes from some of the tourist info and booking offices (p.96).

Maryborough also has the right terrain for cycling. Inquire at the tourist info centre (p.97) about bike hire.

On the water

Both Hervey Bay and the Great Sandy Strait are favoured by boaties. (For those without their own water transport, see pp.93 and 104 for details of cruises, whale-watching trips and fishing charters.)

The sheltered waters of Hervey Bay lend themselves to sea kayaking, and **Splash Safaris** conducts half-day and full-day trips from Urangan to Big Woody Island. The trips include swimming, snorkelling, reef-walking and bushwalking, with all equipment provided. Ph: 0500 555 580

From Urangan, **MV *Krystal Klear*** conducts coral-viewing day-tours in a glass-bottomed boat, with a little snorkelling thrown in (gear provided). Coral-viewing by night is also on offer. Bookings essential. Ph: (07) 4124 0066

Sailboards, canoes, catamarans, and fishing boats and tackle are available at **Torquay Beach Hire** on the Esplanade. Ph: (07) 4125 5528. **Gataker Bay Marine and Boat Hire**, The Esplanade, Point Vernon, also helps people get onto the water. Ph: (07) 4128 1310

Bushwalking

With 165 000ha of wilderness, and landscapes ranging from sandblows to rainforest, Fraser Island is a bushwalkers' paradise.

The island has 43 short walks, ranked from 'easy' to 'challenging'. They set out from 11 sites: Central Station, the Southern Lakes Tourist Drive, Lake Boomanjin, Dilli Village, the Northern Forest Tourist Drive, Lake McKenzie, Dundubara, Kingfisher Bay, Central Lakes Tourist Drive, the eastern beach and Waddy Pt. A map and details are given for all these walks in *Short Walks: Walking Track Guide*, a brochure produced by the Dept of Environment and available from its offices, such as the one at Rainbow Beach, and from the Fraser Island ranger stations.

For the more adventurous, there is the 4-6-day **Forest Lakes Trail**. This is divided into 6 sections: Lake McKenzie-Central Station, Central Station-Lake Benaroon hikers' camp, Lake Benaroon hikers' camp-Lake Boomanjin, Lake Boomanjin-Dilli Village, Dilli Village-Lake Wabby, and Lake Wabby-Lake McKenzie. A brochure, available from offices of the Dept of Environment and the Fraser Island ranger stations, gives details about flora and fauna, the degree of difficulty and the amount of time to allow for each section.

Fishing

Hervey Bay, the Great Sandy Strait and the beaches of Fraser Island are among Australia's best fishing spots.

Fraser is journey's end for tailor as they make their winter spawning run from the south, and in a 'hot bite' the gutters and headlands are lined with anglers.

Hervey Bay is synonymous with whiting; good catches are taken in summer and winter by shore-based anglers from Urangan to Gatakers Bay, or from boats in the sheltered Bay waters. Those who are more ambitious try for pelagics such as mackerel, trevally and queenfish in the deep water at the end of the landmark Urangan Pier.

Off-limits
In Sept, the tailor-spawning area from 400m north of **Waddy Pt** to 400m south of **Indian Head** is closed to fishing as a conservation measure.

Catamarans at Torquay, Hervey Bay

Riding at Susan River Homestead

In the creeks and estuaries from River Heads south through Great Sandy Strait, bream, mangrove jack, cod and sometimes barramundi and threadfin salmon are caught.

Boats that go out to the Bay's reefs, ledges and deep holes take species such as parrot, sweetlip, coral trout, red emperor and snapper, as well as mackerel and trevally.

Many operators run reef-fishing tours in Hervey Bay and out to the continental shelf. Among them are:

- *Eagle Ray* **Smooth Water Reef Fishing**, Ph: (07) 4124 8140
- *Hombre*, Ph: (07) 4125 7800
- *Imagine* **Reef and Game Fishing Charters**, Ph: (07) 4124 7220
- MV *Day Tripper*, Ph: (07) 4125 7567
- MV *Princess II*, Ph: (07) 4124 0400
- *Seaspray* **Reef Fishing Adventures**, Ph: (07) 4125 3586
- *Snapper I*, Ph: (07) 4124 3788

MV *Fighting Whiting* conducts calm-water fishing trips. Ph: (07) 4124 9555

Fishing, Urangan Pier

Go-kart racing

The whole family is catered for at **Hervey Bay Go Kart Track**, Maryborough–Hervey Bay road, Nikenbah. Tandem karts are

Whale-watching tours

Among the tour-operators are:

★ *Bayrunner*, Ph: (07) 4125 3188

★ *Dawn* **Whale Watch**, Ph: 1800 800 862

★ *Hombre* **Whale Watch**, Ph: 1800 064 633

★ MV *Islander* **Whale Watch Cruises**, Ph: 1800 249 122

★ *Mikat*, Ph: 1800 644 393

★ *Princess II*, Ph: (07) 4124 0400

★ *Seaspray* **Whale Watch**, Ph: 1800 066 404

★ *Spirit of Hervey Bay*, Ph: 1800 642 544

★ *Tasman Venture II*, Ph: 1800 620 322

★ **Whalesong Cruises**, Ph: 1800 689 610

★ **Whale Watch Safari**, Ph: 1800 644 393

★ **Whale Watch with Mimi Macpherson**, Ph: (07) 4124 7247

available so that small children can ride with a parent on board. Open Sun–Thurs, 9.30am–5pm; Fri–Sat, 9.30am–9pm. Ph: (07) 4128 1180

Horseriding

Wide Bay Equestrian Park, Lot 5, Noble Rd (off the Maryborough–Hervey Bay road) is 80ha of bushland with a range of horseriding facilities. The park specialises in catering for nervous riders and beginners. Day visitors are welcome. (Bookings essential.) Open daily (weather permitting). Ph: (07) 4122 4618

    Susan River Homestead, on the Maryborough–Hervey Bay road, has 2½ hr rides following 100-year-old cattle trails (p.102). Ph: (07) 4121 6846

Scuba diving

Favoured diving spots in Hervey Bay include Roy Rufus Artificial Reef, Moon Ledge and Rooney's Hole. Try **Divers Mecca,** 403 The Esplanade (Ph: 1800 351 626) and **Wizzer Dive Services,** Buccaneer Ave, Urangan (Ph: (07) 4128 9033).

Swimming

The Fraser Island surf is not ideal for swimming as the beaches are unpatrolled and sharks frequently cruise the shallows. However, Eli Creek and some of the lakes, particularly Lake McKenzie, are idyllic spots to take a dip.

Whale-watching

Hervey Bay is the premier whale-watching site in Qld — and, some say, the world. Over 80 000 people come each year to observe the slow-motion frolicking of the great humpback whales as they rest here in Aug–Oct, before returning to Antarctica for the summer.

    Many businesses offer whale-watching tours. Tour operators are required to follow strict guidelines to ensure that the whales are not subjected to undue stress. Lucky visitors will be treated to pec-slapping, spy-hopping, tail-slapping and full, acrobatic breaches.

Listening in
Many whale-watch vessels in **Hervey Bay** have hydrophones, so that passengers can hear the song of the humpback.

Fun for the young

★ Cycling on the Hervey Bay foreshore (p.102)

★ Golf 'n' Games Waterslide, Torquay (p.96)

★ Hervey Bay Go Kart Track, Nikenbah (p.104)

★ Hervey Bay Natureworld (p.96)

★ M & K Model Railway and Miniature Village, Hervey Bay (p.96)

★ Mini-train rides in Queens Park, Maryborough (p.97)

★ Neptune's Reefworld, Urangan (p.96)

★ Swimming in Eli Creek and Lake McKenzie, Fraser Island (pp.100, 101)

★ Vic Hislop's Shark Show, Urangan (p.96)

★ Whale-watching (p.104)

Hervey Bay Natureworld

Suggested tours – Map 18

Great Sandy Strait villages tour

Approximate distance

160km from Brisbane CBD to Gympie; return trip tour Gympie-River Heads – 380km

About the tour

On the way to Hervey Bay, an alternative to travelling from Gympie to Maryborough on the Bruce Hwy is to turn off onto the Tin Can Bay road at Gympie. Various diversions from the Maryborough-Cooloola Rd then allow you to explore the secluded fishing villages of Great Sandy Strait. Picnic on a foreshore and wet a line if there's time. This route also allows a quick detour to Tin Can Bay or Rainbow Beach if desired. An overnight stop would allow more leisurely enjoyment of the many attractions of Hervey Bay and Maryborough.

Places of interest

❶ **Tinnanbar** (p.99)
❷ **Poona** (p.98)
❸ **Boonooroo** (p.95)
❹ **Tuan** (p.99)
❺ **Maaroom** (p.97)
❻ **River Heads** (p.98)

Side trip

Ⓐ **Tin Can Bay** (p.75)
Ⓑ **Rainbow Beach** (p.74)

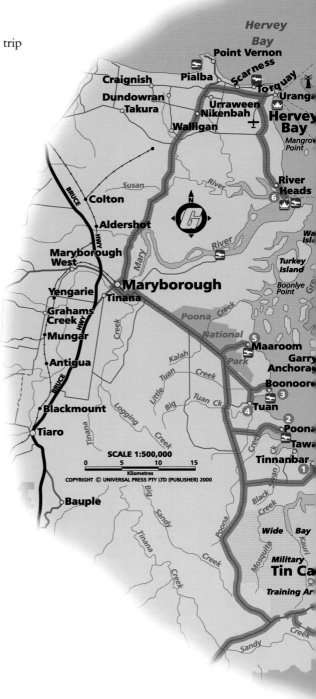

A 'Qld house', Maryborough

Fraser Island lakes 4WD tour

Approximate distance

80km round trip (including beach section)

About the tour

Allow about 4hrs for the inland section of this 4WD trek from Dilli Village to Central Station, on to Lake Wabby and back to the ocean beach. See the unique shapes and colours of the dune lakes, the crystal water of Wanggoolba Creek, the satinays of Pile Valley, and the eerie expanse of Stonetool Sandblow.

Don't miss the way the view unfolds on the walk to the Lake Wabby lookout: first a strip of ocean, then a vast desert of sand, and finally the lake itself, slowly succumbing to the advance of Hammerstone Sandblow.

Places of interest

❶ **Dilli Village** (p.94)
❷ **Lake Boomanjin** (p.100)
❸ **Lake Benaroon** (p.100)
❹ **Lake Birrabeen** (p.100)
❺ **Lake Jennings** (p.100)
❻ **Central Station** (p.100)
❼ **Pile Valley** (p.100)
❽ **Lake McKenzie** (p.100)
❾ **Lake Wabby** (p.100)
❿ **Eurong** (p.95)

Lake McKenzie, Fraser Island

SUNSHINE COAST™

South East Queensland
COUNTRY
WAKE UP TO THE BEAUTY OF IT.

Left: **Sunrise,**
Glass House Mts
Right: **Montville**
Rose Boutique

Gympie, Mary Valley and the Blackall Range

Heading north. The suburbs of greater Brisbane have fallen away behind; the Bruce Hwy rolls out ahead, cutting a swathe through slash-pine forests and coastal scrub. Suddenly the unlikely shapes of the Glasshouse Mts rear over the tree line. They mark the way like fanciful beacons, heralding a landscape where form is more extravagant and colour more bold.

There is a hint of the heady tropics in the air — hills are cross-hatched with rows of pineapples, avocados hang heavily under canopies of glossy green and palms appear in clumps of roadside bush.

Near Gympie the traveller meets the long Mary River, carving a course between high banks and skirting the town in its crowd of hills. Mining headframes, old and new, testify to the eternal allure of gold. Upstream the pastures turn to timbered slopes, the valley narrowing as the ranges close in.

From the wild Conondale Ra, where bolts of water descend into mountain pools and the chimes of bellbirds startle the ear, north to the Mary River floodplain, and south again to the Blackall Ra, land of galleries, eateries and sparkling vistas, nature is lavish and the tourist enticements are richly diverse.

Tourist information

Cooloola Region Visitors Information Centre
Dept of Environment and Heritage Building,
Lake Alford, Bruce Hwy, Gympie 4570
Ph: (07) 5482 5444
www.cooloola.org.au

Dept of Natural Resources Office
(info on state forests)
Sunday Creek Rd, Kenilworth 4574
Ph: (07) 5446 0925

Maleny Tourist Information Centre
Community Hall, Maple St,
Maleny 4552
Ph: (07) 5499 9033

Montville Tourist Information Centre
202 Main St, Montville 4560
Ph: (07) 5478 5544

Naturally Queensland Information Centre (EPA)
(info on national parks)
Ground Floor, 160 Ann St,
Brisbane 4000 Ph: (07) 3227 8185
www.env.qld.gov.au

Must see, must do

★ **Glass House Mts** (p.122)
★ **Lake Borumba Fish Display** (p.126)
★ **WoodWorks Forestry and Timber Museum** (p.115)
★ **Mary Cairncross Park** (p.118)
★ **Wild Horse Mt Lookout** (p.123)

Radio stations

ABC Radio Wide Bay: AM 156.6

Gympie 4GY: AM 558

ABC Coast FM: FM 95.3

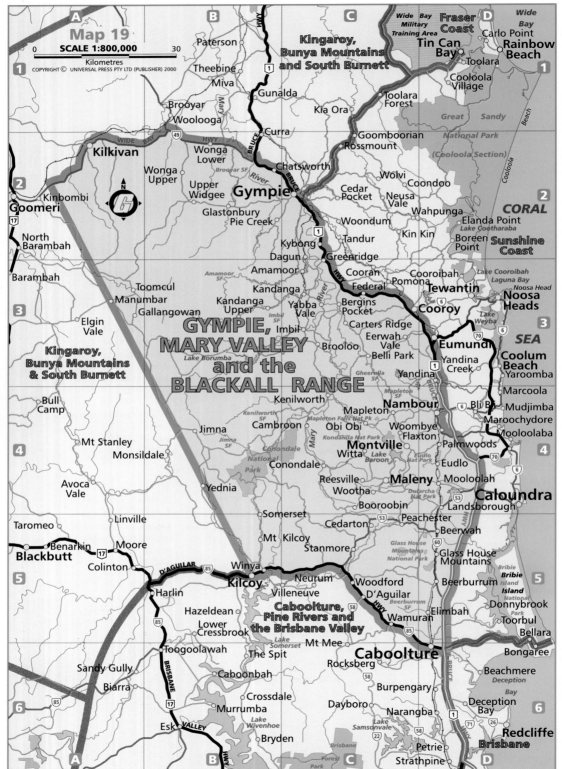

Map 19

SCALE 1:800,000

0   30

Kilometres

COPYRIGHT © UNIVERSAL PRESS PTY LTD (PUBLISHER) 2000

Kingaroy,
Bunya Mountains
and South Burnett

Paterson

Theebine

Miva

Gunalda

Brooyar

Woolooga

Curra

Kia Ora

Kilkivan

Wonga Lower

Wonga Upper

Upper Widgee

Chatsworth

Gympie

Goomboorian

Rossmount

Wolvi

Coondoo

Cedar Pocket

Neusa Vale

Wahpunga

Glastonbury

Pie Creek

Woondum

Kin Kin

Elanda Point

Lake Cootharaba

Boreen Point

CORAL

Kinbombi

Goomeri

North Barambah

Barambah

Kybong

Dagun

Tandur

Greenridge

Amamoor

Amamoor

Cooran

Federal

Pomona

Cooroibah

Lake Cooroibah Laguna Bay

Noosa Head

Tewantin

Noosa Heads

Sunshine Coast

Toomcul

Manumbar

Gallangowan

Kandanga

Kandanga Upper

Yabba Vale

Imbil

Bergins Pocket

Carters Ridge

Eerwah Vale

Brooloo

Belli Park

Cooroy

Eumundi

Coolum Beach

Yaroomba

Elgin Vale

GYMPIE, MARY VALLEY and the BLACKALL RANGE

Lake Borumba

Yandina Creek

Yandina

SEA

Kingaroy, Bunya Mountains & South Burnett

Gheerulla

Marcoola

Bull Camp

Kenilworth

Mapleton

Nambour

Bli Bli

Mudjimba

Maroochydore

Mooloolaba

Jimna

Cambroon

Obi Obi

Woombye

Flaxton

Palmwoods

Mt Stanley

Monsildale

Montville

Witta

Lake Baroon

Eudlo

Conondale

Conondale

Reesville

Wootha

Maleny

Mooloolah

Caloundra

Avoca Vale

Yednia

Somerset

Booroobin

Landsborough

Peachester

Beerwah

Taromeo

Linville

Mt Kilcoy

Stanmore

Cedarton

Glass House Mountains National Park

Glass House Mountains

Benarkin

Moore

Blackbutt

Colinton

Winya

Kilcoy

Neurum

Woodford

D'Aguilar

Beerburrum

Bribie Island

Harlin

Villeneuve

Beerburrum SF

Donnybrook

Hazeldean

Lower Cressbrook

Caboolture, Pine Rivers and the Brisbane Valley

Wamuran

Elimbah

Toorbul

Bellara

Toogoolawah

The Spit

Lake Somerset

Mt Mee

Rocksberg

Caboolture

Bongaree

Sandy Gully

Caboonbah

Burpengary

Beachmere

Deception Bay

Biarra

Crossdale

Murrumba

Dayboro

Narangba

Deception Bay

Esk

Bryden

Lake Wivenhoe

Lake Samsonvale

Petrie

Redcliffe

Brisbane

Strathpine

Natural features

The Mary River rises where the Conondale Ra swerves east to meet the Blackall Ra, and flows north, rambling through the round hills and river flats of Gympie. NW of the Mary's source the Conondales merge with the Jimna Ra, a heavily forested band of rugged country. These are ancient formations, with outcrops of greenstone and metamorphic rock. The virgin forests are still harvested here, and timber towns are scattered through the mountains.

To the east is the green razorback of the Blackall Ra, a chain of high, fertile hills formed in comparatively recent times by the basalt rock of lava flows. The deep, red soil and the high rainfall produce a luxuriant growth of forest, pasture and fruit-bearing trees.

Spurs run east from the Jimna Ra, nudging the Mary River towards the coast. The valleys between them carry mountain torrents and minor creeks down to join the river. Two of these — Yabba and Kingaham Creeks — have been dammed at their confluence to form Lake Borumba, a reservoir for the district. Further south, at the head of Obi Obi Creek, is Lake Baroon, which is piped through the Montville razorback to supply Maroochy Shire and Caloundra city.

Back towards Brisbane, the knobs of the Glass House Mts stud the plain. The most prominent are the plugs of ancient volcanoes.

History

Before European settlement, the Blackall Ra and the upper Mary Valley were part of the traditional lands of the Kabi Kabi Aborigines, who hosted a great bunya-nut festival on the banks of Obi Obi Creek.

Nearly 30 years after Cook's fateful voyage, Matthew Flinders explored Moreton Bay and trekked across country to the Glass House Mts.

By the 1850s, pastoral holdings were being taken up on the Mary River. Then, in 1867, a penurious James Nash found gold in a dry creek bed at Gympie, and the great Gympie gold rush began. The find brought wealth to the area and a huge surge in population — and saved the newly independent colony of Qld from bankruptcy. The town prospered, and became the centre of a rich agricultural district, producing beef, dairy products, tropical fruit and vegetables.

The earliest incursions into the rugged high country of the Blackall Ra were by timbergetters. By the early 1870s, a blacksmith's shop and timber mill had been established at Maleny. After them came the dairy farmers and orchardists, who cleared the remaining forest on all but the most inaccessible land.

Today, the Blackall Ra is a cool mountain retreat for tourists seeking respite from the bright lights of the Sunshine Coast. To the west, in the Conondale and Jimna Ranges, the timber companies still work the forests.

Blackall Ra

Getting there

By road

Take the Bruce Hwy north from Brisbane through the Sunshine Coast hinterland. The highway now bypasses all the towns until it reaches Gympie, 167km from Brisbane. The other towns discussed in this chapter are to the west of the highway, and can be approached by deviating at any of several points along the way.

For close-up views of the Glass House Mts, take the Beerburrum turnoff from the Bruce Hwy, or follow Beerburrum Rd north from Caboolture to Beerburrum and then Glass House Mts Rd via Glass House Mts township and Beerwah to Landsborough. The road then swings NE to rejoin the Bruce Hwy.

To reach the towns of the Blackall Ra, Kondalilla NP, Lake Baroon, Kenilworth and the Conondale Ra, take Glass House Mts Rd to Landsborough, and then the western turnoff up the range towards Maleny. One road follows the spine of the Blackall Ra, passing through or near the townships to Mapleton in the north. The Maleny-Kenilworth road and the Obi Obi Rd (between Kenilworth and Mapleton) complete the circuit. Alternatively, travellers can reach Montville and the northerly towns of the Blackall Ra more directly by continuing along the Bruce Hwy and taking the road west through Palmwoods or from Nambour.

The Amamoor State Forests and Lake Borumba can be most easily reached by taking the turnoffs west from the Bruce Hwy between Cooroy and Gympie; alternatively, take the road north from Kenilworth.

Kilkivan is on the Wide Bay Hwy, which branches west off the Bruce Hwy 12km north of Gympie.

For easiest access to Jimna State Forest, take the D'Aguilar Hwy from Caboolture to Kilcoy and then drive north on the Kilcoy-Murgon road.

McCafferty's Express Coaches leave the Roma St Transit Centre in Brisbane 6 times a day every day for Gympie. Stops on some services include Nambour and Cooroy. Ph: 131 499

Greyhound Pioneer coaches run 5 times a day every day from the Transit Centre to Gympie, some services stopping at Nambour and Cooroy. Ph: 132 030

Glass House Mts Country Coaches run between Landsborough and Maleny 5-6 times a day, Mon-Fri. Ph: (07) 5496 9249

By rail

Electric trains run through the coastal hinterland towns as far as Gympie. There is 1 train a day to Gympie and trains every hour or half hour as far as Nambour. Ph: 131 230. The Tilt Train also stops at Gympie on its way north. To reach the Blackall Ra, take the train to Landsborough and then the connecting bus to Maleny (see above).

Getting around

Fair Dinkum 4WD Tours operates a Conondale Ra day tour as far as Jimna State Forest, with pick-ups at Bribie Island, Caboolture and Brisbane CBD. Ph: (07) 3408 0628

The coaches of **Storeyline Tours** take visitors on various day tours — for example, the Mountain Village Tour (shopping at Montville and taking in the views of the Blackall Ra), the Hinterland and Rainforest Tour (Mapleton Falls, Mary Cairncross Park and other Blackall Ra highlights), and the Gympie Gold Tour (Gympie, Kenilworth township and Kenilworth Bluff Winery). There are pick-ups at Coolum, Peregian and Noosa. Ph: (07) 5474 1500

Noosa Hinterland Tours offers day tours from Noosa in air-conditioned minibuses. There are 2 Blackall Ra tours — one a shopping and lunch tour to Montville, and the other visiting Mapleton Falls NP, Flaxton Barn, Montville and Mary Cairncross Park, before returning to Noosa via Buderim and Bli Bli. Ph: (07) 5474 3366

Around the Back Roads offers 3 different forest drives in a 4WD bus, visiting various scenic places, including the Blackall, Conondale

Relaxing in the Blackall Ra

The Valley Rattler

and Jimna Ranges, Kenilworth and the Cooloolabin Dam, and stopping for bushwalks and picnic lunches. Pick-ups Caloundra–Maroochydore. Ph: (07) 5494 5219

A free **shuttle bus** is a comfortable alternative to the steep walk up to Wild Horse Mt Lookout, east of the Glass House Mts. A bus leaves on the hour from 2 Mobil service stations on the Bruce Hwy – Moby Vic's (North) and Moby Vic's (South) – running daily, 10am–2pm (10am–3pm during Qld school and public holidays). Ph: (07) 5496 9666 for Moby Vic's (North) or (07) 5496 9777 for Moby Vic's (South).

The **Valley Rattler** steam train runs every Sun along the historic Mary Valley line from Gympie to Imbil, via Dagun, Amamoor and Kandanga, in combination with the **Rattler Railmotor**. Ph: Mary Valley Heritage Railway Museum Association, (07) 5482 2750.

When possible, a steam train runs from **Brisbane to Landsborough** on William Landsborough Day (see below). **Southern Cross Motorcycle Tours** takes passengers on the back of a Harley Davidson for trips to the Blackall Ra. Passengers choose their own schedule and destination. Ph: (07) 5445 0022

Festivals and events

Kilkivan Great Horse Ride
Every Easter school holidays, hundreds of riders follow various routes through the countryside and converge on Kilkivan's main street on the day of the Great Horse Ride. The event concludes with a concert and BBQ at night. Ph: (07) 5484 1133

William Landsborough Day
The Landsborough townsfolk celebrate their heritage on the 4th Sat of Jun. If it can be arranged, a steam train runs from Brisbane to Landsborough for the festival. Ph: (07) 5494 1755

Gympie National Country Music Muster
Country music artists and bush poets come from far and wide to perform at this event, and people flock to hear them. They set up camp on the last weekend in Aug at Amamoor Creek State Forest Park. Ph: (07) 5482 6788

Mapleton Yarn Fest
This Oct event, held at the Mapleton Lilyponds and the tavern, began unusually – as a party celebrating the provision of public toilets in the town. Performers of the spoken word now journey from all over Australia to attend. Ph: (07) 5478 6263

Kilkivan Great Horse Ride

Gympie Gold Rush Festival

This week-long festival in Oct celebrates James Nash's discovery of gold in 1867. It includes rock-drilling demonstrations, carnivals and a parade down Mary St. Ph: (07) 5482 5444

Festival of Colour

This hugely popular garden and art festival is held at various locations across the **Maleny** district in Nov. Numerous local gardens are open to the public, and potters, painters and musicians take part. Contact Maleny Tourist Info Centre for details (p.109).

Main towns

For ease of reference, towns have been listed alphabetically in 2 sections: the Mary Valley and the surrounds.

The Mary Valley

Gympie *Map 19 C2*

Gympie, the largest town in the upper Mary Valley, straggles over the hummocks and hills that border the river flats. Its main street runs along the old creek bed where the Gympie gold rush began. Today it is the centre of a rich agricultural region producing beef, pork, dairy products and a wide variety of tropical fruits and nuts.

The Cooloola Visitors Info Centre, on the Bruce Hwy next to Lake Alford, has a comprehensive tourist info section, along with an impressive natural-history display. The centre stocks a series of detailed guides to tours through the surrounding district, collectively called 'Travellin' Round'. Pick up the leaflets on the Mary Valley, Gympie and Kilkivan Shire tours. Open daily, 8.30am–3.30pm. Ph: (07) 5482 5444

Though almost all gold mining had ceased in Gympie by the 1920s, reminders of the town's mining heritage are everywhere. One is the **Gympie and District Historical and Mining Museum**, 215 Brisbane Rd, on the eastern side of Lake Alford. Open daily, 9am–4.30pm. Ph: (07) 5482 3995

A large **statue** at Lake Alford celebrates the Gympie gold miners as saviours of the state. Outside the Town Hall, in Mary St, is another salute to Gympie's golden heritage – the granite **memorial** to James Nash.

A fossicking area has been set aside by the Dept of Minerals and Energy at

Stinging title

First called 'Nashville' after its founder, **Gympie** received its present name in 1868 in honour of the stinging tree, known to the local Aborigines as *gimpi gimpi*.

Gold diggers' memorial, Lake Alford, Gympie

Mining Museum, Gympie

reopened in 1988. Another old mine, the Scottish Gympie No. 1 Shaft, in Brisbane Rd, was reopened in 1998. In its grounds is the restored **Retort House**, the only surviving mine building from the old days.

On the left of the Bruce Hwy near the city centre is **Gympie Golden Gem**. Its mineral and gem display includes samples of 'gympieite', the unique local rock. Open daily, 9am–4.30pm. Ph: (07) 5482 7133

Gympie's timber heritage is remembered in the **WoodWorks Forestry and Timber Museum**, on the northern outskirts (cnr Bruce Hwy and Fraser Rd). The evocative and well-documented displays are made all the more lively by working demonstrations and an invitation to visitors to have a go with a crosscut saw. The old steam-driven sawmill chugs into life on certain days during Qld school holidays (phone for dates). The souvenir shop sells a variety of timber products, from rustic coffee tables to curiosities such as boxes of timber samples. Open Mon–Fri, 9am–4pm; Sun, 1pm–4pm. (Demonstrations of pit-sawing and crosscut-sawing are held on Wed at 10am and 1pm, and on Sun at 2pm.) Ph: (07) 5483 7691

Deep Creek, on the southern side of the town. **Fossicking permits** are issued by the Cooloola Visitors Info Centre, and panning equipment can be hired there.

Visitors to Lake Alford are standing above modern gold-miners working at depths of up to 900m in the old West of Scotland Shaft in Hall Rd, which was

Historic home
In the Historical and Mining Museum is **Andrew Fisher House**, home of the Gympie engine-driver who, in 1908, became Australia's first Labor prime minister.

Fossicking, Deep Creek

Town Hall, Gympie

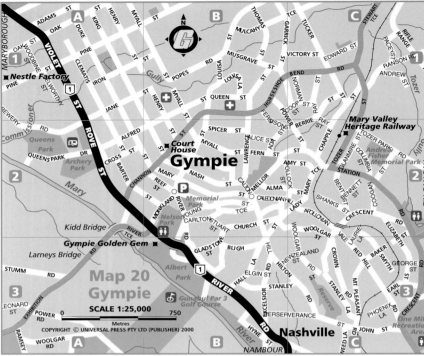

Evidence of Gympie's history is not confined to museums. Many of the impressive buildings of its early days remain. The **Lands Office** (1873) in Channon St was the first substantial government building on the goldfields. The **Gympie Courthouse**, cnr Channon and King Sts, is a turn-of-the-century brick building in Georgian style, with a landmark tower. For details of the town's historic buildings, consult the *Heritage Walk* brochure available from the Cooloola Visitors Info Centre.

Among Gympie's many parks and gardens are **Lake Alford** (at the southern entry to the city, on the Bruce Hwy), **Nelson's Reserve** (near the city centre, with picnic facilities, playground, skatebowl and nearby swimming pool) and **Memorial Park** (a shady retreat with a rotunda and another James Nash memorial, in the heart of the city).

Imbil *Map 19 C3*

Imbil, in the upper Mary Valley, has an air of quiet rural grace. It is the terminus of the **Valley Rattler** steam train (p.113), and the **Imbil Railway Market** is held every Sun, 9am–2pm, in the Village Centre.

The town **lookout**, 240m above sea level, is reached by turning into Elizabeth St and driving up a steep slope (not suitable for caravans or trailers). The lookout has BBQ facilities and a tablet identifying various features in the landscape.

Island Reach Camping Resort, on the eastern side of the town, offers canoeing on Yabba Creek, swimming and wagon rides. The resort can also be used as a base by riders of both mountain bikes and horses. Ph: (07) 5484 5247

Kenilworth *Map 19 C4*

Kenilworth, in the upper Mary Valley just west of the Blackall Ra, is known as a base for bushwalkers exploring Kenilworth State Forest (p.124) and Conondale NP (p.122). In the main street (Elizabeth St), cafe umbrellas mushroom among the shade trees. The library has a tourist-info section.

Opposite the Kenilworth library is the **Town Park**, with a well-equipped adventure playground. Along with the usual array of swings and slippery slides are pedal-powered rides and a flying fox. A safe play area has been fenced off for toddlers.

Camping, Little Yabba Creek, Kenilworth State Forest

The **Kenilworth Country Foods Cheese Factory** (cnr Elizabeth and Charles Sts) offers guided tours and tastings of its hand-crafted cheeses and yoghurts. Open Mon–Fri, 9am–4pm; Sat and Sun, 11am–3pm. Ph: (07) 5446 0144

At the historic **Kenilworth Homestead**, just north of the town, holiday-makers go swimming, fishing and canoeing on the Mary River. For the kids, there are pony rides, getting to know the farm animals, and water slides and grass slides. Day visits by appt. Ph: (07) 5446 0488

About 10mins' drive north of the town, look for the signpost to **Kenilworth Bluff Wines**, in Bluff Rd. Recent vintages are 100% local in origin. Cellar-door sales Fri–Sun, 10am–4pm; other times by appt. Ph: (07) 5472 3723

Kilkivan *Map 19 A2*

Kilkivan is one of the few towns on the **Bicentennial National Trail**, which runs along old coach and stock routes, packhorse tracks and forest trails from Cooktown, in North Qld, to Healesville, in Vic. The trail was designed for horseriders and walkers, but it can also be used by riders of mountain bikes. Ph: (07) 3878 9747

The **Kilkivan and District Historical Society Museum**, at Rise and Shine Cottage in the main street, is a folk museum with a collection that traces the mining and pastoral background of the shire. Open Tue and Sat, 12–3pm; other times by appt. Ph: (07) 5484 1140, (07) 5484 1191 or (07) 5484 7131

On the unsealed Rossmore Rd (turnoff 1.5km east of Kilkivan) is the original site of Kilkivan township (where gold was discovered in 1868), **Kilkivan Cemetery** and, 5km from the turnoff, the **Prophet Mine**, where visitors can pan for gold (p.126). A little further along the road is **Rossmore Caravan Park** (p.127). Rossmore Rd follows the creek for 15km to an old copper smelter at the foot of Mt Clara. Only high-clearance vehicles should attempt the last 1.5km.

The surrounds
Flaxton *Map 19 C4*

Flaxton, high on the northern Blackall Ra, is a sedate residential settlement. Many of the old timber houses, with the wide verandahs and single-skin tongue-and-groove construction typical of their period, have been preserved or faithfully restored.

Flaxton Barn and Model Railway, at 445 Flaxton Dr, offers light meals, craftworks, old wares, books and videos about trains, and a working display of model trains operating in a miniature German landscape, showing features of the culture. Open daily, 10am–5pm. Ph: (07) 5445 7321

Perched on the escarpment on Flaxton Dr is **Flaxton Gardens Cellar and Vineyard, Restaurant and Pottery**, a complex of wine cellar (the 2nd cellar door for the Mt Tamborine Winery), working pottery, craft shop and restaurant/tea gardens based around a colonial homestead. There is a breath-taking view. Open daily, 9am–5pm; 10am–4pm for cellar-door sales. Ph: (07) 5478 6555 (wine cellar), (07) 5445 7461 (pottery), (07) 5445 7450 (craft shop), or (07) 5445 7400 (restaurant).

The **Miniature English Village**, on Flaxton Dr, has tiny reconstructions of old English buildings, a 'Pickwick Theatre', chandler's, apothecary, medieval memorial brasses, a set of old English stocks, and historic and heraldic gifts and souvenirs. Open daily, 9.30am–5pm. Ph: (07) 5445 7225

In favourable weather, hang gliders and para-gliders swoop and soar in the thermals that ascend the escarpment from the coastal hills below.

Mt Clara chimney
The **Mt Clara** smelter operated in the 1870s, and this surprisingly elegant stone-and-brick chimney, believed to have been built by Cornish miners, has been fully restored.

Flaxton Gardens

Landsborough *Map 19 D4*

This old Cobb & Co staging post is 9km west of the Bruce Hwy. Among the tall eucalypts on the southern side of the town a sawmill still scents the air with woodsmoke.

Landsborough's superb **Historical Museum** is at 4 Maleny St, 300m west of the railway line. On William Landsborough Day (4th Sat of Jun each year) and at other special events, many of the old machines on display are shown in operation. Open daily, 10am–4pm. Ph: (07) 5494 1755

De Maine Pottery and Gallery, on Maleny Rd, has a collection of work by a master potter and clay artist. Open Wed–Mon, 9am–4.30pm. Ph: (07) 5494 1458

Maleny *Map 19 C4*

The old timber and dairying township of Maleny has preserved its individuality by adding an 'alternative' atmosphere to its rural charm. Maple St, the town's main street, is lined with interesting shops selling books, handcrafts and organic produce. There are also eateries with distinctive menus. A tourist info centre operates from a booth in the Community Hall. Open daily, 10am–3pm. Ph: (07) 5499 9033

The **Sunday Handcraft Markets**, held in the RSL Hall, opposite the Maleny Hotel in Bunya St, offer high-quality handcrafts, fresh organic produce, home-cooked food, and native plants and herbs. Open Sun, 9am–2pm. Ph: (07) 5493 2958

Up Front Licensed Club Cooperative, 31 Maple St, has garden seating at the rear. Open Mon and Fri, 8.30am–10pm; Tue–Thurs and Sat–Sun, 8.30am–5.30pm. Ph: (07) 5494 2592. Next door is the **Cooperative Organic Shop**. Open Mon–Fri, 9am–5.30pm; Sat, 9am–11am; Sun, 10.30am–3pm. Ph: (07) 5494 2088

Peace of Green Gallery, across the road at 38 Maple St, is a collective art and craft gallery showing unique local works. Open daily, 9am–5pm. Ph: (07) 5499 9311

The **Celtic Tea Room of Maleny**, south of the town on Mountain View Rd, offers morning and afternoon teas and light lunches, with Celtic music on Sun afternoon. Open Wed–Sun, 10am–4pm. Ph: (07) 5499 9426

Further west along Mountain View Rd is **Mary Cairncross Park**, which has one of the most spectacular views in SE Qld — a splendid prospect over the Glass House Mts and Moreton Bay, with a viewing telescope provided. There are walks

Mary Cairncross Park

It was the far-sighted generosity of Mary Thynne Cairncross, an early conservationist, that has preserved the natural beauty of this part of the Blackall Ra.

Maleny's rich dairy pastures

through the rainforest at the rear of the park, and a kiosk supplying morning and afternoon teas, light meals, picnic baskets, umbrella hire, souvenirs, film and other useful items. Open 7am–7pm in summer; 7am–6pm in winter. Ph: (07) 5494 2287. The associated **Thynne Natural History Education Centre** is open daily (weather permitting), Mon–Sat, from 11am; Sun, from 10 am; closing times vary. Ph: (07) 5499 9707

For more vistas, continue along Mountain View Rd to **Macarthy's Lookout**, and (via Reesville Rd) **Howell's Knob Lookout**.

At 58 Montville Rd is **Maleny Touch Wood**, where visitors can watch a wood-turner at work and browse in the showroom. Open daily, 9am–5pm. Ph: (07) 5499 9166

Deep in the valley to the west is **Lake Baroon** (p.125).

Mapleton *Map 19 C4*

At the northern end of the Blackall Ra is Mapleton, a mountain village with sweeping views and a forest backdrop. The village is known for the **Mapleton Lilyponds**, created by a local resident and loved by waterbirds and the public to whom they were bequeathed. They can be found in Delicia Rd, just behind the main shopping centre. The picnic grounds that surround the ponds have electric BBQs and a fenced-in children's playground.

About 5km along the Obi Obi Rd is **Mapleton Falls NP** (p.125) and about 2km north of the town is **Mapleton State Forest** (p.125).

Montville *Map 19 C4*

Montville is a ridgetop village that once serviced the citrus-growers who settled here in the late 19th century, after the timbergetters had moved on. It is intimate in scale, with a small village green and garden paths replacing the usual grid of streets and pavements.

The centre of the village is a mazy collection of old and new establishments bordering Main St — coffee shops, potteries, art and craft galleries, inns and eateries, many with rustic adornments of studied quaintness. To fully appreciate

Camphor Cottage, Montville

Montville's village charm, be sure to walk both sides of Main St, as shown in map 21.

A signposted **Heritage Trail** leads through the village, explaining the historical significance of various sites. As well, a **Senses Trail** for the visually impaired leads from the Village Hall out around the **Razorback Lookout**. Braille notices along the trail explain various features.

Cadman Cottage – House of Chimes, in Main St, sells award-winning musical chimes, books and gifts. Open daily, 8.30am–5pm. Ph: (07) 5442 9300

Coffee, lunch, jams and gifts are on offer at **Camphor Cottage**, 190 Main St. Open daily, 9am–5pm. Ph: (07) 5442 9300

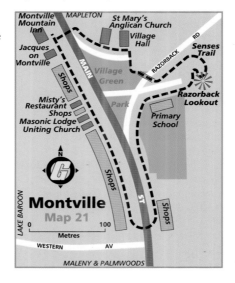

Montville
Map 21
0   100
Metres

Life on the edge
Because of its location — on a narrow ridge about 450m above the Obi Obi Valley on one side and the coastal plain on the other — **Montville** was known as Razorback until 1897.

Black Forest Hill Cuckoo Clock Centre

Next door is the **Herb Garden**, a vine-covered Tudor-style cottage with a pathway winding through an apron of aromatic herb beds. Open daily, 9.30am–5pm. Ph: (07) 5442 9190

The **Rainbird Gallery**, opposite the Village Green, has paintings, craftworks and sculpture. Open daily, 10am–5pm. Ph: (07) 5442 9211

Gumnuts and Lace deals in wonders and enchantments. Visitors will find themselves in a den of shimmering charms and twinkling mobiles. Open daily, 8.45am–5.15pm. Ph: (07) 5442 9324

For Celtic paraphernalia – music, books, hats, ties, jewellery and sweets – there is the **Irish and Scottish Shop** in Connemara Cottage. Open daily, 9.30am–4.30pm. Ph: (07) 5442 9169

Not Just Dolls stocks an assortment of dolls, teddies and other toys for collectors and children. Open daily, 9am–5pm. Ph: (07) 5442 9577

The **Black Forest Hill Cuckoo Clock Centre**, 194 Main St, sells grandfather, cuckoo and wall clocks. Open Mon–Sat, 9.30am–5pm; Sun, 12.30pm–5pm. Ph: (07) 5442 9409

Misty's Mountain Restaurant is a Montville landmark. The building that has housed it since 1975 was built in 1918 as a fancy goods store and lolly shop, and a meeting place for locals. The restaurant is open daily for lunch, morning and afternoon tea and dinner (BYO). Ph: (07) 5442 9264

North of Montville, turn west off the Montville–Mapleton road into Kondalilla Falls Rd for **Kondalilla NP** (p.125).

South of Montville is **William and Mary Gerrard Lookout**, on the edge of the razorback, with commanding views of the coast south from Noosa. There is no signpost on the roadway, so keep an eye out for the shelter-shed. **Balmoral Lookout**, a little further south along the road, has shady trees, picnic facilities and a view SE to the sea.

National parks and state forests

This is a region of blue ridges, eucalypt forests, palm-filled gullies, basalt outcrops and gushing streams. Its state forests and national parks are home to hundreds of species of birds, reptiles, mammals and aquatic life.

Most state forests and national parks have walking tracks, swimming holes, lookouts, picnic areas and, with a few exceptions, camping facilities.

Some are suitable for horseriding (p.127), and Gheerulla State Forest has official trailbike tracks (p.122).

Amamoor State Forests (incorporating Imbil State Forest)
Map 19 B3

South of Gympie is a series of state forests in the rugged country between the Mary River and the Jimna Ra, the most accessible being the Amamoor and Imbil state forests. High-quality hoop and bunya pine from the forest plantations is processed at 2 large sawmills near Imbil.

The forests, which include rainforest and open eucalypt forest as well as hoop-pine plantations, have walking tracks, camping and picnic areas, swimming holes, scenic lookouts, recreational drives and a host of forest wildlife, from bellbirds to platypuses.

The scenic **Imbil Forest Drive** from Imbil to Lake Borumba (p.126) leads 14km through varied forest. Along the way there are 9 info stops, a short walk and a lookout.

Platypus

Rainforest, Blackall Ra

The **Amama Day Use Area**, on Amamoor Creek, has picnic facilities, an open area suitable for ball games, walking tracks, and resident platypuses. The walks vary in length from 300m to 2.2km return. The 300m **Platypus Walk**, which leads to a platypus viewing platform, is suitable for wheelchairs along its entire length.

Further along Amamoor Creek Rd, past the Amamoor Info Shelter, camping is available at **Cedar Grove** and **Amamoor Creek**. Cedar Grove has a rainforest walk (1km return), a hiking trail (4.6km return) and a deep swimming hole. Many trees on the rainforest walk, such as the imposing specimens of red cedar, are labelled for easy identification and can be seen close-up. A further 4km along the road, the **Amamoor Creek Camping Area** is the gathering point for the annual Gympie National Country Music Muster, held in Aug. Dogs are allowed here if on a leash. Bookings not necessary. For more info, contact the Dept of Natural Resources Office, Sunday Creek Rd, Kenilworth. Ph: (07) 5446 0925

Bellbird habitat
South of Imbil on the Imbil–Kenilworth road is the **Burtenshaw Feature Protection Area**, where a colony of bellbirds fill the forest with their chimes.

Beerburrum State Forests

See Glass House Mts NP and Beerburrum State Forests.

Brooyar State Forest *Map 19 B2*

The **Brooyar Forest Drive**, a single-lane gravel road with self-guiding arrows and info signs, leads through hardwood forests, past 2 lookouts with views of the Widgee Valley. These are favoured abseiling spots (p.126). At **Glastonbury Creek Forest Recreation Area**, there are tent sites, camping facilities and a picnic area, with a waterhole nearby.

Conondale NP *Map 19 B4*

This national park, gazetted in 1995, protects pristine rainforest and old-growth eucalypt forest in a rugged region of gorges, cascades and rare fauna species such as the marbled frogmouth and the yellow-bellied glider. Bushwalking books on the Conondales, giving the history, maps and descriptions of walks, are available from the Maple St Co-op, Maleny, and the Craft Shop in Kenilworth.

Gheerulla State Forest *Map 19 C3*

On the bank of **Gheerulla Creek**, 2km from the road, there is a camping area equipped with toilets, drinking water, picnic tables and BBQs. Here the dense eucalypt forest is interrupted by dramatic cliffs and strange rock formations.

Trailbike-riding is permitted in the forest — one of the few official trailbike areas in Qld. A short beginners' track complements the more challenging 34km route for experienced riders (p.126).

Glass House Mts NP and Beerburrum State Forests *Map 19 C5*

There are 13 peaks in the dramatic Glass House group, only 3 of which were actual volcanic cores — Beerwah (556m), Tibrogargan (364m) and Coonowrin, or Crookneck (377m). The others were formed when deposits of molten rock cooled in the surrounding surface rock, which was then weathered away.

The **Glass House Mts NP** protects 7 of the peaks — Beerwah, Tibrogargan, Ngungun, Coonowrin (Crookneck), Miketeebumulgrai, Elimbah (Saddleback) and Coochin Hills, along with the Blue Gum Creek section.

Tracks suitable for climbers lead from base to summit of the main peaks. **Mt Ngungun** is the most accessible peak, with a 1–2hr return climb suitable even for inexperienced climbers. The trails to the top of **Mts Beerwah** and **Tibrogargan** should be tackled only by those who are fit and experienced in bushwalking and climbing (2–3hr return). The **Mt Coonowrin (Crookneck)** trail is the most demanding of all, and should be left to experienced rockclimbers, who can expect to take at least half a day for the climb and descent.

The parks are known for the wildlife that abounds there — look out for koalas,

Glass House Mts from Mary Cairncross Lookout

The Legend of Coonowrin

Father Tibrogargan and Mother Beerwah had many children: Coonowrin, the eldest and tallest, the Tunbubudla twins, Beerburrum, Coochin, Ngungun, Tibberoowuccum, Miketeebumulgrai and Elimbah.

One day, looking out to sea, Tibrogargan noticed that the waters were suddenly rising. He called out to his eldest son to help his mother and the younger children to safety on the mountains further inland. But Coonowrin ran off to save himself. Tibrogargan was so angry that he struck Coonowrin and dislocated his neck.

Today, Tibrogargan gazes out to sea with his back turned sorrowfully on the shameful Coonowrin, who is still unable to straighten his neck.

Sacred ground
On your way to Wild Horse Mt, follow the signs along Bowen and Johnston Rds to the remains of a **bora ring** once used by the Kabi Kabi people.

forest birds, echidnas, lizards and wallabies. Camping is not permitted. For more info on the national parks, contact the Qld Parks and Wildlife Service, 61 Bunya St, Maleny 4552. Ph: (07) 5494 3983

The **Beerburrum State Forests** cover most of the coastal lowlands from Caboolture to Caloundra and include the **Bellthorpe State Forest** at the southern end of the Conondale Ra. **Beerburrum Forest Drive**, which can be accessed from either Beerburrum or Glass House Mts township, is a partly sealed road running through some patches of open country, where there are magnificent views of the Glass House Mts.

There are 2 lookouts along the drive. **Beerburrum Mt Lookout,** just off Beerburrum Rd near Beerburrum township, has a fire tower with commanding views; the 700m walking track to the lookout is sealed but steep. The **Glass House Mts Lookout,** at the top of a sandstone scarp, surveys the stony flanks of the surrounding peaks. The fire tower at this lookout is usually open to the public at weekends. Signs at the lookouts help to identify the various peaks.

On the eastern side of the Bruce Hwy, **Wild Horse Mt Lookout** is an impressive octagonal structure at the summit of a 123m peak due east of Glass House Mts. The lookout — a joint DPI Forest Service and Telstra project — has an instructive display that runs around every face of the octagon's roof. There is a carpark at the base of the peak, and a steep 700m walk to the top. (Alternatively, park at either of Moby Vic's North and South Mobil service stations on the highway and take the free shuttle bus — p.113.) The walk is only sparsely shaded and can be very hot, but it has some interesting native plants to reward the hiker.

Mt Tibrogargan

Imbil State Forest
See Amamoor State Forests.

Jimna State Forest *Map 19 B4*
Jimna State Forest can be reached via the Kilcoy–Murgon road or (in dry weather only) by turning off Kenilworth Forest Drive (see below). It has much to offer visitors — plantations of hoop pine, stretches of dense eucalypt forest, mountain vistas, cool streams and over 140 species of birds and animals.

Peach Trees Camping and Day Use Area, on Yabba Creek north of Jimna township, has picnic facilities, toilets and hot and cold showers. Overnight hikers can also obtain a **permit** to camp in other parts of the forest. Contact the Dept of Natural Resources Office, Sunday Creek Rd, Kenilworth, Ph: (07) 5446 0925. At Peach Trees there are 4 walking tracks of varying length and difficulty, and swimming holes in Yabba Creek.

Jimna Fire Tower is the tallest fire tower in Qld. Visitors can climb 241 steps to the viewing platform, 44m high, to survey the surrounding forest. The day-use area at the foot of the tower has picnic facilities, toilets and drinking water.

The **Marumba viewing area**, on the Kilcoy–Murgon road, looks out over hoop-pine plantations. There are picnic tables, BBQs and wood provided here, but no drinking water or toilets.

Yednia Lookout is at the top of Red Bluff, above the valley of Sheep Station Creek and Yednia Sawmill.

The DPI Forestry Office at Jimna has more info about the forest, including maps of the area and details about the various points of interest. It is open both during and outside normal office hours.

See p.126 for details of **Landcruiser Mountain Park**, 22km north of Jimna.

Kenilworth State Forest *Map 19 B4*
This 20 000ha state forest in the upper Mary River catchment area encompasses a variety of landscapes, from rainforests, hoop-pine plantations and high blue-gum ridges to rocky gullies scoured by rushing streams. The forest has a signposted drive, picnic and camping areas, walking tracks, swimming holes, scenic lookouts and facilities for horseriding and mountainbike-riding. Inquire at the Dept of Natural Resources Office, Sunday Creek Rd, Kenilworth. Ph: (07) 5446 0925

The **Kenilworth Forest Drive** winds through different forest types for about 40km and passes through a section of the **Conondale Ra NP** before returning to the Maleny–Kenilworth road. Signposts identify points of interest. The road is

Wood wizardry
The **Jimna Fire Tower** was built over 3 years by a father-and-son team, who spliced together 2 ironbark logs for each leg, and braced them with a network of timbers and zigzag stairs.

Kenilworth State Forest

unsealed, with sharp curves and steep grades, and should not be used in wet weather. It is not suitable for caravans or coaches.

Charlie Moreland Camping and Day Use Area on **Little Yabba Creek** has picnic facilities, horse yards, 3 walking tracks, including a 4.4km hike (1-way) to the fire tower at Mt Allan (593m), and swimming holes. **Booloumba Creek Camping and Day Use Area** is set in a patch of rainforest with nearby swimming holes, rocky gorges, walking tracks and scenic lookouts. Campers have a choice of individual sites in the forest and open-area camping. Bookings are unnecessary at both sites, but there are self-registration facilities at the entrances, where campers are required to lodge their camp details and fees.

There are also picnic facilities and walking tracks at **Peters Creek**, among Sydney blue gums, and **Booloumba Falls and Gorge**, where Booloumba and Peters Creeks meet amid rocky outcrops and cascades.

Back on the Kenilworth–Maleny road just north of Little Yabba Creek bridge is the wheelchair accessible **Fig Tree Walk** (1.2km return), featuring giant Moreton Bay figs.

Kondalilla NP *Map 19 C4*

Kondalilla NP is 327ha of rainforest remnants and wet eucalypt forest. A 2km circuit track leads from the park entrance to the **Kondalilla Falls**, where Skene Creek plunges 90m over the western rim of the Blackall Ra. The full circuit, taking in the base of the falls, is 4.8km.

In 1972 the rare gastric brooding frog was found in Kondalilla NP, but it has not been seen since 1979.

Camping is not permitted in this national park. For further info, contact the Qld Parks and Wildlife Service, 61 Bunya St, Maleny 4552. Ph: (07) 5494 3983

Mapleton Falls NP *Map 19 C4*

This tiny park temporarily has only 1 walking track (the Mapleton Falls Lookout Track has been closed for safety reasons). It leads to a pleasant picnic area and then on to the **Wompoo Circuit** (1.3km), through a piccabeen (bangalow) palm grove and wet eucalypt forest. **Peregrine Lookout**, just off the track, gives views over the palm-filled Obi Obi Valley. Camping is prohibited in the park. For further info, contact the Qld Parks and Wildlife Service, 61 Bunya St, Maleny 4552. Ph: (07) 5494 3983

Mapleton State Forest *Map 19 C4*

About 2km from Mapleton, at the northern end of the Blackall Ra, the **Mapleton Forest Drive** leads past the picnic facilities of the **Mapleton Day Use Area** through walls of blackbutt forest. There are short walks and scenic lookouts along the drive, which passes **Cooloolabin Dam**, a source of water for the Sunshine Coast. At the northern end of Mapleton State Forest is **Point Glorious**, a rocky outcrop with views of the coast and hinterland.

Other attractions

Crystal Waters Permaculture Village

Outside the township of **Conondale** is this permaculture village, where theories of environmentally sustainable food-crop production are practised. The village conducts 2hr overview tours and regular **Motivating Edge Tours** from 9.30am to 1.30pm on the 1st and 3rd Sats of each month. Bookings essential. Ph: (07) 5494 4721. Longer-staying visitors are catered for with camping facilities, a bunkhouse, cabins and educational courses, all in a bush setting. Bookings essential. Ph: (07) 5494 4620

Lake Baroon *Map 19 C4*

This lake, which supplies the Maroochy Shire and Caloundra city with water and visitors with a spot to picnic, sail, fish, canoe and swim, lies deep in the valley between the Blackall and Conondale ranges. The kiosk has Devonshire teas, and boats for hire. Open weekends, public holidays and school holidays (except Tue) from 10am. Ph: (07) 5499 9333

Sound of water
The name **Kondalilla** comes from an Aboriginal word meaning 'rushing waters'.

A vanishing species
The tadpoles of Kondalilla's gastric brooding frog develop in the female's stomach. There they produce a substance that stops her from secreting digestive juices.

Lake Baroon

Lake Borumba *Map 19 B3*

In the state forest SW of Imbil is Lake
Borumba, a reservoir enclosed by forested
hills. There is a picnic area on its shore,
where wallabies graze, and a camping
ground (Ph: (07) 5482 2555). Waterskiing
and fishing are permitted at the lake, which
is stocked with various fish species. At the
hatchery nearby is the **Lake Borumba Fish
Display**, an aquarium stocked with many
species of freshwater fish and equipped
with a push-button video commentary.

Prophet Mine *Map 22* 🔵

This is a working gold mine and
quarrying operation where day-trippers
are invited to pan genuine gold-bearing
dirt. There are demonstration gold pours
Sat and Sun at 2pm, and night-time gold
pours by appt. Bookings essential for
group tours (Mon–Thurs only). Open
Sat–Thurs, 9am–5pm. Ph: (07) 5484 1226

Teamsters Way Stop Slab Hut

This complex (cnr Old Gympie Rd and
Mt Beerwah Rd) was built as a tribute
to the teamsters, bullockies, wheelwrights
and coachbuilders of yesteryear. Visitors
can watch a blacksmith at work or book
for the **Sunset Tour** — a trip in a horse-
drawn coach among the Glass House Mts,
returning to a campfire meal.
Open Tue–Sun, 9am–3.30pm.
Ph: (07) 5496 9588

Real gold

At the **Prophet Mine**,
ask John Parsons, a
gold-miner with a
philosophical
approach, to describe
how the mine offers
visitors the *'real* gold
experience'.

Recreational activities

Action

Eagle Nest Lookout and Point
Pure Lookout, in the Brooyar State
Forest (p.122), are both well-
known **abseiling** locations. (DPI Forest
Service **authorisation** is required —
Ph: (07) 3224 2928 — and group
leaders must be qualified.)

Landcruiser Mountain Park is a
working cattle property and privately
owned wilderness park designed for
off-road and bush camping enthusiasts.
There are 200km of specially designed
4WD trails to test both novices and
experts. (For 2WD vehicles, there is
access to 2 camping areas, in dry weather
only.) Turn off the Kilcoy–Murgon road
16km north of Jimna as signposted.
Ph: (07) 5497 3164

Gheerulla State Forest has official
trailbike tracks. Permits are required.
Contact the Dept of Natural Resources
Office, Sunday Creek Rd, Kenilworth.
Ph: (07) 5446 0925

In the air

Wind Dancer takes passengers for
45min–1hr balloon flights over the
Glass House Mts. Ph: (07) 5495 2815

Skydrifter balloon flights with
champagne and chicken breakfast
leave from Caboolture Airfield.
Ph: (07) 5495 6714

Abseiling, Glass House Mts

Fun for the young
★ Flaxton Barn Model Railway (p.117)
★ Playground at Mapleton Lilyponds (p.119)
★ Nelson's Reserve, Gympie (p.116)
★ Not Just Dolls, Montville (p.120)
★ Town Park playground, Kenilworth (p.116)

Bushwalking

The state forests and national parks of this region are well supplied with walking tracks, ranging in difficulty and duration from a gentle stroll along a boardwalk to long-distance hiking trails (pp.121–25).

The **Bicentennial National Trail**, which follows old stock routes and forest trails from North Qld to Vic, passes through the Brooyar State Forest and crosses the Wide Bay Hwy near Kilkivan. The trail can be used for a short walk or for long-distance hiking. Ph: (07) 3878 9747

Fossicking

Just beyond the original site of the old mining town of Kilkivan on Rossmore Rd is **Rossmore Caravan Park** at Fat Hen Creek, where fossickers can camp and search for jasper, garnet and gold (p.117). Also on Rossmore Rd is the **Prophet Mine**, where visitors can pan for gold (p.126).

Horseriding

Glass House Mts Trail Rides provides horses for small groups of riders to explore the trails that run through the Glass House Mts. Ph: (07) 5496 9588

Marlin Park Ride a Way, in the Mary Valley between Imbil and Kenilworth, has guided half-day and full-day treks on quality horses. Ph: (07) 5484 5165

Kenilworth State Forest has facilities for horseriding at the **Charlie Moreland Camping and Day Use Area**. Inquire at the Dept of Natural Resources Office, Sunday Creek Rd, Kenilworth. Ph: (07) 5446 0925

On the water

Unpowered boats – **sailing boats, rowing boats** and **canoes** – are permitted on Lake Baroon (p.125) and **waterskiing** is allowed on Lake Borumba (p.126).

Lake Borumba is also a popular **fishing** spot, stocked with golden perch, silver perch, bass, saratoga and the endangered Mary River cod.

Nelson's Reserve, Gympie

Suggested tours – Maps 22a and b

'Glass House Mts Close-ups' tour - Map 22a

Approximate distance

180km return from Brisbane CBD

Sunset, Glass House Mts

About the tour

After leaving the Bruce Hwy, this leisurely drive runs NW to Beerburrum and then explores the forests and pineapple farms that surround the Glass House Mts. (Sections of the road are unsealed.) The tour gives extreme close-ups of the main Glass House peaks as well as panoramic views from the Glass House Mts Lookout. After circling back past Tibrogargan to the Glass House Mts township, the road branches off to take in Mt Beerwah, and then Mts Ngungun and Coonowrin. The tour finally heads east past a bora ring and on to the Wild Horse Mt Lookout, another commanding vantage point.

Places of interest

❶ **Beerburrum Mt Lookout** (p.123)
❷ **Glass House Mts Lookout** (p.123)
❸ **Mt Tibrogargan** (p.122)
❹ **Mt Ngungun** (p.122)
❺ **Mt Coonowrin** (p.122)
❻ **Mt Beerwah** (p.122)
❼ **Bora ring** (p.123)
❽ **Wild Horse Mt Lookout** (p.123)

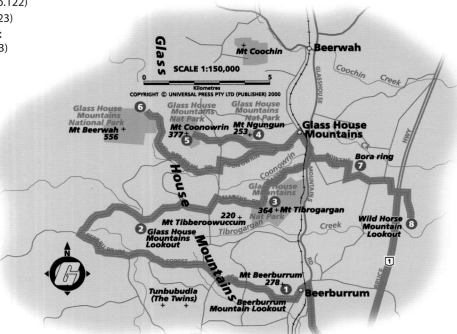

Forests and fossicking tour – Map 22b

Approximate distance

160km from Brisbane CBD to Gympie; round trip tour
from Gympie — 150km

About the tour

This drive from Gympie to Kilkivan includes a diversion
down Rossmore Rd past the site of the original Kilkivan
gold strike, the modern Prophet Mine and the Rossmore
Caravan Park fossicking area to the old Mt Clara copper
smelter (2WD in dry weather only). Here also is the site of
a market garden established during the gold rush days, and

Prophet Mine

the grave of one of the Chinese gardeners. The return trip includes a loop through the Brooyar
State Forest, with views west to the Black Snake Ra and down over Glastonbury Creek.

Places of interest

❶ **WoodWorks Forestry and Timber Museum** (p.115)
❷ **Kilkivan and District Historical Society Museum** (p.117)
❸ **Old Kilkivan township and cemetery** (p.117)
❹ **Prophet Mine** (p.126)
❺ **Rossmore Caravan Park** (p.127)
❻ **Mt Clara Smelter** (p.117)
❼ **Eagle Nest Lookout** (p.126)
❽ **Point Pure Lookout** (p.126)
❾ **Glastonbury Creek Forest Recreation Area** (p.122)

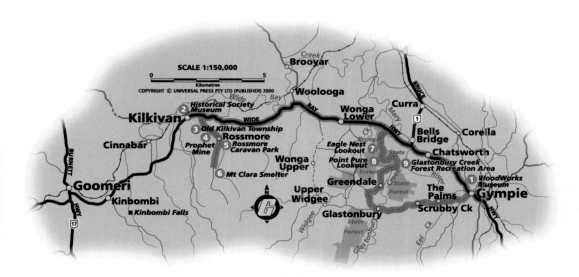

The Brisbane Valley, Caboolture and Pine Rivers

Follow the Brisbane River upstream, and the country opens out into a familiar Australian landscape — faded khaki paddocks stretching away to navy hills and, on the far horizon, a dramatic line of crags and peaks. Over a ridge and the character of the land changes, the flinty light giving way to the deeper colours of the cultivated earth. Further on, in the upper Brisbane Valley, are the snaking reaches of the Wivenhoe and Somerset Dams.

NW of Brisbane, the D'Aguilar Ra rises through eucalypt woodland to the lush uplands of Mt Glorious and Mt Mee. Here rainforests edge the rolling pastures, and tea houses perch at the top of the scarp. These heights have long been the haunt of day-trippers escaping the heat of the city. In many places, walking trails lead off into the cool depths of the forest, returning to grassy expanses, picnic tables and the aroma of food cooking over fires.

To the traveller, the region is a shifting scene, with its river cliffs and mighty dams, its tucked-away townships and ridgetop forests, its ironbarks and anthills, and its shimmering vistas of the distant city.

ℹ Tourist information

Caboolture Community Information Centre
55 King St, Caboolture 4510
Ph: (07) 5495 3122

Esk Shire Council
2 Redbank St, Esk 4312
Ph: (07) 5424 1200

Kilcoy Tourist Information Centre
Craft Cottage, Yowie Park,
Kilcoy 4515 Ph: (07) 5497 1888

Naturally Queensland Information Centre (EPA)
(info on national parks)
Ground Floor, 160 Ann St,
Brisbane 4000 Ph: (07) 3227 8185
www.env.qld.gov.au

Tourism Pine Rivers Information Centre
Cnr South Pine and Gympie Rds,
Strathpine 4500 Ph: (07) 3205 4793

Victory Cafe and Tourist Information Centre
96 Archer St, Woodford 4514
Ph: (07) 5496 1430

Must see, must do

★ **Australian Woolshed,**
  Ferny Hills (p.142)
★ **Brisbane Forest Park** (p.141)
★ **Caboolture Historical Village**
  (p.137)
★ **Lakes Wivenhoe and**
  Somerset (p.143)
★ **Woodford Folk Festival** (p.135)

Radio stations

4QR ABC: AM 612
Radio National: AM 792
ABC FM: FM 106.1.
Caboolture 4OUR FM:
FM 101.5

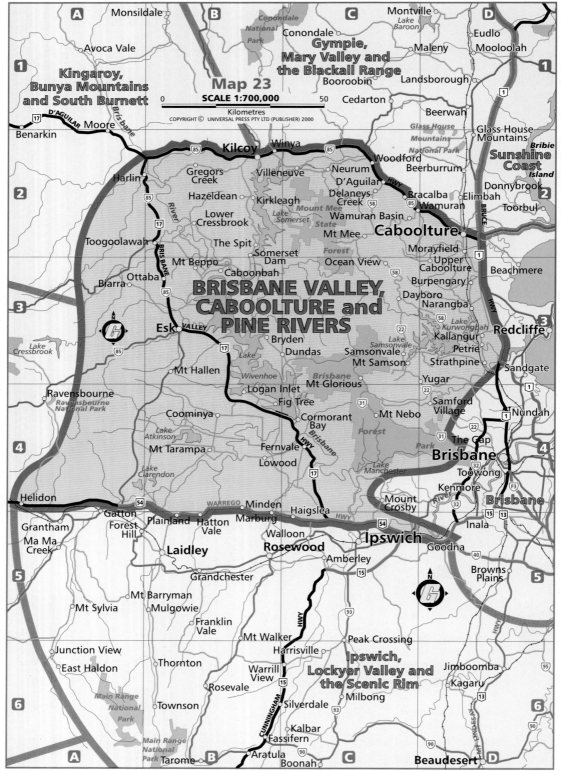

Map 23

SCALE 1:700,000

Kilometres
COPYRIGHT © UNIVERSAL PRESS PTY LTD (PUBLISHER) 2000

BRISBANE VALLEY, CABOOLTURE and PINE RIVERS

Kingaroy, Bunya Mountains and South Burnett

Gympie, Mary Valley and the Blackall Range

Ipswich, Lockyer Valley and the Scenic Rim

Natural features

East of the Great Divide, the Brisbane River and its tributaries, such as the Stanley, elbow their way through rugged hills and widen into sinuous lakes above the Somerset and Wivenhoe Dams. Downstream, the river cuts through a Streeton landscape of wide, pale hills against a backdrop of mountains, then edges past the D'Aguilar Ra to unite with the Bremer River and enter the sprawling suburbs of the Ipswich–Brisbane conurbation.

NW of the Brisbane CBD, the suburbs clamber into the eastern foothills of the D'Aguilar Ra, before conceding to eucalypt forest. At Mt Nebo, Mt Glorious and Mt Mee, the range arcs around the amphitheatre-like valleys of Samford and Dayboro. The North and South Pine Rivers rise on the eastern slopes of this range and flow through belts of rich, red-soil country before converging near the coast.

History

Before European settlement, the Brisbane Valley was a major winter hunting and food-gathering ground for the Aborigines of the district. Despite their resistance, their hold over the territory loosened with European penetration of the area. Disease and forced removal hastened the process of dispossession.

European explorers such as Oxley, Lockyer and Cunningham ventured up the Brisbane River in the period 1823-29 searching for navigable waterways and pastoral country. In 1830, returning from an expedition up the Brisbane Valley and the Stanley River, Capt Patrick Logan met his death at the hands of Aborigines.

Oxley also explored the Pine Rivers area in 1823, returning the following year with Cunningham to cut the impressive hoop pines for spars. By 1840, pastoralists were taking up land in the Woodford area, leading to prolonged clashes with the local Aboriginal clans. Later in the 19th century, rainforest was cleared for dairying, especially on the floodplains and around Mt Glorious, Mt Mee and Dayboro, and hillside forests were replaced by plantations of bananas, pawpaws and pineapples.

Pastoral settlement of the upper Brisbane Valley began in the early 1840s, with more intensive occupation after 1842, when the ban on settlement within 50 miles of the Moreton Bay penal station was lifted. The soldier-settlement schemes instituted after WWI broke up many of the larger pastoral holdings and led to further diversification of agriculture. Today, the main product is beef, though grain, fodder and small crops are also important.

Suspicion
It was rumoured that the convicts who accompanied Logan, made mutinous by his cruelty, were implicated in his death.

The Brisbane Valley

In-depth guide
Living with the Environment in the Pine Rivers Shire, by John Bowden, gives unmatched coverage of the Pine Rivers area. Available at the Tourism Pine Rivers Info Centre.

Getting there

By road

The Brisbane Valley Hwy (Hwy 17) turns north off the Warrego Hwy about 16km past the Ipswich turnoff. It passes through Fernvale and skirts Lake Wivenhoe before running north through Esk and Toogoolawah to meet the D'Aguilar Hwy. To take the scenic route to Kilcoy, turn right 4km north of Esk, cross the upper reaches of Lake Wivenhoe just past Caboonbah, and follow the winding mountain road along the western shore of Lake Somerset.

An alternative northern approach to the Brisbane Valley is to travel from Brisbane on the Bruce Hwy, turn off through Caboolture and take the D'Aguilar Hwy via Woodford to Kilcoy.

For a 'backblocks' route to Mt Mee, take Samford Rd from Brisbane and drive north through Samford and Dayboro.

Brisbane Bus Lines has a morning service running Mon–Fri and Sun through the main towns of the Brisbane Valley, terminating at Moore. An afternoon service to Kilcoy goes via Caboolture and Woodford, along the Bruce and D'Aguilar Hwys. The buses also run several times a day to Dayboro, Petrie and Strathpine. Ph: (07) 3354 3633

By rail

Queensland Rail has a frequent Citytrain service to Caboolture; stops include Petrie and Strathpine. Ph: 131 230

Getting around

North South Tours and Travel offers bus tours in the region: the full-day Australian Animal Adventure tour through the Samford Valley stops at a deer farm, an emu farm and the Alma Park Zoo; the full-day Pioneer Tour takes in the Caboolture Historical Village, the Caboolture Warplane Museum and an art gallery showing Australian colonial and Aboriginal works; the half-day Australiana Tour goes to Walk-about Creek and the Mt Samson Emu Farm. The same company also runs a half-day tour which includes a cruise aboard the MV *Pelican*

on the Pine River estuary and, time permitting, a visit to Osprey House Environmental Centre. Bookings essential. Ph: (07) 3325 0322

The **Samford Valley Mini Bus** takes visitors sightseeing in the Samford Valley. Ph: (07) 3289 2260

Festivals and events

The Grape and Watermelon Festival

A 1-day festival celebrating the local produce. Held in or near **Coominya** every 2 years in Jan. There are stalls, seed-spitting competitions, a band and fireworks. Ph: (07) 5426 4356

Pine Rivers Festival

This festival packs a broad range of cultural and fun activities into 12 or so days in late May–early Jun. Ph: (07) 3205 0549

Freaky Arts Festival

This Jun festival of youth culture is part of the Pine Rivers Festival. It features young local bands and film-makers, and workshops in music, circus performance and visual arts. The climax is a day of performance in the **Pine Rivers Park**. Ph: (07) 3864 3021

By the back door
A scenic route to **Lake Wivenhoe** from Brisbane is via the Samford/Mt Glorious road and the Northbrook Parkway, which joins the Wivenhoe–Somerset road.

Feeding deer, Alma Park Zoo

Small-crop farming, Brisbane Valley

Bos Camel Races

Lots of family entertainment is on offer at the Bos Camel Races, held at **Coominya** in Sept. Ph: (07) 5426 4157

Esk Multicultural Festival

The many different cultural traditions in the Esk community are celebrated in Sept with a street parade, concert, food and craft stalls, games and rides. Ph: (07) 5424 1643

Kirkleagh Klassic Fishing Comp

The largest fishing contest in Qld is held at Kirkleagh, **Lake Somerset**, in Oct. Ph: (07) 3281 4723

Woodford Folk Festival

This music festival, held 27 Dec–1 Jan at **Hidden Valley**, 5km from Woodford, brings 2000 performers and huge audiences from all over Australia. Ph: (07) 5496 3196

Main towns

For ease of reference, towns have been listed alphabetically in 2 sections: the Brisbane Valley and the Caboolture and Pine Rivers areas.

The Brisbane Valley

Coominya *Map 23 B4*

This is a small town with a turn-of-the-century streetscape set among cattle properties and small-crop farms against the backdrop of the Toowoomba Ra. It is 5km off the Brisbane Valley Hwy and a few km from Lake Wivenhoe.

Among the many heritage buildings in the township is **Bellevue Homestead,** dating from 1868. Today, thanks to volunteers of the National Trust, it stands opposite the historic Coominya Railway Stn, but its original site was the valley now flooded by the Wivenhoe Dam. Built by pioneers Joseph and William North, it is a single-storey building made of mud-brick and timber. Bellevue is 1 of only 2 homesteads of its era in the Brisbane Valley to survive the break-up of the early land holdings. (The other is Caboonbah, on the Wivenhoe Dam.) Open Mon–Wed and Sat–Sun, 10am–5pm. Group bookings welcome. Ph: (07) 5426 4209

Just outside the township, at 14 Wills Rd, is **Coominya Collectors Museum**. Its collection includes some unusual items: die-cast models of cars, trucks and aeroplanes, genuine US police patches, FBI 'Wanted' posters, and a plate collection. Open Wed–Sun, 9am–4pm. Ph: (07) 5426 4630

At 50 Larsen's Rd is the **Wivenhoe Deer Farm**, where visitors are invited to learn about deer-farming by touring the property, viewing a video and hand-feeding the deer. Refreshments are available. The farm is open every day, but visits are by appt only. Ph: (07) 5426 4106

Esk *Map 23 B3*

The town of Esk nestles beneath a ridge crowned by a craggy bluff. Hwy 17 leads the traveller through tree-clad ridges down into an intimate settlement of old pubs, churches, shops, colonial houses, creeks and bunya pines.

Royal strain
Deer were introduced into Qld in 1873, when Queen Victoria presented the Acclimatisation Society of Qld with 2 stags and 4 hinds. They were released in Esk Shire.

The **Old Rectory**, at 85 Ipswich St, shaded by camphor laurels, has multiple attractions: refreshments on its wide verandahs, a gallery of paintings by the resident artist, a display of baskets and pottery, a collection of local maps and a wealth of info about the district. Open Tue–Sun (variable hours). Ph: (07) 5424 2025. Also in Ipswich St is the Esk **war memorial**, erected in 1920.

Glen Rock is the crag that looms above the town. It is said that in stormy weather the ironstone in the rock attracts fearsome bolts of lightning.

Out along the Gatton road is the **Brisbane Valley Ostrich Farm**, offering guided tours by appt. Ph: (07) 5424 1146

Fernvale *Map 23 C4*

The small township of Fernvale, on the Brisbane Valley Hwy, is at the entrance to Esk Shire, 15km north of the turnoff from the Warrego Hwy. This is a growing town, both residentially and commercially, and several new shops have recently been added to the traditional streetscape of timber buildings.

Fernvale Hall, in Simpson St, was built in 1934 as a venue for dances and public meetings. It is now an antique gallery. **Fernvale Memorial Park**, on the highway, has a war memorial and a large tourist map that locates the points of interest in the surrounding district.

The popular **Fernvale Markets** are held on the town's outskirts every Sun, 6am–noon. Ph: (07) 5464 3863

Kilcoy *Map 23 B2*

The first glimpse of Kilcoy is from the winding road that skirts Lake Somerset. The town lies in a wide valley, beyond the northern shores of the lake. There is a feeling of repose here, with the houses dotted loosely over the hills that surround the town centre.

The 1st European settlement at Kilcoy was the McKenzie brothers' pastoral lease, selected in 1841. More settlers followed, raising dairy herds and beef cattle on the banks of Kilcoy and Sandy Creeks, and the forests yielded rich harvests of timber. Today, the Kilcoy Pastoral Company, which exports high-quality beef, is the town's main employer.

The Kilcoy yowie

Like the Himalayan yeti and the Bigfoot of the Rocky Mts, the yowie dwells somewhere in those dark regions between mountain forests and the human subconscious. The yowie, half-man, half-beast, has an ancient lineage, reaching far back into Aboriginal legend. Since European settlement, many people working or travelling in rugged country have returned with stories of glimpsing a strange, hairy, man-like creature in the dim light of the forest. Between 1975 and 1979 there were more than 3000 reported sightings of the yowie throughout Australia. The last sighting of the Kilcoy yowie was in 1979, when 2 schoolboys encountered a tall, hairy, 'kangaroo-like' being while pig-shooting north of the town.

A focal point of the town is the **lagoon** in **Yowie Park**, where an emasculated statue of the local yowie stands. Many species of water bird busy themselves on the lagoon or idle on its banks.

Next to Yowie Park is the **Craft Cottage**, an old dwelling where local arts and crafts, home-made cakes, sweets and preserves, garden produce and plants are sold. It also houses the tourist info centre, open daily, 9am-4pm. Ph: (07) 5497 1888

Just up the road, at 26 Mary St, is the **Old Cordial Factory**, now an art studio showing decorative and folk arts and crafts, including blacksmithed and woodcrafted items. Open Mon-Wed, 9am-6pm; Thurs-Fri, 9am-5.30pm; Sat-Sun, 10am-4pm. Ph: (07) 5497 1400

Historical Village, Caboolture

Lowood *Map 23 B4*

Many travellers break their journey with a picnic on the banks of the Brisbane River near Lowood, 7km west of Fernvale. The town has craft and antique shops alongside a range of modern facilities.

Toogoolawah *Map 23 B2*

The highway north to Toogoolawah descends into a valley of green paddocks surrounded by rolling hills and deeply folded mountains. Toogoolawah is the commercial centre for the northern part of Esk Shire. It is a pleasant, unhurried little town, the old shops, pubs and houses preserving a strong sense of continuity with the past.

In Cressbrook St is **Alexandra Hall**, built in 1912 as a venue for town gatherings, from dances to community meetings. After 1931 it was used as a picture theatre. The **ANZ Bank** building, also in Cressbrook St, and the **bandstand** in Toogoolawah Park both date from 1924.

St Andrews Church, bounded by Gunya, Mangerton and Cressbrook Sts, near McConnel Park, was built in 1912. It was designed by the architect Robin Dods, and is now listed with the National Trust. The church has a shingle roof.

The **war memorial**, in Cressbrook St, was erected in 1920.

The Caboolture and Pine Rivers areas

Caboolture *Map 23 D2*

Caboolture is now almost a satellite of Brisbane, with a town centre that is full of bustle, designed streetscapes and modern municipal buildings. South of the main street, on Morayfield Rd, the **Centenary Lakes** parks have waterfalls, walking paths, gardens, picnic areas and a children's playground.

The Caboolture Community Info Centre, 55 King St, has a well-organised tourist-info section staffed by volunteers. Ph: (07) 5495 3122

The displaced buildings of old Caboolture have been re-erected at the **Historical Village**, a 4ha site 2.5km north along Beerburrum Rd. The village is a complex of over 50 restored buildings, including the Caboolture Riverview Hospital, the post office and the shire hall, and caters for the whole family, with a miniature train (operating daily), wagon rides, a licensed bush pub, tea-room, picnic facilities, carpenter's shop, pottery and craft shop. 'Special days' include Australia Day and Father's Day. Wheelchair accessible. Open daily, 9.30am-3.30pm. Ph: (07) 5495 4581

Centenary Lakes, Caboolture

Caboolture Warplane Museum

The **Caboolture Warplane Museum**, at Caboolture Airport, McNaught Rd, displays fully restored aircraft in flying condition and warplanes under restoration: Wirraway, Winjeel, Tiger Moth, Mig 17, Mustang and many others. Video re-enactments are screened hourly. Scenic flights can also be arranged. Open daily, 10am–4pm. Ph: (07) 5499 1144

Dayboro *Map 23 C3*

Set in a cultivated valley bounded by an arc of the D'Aguilar Ra, Dayboro occupies a small hill on the banks of Terrors Creek. To the north, the road winds up to Mt Mee, 22km away.

The town is neat and well cared-for, with cherished early buildings, such as the **Crown Hotel** (1913) and **St Francis Xavier Uniting Church** (1898), gracing its streets. Some of the old shops in the tree-lined town centre have been converted to cafes and restaurants, and both the old butter factory and the old plumber's shop have become arts centres.

Arts and crafts also feature in the **Hay Cottage Info Centre** in Cruice Park (Williams St), along with a small historical collection. The cottage itself was built in 1872 on land that is now flooded by Lake Samsonvale. Open daily, 10am–3pm. Ph: (07) 3425 1788

Cruice Park has a well-equipped community centre, with tennis courts, heated pool and children's playground. A 'Bush Barbie Breakfast' is held here every

Sun, and on other days by arrangement (for a minimum of 20 people). Ph: (07) 3425 3470

Mt Glorious *Map 23 C3*

This is a small settlement with a handful of restaurant/tea-rooms, galleries and views over the Samford Valley to the sea. The **Maiala Rainforest Teahouse** (the original Mt Glorious Teahouse) has a fire going on rainy afternoons. Open Mon–Fri, 10am–4pm; Sat, 10am–5pm; Sun, 9.30am–5pm. Ph: (07) 3289 0100. The township is bordered by the rainforest of the Maiala section of D'Aguilar NP (p.141).

Mt Mee *Map 23 C2*

Perched at the northern end of the D'Aguilar Ra, on the Dayboro–Woodford road, are the weathered grey farmhouses and lush dairy pastures of Mt Mee, with panoramic views of the Glass House Mts and Moreton Bay to Moreton Island. South of Mt Mee is the turn-off to Mt Mee State Forest (p.142).

Mt Nebo *Map 23 C4*

The Brisbane Forest Park township of Mt Nebo is a community among the trees, where bellbirds tinkle like wind-chimes. New houses are spreading out from the village centre along the heavily wooded spurs, among them some 'alternative-style' structures. Try the local cafe/shop for visitor info.

Wild horse at Dayboro

The name **Terrors Creek** suggests a fear-filled incident, but is in fact a corruption of 'Terah', the name of a wild stallion that once roamed the area.

Art gallery, Mt Glorious

Alma Park Zoo

Garden of Eden
The **North Pine River** was originally named the Eden River by Robert Dixon, an early surveyor of the district, who was clearly struck by its beauty.

Petrie *Map 23 D3*

Once a small paper-mill township surrounded by farmland, Petrie has now been engulfed by suburbia. Reminders of the old settlement remain, however — the North Pine River, bordered by the stately hoop pines that gave it its name, still flows by on its way to Bramble Bay, and the mill operates in its old location.

Nearby **Lake Samsonvale** (p.144) is an aquatic playground for Petrie residents (blue-green algae permitting).

North Pine Country Park, on Dayboro Rd SE of Lake Kurwongbah, has multiple attractions — a heritage village, the North Pine Hotel (a replica of the original hotel at Petrie), and much more — and is home to the **North Pine Country Markets**, held 8am–2pm every Sun. Ph: (07) 3285 3138. A free market bus connects with the Petrie railway station (Ph: 131 230 for train and bus times). The North Pine Bush Poets Group invites visitors to taste country culture with **Dad and Dave's Billy Tea and Damper** on Sun, 8am–2pm; other days by appt. Ph: (07) 3886 1552

High-speed thrills are the hallmark of **Lakeside International Raceway** on Lake Kurwongbah's NE shore, where major motor-sport events are staged. Ph: (07) 3285 3333

At Kallangur, north of Petrie, is **Alma Park Zoo**, where visitors are invited to get close to the animals, both exotic and native. The park has picnic facilities, BBQs and tropical gardens. To get there, follow Old Gympie Rd north, and turn left at Alma Rd, or take the Citytrain to Dakabin Stn, where the zoo bus connects at 9.50am. Wheelchair accessible. Open daily, 9am–5pm. Ph: (07) 3204 6566

Samford Village *Map 23 D4*

In the rolling hills of Samford Valley, with its high backdrop of the D'Aguilar Ra, is Samford Village. Although residential development has spread over the valley, old buildings, such as the 2-storey **Farmers' Hall** (1918), the **Golden Valley Hotel** and **St Paul's Anglican Church**, have been preserved, alongside new restaurants, antique shops and gift shops.

The **Samford Valley Arts and Craft Collective**, in Main St, exhibits work by local artists. Open Mon–Fri, 10am–3pm; Sat–Sun, 10am–5pm. Ph: (07) 3289 7239

Samford District Historical Museum, in Station St, features displays and historical records. Open Sun, 10am–4pm; other days by appt. Ph: (07) 3289 1550

A tourist map in **John Scott Park**, Main St, shows the locations of the district's attractions.

Country music
The Pioneer Village Country Music Club, at North Pine Country Park, puts on a **Sunday Arvo in the Country** every second and fourth Suns in the month.

Strathpine *Map 23 D3*

Light industry now lines the stretch of Gympie Rd that runs through Strathpine, but parkland greens the banks of Four Mile Creek and sections of the South Pine River. **Pine Rivers Park** has picnic facilities, a playground and bikeway. This is the site of the Freaky Arts Festival (p.134).

The Tourism Pine Rivers Info Centre, cnr South Pine and Gympie Rds, has info about the Pine Rivers district and beyond. Open Mon–Fri, 9am–4pm; Sat–Sun, 9am–2pm. Ph: (07) 3205 4793

Woodford *Map 23 C2*

Woodford is known Australia-wide for its Folk Festival, held on 27 Dec–1 Jan each year. Just an hour's drive north of Brisbane and surrounded by state forest, mountain ranges, dairy and beef cattle properties and distant volcanic peaks, Woodford is ideal for a day trip.

Archer St, the spacious main street, is lined with memorial trees, BBQs and picnic tables. The many original buildings, such as the **school** (1882), **police station** (1885), **St Mathias Anglican Church** (1891) and the still functioning **cattle yards**, preserve the rural atmosphere of the town.

Tilney's Restaurant, in a restored Queenslander (101 Archer St), houses **Gallery 101**, where the Woodford Community Art Group meet for workshops and display their art. A major exhibition is held here each year in Nov. Ph: (07) 5496 1878

At Woodford, the Australian Narrow Gauge Railway Museum Society runs **steam train rides** on the **Durundur Railway** each Sun throughout the year and every day of the Woodford Folk Festival, 10am–4pm. Ph: (07) 3202 6582 or (07) 3265 6834. The train leaves from Margaret St, Woodford and stops at the Woodford Herb and Cottage Gardens, 71 Peterson Rd, where Devonshire teas, light meals, nursery plants and crafts are available. Ph: (07) 5496 1316

Group tours (by appt) are welcomed at 2 hydroponic farms in the area – **Timbertop Hydroponic Farm,**

Woodford steam train

Kauri Ct, Woodford (Ph: (07) 5496 1963) and **Stony Creek Hydroponic Farm,** Fletchers Rd, Stony Creek (Ph: (07) 5496 1447).

There are 2 **alpaca studs** on Sirl Rd at Stony Creek, 9km from Woodford, both welcoming bus tours and individual visitors by appt. You are invited to strike up an acquaintance with these winsome animals, and watch the shearing and spinning of their fine wool, at **Durundur Alpaca Stud** (Ph: (07) 5496 1840) and **Holmwood Alpaca Stud** (Ph: (07) 5496 1331).

Delaneys Creek Winery and Vineyard, near D'Aguilar (cnr Buckingham and Hennessey Rds), invites visitors to sample its white and red table wines 10am–5pm daily. Their muscat rosé is a perfect summer accompaniment to the area's tropical fruit. Ph: (07) 5496 4925

For more info about Woodford and the surrounding area, call in at the Victory Cafe and Tourist Info Centre, 96 Archer St. Ph: (07) 5496 1430

Fruit fit for the King

Elvis Parsley's Grapelands, a greengrocery at 87 Archer St, is adorned with Elvis posters, and the service comes with a song. Open Mon–Fri, 8am–5pm; Sat, 8am–noon. Ph: (07) 5496 1309

National parks, regional parks and state forests

Brisbane Forest Park *Map 25*

Brisbane is backed by mountains and bushland, much of which is preserved in the 28 500ha Brisbane Forest Park. This encompasses state forests, council reserves and sections of the D'Aguilar NP.

Major attractions include **Bellbird Grove**, with its picnic areas and walking trails (see map 24) that have the gold-rush days and Aboriginal interaction with the environment as their themes; **McAfee's Lookout**, with views over the Brisbane River mouth and Moreton Bay; **Camp Mt**, overlooking the Samford Valley, with views north over Lake Samsonvale to the Glass House Mts, and east to the city; **Jolly's Lookout**, a formal lookout area built in the 1930s, with a geological display showing the major rock types within the park, and a view over the Samford Valley to Deception Bay; **Boombana**, a picnic area set in lush forest and a starting point for walks; **Manorina Bush Camp**, a forest picnic and camping area with self-guided walks; **Westridge Outlook**, with an info shelter, an elevated boardwalk around a rocky knoll, and views west over the range to the Lockyer Valley in the distance (glimpses of Lake Wivenhoe); **Maiala**, the protected heart of Mt Glorious, with a grassy picnic area on the site of an old sawmill and walks leading deep into the rainforest; **Wivenhoe Outlook**, a picnic area with steps leading down to a platform lookout and small tiered amphitheatre,

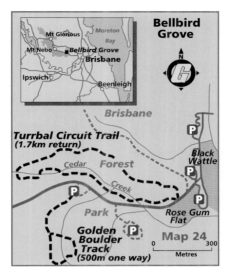

looking through hills to Lake Wivenhoe; **Cedar Flats**, a picnic area along Northbrook Parkway, connecting to the Wivenhoe-Somerset road; and, on Samford Rd, **Lomandra** and **Ironbark Gully**, established picnic areas at the entrance to Samford Valley, 'Home of the Powerful Owl'. In the SW is **Lake Manchester**, which is approached via Mt Crosby Rd.

An info centre at the park head-quarters at 60 Mt Nebo Rd, the Gap, supplies a brochure with details of all these areas, and a bushwalking guide mapping all the walks. The Walk-about Creek Freshwater Study Centre (p.144) is part of the headquarters complex. Ph: (07) 3300 4855

Brisbane Forest Park

Signs of ages past
Signposts along
Mt Nebo Rd mark
the geological features
that can be seen in
Brisbane Forest Park.

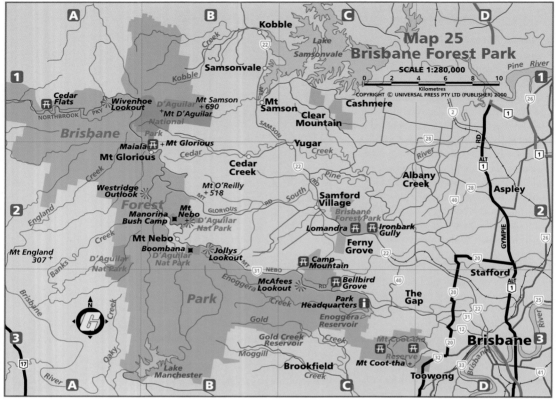

Mt Mee State Forest *Map 23 C2*

This area of 14 000ha of rainforest, dry eucalypt forest and pine plantations is reached by taking the signposted turnoff along Sellin Rd to the **Mt Mee Forest Station** and the **Gantry Day Use Area**. The day use area has a picnic ground and toilets, and the 1km (return) **Piccabeen Walk** (wheelchair accessible) begins here. About 6km along Neurum Creek Rd is the **Neurum Camping Area**, with 12 individual forest campsites (also wheelchair accessible). The **Falls Lookout** and the 1.3km (return) **Mill Rainforest Walk** are features of the drive in to Neurum Creek.

     Archer Camping Area is a new remote campsite (9 sites) and **trailbike-riding** area 16km along Lovedays Rd. **Permits** are needed to enter the area. Contact the Dept of Natural Resources. Ph: (07) 3224 2928

Other attractions

Australian Woolshed

This lavish tourist establishment, at 148 Samford Rd, **Ferny Hills**, has a 'timber, tin and gum leaves' atmosphere, and gives its customers concentrated Australiana. Among its many attractions are native and farm animals, a working dog show, a shearing show, a whip-cracking display and an experiential learning centre. Open daily, 8.30am–4pm. Ph: (07) 3351 5366

Caboonbah *Map 26* ❿

Caboonbah Homestead, on the Esk-Kilcoy road, was built in 1889-90 as the home of Katherine and Henry Plantagenet Somerset, pioneer settlers in the area. On a river cliff, high above a reach of the Brisbane River now flooded by the Wivenhoe Dam, the homestead looks out over rolling pastoral country.

     Caboonbah is the headquarters for the Brisbane Valley Historical Society, and several other historic structures have been moved to the site: 2 **cottages** and a **cell block** dating from the early 20th century, and the 1928 **Esk courthouse**. The complex is open to the public Thurs–Sun, 10am–4pm; other times by appt. Ph: (07) 5423 1553

Cedar Creek *Map 25 B2*

Scenic Cedar Creek Rd turns west off the Samford–Dayboro road and follows the boulder-strewn valley of Cedar Creek deep into the Fahey Ra, below Mt Glorious. **Andy Williams Park**, an open lawn area on the creek bank, is the only official picnic area, and is equipped with BBQs and other facilities. The public road ends at the boundary of a private retreat.

Clear Mt *Map 25 C1*

Clear Mt Rd is a steep gravel road that climbs through eucalypt forest from Winn Rd and leads past the Clear Mt Resort. It has views over Lake Samsonvale to the north, south to the city, east to Moreton Island and west to the D'Aguilar Ra.

Lake Atkinson *Map 23 B4*

The Brisbane Valley earns its appellation of 'the Valley of Lakes' with the magnificent dams that straddle the upper reaches of the river. Lake Atkinson, the smallest of the 3 dams, is on a tributary of the Brisbane River near Coominya. At the lake are toilets, shelter sheds, BBQs and a boat ramp for launching speedboats and other craft.

Lake Somerset *Map 23 B2*

Lake Somerset reaches north into the rugged D'Aguilar Ra. The lake is suitable for water activities of all kinds – fishing, swimming, boating and waterskiing. At **Kirkleagh** there are boat ramps and camping and picnic facilities. **The Spit** also has a boat ramp and BBQs for day-trippers. **Somerset Park** has camping, caravan and picnic facilities.

Take the Esk–Kilcoy road around the western shores of the lake for a trip through ridges clothed with dense eucalypt and hoop-pine forest, and gullies dark with rainforest.

Lake Wivenhoe *Map 23 B3*

Lake Wivenhoe has a water-carrying capacity over twice that of Sydney Harbour, and stretches from the dam wall far up into the upper Brisbane Valley. Pelicans, swans, cormorants, wood ducks and a host of other water birds visit its waters. Along its banks are numerous picnic areas, and there are camping facilities, a kiosk, boat hire and a boat ramp at **Logan Inlet**. As a precaution, some areas are closed to swimming because of the risk of contamination by blue-green algae. Power boats (other than those with an electric motor) are not permitted. At the southern end of the lake is **Cormorant Bay**, which has an elegant restaurant and picnic grounds.

Australian Woolshed

Lake Wivenhoe

The Lake Wivenhoe Info Centre, near the dam wall, has natural-history displays and material on everything you ever wanted to know about the valley's big dams. Open daily, 8.30am–5pm. Ph: (07) 5427 8100

Lake Samsonvale *Map 23 D3*

In the South Pine district are **Lake Samsonvale**, on the North Pine River, and the smaller **Lake Kurwongbah**. At Lake Samsonvale, the main picnic areas are at MacGavin View, Bullocky Rest and Forgan Cove, with playgrounds at MacGavin View and Bullocky Rest. **MacGavin View** is a well-equipped area with young trees, and looks across to a small island. At **Bullocky Rest**, the numerous picnic tables are set among mature eucalypts, with a mountain backdrop west across the lake. This area has wheelchair access, and a 4.2km (1-way) walking trail to **Forgan Cove**.

Lyell Deer Farm *Map 26* ⊙

This working deer farm, tucked in under the mountains, offers venison BBQs, souvenirs and hand-feeding sessions. Turn west off Mount Samson Rd into Old Mt Samson Rd, and then right into Foggs Rd, following it to the end. Farm tours by appt only. Ph: (07) 3289 4270

Mt Samson Emu Farm *Map 26* ⊙

Turn off Mt Samson Rd into Winn Rd for this tourist-friendly emu farm. Among its other attractions are traditional farm animals, kangaroos, an animal nursery, horseriding, the Bushman's Bar and Grill and country vistas. Open Sun and public holidays, 10am–5pm; other days by appt. Ph: (07) 3289 4264

Walk-about Creek Freshwater Study Centre *Map 26* ❶

Most people will find something to interest them at this centre, which is part of the headquarters complex of **Brisbane Forest Park**, 60 Mt Nebo Rd, the Gap. Its aim is to give visitors a glimpse of the world of freshwater wildlife. Of particular interest are the platypus display and the activities for children. Open Mon–Fri, 9am–4.30pm; Sat–Sun and public holidays, 10am–4.30pm. Ph: (07) 3300 4855

Recreational activities

Action

Di Zischke, the 'Camel Lady', offers **camel-back tours** of **Balara**, a working cattle and camel property near Coominya. Rides last from an hour to 5 days (camp out on the longer rides). Ph: (07) 5426 4157

The Archer Camping Area in Mt Mee State Forest has special **trailbike** areas. A **permit** is required (p.142).

In the air

Ramblers Parachute Drop Zone, just north of Toogoolawah, offers weekend tandem skydiving for beginners or

Brisbane Forest Park headquarters

professionals, parachute training and, for fear-sharpened appetites, a snack bar, picnic area and BBQs. There is also a pool. Ph: (07) 3399 6400

Skydive Sunshine, at the Caboolture Aero Club, Caboolture Airport (McNaught Rd), organises drops over a rural landscape. Student training and tandem jumps available. Ph: 0500 522 533

Bushwalking

At **Lake Wivenhoe** there are walking trails at Cormorant Bay (1.4km 1-way) and between Fig Tree Lookout and Sheepstation Inlet (7km round trip).

Brisbane Forest Park has numerous walking tracks in varied terrain, including dense rainforest (p.141).

Interpretive walking tracks (some wheelchair accessible) are a feature of **Mt Mee State Forest** (p.142).

Cycling

Most of the townships throughout the region cater for bikes, and **Brisbane Forest Park's** forestry roads allow more adventurous cyclists to explore wild places in parts of the D'Aguilar Ra. **Permit** required. Ph: (07) 3300 4855

Fishing

Lakes Wivenhoe, **Somerset** and **Atkinson** have been stocked with native species such as golden perch (yellowbelly), silver perch and bass. For details of fishing regulations, contact the Lake Wivenhoe Info Centre (Ph: (07) 5427 8100). **Lake Samsonvale** has specially allocated areas for shore fishing.

Horseriding

The **Bicentennial National Trail**, which skirts the Brisbane Valley, follows old coach and stock routes, and is ideal for horseriding. Ph: (07) 5466 7200

Mountain Lake Adventures, a cattle property on the Esk–Kilcoy road via Lake Somerset, offers 1hr, 2hr, half-day or 2-day horseback tours of scenic country overlooking Lake Wivenhoe. Visitors on the 2-day trail ride stay overnight at a stockmen's camp. Ph: (07) 5423 1645

Mt Mee Range Riding, at Oceanview, 11km north of Dayboro along Mt Mee Rd,

has rides ranging from 2hrs to a full day. Ph: (07) 3425 3053

With its network of forestry roads, **Brisbane Forest Park** is perfect for horseriding, but a **permit** is needed. Ph: (07) 3300 4855

On the water

The huge dams and rivers of the Brisbane Valley make this an ideal place for water-based sports. Paddle boats, canoes, catamarans and surf skis are available for hire at **Yupi Kiosk**, Logan Inlet, on Lake Wivenhoe. Open Mon, 12.30pm–5pm; Thurs, 8am–2pm; Fri–Sun, 8am–5pm (Ph: (07) 5426 4475). Check with the Lake Wivenhoe Info Centre (Ph: (07) 5427 8100) for restrictions applying to fuel-powered boats. (See pp.143–44 for further info on Lakes Atkinson, Wivenhoe and Somerset.)

Rainbow Safaris invites canoeists, experienced and beginners alike, on a day-long tour of the upper Brisbane River every Sat and Sun. Ph: (07) 3396 3141

For 1-day and 2-day eco-adventures, join **Kayak Escapes** on the upper Brisbane River. The trail runs for 55km through gentle rapids, log jams and quiet pools. Ph: (07) 3359 3486

Water activities on Lake Samsonvale in the South Pine district may be restricted because of problems with blue-green algae.

Fun for the young

★ Alma Park Zoo, Kallangur (p.139)

★ Australian Woolshed, Ferny Hills (p.142)

★ Caboolture Historical Village (p.137)

★ Cruice Park, Dayboro (p.138)

★ Logan Inlet, Lake Wivenhoe (p.143)

★ Mt Samson Emu Farm (p.144)

★ North Pine Country Park (p.139)

★ Walk-about Creek Freshwater Study Centre (p.144)

Emu chicks

Suggested tours – Map 26

'Valley of Lakes' tour

Approximate distance

280km return from Brisbane CBD

About the tour

Explore the scenic attractions and recreation facilities of the Brisbane Valley lake country with a 1-day or 2-day driving tour to Lakes Atkinson, Wivenhoe and Somerset. This tour approaches the Brisbane Valley via Ipswich and returns to Brisbane on the Bruce Hwy. As well as the scenery, there are historic homesteads, camel rides, a deer farm, parachuting, horseriding, museums, picnic spots, restaurants and water activities of various kinds. At the lakes, keen anglers can wet a line for yellowbelly, silver perch or bass.

Places of interest

❶ **Cormorant Bay** (p.143)
❷ **Bos Camel Co, Balara Homestead** (p.144)
❸ **Bellevue Homestead** (p.135)
❹ **Wivenhoe Deer Farm** (p.135)
❺ **Coominya Collectors Museum** (p.135)
❻ **Lake Atkinson** (p.143)
❼ **Brisbane Valley Ostrich Farm** (p.136)
❽ **Ramblers Parachute Club** (p.144)
❾ **Mountain Lake Adventures** (p.145)
❿ **Caboonbah Homestead** (p.142)
⓫ **Yowie Park** (p.137)

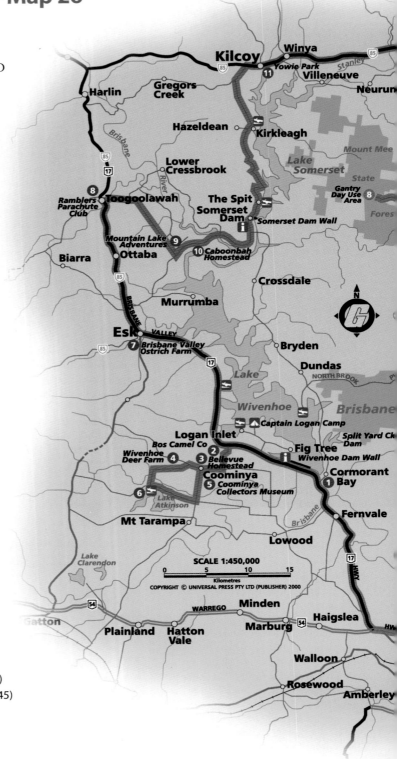

Mountaintop tour

Approximate distance

200km return from Brisbane CBD

About the tour

Pack a picnic lunch and drive from the Gap to Mt Nebo (617m) and Mt Glorious (619m) to traverse Brisbane Forest Park, before descending into the Samford Valley and running north past Lake Samsonvale to Dayboro. Then climb again to Mt Mee, making sure to explore the secluded old-growth areas of Mt Mee State Forest. To return, continue north to the D'Aguilar Hwy on Mt Mee Rd and drive through Caboolture to the Bruce Hwy. Attractions such as the Alma Park Zoo and North Pine Country Park in the Pine Rivers district can be visited on the return journey.

Places of interest

❶ **Walk-about Creek Freshwater Study Centre** (p.144)

❷ **Boombana** (p.141)

❸ **Manorina Bush Camp** (p.141)

❹ **Maiala** (p.141)

❺ **Lyell Deer Farm** (p.144)

❻ **Mt Samson Emu Farm** (p.144)

❼ **Gantry Day Use Area, Mt Mee State Forest** (p.142)

❽ **Delaneys Creek Winery and Vineyard** (p.140)

❾ **Caboolture Historical Village** (p.137)

❿ **Alma Park Zoo** (p.139)

⓫ **North Pine Country Park** (p.139)

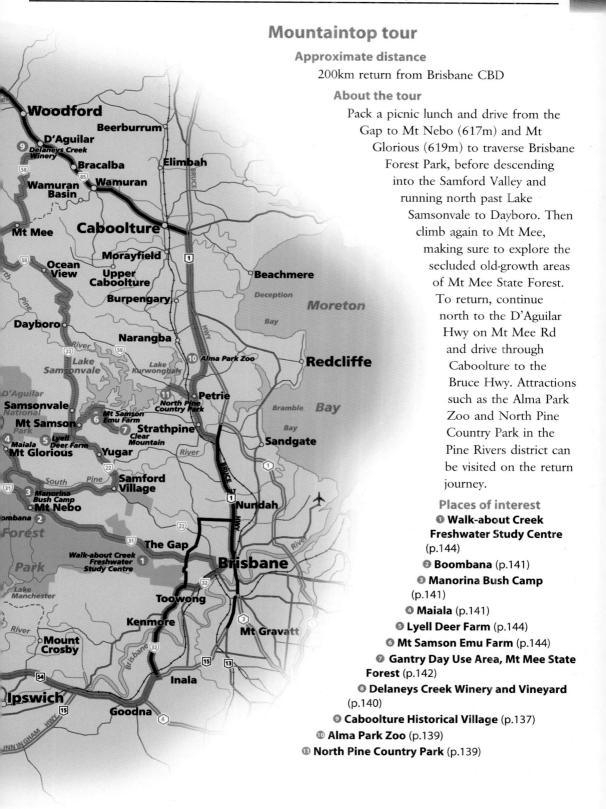

South East Queensland
COUNTRY
WAKE UP TO THE BEAUTY OF IT.

*Left: **Bunya tree***
*Right: **Kingaroy:***
Peanut Country

Kingaroy, the Bunya Mts and the South Burnett

North-west of Brisbane are the grand escarpments of the Bunya Mts and, spread before them, the rolling red-soil country of the South Burnett. It is a region of forests and farms, ranges and rivers, and rich alluvial plains.

Blackbutt forests dominate the high country to the east. Below are the swirling contours and neat geometry of farmland, where verdant crops abut paddocks of turned earth, and a feathery puff of red dust follows the plough. Around them are low ridges stippled with olive groves.

This is a bountiful place; the bunya-nut feasts of bygone times, the gold-flecked creeks, the hoop-pine forests and young vineyards, the monumental peanut silos marking the town of Kingaroy, and the steaming towers of the coal-fired power station at Tarong — all these tell of the plenty that has drawn people here since the Dreamtime.

Today, visitors come for the charm of the country towns and the restorative quiet of farms under a large sky. There are gullies to fossick in, wines to sample and, in high and compelling contrast, the cloud-wrapped forests of the Bunya Mts to explore.

ℹ Tourist information

Cherbourg Council Offices
Barambah Ave, Cherbourg 4605
Ph: (07) 4168 1866

Kingaroy Tourist Information Centre
128 Haly St, Kingaroy 4610
Ph: (07) 4162 3199

Murgon Tourist Information Centre
118 Lamb St, Murgon 4605
Ph: (07) 4168 1984

Nanango Shire Council
48 Drayton St, Nanango 4615
Ph: (07) 4163 1307

Naturally Queensland Information Centre (EPA)
(info on national parks)
Ground Floor, 160 Ann St,
Brisbane Qld 4000
Ph: (07) 3227 8185
www.env.qld.gov.au

Wondai Shire Council
31 Scott St, Wondai 4606
Ph: (07) 4168 5155

Must see, must do

★ **Bunya Mts** (p.158)
★ **Coomba Falls** (p.160)
★ **Peanut Van, Kingaroy** (p.154)
★ **South Burnett wineries** (p.163)
★ **Tarong Power Stn** (p.162)

Radio stations

4QS (ABC): AM 747
4SB Kingaroy: AM 1071
FM 87.6 Kingaroy (tourist info)

KING **A** GRADE

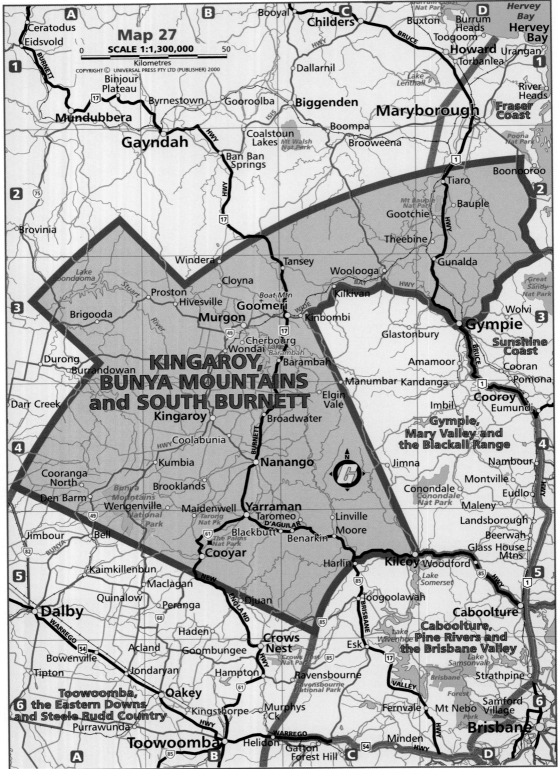

Map 27

SCALE 1:1,300,000

0   50

Kilometres

COPYRIGHT © UNIVERSAL PRESS PTY LTD (PUBLISHER) 2000

KINGAROY, BUNYA MOUNTAINS and SOUTH BURNETT

Ceratodus
Eidsvold
Binjour Plateau
Mundubbera
Gayndah
Byrnestown
Gooroolba
Ban Ban Springs
Coalstoun Lakes
Mt Walsh Nat Park
Biggenden
Boompa
Brooweena
Maryborough
Booyal
Childers
Buxton
Toogoom
Burrum Heads
Howard
Torbanlea
Urangan
Hervey Bay
River Heads
Fraser Coast
Dallarnil
Lake Lenthall
Boonooroo
Tiaro
Bauple
Gootchie
Theebine
Gunalda
Brovinia
Lake Boondooma
Windera
Tansey
Woolooga
Proston
Cloyna
Hivesville
Goomeri
Boat Mtn
Kilkivan
Kinbombi
Gympie
Wolvi
Great Sandy Nat Park
Murgon
Brigooda
Durong
Burrandowan
Cherbourg
Wondai
Barambah
Barambah
Glastonbury
Amamoor
Kandanga
Cooran
Pomona
Sunshine Coast
Darr Creek
Manumbar
Elgin Vale
Imbil
Cooroy
Eumundi
Kingaroy
Broadwater
Coolabunia
Kumbia
Nanango
Jimna
Gympie, Mary Valley and the Blackall Range
Nambour
Montville
Eudlo
Cooranga North
Den Barm
Brooklands
Bunya Mountains National Park
Wengenville
Maidenwell
Tarong Nat Pk
Yarraman
Taromeo
Linville
Moore
Conondale
Conondale Nat Park
Maleny
Landsborough
Beerwah
Glass House Mtns
Jimbour
Bell
Blackbutt
Benarkin
Cooyar
Harlin
Kilcoy
Woodford
Lake Somerset
Kaimkillenbun
Maclagan
Djuan
Toogoolawah
Caboolture
Quinalow
Peranga
Caboolture, Pine Rivers and the Brisbane Valley
Dalby
Haden
Crows Nest
Esk
Lake Wivenhoe
Lake Samsonvale
Strathpine
Bowenville
Acland
Goombungee
Crows Nest Nat Park
Ravensbourne
Ravensbourne National Park
Brisbane Forest
Tipton
Jondaryan
Hampton
Fernvale
Mt Nebo
Samford Village
Toowoomba, the Eastern Downs and Steele Rudd Country
Oakey
Kingsthorpe
Murphys Ck
Minden
Brisbane
Purrawunda
Toowoomba
Helidon
Gatton
Forest Hill

Natural features

The South Burnett is an area of red-soil hills and rich floodplains flanked in the SW by the Bunya Mts, and to the south and east by a series of spurs and ranges. Several minor streams drain the region before uniting with the Burnett River and flowing northwards to the sea. Some have been dammed to supply the district's farms with irrigation water and to cool the steam that drives the turbines of Tarong Power Stn.

The alluvial soils of the river valleys and the red loams of the highlands once supported rainforests and thick eucalypt woodlands. With European settlement, much of the forest was felled for timber and to make way for grazing and farming. Now the country is a rich patchwork of contour-ploughed paddocks in deep reds and greens, rising here and there to a tree-dotted ridge.

The Bunya Mts, an isolated section of the Great Divide, is a ridge of ancient basaltic rock that rises abruptly above the surrounding countryside. Drier rainforests with hoop-pine and vine thickets clothe its lower slopes, and moist rainforest its crest. The dark domes of bunya pines dominate the higher forests, butting through the canopy like pagodas.

History

The Aboriginal people of the South Burnett, many of whom belonged to the Waka Waka language group, celebrated seasonal abundance with inter-tribal gatherings. One of these was the bunya-nut feast, held on the Bunya Mts every 3 years or so. It was a time of song and dance and socialising — a chance to renew old ties, trade goods, exchange news and ideas, and settle disputes, sometimes in ritual combat.

With the first trickle of European settlers, Aboriginal society came under threat. The people were violently displaced, their communities were ravaged by disease, and their access to traditional lands was forbidden. Cherbourg, the site of an Aboriginal settlement established in 1904, is now home to the descendants of clans from near and far, among them the original owners of these rich lands.

The first pastoral properties were taken up in 1842, and within 10 years sheep stations covered the whole region. When disease depleted their flocks, the pastoralists turned to cattle.

In 1865, James Nash found gold at Nanango, and for a short while prospectors rushed to the find. A century later, enormous coal deposits were revealed at nearby Meandu Creek, and production began in 1983 to supply the coal-fired Tarong Power Stn.

The late 19th century brought timbergetters and sawmills, soon followed by the railway, closer settlement and new towns. Dairying, pig-farming and crops such as peanuts and maize became a vital part of the region's agricultural wealth.

Bonye to bunya
In the Waka Waka language, *bonye bonye* was the name given to the bunya nut festival.

Dandabah, Bunya Mts

Getting there

By air

No airline has regular flights to the South Burnett region. However, **Pratt Air Services** at Kingaroy provides a charter service for the district and flights from Brisbane can be arranged.
Ph: (07) 4162 2629

By road

For a scenic approach from Brisbane, take the Ipswich Mwy, turn off 15km past Ipswich onto the Brisbane Valley Hwy (Hwy 17), and travel through Esk to the D'Aguilar Hwy. Alternatively, take the Bruce Hwy to Caboolture and then the D'Aguilar Hwy through Kilcoy.

The D'Aguilar Hwy winds up the Blackbutt Ra through hoop-pine forest, and then descends into the South Burnett Valley, terminating in Kingaroy. From Kingaroy, the Bunya Hwy runs SW past the Bunya Mts and ultimately to Dalby, and north to join the Burnett Hwy (Hwy 17), which connects Nanango with Goomeri.

Tiaro, on the Bruce Hwy, is the most northerly town in this region.

Brisbane Bus Line coaches leave the Brisbane Transit Centre in Roma St twice daily, Sun–Fri, and once on Sat, passing through the major towns, including Kingaroy, as far as Murgon. The service extends once daily to Goomeri, Tue–Sat.
Ph: (07) 3355 0034

By rail

There is no longer a regular passenger rail service between Brisbane and the South Burnett region. Qld Rail organises occasional steam-train rides from Gympie to Murgon and/or Kingaroy and back.
Ph: (07) 3235 2222

Getting around

Pursers Coaches runs a full-day South Burnett winery tour each Sun, with pick-up points throughout the district.
Ph: (07) 4168 1533

Pratt Air Services offers scenic flights over the South Burnett every day from Kingaroy Aerodrome, Goodger Rd. Charter flights available. Ph: (07) 4162 2629

Festivals and events

Blackbutt Country Markets

Stalls displaying local crafts and produce line Blackbutt's main street at the town's markets, held on the 3rd Sun of each month.

Peanut Festival

Every 2 years, in Mar or Apr, the townsfolk of **Kingaroy** gather to pay homage to the humble peanut, the source of much of the region's wealth. They celebrate the harvest with a Peanut Ball, thanksgiving service, concerts, an art exhibition, heritage day and trade fair.
Ph: (07) 4162 3199

Goomeri Show

The Goomeri Show is held in Mar or Apr in the Goomeri Showgrounds. Here locals display their produce, livestock and craftwork, watch ring events and sample the attractions of Sideshow Alley.
Ph: (07) 4168 4177

Burrandowan Picnic Races

The Burrandowan Picnic Races are held in May on the site of one of the district's first stations, about 50km west of Kingaroy, established by explorer and squatter Henry Stuart Russell in 1843.
Ph: (07) 4162 3199

Town of 1911 Pumpkin Festival

This festival celebrates **Goomeri's** transition to townhood, which occurred

Approach to Bunya Mts NP

in 1911 with the great land sale. There are stalls, bush bands, bush poets, historical displays, fairground rides, line dancing, tours to the local historic homesteads, and the Great Australian Pumpkin Roll down Policeman's Hill. It is held on the last weekend in May. Ph: (07) 4168 4023

Nanango Pioneer Festival
This event in historic Nanango is held in Oct, when the townsfolk gather to celebrate the town's origins with a parade of wagons and bullock teams. Ph: (07) 4163 1307

Taabinga Spring Music Festival
This has become a spring tradition in SE Qld music circles. It is a festival of chamber music held in early Oct at historic **Taabinga Homestead** (p.162), south of Kingaroy. Ph: (07) 4164 5531

Main towns

Blackbutt *Map 27 B5*
Blackbutt is a timber town at the top of the Blackbutt Ra. Together with the nearby hamlet of Benarkin, it stands at the SE entrance to the South Burnett.

Blackbutt is in many ways typical of the townships of the district, with its neat gardens, wide streets, a war memorial, a small church, and an old 2-storey timber pub with broad verandahs. Less typical are the **Centennial Clock** in the main street and the **bakery** with wood-fired oven.

The **Butt Pots Gallery**, at Lot 1, Blackbutt Gardens Estate, displays handmade and wheel-thrown pots by local craftspeople. Ph: (07) 4163 0135

There are more reminders of pioneer times in the replica of an **old slab hut**, in Hart St, beside Les Muller Park.

Just 10min out of town is the **Art Academy**, where students can work under the tutelage of painter John Spies. Original watercolours and prints depicting nocturnal wildlife are on display. Visits by appt only. Ph: (07) 4163 0621

In Cherry Creek Rd, about 7km from town, is the **Cherry Creek Garden** (p.160).

Taromeo Stn, outside Blackbutt, was the original settlement in the area. It was established by Simon Scott in 1842 and became a stage post on the coach route from Moore to Nanango. Several of the original buildings remain, among them a blacksmith's shop, stables, a travellers' bath house and a stone storehouse, now a museum. The nearby family cemetery, surrounded by stone walls, has National Trust classification. To find Taromeo, turn left off the highway 7km east of Blackbutt and follow the road for 2.5km, past the timber mill. Visits by appt only. Ph: (07) 4163 0142

Sandy Forest Fire Tower has a commanding view of the surrounding hoop-pine plantations, and beyond to Tarong Power Stn, the Glass House Mts and the sea. Take the Taromeo Rd for 1.5km, and then follow the road leading off to the right for 200m. There is public access to the lower landings of the tower, but permission is required for group access. Ph: (07) 3224 2928

Benarkin State Forest, on the highway 4km east of Blackbutt opposite the hamlet of Benarkin, has picnic and BBQ facilities. From the picnic area a 30km round trip on the Forest Drive leads to the Emu Creek camping ground, which has deep waterholes for swimming and fishing.

Cherbourg *Map 27 B3*
Originally established as an Aboriginal settlement in 1904, Cherbourg is now an independent community of over 1000 people who run local affairs through the Cherbourg Community Council.

Cherbourg's main industry is the **emu farm** established by the community in 1989 — the first commercial emu farm in Qld. The farm now has over 1400 birds, and supplies meat to the restaurant trade and breeding stock to other farms. Visitors are invited to tour the farm with a guide, watch a demonstration of emu-egg carving, and view the Aboriginal paintings and artefacts for sale. Open daily, 8am–3pm. The 40min tours are conducted by arrangement Sat–Sun at 9.30am, 11am and noon. Ph: (07) 4168 2655

Main street, Blackbutt

Tree fact
The bark on the lower trunk of the *Eucalyptus pilularis* is black as though burnt in a bushfire — hence its common name of 'blackbutt'.

Emu farm, Cherbourg

Goomeri *Map 27 C3*

Goomeri (pronounced locally as *G'mary*) is a centre for pastoral, agricultural, dairying and timber-getting activities. A walking map, available from the visitors info centre in Boonara St, details points of interest, including the **Hall of Memory** next door (dating from 1926), the **Memorial Clock** in the town's centre (the face of which does not have numbers but spells out the words *Lest we forget*), 6 churches, antique shops, parks, coffee shops, old homes and prize-winning gardens.

The **Boat Mt Environmental Park** is easily reached from Goomeri (p.156). See p.160 for the **Elgin Vale Mill**, SE of Goomeri.

Kingaroy *Map 27 B4*

Prosperous Kingaroy sprawls among green paddocks in the red-soil heart of the South Burnett region. Its surrounding farms yield abundant harvests of peanuts, which are stored in the towering silos in the centre of town, and navy beans, known to consumers as 'baked beans'. Three-quarters of Australia's navy beans are now grown around Kingaroy.

A video about the peanut industry is screened in the Kingaroy Tourist Info Centre at 128 Haly St, opposite the peanut silos. Open Mon–Fri, 9am–5pm; weekends and public holidays, 10am–2pm. Ph: (07) 4162 3199

The **Peanut Heritage Museum**, next to the tourist info centre, records the pastoral and agricultural history of the area. Part of the museum complex is the first shire council office, built in 1913. Open Mon–Fri, 9am–4pm; Sat–Sun, 9am–2pm; other times by appt. Ph: (07) 4162 4953

Across the street from the old shire council chambers is **Carroll Cottage**, built in 1901, and the 1st house in what was to become Kingaroy. Open by appt; 24hr notice. Ph: (07) 4162 4953

Ultra-fresh A-grade peanuts stack the shelves of the famous **Peanut Van** in Kingaroy St, which has been dispensing premium peanuts to tourists for over 25 years. A mail-order service is available. Ph: (07) 4162 8400

Tours of the local peanut-processing factory, **Kingaroy Toasted Peanuts**, at Taabinga Industrial Estate in Kingaroy St, are conducted at 10am and 3pm, Mon–Fri. Ph: (07) 4162 2272. (The landmark peanut silos in Haly St are not open to the public.)

At **Kingaroy Wines**, 67 William St, near the town centre, visitors can taste and buy semillon, chardonnay and shiraz from South Burnett growers, bottled under the Stuart Range Estates label. Winery tours lasting 15–30min are conducted at 10am and 2pm daily, and hour-long guided tours are available by appt. Open daily, 9am–4pm. Ph: (07) 4162 3711. See p.163 for details of the nearby **wineries** in the Booie Ra.

Mom's beans

Navy beans were first planted on farms near **Kingaroy** during WWII, when American fliers stationed in the town pined for their customary diet.

Carroll's Nature Reserve is a hilltop patch of natural vegetation just outside the town centre, in Fisher St. Here there is an elevated lookout with wheelchair access. The nearby **Kokoda Track walking path** commemorates the 50th anniversary of victory in the Pacific in WWII.

For panoramic views of Kingaroy and the surrounding farmland, drive west along Haly St and turn right to the picnic area at **Mt Wooroolin**, 3km from the town centre. At the summit, there is a lookout with wheelchair access. The vista includes **Gordonbrook Dam** (p.161).

A short drive north of Kingaroy is **Hillview Crafts and Garden**. Take Devonshire tea or a light lunch, and inspect the folk art and local crafts on display. Open Tue-Sat, 9.30am–4.30pm. Ph: (07) 4162 1727

Kumbia *Map 27 B4*

Pretty Kumbia, on the road from Kingaroy to the Bunya Mts, has facilities for drivers to leave caravans and trailers before making the steep ascent to the mountains.

Murgon *Map 27 B3*

North of Kingaroy is the large and prosperous town of Murgon, centre of the South Burnett's beef and dairy

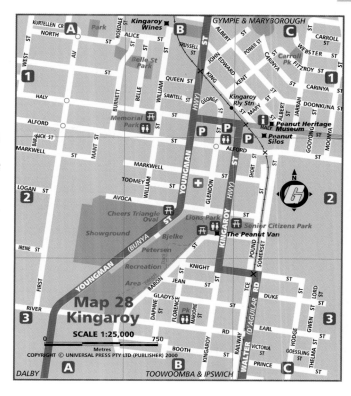

Map 28
Kingaroy
SCALE 1:25,000
COPYRIGHT © UNIVERSAL PRESS PTY LTD (PUBLISHER) 2000

country. Recently, unreliable rainfall has obliged local farmers to diversify, and many now include among their crops olives, wine-grapes, sunflowers, cotton and duboisia (a native plant grown for its medicinal properties).

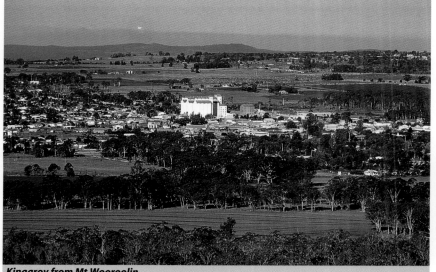

Kingaroy from Mt Wooroolin

Hillview Crafts and Garden

Main street, Nanango

The **Qld Dairy Industry Museum**, on the Murgon-Gayndah road, focuses on the changes in the dairy industry since the late 19th century. It houses a display of old-time dairying equipment — separators, butter churns, cheese presses — and the state-of-the-art machinery that replaced it. The display includes a working dairy, and demonstrations of butter-making can be arranged. Open Sat–Sun, 1pm–4pm; other times by appt. Ph: (07) 4168 1499 or (07) 4168 1984

For wine-lovers, there are the nearby **Barambah Ridge Winery, Rodericks Fine Wines** and the **Bridgeman Downs Cellars** (p.163).

Fossickers are welcome at the **Jasper Fields**, Cloyna, 25km NW of Murgon, and at **Nambadi**, Windera (p.164).

Take the Murgon-Gayndah road for 6km and turn right for the **Tableland Scenic Drive** (a 24km circuit). This leads to **Kapernick Park**, with panoramic views, and then to **Boat Mt Environmental Park**, which has walking tracks and lookouts, and the **Jack Smith Scrub Environmental Park**, with spectacular views and a 1km circular walking track. Duboisia plantations can be seen from the road.

Near the Burnett Hwy 12km SE of Murgon is **Lake Barambah** (also called Bjelke-Petersen Dam), a major watersports venue (p.161).

Nanango *Map 27 B4*

Founded in 1848, Nanango is one of Qld's oldest towns. The original slab homestead of the **Tarong sheep station** still stands, the spear marks on an old shed a graphic reminder of the conflict caused by European occupation of the area.

It was here, in 1848, that James Goode built the hut that was to become Goode's Inn, the first commercial establishment in the South Burnett district. Many of the inn's trappings are displayed in **Berlin's Gem and Historical Museum** (p.160).

The discovery of alluvial gold in 1865 brought a wave of prospectors when the find was made public 2 years later, but the field was not a rich one. In the 20th century, mining helped to restore the town's fortunes when the Meandu coal mine was developed to supply Tarong Power Stn, which became fully operational in 1986 (p.162).

Ringsfield House, in Alfred St, was built in 1908 and is currently being restored. Open Wed, 10am–4pm; Sat, noon–4pm; Sun, 10am–4pm, or by appt. Ph: (07) 4163 7132 or (07) 4163 1491

Nearby are the **East Nanango State Forest Park** and the **Emu Creek State Forest Park** (p.159).

Cotton fields, Murgon

Proston *Map 27 B3*

Proston was originally part of the Wigton property, selected in 1850. A 1910 land ballot dividing the brigalow scrub into smaller blocks opened the way for denser settlement. With the arrival of the railway from Murgon in 1923 the town prospered, and a decade later a butter factory was built there. It has recently closed.

Duboisia grows naturally in this area in pockets of acidic red soil, and a hybrid form, used in the manufacture of pharmaceuticals, is now grown commercially.

In 1980 work began on the nearby **Boondooma Dam**, built to supply Tarong Power Stn (p.162).

Boondooma Homestead, on the Durong–Mundubbera road, is an old stone building dating from the mid-19th century. It now has National Trust listing and is being restored. Visits by arrangement with members of the Restoration Committee. Contact Phil Seiler (Ph: (07) 4168 0244) or Buddy Thomson (Ph: (07) 4168 0168).

About 24km SW of Proston are the **Leura-Joy Gemfields, Brigooda** (p.164).

Tiaro *Map 27 D2*

Tiaro, a small settlement in gently rolling pastures, is the most northerly town in this region. The **Hideaway Station Hotel**, on the opposite side of the railway line from the hwy, is an old country pub with sunset views. It was built over 100 years ago, and old photographs and vintage advertisements adorn its walls.

Wondai *Map 27 B3*

Originally a turn-of-the-century railway depot serving settlers and timbergetters, Wondai is now a centre for the surrounding farms. Peanuts and grains are the chief crops, and beef is a major product.

The first hospital of the region was built here in 1915. The **Wondai Museum**, behind the library in Mackenzie St, preserves the original hospital operating theatre as part of its structure. It also houses a collection of items from pioneering times, including farm machinery, a church organ, a fire engine, a manual telephone exchange and early photographs. Open Mon–Fri, 10am–12.30pm and 1.30pm–4pm; on weekends by appt. Ph: (07) 4168 5402

A round-trip scenic drive, leading from Wondai through Durong to Proston and back to Wondai, runs close to **Boondooma Homestead**, the **Brigooda gemfields** (p.164) and **Boondooma Dam** (p.160). It takes about 3 hours at a leisurely pace.

Sidcup Castle
On the way into **Proston**, pull over to admire this fanciful wooden replica of the original owner's Kentish home.

Historic hotel, Wondai

Ahead of its time
Behind **Boondooma Homestead** is a stone building — the first in Qld to be erected using metric measurements. Its builder was Flemish, and he used the methods of his homeland.

Yarraman *Map 27 B5*

Yarraman's houses are scattered about on hills overlooking the Yarraman Creek valley. This is an old timber town. A huge mill was built here in 1912, and a burly pillar of rough-hewn timber stands as a monument in the main road. A timber mill still operates, processing hoop pine from the local forests.

The **Yarraman Bacon Factory**, at the top of the main street, sells old-fashioned country-style hams and bacon to the public. Open Mon–Fri, 8am–5pm. Ph: (07) 4163 8260

The **Palms NP**, about 18km from Yarraman along the New England Hwy towards Cooyar, has an easy circuit walk and a picnic area (p.159).

Just north of Yarraman, off the D'Aguilar Hwy, is **Yarraman Forest Drive**, an unsealed road running through the half-light of mature hoop-pine plantations and native woodland. There are several picnic areas and walks along the way. The Forest Drive leads to a lookout over the Meandu open-cut coal mine and connects with the road that descends to **Tarong Power Stn** and the mine (p.162).

National parks and state forest parks

Bunya Mts NP *Map 29*

The Bunya Mts, part of the Great Dividing Ra overlooking the South Burnett basin, were declared a national park in 1908. The park now covers 11 700ha. Access is via the Bunya Hwy from Kingaroy or, for those approaching from Nanango or Yarraman via Maidenwell, up a steep road, some of which is unsealed. Either way, the climb is long and very steep, and caravans and trailers are not recommended. There is no petrol or diesel available on the Bunya Mts.

The wet rainforest that covers the higher ridges is topped by lofty bunya pines, with hoop pine replacing the bunyas towards the foothills. Areas of naturally treeless grassland, known as 'balds', are scattered throughout the park. Rare native grasses grow here.

At **Dandabah**, near the SE entrance to the park, there is a privately run kiosk and a licensed restaurant, **Rosella's Rainforest Brasserie**. Nearby is the ranger's office info centre, open daily, 7.30am–4pm; staffed 2–4pm. Ph: (07) 4668 3127. The office dispenses **camping permits**, walking maps and comprehensive info about the Bunya Mts, including its history, flora and fauna. It also houses a collection of scholarly articles on the area and a natural-history display.

Tame red-necked wallabies abound in the open areas. The shyer swamp wallabies, pademelons, antechinus and echidnas are less frequently seen. Brush turkeys strut about the picnic areas, and the forest rings with the call of whipbirds and currawongs. There are also crimson rosellas, king parrots, regent and satin bower birds, rifle birds, superb blue wrens, and many others.

Well-signposted tracks lead off the bitumen Bunya Mts Rd, which runs from one end of the park to the other (see map 29). The 9 walks, ranging from 500m return to 10km return, allow the visitor to enjoy the Bunyas' panoramic outlooks and distinctive variations in vegetation.

There is plenty of privately run accommodation nearby, ranging from campsites to guesthouses and log cabins, but the Bunyas are so popular that it is essential to book well in advance. Camping in the national park is permitted at Dandabah, near the ranger's office, where **permits** are available, and at Westcott and Burton's Well. Ph: (07) 4668 3127

A 'bald' in the Bunya Mts

between 2pm and 4pm daily. It is advisable to book campsites in advance.

East Nanango State Forest Park

This state forest park, on the Nanango–Mt Stanley road 8km from Nanango, has hoop-pine forest, a small native forest, a playground, BBQs, tables and a garden.

Emu Creek State Forest Park

Emu Creek is reached by travelling 4km east of Blackbutt to the Benarkin State Forest picnic area and then following the 'Forest Drive' signs (a 30km round trip). A clear stream runs between sandy banks, here and there widening into deep holes. The picnic and camping areas are well equipped, and the BBQs supplied with wood. Ph: (07) 3224 2928

The Palms NP *Map 27 B5*

This is a small national park about 18km SW of Yarraman, a short distance from the New England Hwy. Its gentle circuit walk leads to a spring-fed gully through a dense forest of piccabeen palms, with hoop pines and figs towering overhead. The silence is broken by the occasional shriek of a sulphur-crested cockatoo.

Tarong NP *Map 27 B5*

This 1940ha area near Maidenwell was recently gazetted as a national park because of its high conservation value. It has rainforest, emergent hoop pines and narrow-leaved ironbark open forest, with several rare or endangered flora species in the understorey. However, there are no facilities for visitors: no tracks, signposting or picnic or camping areas.

Loving wildlife to death

Info at the **Bunya Mts** ranger's office explains the damage caused by feeding sunflower seeds, bread and other food to the park's birds and animals. The advice is: look, but don't feed.

Map 29
Bunya Mountains
National Park
SCALE 1:85,000

0   1   2   3
Metres
COPYRIGHT © UNIVERSAL PRESS PTY LTD (PUBLISHER) 2000

— **1** — Bunya Bunya Track (500m)
— **2** — Scenic Circuit Track (4km return)
— **3** — Barker Creek Circuit Track (10 km return)
— **4** — Barker Creek Lookout Track (5.4km return)
— **5** — Westcliff Track (3.2km & 1.5km return along road)
— **6** — Koondaii Lookout Circuit Track (2.5km return)
— **7** — Westcott Plain Track (4.8km & 1.8km return along road)
— **8** — Cherry Plain Track (6km & 2.4km return along road)
— **9** — Mt Kiangarow Track (2.3km return)

KINGAROY
A   **B**   **C**   **D**

1
+ Mt Kiangarow
1135
9

Burtons Well

Bunya

Ghinghion
Lookout
8

2
Mountains

Bottle Tree
Bluff

Cherry Plain

Cherry Plain
Lookout
7

National

Barker Creek
Lookout

Big Falls
Lookout

Pine Gorge
Lookout

Creek

Valley View
Lookout

Westcott

Big Falls

Saddle-tree

Koondaii
Lookout
6

Little
Falls

Paradise
Falls

Tim Shea
Falls

2

3
Westcliff
Lookout
5 **Paradise**

Festoon
Falls

Dandabah

Kingaroy   17
Kumbia   Nanango

Bunya Mountains
National Park
Bell   Yarraman
Maidenwell
Cooyar
Kaimkillenbun

Dalby   Maclagan   42
Crows
Nest
Jondaryan   54

Toowoomba

Park

Mt Mowbullan +
1101

Cattle Creek
Falls

Cunjevoi
Falls

J.S. Fisher
Lookout

Munro's
Camp

Russell
Park

+ The Pinnacle
892

ROAD
DALBY
CARBINES SHUTE
WARREGO HWY

Boondooma Dam

Other attractions

Berlin's Gem and Historical Museum *Map 31* ❼

This museum in Berlins Rd, between the Nanango-Yarraman road and the Nanango-Maidenwell road, is in a cottage set among shady trees in a carefully tended garden. One room and an enclosed verandah house a large collection of rocks, minerals, gems and fossils. Next door is a schoolhouse dating from 1866, crammed with memorabilia, including bottles, butter churns, crosscut saws, saddles, telephone equipment, barber's chairs, and an array of items from Nanango's historic Goode's Inn. Open daily by appt. Ph: (07) 4163 7145

Boondooma Dam *Map 27 A3*

Boondooma Dam, 20km west of Proston, on the Boyne and Stuart Rivers, was built in 1983 to supply water to the region's farms and Tarong Power Stn. People come here to camp, fish, waterski and picnic beside its placid waters. The dam has been stocked with bass, yellowbelly, silver perch, saratoga and Murray cod. There is a boat ramp, kiosk, and camping and caravan facilities overlooking the water. Ph: (07) 4168 9133

Cherry Creek garden

In Cherry Creek Rd, about 7km from **Blackbutt**, is the Cherry Creek garden, a member of the Australian Open Garden scheme. The property is also a member of the Kingaroy and South Burnett Host Farm Group (p.162). Ph: (07) 4163 0590

Coomba Falls *Map 31* ❻

Just outside the small township of **Maidenwell** are the Coomba Falls, where a stream descends a dramatic wall of granite rock into a deep pool. A gravel road near the Maidenwell Trading Post and King's Hotel leads 2km down to a carpark. Follow the walking track to the lookout and down a series of steps to the grassy banks of the pool.

Elgin Vale Mill *Map 27 C4*

This mill, SE of **Goomeri**, has been preserved as a memorial to the timber industry, which flourished here for 60 years (1927-87). The hoop and bunya pines that once grew abundantly in the area were brought here for milling. This is one of the overnight campsites on the **Bicentennial National Trail**. For inspection of the mill, Ph: (07) 4168 8128.

Power point

Water from the **Boondooma Dam** is pumped through a pipeline to Tarong Power Stn and used to condense the steam after it has passed through the turbine.

Gordonbrook Dam *Map 31*

Gordonbrook Dam is on the **Stuart River**, 22km from Kingaroy off the Bunya Hwy between Kingaroy and Wondai. The dam is stocked with yellowbelly, silver perch, bass and saratoga. There are picnic tables, wood-fire BBQs, shelter sheds, compost toilets and a boat ramp. For info, Ph: (07) 4162 6230.

Kinbombi Falls *Map 31*

Kinbombi Falls, which flow only after heavy rain, drop into a deep ravine between dark cliffs. At the base is a pool ideal for summer swimming when flushed out by a good flow. There are picnic facilities, a BBQ and toilets in the light shade of an ironbark forest near the carpark.

A walking track leads from the picnic ground down the cliff to rocks near the foot of the falls (see map 30). Another (ill-defined) track runs from the main track through the scrub to a lookout at the top of the cliff, looking back towards the falls. From here the track skirts the edge of the gorge and out onto a spur, where Smith's Steps – 142 of them – descend to Barrow Pt, downstream of the falls.

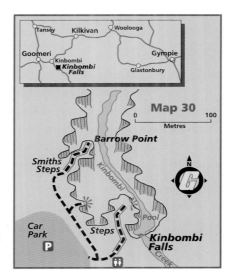

Lake Barambah *Map 27 B3*

Fishing and **watersports** are popular at Lake Barambah (also known as Bjelke-Petersen Dam), 12km SE of Murgon, on **Barkers Creek**. The lake attracts those interested in waterskiing, sailing, freshwater fishing or picnicking. At the **Yallakool Tourist Park**, on the banks of the lake, are facilities for camping, a caravan park, a kiosk, boat ramps, hire boats, picnic

Pool, Coomba Falls

Black-white wars
The **Coomba Falls** are said to have been the site of a battle between local Aboriginal people and the settlers at Tarong Stn.

Mustering near Kingaroy

Host farms

For a taste of authentic country life, stay at one of the many host farms scattered about the South Burnett. These are working properties, where guests are invited to join in farm activities such as milking cows and gathering eggs, or to go bushwalking, horseriding, wine-tasting, fossicking, swimming or fishing. Some, such as Minmore and Taabinga, offer pony rides for children. Many provide special recreational facilities, such as tennis courts and BBQs.

★ **Bridgeman Downs** is 12km from Murgon on Lake Barambah. Bookings essential. Ph: (07) 4168 4784

★ **Cardowan** is a cattle property 40km SW of Kingaroy. Ph: (07) 4164 4260

★ **Cherry Creek**, 7km south of Blackbutt, has an exhibition garden. Ph: (07) 4163 0590

★ **Minmore Homestead** is 20km west of Kingaroy on 7000ha of prime Hereford cattle country. Ph: (07) 4164 3196

★ **Old Boyneside**, in the foothills of the Bunya Mts, on the Bunya Hwy 12km SW of Kumbia, is a cattle and grain property. Ph: (07) 4164 4262

★ **Passchendaele**, 66km NW of Kingaroy, is a working cattle property. Ph: (07) 4164 8147

★ **Springbrook Host Farm**, at Booubyjan, 28km north of Goomeri, runs training courses in farmwork as well as various holiday activities, among them horseriding, bush camping, gold-panning, fossicking, badminton and croquet. Ph: (07) 4168 6106

★ **Surrey Park**, 2.5km NE of Kumbia, is a mixed farm with cattle, pigs, peanuts and grains. Ph: (07) 4164 5507

★ **Taabinga Farm Holidays**, outside Kingaroy off the Bunya Hwy, is a cattle and grain property where guests can stay in a stockman's slab cottage. Ph: (07) 4164 5543

★ Phone the **Kingaroy and Burnett Valley Host Farm Group** on (07) 4164 3196 or (07) 4168 4784 for more info.

areas, a tennis court, bunk houses and self-contained cabins. For bookings, Ph: (07) 4168 4746. Activities such as waterskiing and fishing are prohibited in parts of some of the lakes in the region. Check with the local authority before venturing forth.

The Llama Farm

This farm, out along the Nanango-Yarraman road, runs not only llamas but also alpaca, deer and other exotic animals. Group tours only (by appt). Ph: (07) 4163 7150

Taabinga *Map 31*

Taabinga, 18km south of **Kingaroy**, dates from 1846 and is one of the district's earliest homesteads. The Taabinga Spring Music Festival is held here (p.153), and the homestead is open to the public on the 2nd Sun of each month, Sept-Jun inc; coach and group visits at other times by appt. Ph: (07) 4164 5531. (Taabinga Farm Holidays – see above – is a separate establishment.)

Tarong Power Stn *Map 31* ●

The **Yarraman Forest Drive** (p.158) provides a scenic approach to the Tarong Power Stn and Meandu Mine. More direct access is gained by continuing left along the D'Aguilar Hwy north from Yarraman and turning left into Tarong Power Stn Rd. This descends to the 2 massive cooling towers and the 210m chimney of the power station, which can be seen from as far away as the Bunya Mts, sending blasts of steam and a column of smoke into the sky. The power station is set in bushland, and BBQ and picnic facilities have been provided in the **Community Park** near the dam. The Tarong Visitors Centre has an info display and is open daily, 9am–5pm. Tours of the power station can be arranged by appt, Tue–Fri, 9am–2pm. Ph: (07) 4160 9444

Black coal for the station's boilers comes from the adjacent **Meandu open-cut mine**, operated by Tarong Coal. The mine entrance lookout is reached along Nobby Smith Way, further along the Nanango–Maidenwell road. Mine tours are available Mon–Fri, by appt only. Ph: (07) 4160 7211

Wineries

With the boom in demand for Australian wine, vineyards are here and there replacing the district's traditional crops. All of the wineries below offer tasting and cellar-door sales. Some also offer excellent local cuisine, but intending diners would be wise to book.

Recreational activities

Action

Australiana Camping, a 14min drive south of Blackbutt, offers campsites and

Cellar door, Kingaroy Wines

tracks for **trailbikes, mountain bikes** and **4WDs**. It also provides for **horseriding** (BYO horse) and **bushwalking**. Groups welcome. Bookings essential. Ph: (07) 4163 0864 or (07) 4163 0108

In the air

The **Kingaroy Soaring Club** (Kingaroy Aerodrome, Goodger Rd) offers scenic and trial instructional flights every weekend or by appt. Ph: (07) 4162 2191

Bushwalking

The Bunya Mts are a walker's paradise, with an extensive system of trails to cater for walkers of every age and degree of fitness. You can amble along level paths, hike for miles, or descend into gullies thick with tree ferns (p.158). There are walking tracks in most of the other national parks and recreational areas in the state forests, and also at many of the private host farms (pp.159 and 162).

South Burnett wineries

NAME	ADDRESS	PHONE	OPEN
Barambah Ridge Winery	79 Goschnick's Rd, Redgate via Murgon	(07) 4168 4766	10am–5pm daily
Bridgeman Downs Cellars	Barambah Rd, Moffatdale via Murgon	(07) 4168 4784	10am–4pm Fri–Sun
Captain's Paddock Vineyard	18 Millers Rd (off Crawford–Booie road), Kingaroy	(07) 4162 4534	9am–4pm Sat–Sun
Crane Winery	Haydens Rd, Booie via Kingaroy	(07) 4162 7647	9am–4pm Fri–Tue; groups by appt
Kingaroy Wines (Stuart Range Estates)	67 William St, Kingaroy	(07) 4162 3711	9am–4pm daily; tours 10am and 2pm daily
Rodericks Fine Wines	90 Goschnick's Rd, Redgate via Murgon	(07) 4168 4768	10am–5pm daily

Bicentennial National Trail

There is no better way of getting to know the countryside than by setting out on the **Bicentennial National Trail,** which runs through the Benarkin State Forest north to Kilkivan. This is a recreational trail running 5330km from Cooktown to Healesville, in Victoria. It follows old coach and stock routes, packhorse tracks and forest trails through immensely varied landscapes, from tropical rainforest to snowy peaks. The trail was designed for walkers and horseriders, but it can also be used by riders of mountain bikes. Ph: (07) 3878 9747

Camping

Campsites are provided at the national parks, forest parks, dams and some host farms and fossicking sites.

Fossicking

In the hills and creeks of the South Burnett, the dedicated fossicker can find gemstones, gold, fossils and petrified wood.

At the **Jasper Fields, Cloyna,** 25km NW of Murgon, there are camping facilities and a BBQ area. Search for jasper, agate, crystal, bloodstone, amethyst and petrified wood. Bookings essential. Ph: (07) 4168 6210

At **Nambadi, Windera,** jasper, agate, quartz and petrified wood can be found.

Open daily, but phone first for details. Ph: (07) 4168 6130

Search for garnets at the **Leura-Joy Gemfields** on Les Koy's property at Brigooda, about 24km SW of Proston. A wide range of other gemstones can be found here as well. Both day-trippers and campers are welcome. Open daily. Ph: (07) 4168 0177

Seven-Mile Diggings near Nanango, where James Nash made the first gold discovery in 1865, still draws fossickers searching for alluvial gold and gemstones.

Washing for gemstones

Bunya Mts Horse-Drawn Tours

Top baits
When fishing the dams, fresh bait is good but live is even better. Local shrimps are hard to beat, but earthworms and grubs can also produce good fish.

The diggings, 15km from Nanango out along the original coach route, can be reached only by 4WD.

Horseriding
Several of the host farms (p.162) have horses for riders of various levels of experience. Some organised rides follow old stock routes and timber trails.

At **Bushland Park**, in the foothills of the Bunya Mts, well-trained horses are provided for 1½–2hr rides. Guides lead the riders through red-gum woodland, rainforest and vine thicket.
Ph: (07) 4663 4717

Some may prefer to survey the Bunya Mt scenery in old-world style aboard a horse-drawn wagon. **Bunya Mts Horse-Drawn Tours** has 2 imperturbable Clydesdales that trundle passengers along the old logging track through a private rainforest to a picnic spot, where there is billy tea to be had, and damper with treacle. For youngsters there is a miniature version with Shetland ponies.
Ph: (07) 4668 3115

On the water
Gordonbrook Dam, Boondooma Dam and Lake Barambah (pp.160, 161) are prime spots for **swimming**, **fishing**, **canoeing** and **waterskiing**. In a good season you can also swim in the many waterholes along the streams; Coomba Falls (p.160) and Emu Creek (p.159) are recommended.

Fun for the young
★ Flavoured nuts from the Kingaroy Peanut Van (p.154)
★ Freshwater fishing (pp.160–61)
★ Riding ponies at host farms (p.162).
★ Swimming in Emu Creek waterholes (p.159)
★ Wagon rides in the Bunya Mts (p.165)
★ Wildlife in the Bunya Mts (p.158)

The award-winning Peanut Van, Kingaroy

Suggested tours – Map 31

South Burnett antiques tour

Approximate distance

165km from Brisbane CBD to Blackbutt; round trip tour from Blackbutt — 275km

About the tour

The pioneering heritage of the South Burnett is reflected in the number of antique shops throughout the district. As the map shows, most settlements of any size have one or more outlets offering a broad range of fine antiques, colonial and period furniture, Australiana and assorted collectibles.

Places of interest

❶ **Jon Sebastian's**, 13 Margaret St, Yarraman. Open daily, 9am–5pm. Ph: (07) 4163 8336

❷ **Goode Old Wares**, 47 Fitzroy St, Nanango. Open Thurs–Fri, 9.30am–4.30pm; Sat–Sun, 9.30am–1.30pm. Ph: (07) 4163 3582

❸ **Pottique**, Kingaroy–Nanango Hwy, Coolabunia. Open daily, 9am–5pm. Ph: (07) 4162 2781

❹ **Johno's Collectibles & Secondhand Mart**, 92 Kingaroy St, Kingaroy. Open Mon–Fri, 8.30am–5pm; Sat, 9am–12.30pm. Ph: (07) 4162 7137

❺ **Kumbia Old Age Furniture**, 37 Bell St, Kumbia. Open Thurs–Tue, 10am–5.30pm. Ph: (07) 4164 4331

❻ **Wondai Antiques**, Bunya Hwy, Wondai. Open Wed–Sun, 9am–5pm. Ph: (07) 4168 5200

❼ **Roundabout Antiques**, Old Bank Bldg at roundabout, Bunya Hwy, Wondai. Open daily, 9am–5pm. Ph: (07) 4169 0111

❽ **Rocking Horse Antiques**, Old Bank Bldg, 11 Moore St, Goomeri. Open Thurs–Sun, 10am–5pm. Ph: (07) 4168 4422

❾ **Goomeri Trading Post**, 28 Boonara St, Goomeri. Open Thurs–Sun, 10am–5pm. Ph: (07) 4168 4154

Central Kingaroy

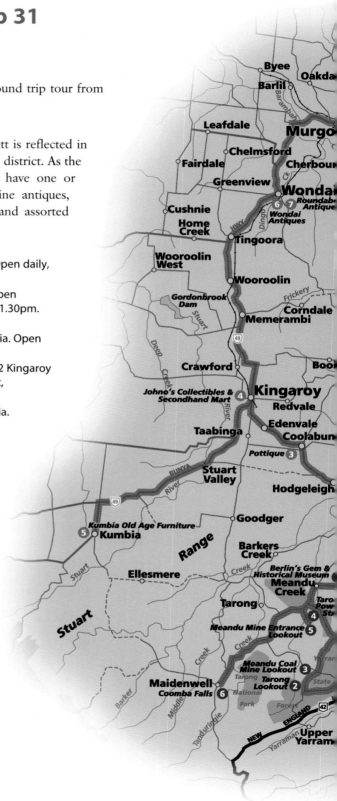

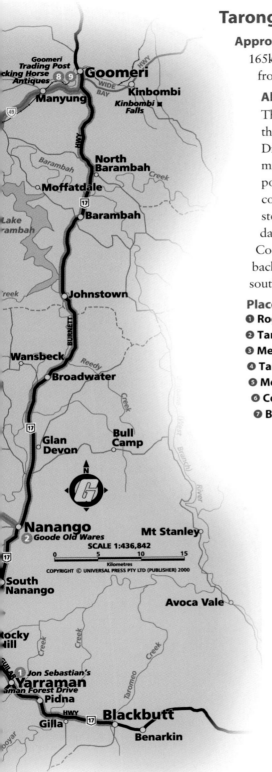

Tarong tour

Approximate distance

165km from Brisbane CBD to Blackbutt; round trip tour from Blackbutt — 100km

About the tour

This tour, which has sections of unsealed road, leads through hoop-pine plantations on Yarraman Forest Drive, and gives unrivalled views over the Meandu coal mine and Tarong Power Stn. It then descends to the power station itself, where the scale of the mighty cooling towers can be appreciated. For a picnic lunch, stop off at the Community Park near the power station dam before heading SW to the Meandu mine and then Coomba Falls near Maidenwell. On the return journey, a back road leads past Berlin's Gem and Historical Museum south of Nanango.

Places of interest

❶ **Rogers Park, Yarraman Forest Drive** (p.158)
❷ **Tarong Lookout, Yarraman Forest Drive** (p.158)
❸ **Meandu Coal Mine Lookout** (p.158)
❹ **Tarong Power Stn** (p.162)
❺ **Meandu Mine Entrance Lookout** (p.163)
❻ **Coomba Falls** (p.160)
❼ **Berlin's Gem and Historical Museum** (p.160)

Tarong Power Stn

Left: **Sunflower fields, Toowoomba**
Right: **Rudd's Pub, Nobby**

Toowoomba, the Eastern Downs and Steele Rudd Country

The Darling Downs are often associated with the grand old pastoralists of SE Qld. Certainly, the fertile plains offer grazing opportunities which have not been overlooked by generations of white settlers. A lesser known fact is that the Downs encompass other terrain, such as the 'sugarloaf' rock formations dotting the Eastern Downs, as well as a variety of lifestyles and attractions.

The Downs are loosely divided into 2 regions: the Eastern Downs and the Southern Downs (p.187). The Eastern Downs include Toowoomba and stretch from Crow's Nest in the north, to Dalby and surrounds in the west, and southwards into the cotton country around Nobby, Cecil Plains and Millmerran. Wineries and national parks punctuate farming land that seems to stretch for ever. This is the home of small blocks and large holdings — typical of the places Steele Rudd described in his famous stories about life on the land. This is a region with horizons lying in the western outback of the state and as much space as one could imagine. This is a place in which to lose — and find — oneself.

ℹ Tourist information

Bell Information Centre
Bell Chimes Art Gallery,
33 Dennis St, Bell 4408
Ph: (07) 4663 1303

Crow's Nest Information Centre
Emu Creek Rd, Crow's Nest 4355
Ph: (07) 4698 1155

Dalby Information Centre
Thomas Jack Park, Dalby 4405
Ph: (07) 4662 1066

Naturally Queensland Information Centre (EPA)
(info on national parks)
158 Hume St, Toowoomba 4350
Ph: (07) 4639 4599
www.env.qld.gov.au

Toowoomba Tourist Information Centre
Cnr James and Kitchener Sts,
Toowoomba 4350
Ph: 1800 331 155 or (07) 4639 3797

Must see, must do

★ **Empire Theatre** (p.176)
★ **Jimbour House** (p.182)
★ **Rimfire Winery** (p.182)
★ **Rudd's Pub** (p.176)
★ **Spring Bluff Railway Stn and gardens** (p.182)
★ **Toowoomba Railway Refreshment Rooms** (p.176)

Radio stations

4QS ABC: AM 747
Radio 4WK: AM 963
(Warwick and surrounds)
Radio FM 88: FM 88
(Toowoomba and Crow's Nest)

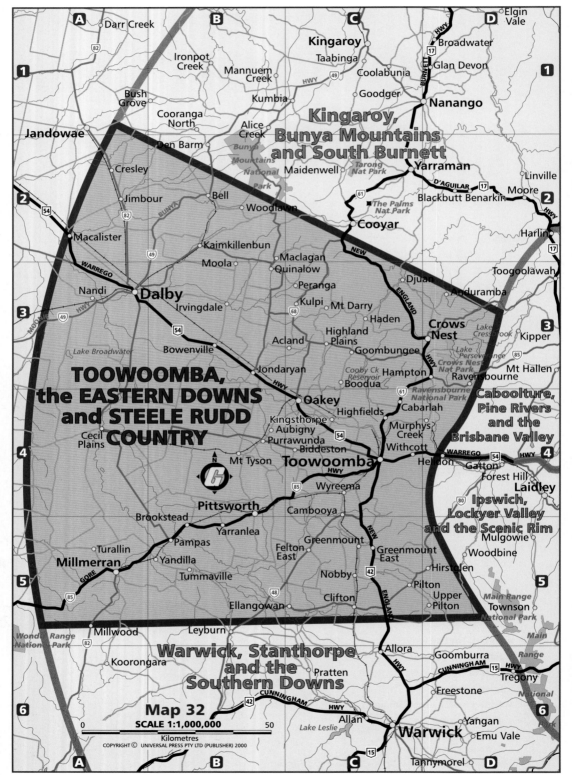

Kingaroy, Bunya Mountains and South Burnett

TOOWOOMBA, the EASTERN DOWNS and STEELE RUDD COUNTRY

Caboolture, Pine Rivers and the Brisbane Valley

Ipswich, Lockyer Valley and the Scenic Rim

Warwick, Stanthorpe and the Southern Downs

Map 32

SCALE 1:1,000,000

0   50

Kilometres

COPYRIGHT © UNIVERSAL PRESS PTY LTD (PUBLISHER) 2000

Natural features

The Darling Downs comprise 72 500km^2 of rich black soil, the result of volcanic activity thousands of years ago. The Great Dividing Ra — a linked series of mountain peaks created by the same activity, which runs down the east coast of Australia from Qld to Vic — marks the Downs' eastern boundary while the granite terrain of the Southern Downs and northern NSW (p.255) signals its southern reach. Westwards lies the 'Golden West' — more extensive plains with variable soils — and to the north, the Bunya Mts (p.149).

The Eastern Downs are made up of grasslands, mountains, forests and national parks, with the Condamine River coursing through its western reaches. Vegetation includes bunya pine, silky oak, stringy bark, red gum, cedar and hoop pine, which encouraged the early growth of a timber industry. Native wildlife includes wedge-tailed eagles, kangaroos and terrapins. Because of its elevation, the region experiences seasonal changes and the temperature can drop to 10°C or under in the winter months.

History

Prior to white invasion the Downs were home to at least 4 Aboriginal groups, including the Jagara, Giabal and Bigambul peoples, for 15 000 years or more. The advent of Europeans was heralded by explorers. Among the most famous of these was the English botanist Allan Cunningham who came here in 1827. As the farming value of the region became evident, settlers moved in to claim large tracts of land and began to build their personal wealth on the back of Australia's most famous export, wool.

Bullock wagons carried goods to and from Moreton Bay (p.39) and towns were established along the bullock routes. Drayton, now a suburb of Toowoomba, was the first such township. Indigenous local people fought to protect their land and rights. While descendants of these original inhabitants still live in the region, their numbers have been severely depleted by European aggression.

As white settlement grew, the Downs were put to other uses. These included growing grain and cotton crops, and establishing cattle stations and a large dairy industry. This diversification led to a further increase in population. Toowoomba became a municipality in 1860 and a city in 1904, and new shires were created on the southern edge of the Eastern Downs in 1913. While the variety of industries has been maintained in the ensuring years, settlement has stabilised and, in some districts, declined over the 20th century. However, the region is still a rich source of income and inspiration for many.

Getting there

By air

Eastland, a Qantas affiliate, provides daily services between Brisbane and

> **History lesson**
> The **Toowoomba Historical Society** (49 Lindsay St) has extensive records of the history of European settlement of the region. Open Mon–Fri, 10am–4pm; Sat (in spring/summer), 1pm–4pm.
> Ph: (07) 4638 7362

Darling Downs: life on the land

*Spring Bluff Stn,
Toowoomba*

Toowoomba. Ph: 131 313. **Flight West
Airlines** offers twice-weekly flights to
Toowoomba. Ph: 132 392

By road

In under 2hrs, motorists can travel an easy
route westwards from Brisbane via the
Western Hwy, which becomes the
Warrego Hwy, into Toowoomba, the
gateway to the region. The Warrego Hwy
bypasses the city of Ipswich and towns
including Gatton and Helidon. From
Toowoomba, the highway continues NW
to Oakey, Jondaryan and Dalby. The
Bunya Hwy links Dalby and Bell. The
New England Hwy snakes from south to
north, with Crow's Nest being its highest
point of reference in the region. Other
towns and landmarks in the Eastern
Downs are linked to these major laneways
by surfaced and unsurfaced roads.

   McCafferty's Bus Service runs daily
between Brisbane and Toowoomba. The
service departs from Roma St Transit
Centre and arrives at the Toowoomba
Bus Terminal, Neil St, in the town centre.
Ph: 131 499. Major interstate coachlines
operating services in the region include
Greyhound/Pioneer and **McCafferty's**.
The **Airport Flyer** offers door-to-door
delivery between Brisbane Airport and
Toowoomba. Ph: 1300 304 350

   The **City Bus** service operates in
Toowoomba and surrounds.
Ph: (07) 4633 1177. Inquire at info centres
or council offices about local bus services.

By rail

Countrylink has twice-weekly services
between Brisbane and Toowoomba,
continuing on through Oakey and Dalby
into the Golden West. Buses at
Toowoomba connect the train with other
district centres. Ph: 132 232

Getting around

Two taxi companies, **Yellow Cabs**
(Ph: 131 924) and **Garden City Cabs**
(Ph: 131 008) operate in Toowoomba.
The latter company also offers organised
or individual tours in its **Heritage
Toowoomba** limousines. Most of the
district centres also have a taxi service.
Inquire at info centres or local services.

Tea for 2
The **Toowoomba
Railway Refreshment
Rooms** are situated in
Toowoomba's oldest
public building, the
railway station,
constructed in 1874.

   Terranova Coach Tours has a day
trip from the Gold Coast to
Toowoomba, taking in a quick spin of
the sights along the way and in town.
Ph: (07) 5538 7113

   Toowoomba Live Steamers offers
steam-train rides each month in Heritage
Park (Spring St, Toowoomba) noon–4pm
(weather permitting) on the 3rd Sun of
the month.

Festivals and events
Cotton Week and Harvest Festival

Over 13 days in Mar, the town of **Dalby**
holds the combined Cotton Week and
Harvest Festival. The program of events
includes a Harvest Festival parade,
fireworks and novelty events such as
cotton-bale rolling. Ph: (07) 4662 1066

Crow's Nest Show

Held in early May, this show gives
Crow's Nest locals the chance to
celebrate their community while tourists
can simply enjoy the festivities.
Ph: (07) 4698 4174. (This is one
of several local shows held annually.
Contact info centres for dates and
details of other regional activities —
including rodeos, which are very popular
in these parts.)

Field Day

This event is held by the **Dalby** Pioneer
Park Museum on the 2nd Sun in May.
It is an opportunity to see the likes of late-
1800s threshers, a 1930s model reaper and
binder, and early hand-driven cornshellers
in motion. Ph: (07) 4662 4760

Working Draught Horse Expo

Over the Queen's Birthday weekend
(Jun), the **Jondaryan Woolshed** puts on a
show which shows these gentle giants of
an earlier era going through their paces.
Ph: (07) 4692 2229

National Open Rendezvous

The town of **Millmerran** is the national
headquarters of the Sporting Shooters
Association of Australia. Biennually
the association gathers in Jul for
a display of shooting skills.
Ph: (07) 4695 4235

Australian Heritage Festival

See the past come alive in 9 days of steam engines, scones and shearing. In late Aug/early Sept the **Jondaryan Woolshed** displays bush crafts and bush skills. Ph: (07) 4692 2229

Agricultural Show

The beginning of Sept heralds the 3-day **Toowoomba** 'Ag' Show. People travel from far and wide to display agricultural produce and machinery in the largest of such exhibitions in Qld. Ph: (07) 4634 1555

Carnival of Flowers

In Sept springtime blossoms in **Toowoomba**. The Carnival of Flowers allows both civic authorities and home gardeners to show off their blooms. There is also a Floral Parade, which in the past has included up to 100 floats. The carnival takes place in the last full week of the month and has been running since 1939. Ph: (07) 4632 4877

Crow's Nest Day

For almost 2 decades **Crow's Nest** has put on this day of fun and festivity. Highlights include the Combantrin Cup for worm-racing, and chainsaw competitions. The day is part of Crow's Nest Shire Week and usually falls on the 2nd-last Sat in Oct. Ph: (07) 4698 1505

Main localities and towns

Bell *Map 32 B2*

Bell *is* the Bunya Mts in a manner of speaking. This tiny town is set in the foothills of the Bunyas and its horizon is dominated by their imposing forms. Once a thriving rail terminus, the township is now a picturesque relic of colonial life, as well as being a regular Tidy Towns winner.

Among Bell's most interesting features are the hand-hewn stone-pitched drains constructed during the Great Depression from local sandstone, the **stone house** built by Scottish stonemasons in 1910, the colonial **Bellview Hotel**, and an enormous bunya tree of indeterminate age. A

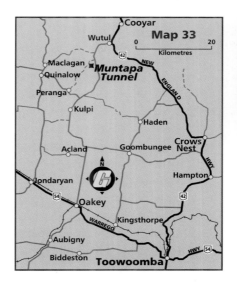

Clydesdale horses, Darling Downs

working **diesel train** (Dennis St) was one of the 1st 12 diesels in Australia. An even earlier historic feature is the **Bell Race Club** (Recreation Reserve). Organised horseracing began in the district before the establishment of the town itself, and quarterly meets still take place here.

Bell is 30min north of Dalby on the Bunya Hwy and is set in grain-growing country – as illustrated by the giant silos beside its railway line.

For more of the district's history, go NE and take a walk through an old railway tunnel. The 300m **Muntapa Tunnel walk** takes about 5min (see Map 33).

Crow's Nest *Map 32 D3, 35* ⑥

The town of Crow's Nest sits astride 2 creeks on the Great Dividing Ra and is consequently subject to seasonal changes, unlike many places in Qld. The pretty tree-lined 40km drive to the town from Toowoomba gives some hint of the pleasures it offers. Established in 1868 as a stopping post for timbergetters and drovers, Crow's Nest is now the district centre. It offers a fascinating insight into 19th-century and early 20th-century rural life as well as providing access to a host of attractions.

The **Crow's Nest Regional Art Gallery** is housed in the Shire Council building (New England Hwy). Open Tue–Sun, 10am–4pm. Ph: (07) 4698 1687

Stone house, Bell

The name of the crow

According to local legend, Crow's Nest got its name from an indigenous local called Jimmy Crow who lived in the area in the 1860s. He was said to live in a hollow tree, from which he greeted stockmen as they came into the newly established settlement. The land on which Jimmy Crow resided was used as a camping ground and became known as Jimmy Crow's Nest. Although there is a replica of the tree and a statue of 'Jimmy' in the town centre, at Centenary Park, these days locals are mindful of the complicated history of white settlement and, also, of the probable exaggeration of the original facts. Nonetheless, the name has now well and truly stuck. Perhaps in an effort to move away from its 'historical' meaning, the town has adoped a crow as its motif along with the line, 'Have a sticky beak at Crow's Nest'.

Town mural
The **Dalby Potters Mural**, located near the info centre and created for its opening in 1988, comprises 3 tablets representing the motto of the town:
Respice (look back)
Aspice (look around)
Prospice (look forward).

Not far away is the **Country Women's Association Hall** (New England Hwy), an attractive white timberboard edifice with blue trim. Next door is **Salts Antiques** (New England Hwy), housed in a double-fronted shop. Open Sat–Sun, 10am–4pm; weekdays by appt.
Ph: (07) 4698 1266

Only 1.5km down the New England Hwy lies the **Carbethon Folk Museum and Pioneer Village**. The centrepiece of the Pioneer Village is 'Carbethon', a house built over 130 years ago which sits alongside a shingle-roofed slab hut, butcher's shop, working printery and much more. The village is laid out as a street, allowing visitors a walk back in time. Partly wheelchair accessible. Open Thur and Sun, 1pm–5pm; public holidays, 10am–5pm. Ph: (07) 4698 1776

Dalby *Map 32 A3*

The road westwards to Dalby gives a sense of the town's frontier status as the silhouettes of power poles eerily punctuate the unending horizon. Settled in 1841, the town itself seemingly contains few traces of its pioneer status. The former **Ogden's Drapery** (now Thrifty's Fabrics, in Cunningham St), built in 1886, is the only shop retaining its original shopfront. It also houses its original cash railway (an apparatus moving money from one part of the

shop to another), only recently taken out of use.

However, what Dalby lacks in bricks and mortar it makes up for in an array of historical museums and memorabilia. Among these is the **Dalby Pioneer Park Museum** (3 Black St), which displays what is claimed to be the largest collection of working tractors and agricultural machinery in Qld. The museum also houses original colonial buildings which have been moved onsite and a dinosaur egg found in the district. Wheelchair accessible. Open daily, 9am–3pm. Ph: (07) 4662 4760

A unique memento of the past is what is said to be the only cairn to have been erected in commemoration of an insect. This is the **Cactoblastis Memorial Cairn** (Marble St), erected in 1965 by the Qld Historical Association in memory of the Cactoblastis moth's successful battle against the prickly pear infestation in the 1920s and 1930s.

Visit **Dalby Regional Gallery** (107 Drayton St) which exhibits the works of local artists in an ever-changing program of shows. Open Tue–Fri, 10am–4pm; weekends, 1pm–4pm. Ph: (07) 4660 6100

Dalby was officially founded and named by Captain Perry, Assistant Surveyor to the Colony of NSW. The name derives from the Swedish words

Jondaryan Woolshed, Jondaryan

dal, meaning 'dale', and *by*, 'town', and was purportedly chosen by Perry to commemorate a 'pretty little village' in the Isle of Man conquered by Vikings long ago. However, a man called Henry Dennis initially 'discovered' the site when he and a local Aborigine camped at what is now the **Crossing Monument** (near Edward St weir). Dennis called the site, and the creek that runs through the town, Myall Creek.

Dalby has an 18-hole golf course (p.183), a racecourse and bikeway and is the district centre for services and facilities.

Jondaryan *Map 32 B3*

Jondaryan is a stopping post on the way to several tourist attractions. SW of town is the **Jondaryan Woolshed**, a sheep station built in 1859 with space for 88 blade shearers to handle some 200 000 sheep a season. Here are gathered buildings from colonial life, such as a single-roomed schoolhouse, a bank and a cheese factory, as well a range of activities such as blacksmithing and sheepdog demonstrations. Damper and billy tea, as well as other refreshments, are available, and there is simple accommodation for those who wish to

DIY damper
Jondaryan Woolshed recipe
Ingredients
4 cups self-raising flour
2.5 cups cold water
pinch salt
Method
Bind ingredients together in a bowl with a knife until the dough leaves the side of the bowl. Do not knead. Cook in a hot oven for 45 mins. When cooked, turn upside-down to cool. When cool, cut and spread damper with butter and golden syrup.

Pioneer Park Museum, Dalby

The Empire
The **Empire Theatre**'s auditorium holds 1567 seats. As well as stage space, the Empire houses bars, function rooms, and a cafe and restaurant.

try life on the land. Wheelchair accessible. Open daily, 9am–4pm; tours 1pm (10.30am weekends). Ph: (07) 4692 2229

Nobby *Map 32 C5*

Nobby has 2 boasts to make: it is the one-time residence of 'Steele Rudd' (Arthur Hoey Davis) and the home of Sister Elizabeth Kenny, the nurse who developed a revolutionary treatment for polio victims in the mid-20th century. Davis, who lived from 1868–1935, had a block in the district for several years. He is best remembered for his 'Dad 'n' Dave' tales of a couple of small-time selectors doing it hard on the land.

At **Rudd's Pub and Museum** visitors can enjoy the Dad'n'Dave fittings and public readings from Rudd's work. Ph: (07) 4696 3211. Nearby is the **Sister Kenny Memorial**. Alternatively, walk through the tiny village or drive through the rich farmlands surrounding it. Sunflowers, sorghum and peanuts are just some of the crops grown here.

Oakey *Map 32 C4*

The little town of Oakey (pop. 4200) has as its main claim to fame the Army Aviation Centre, a major aviation defence facility initially established during WWII as an RAAF station. Within its grounds sits the **Flypast Museum of Australian Army Flying**. Here, aircraft from Australia's wartime history are on display, including the Bristol Boxkite, a plane used in WWI training, and the Blackhawk helicopter. Wheelchair accessible. Open Wed–Sun, 10am–4pm. Ph: (07) 4691 7666. The small **Oakey Historical Museum** is open on weekends.

Toowoomba *Map 34*

Toowoomba, also known as the 'Garden City of the West', is an oasis perched on the top of the Great Dividing Ra between a valley and a plain. Only 90min west of Brisbane, this regional centre has over 150 parks and gardens as well as a university and a sizeable commercial sector. Of especial renown are the camphor laurels lining its main streets and the Carnival of Flowers (p.173). Toowoomba is a city large enough to

divide itself into suburbs and yet small enough to retain its country charm.

One of Toowoomba's famous sights is the heritage-listed **Empire Theatre** (56 Neil St), the largest regional theatre in Australia. It features a grand proscenium arch believed to be the only one of its kind left in the world. The Empire opened as a silent movie house in 1911, burned down in 1933 and was rebuilt with an Art Deco design. With the advent of television the theatre was forced to close. It was reopened, after restoration, in 1996. Wheelchair accessible. Ph: 1300 655 299. www.toowoomba.qld.gov.au/Empire/

The **Toowoomba Railway Refreshment Rooms** (Railway St) is a charming spot to sit and sip tea. This Victorian edifice houses the only railway dining room left in Qld. Between noon and 2pm, Mon-Fri, counter lunches and silver service are offered. Wheelchair accessible. Ph: (07) 4631 3223

As settlement grew, the famous transport company Cobb & Co extended its business into the region. At the **Cobb & Co Museum** (27 Lindsay St), visitors can view the coaches that crossed both mountains and plains. Farm wagons, buggies and phaetons, and more than 45 horse-drawn carriages are also on display. Wheelchair accessible. Open daily, 9am–4pm. Ph: (07) 4639 1971

Road rage
Cobb & Co had rules for passengers displayed on notices in its carriages. These included no discussion of bushrangers, accidents, politics or religion, and no snoring or removal of shoes.

Cobb & Co Museum

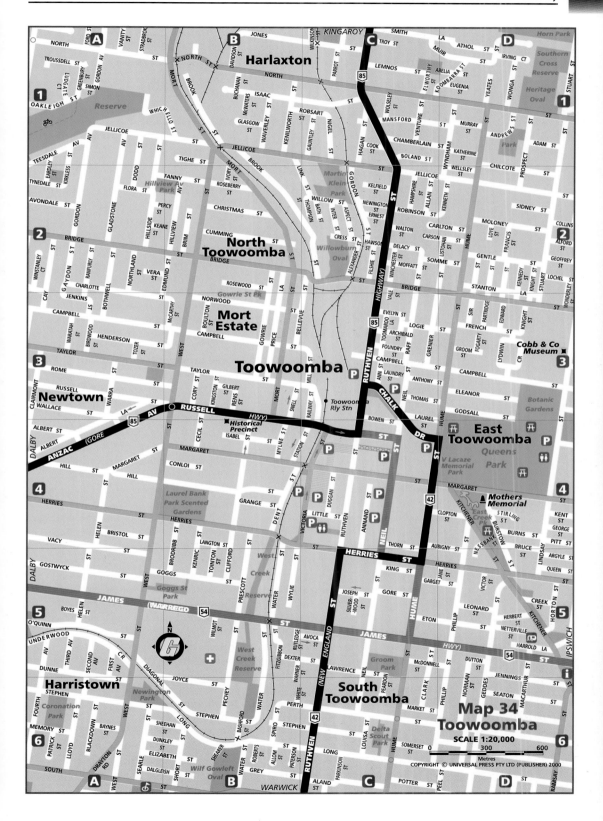

Map 34
Toowoomba

SCALE 1:20,000

0   300   600
Metres
COPYRIGHT © UNIVERSAL PRESS PTY LTD (PUBLISHER) 2000

Toowoomba, 'Garden City of the West'

Toowoomba is also home to many antique shops and artists. A brochure, *Toowoomba: Queensland Centre for Antiques and Art*, lists dealers and galleries and includes a guide map. The **Toowoomba Regional Art Gallery** (531 Ruthven St) is the oldest public art gallery in Qld. Established in 1938, the new gallery building was opened in 1994 and includes a library of rare books and manuscripts. There is a considerable holding of Australian art, including works by Tom Roberts and Lionel Lindsay. Wheelchair accessible. Open Tue-Sat and public holidays, 10am-4pm; Sun, 1pm-4pm. Ph: (07) 4688 6652

Toowoomba's history is well documented and there are plaques in many of its inner-city streets denoting the events and figures of the past. The pamphlet *A Walk Through History* takes visitors on a self-guided tour of the area where early settlement took place. Another pamphlet, *Toowoomba's Caledonian Estate Heritage Trail*, focuses on a walk through a slightly different area of the town, while *Tourist Drive 1* incorporates a short walk along Russell St into its larger walking/motoring survey of the town and its surrounds. Among Russell St's attractions is a 1919 urinal, which was Toowoomba's 1st sewerage connection. All pamphlets are available from the info centre or from public buildings such as the Art Gallery.

National parks, reserves and conservation parks

Crow's Nest NP *Map 32 D3*

A short drive east of Crow's Nest lies Crow's Nest NP. This is an enchanting spot for children of all ages with its easy walking tracks, waterfalls, a swimming hole and the famous **Valley of Diamonds** — a reference to the sparkling effect of sunlight on the rockface of a gorge not far inside the park entrance.

The 492ha of the **Falls section** of the park was established in 1905 as a recreation reserve and came under federal jurisdiction in 1967. Such care is rewarded by the abundance of native creatures such as rosellas and rock wallabies. Access to the park is from Crow's Nest. Camping is permitted, and there are BBQs, picnic tables and other facilities for day visitors. Wheelchair accessible. Ph: (07) 4639 8333

Lake Broadwater Conservation Park *Map 32 A3*

Lake Broadwater, located 30km SW of Dalby, is the only naturally occurring lake on the Darling Downs. It is situated in the Lake Broadwater Conservation Park, established in 1994. The park includes 870ha of vegetation and over 240 species of birds, including migrants from the Northern Hemisphere. Camping, boating, swimming and picnicking are all permitted. There is also a **natural-history museum**. Wheelchair accessible. Access is by a sealed road from Dalby.

Mt Basalt Reserve *Map 32 A5*

The geological formations pushing through the volcanic soils of the Mt Basalt Reserve, 19km south of Millmerran, distinguish this park. The reserve includes 7ha of scrub and several walking tracks. There are views of the surrounding farmlands as well as glimpses of the Condamine and MacIntyre catchments.

Ravensbourne NP *Map 32 D3*

Before the encroachment of white settlers, the Great Dividing Ra and its surrounds supported a number of natural environments, including rainforest, red

Crow's Nest NP

cedar forest and open eucalypt forest. Clearing by timbergetters and graziers razed these environments and destroyed much of the wildlife in them. The 440ha area, declared a national park in 1922, preserves an environment rich in flora and fauna now largely lost elsewhere.

Ravensbourne sits on a spur of the Great Dividing Ra between Toowoomba and Esk (p.133). It is easily accessible for daytrippers and most walks are less than 1km. Access is via Hampton on the New England Hwy or from Esk. Picnic

facilities, including fireplaces and BBQs, are available. Wheelchair accessible.

Toowoomba Bicentennial Waterbird Habitat *Map 32 C4*

This acclaimed reserve (cnr Alderley and Mackenzie Sts, Toowoomba) is the result of the vision of a single man, Ken Ferrier. He saw the possibility of restoring the 7.6ha site to its original state: a wetland environment of lakes, mudflats, marshes, islands and grasslands. In 1988 the city council completed the restoration project

Condamine Bell

Bullock trains were last century's diesel trucks. They carried timber and wool out of the Downs and brought back essential supplies. Bells for the bullocks were required so that a teamster could locate his animals after they were unyoked for the night. The greater the carrying sound of the bell, the more effective it was.

In the little town of Condamine — sharing its name with the Condamine River which winds its way through the Downs — a bell was made in the 1860s or 70s by the local blacksmith, S W Jones. This bell was famous for the quality of its carrying power and became known as the Condamine Bell. Some claimed that they could hear its ring 6 or 7 miles away. The model was distinguished by the stamp on its tongue. Orders for it came from as far afield as Western Australia — a feat all the more remarkable given that Australia, or the colonies that eventually made up the federation, was at that time still being settled by the British.

Lake Broadwater Conservation Park

A beer a day ...
The **Farmers Arms Tavern** at Cabarlah, established in 1863, is Qld's oldest surviving hotel.

and today its commitment to Ferrier's vision can be enjoyed by everyone.

Birds living in the habitat include the white-faced heron, Australian pelican, black-winged stilt and sacred ibis. There are platforms and a hide for birdwatchers. Wheelchair accessible (in part).

Parks and gardens

Brindabella Country Gardens *Map 32 C4*

Old World charm meets New World panache at these English-style gardens (cnr New England Hwy and Quinlan Rd) 2km north of **Toowoomba**. The gardens, with a nursery attached, include a maple walk, formal rose garden and rhododendron woodland. Wheelchair accessible. Open Fri–Sun and public holidays, 9am–5pm. Ph: (07) 4696 8440

Ensor Park *Map 32 B2*

Ensor Park, in the pretty town of **Bell**, was originally the site of the town water supply. The water proved too brackish for use so locals had to depend on rainwater. These days the park is a picnic spot, with tables and BBQs. Wheelchair accessible.

Japanese Gardens *Map 32 C4*

Sink into the stillness of the beautiful Japanese Gardens (West St, **Toowoomba**), located at the **University of Southern Qld**. These are the largest Japanese gardens in Australia and are a perfect place to rest feet, eyes and mind. Wheelchair accessible. Open daily, 7am–7pm. Ph: (07) 4631 2100

Lake Cooby *Map 32 C3*

Loveday Cove, at Lake Cooby, is the site of the Darling Downs Sailing Club, one of the many features of this pretty artificial lake. Walking, fishing and boating are all permitted, and picnickers are welcome to loll on the grassy surrounds.

Lake Cooby is 28km north of **Toowoomba**, with a turnoff from the New England Hwy at either Highfields or the Borneo Barracks, Cabarlah. Picnic tables and BBQs are available and there is some wheelchair accessibility.

Lake Cressbrook *Map 32 D3*

The newest of the 3 lakes created for Toowoomba's water supply, Lake Cressbrook offers a range of outdoor activities such as camping, fishing, sailing, rowing and windsurfing. There is also a playground with basketball hoop and a volleyball court. The lake is set in native bushland 58km NE of **Toowoomba**, not far from Crow's Nest. Some wheelchair accessibility.

Lake Perseverance *Map 35* ❽

Lake Perseverance is an artificial lake located 53km NE of **Toowoomba**. As well as being used for the supply of water to Toowoomba, Lake Perseverance is a great spot for waterskiing, walking and picnicking. Tables and wood BBQs are supplied; some wheelchair accessibility.

Laurel Bank Park *Map 34 B4*

Tucked away in the SE corner of this park (Herries St, **Toowoomba**) are the **Scented Gardens**, especially designed for the enjoyment of the visually impaired. The park has good recreational facilities, including picnic tables. Wheelchair accessible.

Queens Park *Map 34 D4*

Take a stroll through Queens Park (Margaret St, **Toowoomba**), home of the city's Botanic Gardens. The 60ha park is located in one of the older parts of town and sits between tree-lined streets filled with gracious colonial homes. There are stands of giant camphor laurels, and one area (bounded by Campbell and Lindsay Sts) features magnificent flower displays in spring and summer.

There are also picnic tables, BBQs, bikeways and an array of play equipment, and cafes are close at hand. Wheelchair accessible. On the 3rd Sun of every month a **craft fair** is held here, offering a range of handmade wares, carriage rides and fun for the whole family.

Picnic Pt *Map 35* ❶

Look out on the Lockyer Valley and Tabletop Mt from this favourite local picnic spot. Grimmer memories reside in the rockface: basalt rocks quarried here

Queens Park, Toowoomba

were used to build the Toowoomba Gaol, opened in 1864. A more notable feature these days is the mushroom-shaped watertower. Picnic Pt, at an altitude of 710m, has walking tracks, parklands, picnic and dining facilities. Wheelchair accessible.

Table Top Park *Map 32 C4*

This escarpment park, on the eastern edge of **Toowoomba**, is also the site of one of the most bloody battles of resistance by the original inhabitants of the area, the Jagara people, led by Multuggerah, in 1843. Now it is a place for walkers. The naturally treeless summit is a 1.9km return trek.

Thomas Jack Park *Map 32 A3*

Thomas Jack Park (Drayton St, **Dalby**), named after a prominent local business-man who was mayor of the town for many years, houses the district's tourist info centre and offers 4ha of parklands for play and picnicking. It features a playground, lily pond, picnic tables and gas BBQs, as well as shady foliage for hot travellers. Wheelchair accessible.

Other attractions

Acland Coal Mine Museum *Map 35* ❶

At the time of its closure in 1984, the Acland coal mine (Francis St, **Acland**) was the last (and smallest) colliery in Australia to winch up coal in small skips. It is now a museum, and guided tours are offered. Open Mon–Tue (and in Feb) by appt; Wed–Sun, 9am–5pm. Ph: (07) 4691 5703

Black Forest Hill *Map 35* ❷

This unusual attraction on the New England Hwy, at **Cabarlah**, is a little bit of Germany far from home. Located between Toowoomba and Crow's Nest, the commercial centre features handcarved cuckoo clocks in all shapes and sizes as well as steins and strudel. Wheelchair accessible (in part). Open daily, 9am–5pm. Ph: (07) 4696 6100

Danish Flower Art *Map 35* ❸

A working farm 13km north of Toowoomba, Danish Flower Art (New England Hwy, **Highfields**) has flower

Danish Flower Art, Highfields

and garden walks, a hothouse, picnic and playground areas, and amazing dried flower displays. Wheelchair accessible. Open daily, 9am–5pm. Ph: (07) 4640 8211

Highfields Old School Gallery *Map 32 C4*

The original schoolhouse of the district (New England Hwy, **Highfields**), built in the 1870s, now houses works by local artists, as well as the Chocolate Cottage and Cafe. Wheelchair accessible. Open Wed–Mon, 10am–5pm (8.30am on Sun for breakfast). Ph: (07) 4630 8729

Highfields Orchid Park *Map 32 C4*

This park at Highfields Rd, **Highfields**, has one of the largest orchid displays in Australia. The flowering season is from Apr–Oct, peaking Jul–Sept. Wheelchair accessible. Open daily, 8am–5pm. Ph: (07) 4630 8220

Highfields Pioneer Park and Museum *Map 32 C4*

One of the more unusual attractions at the Highfields Pioneer Park and Museum (Wirraglen Rd, **Highfields**) is the 40 000 seashells and coral pieces making up the Rose Peters Shell and Coral Collection, said to be one of the largest such collections in Qld. The Pioneer Park and Museum also houses one of the 1st Toowoomba fire trucks, the tiny boot repair premises of an early resident of the area, and a chapel used for much of this

**Flower power
Geranium Oil Farm**
(Robinson Rd, Geham) sells essential oils and other aromatic products made from farm produce. Open daily. Ph: (07) 4696 6125

Agricultural history

The antique tractor on the roof of **Jimbour Public Hall** was the first tractor to be used on the Jimbour plains.

Highfields Pioneer Park

century in nearby Meringandan. Picnic tables and large grounds are available. Wheelchair accessible. Open daily, 10am–4pm. Ph: (07) 4696 6309

Home of Herbs *Map 32 C4*

Winner of the 1996 and 1997 Carnival of Flowers industrial garden competition, these gardens, at Greenridge Botanicals (17 Freighter Ave, **Toowoomba**), give a fascinating glimpse into the healing power of herbs. The gardens are divided into culinary, aromatic and medicinal herbs, with more than 300 varieties. Wheelchair accessible. Open for weekend or group tours (with educational talk) by appt. Ph: (07) 4633 1202

Jimbour House *Map 32 A2*

In 1874–76 a 40-room mansion was built at **Jimbour Stn**, a giant holding claimed as pastoral land in 1841. The name comes from the local word *jimba* or *gimba*, meaning 'good pastures'. The German explorer Ludwig Leichhardt, immortalised in Patrick White's novel *Voss*, organised his last ill-fated expedition to cross Australia from the property in 1848.

In the 20th century the mansion and its grounds have been maintained by the Russell family, who bought the station in 1923. As a result of the Russells' vision

and generosity, visitors are now able to stroll through the gardens and admire the imposing edifice of the house, made from local sandstone and lime, and cedar from the Bunya Mts. The approach is by Jandowae Rd from Dalby or via Bell.

Rimfire Vineyards and Winery *Map 32 C2*

Located just 35km north of Jondaryan on Bismarck St, **Maclagan**, the winery's label depicts its lovely surrounds in the form of a bunya tree, an expanse of fertile croplands and the Bunya Mts on the horizon. Open daily for tastings, refreshments and wine sales, 10am–5pm. Wheelchair accessible. Ph: (07) 4692 1129

Spring Bluff Railway Stn and gardens *Map 35* ❷

In 1914 Qld Railways launched a competition to encourage railway staff to beautify stations. The stationmaster and staff of Spring Bluff, a little station on a steeply sloped part of the Ipswich-Toowoomba line near **Toowoomba**, took up the challenge and over many years built magnificent landscaped gardens. It is estimated that over 22 000 working hours were put into the effort.

Today, the gardens are a major tourist attraction and the station and surrounding dwellings, such as the

Claim to fame

Jimbour House was used as a setting for the 1980s Australian TV miniseries 'Return to Eden', which starred Rebecca Gilling and James Reyne.

Bargain hunting

Markets in the region include:

★ **Every Sun:** PCYC Markets
(219a James St, Toowoomba)
and Wilsonton Undercover Markets
(Wilsonton Shopping Centre,
Toowoomba)

★ **1st Sun of the month:** Boulevard
Craft Markets (Margaret St,
Toowoomba) and USQ Markets
(USQ, West St, Toowoomba)

★ **3rd Sun of the month:** Queens Park
Craft Markets (Queens Park, Margaret
St, Toowoomba)

★ **4th Sun of the month:**
Cabarlah Country Markets (Cabarlah
Sports Ground, New England Hwy,
Cabarlah).

stationmaster's residence, have been
restored. A steam train runs from
Toowoomba to Spring Bluff during
the Carnival of Flowers (p.173), with
additional specials from Brisbane.
The gardens are wheelchair accessible.
Ph: (07) 4688 6644

Recreational activities

Action

Bushland Park, only 1hr from
Toowoomba at the foot of the Bunya
Mts, offers a chance to get away from it
all in redgum forest mixed with rainforest
and vine scrub. Camping, horseriding and
guided walks are among the organised
attractions. Ph: (07) 4663 4717

For a faster pace, try **Toowoomba
Indoor Race Karts** (7 Freighter St,
Toowoomba). Open daily; times vary.
Ph: (07) 4633 2980

In the air

Get a bird's eye view of the Downs with
the **Darling Downs Soaring Club**.
Located between Jondaryan and
Bowenville on Mason's Rd, the club
offers joy flights, tuition and
accommodation for individuals and groups

wishing to take extensive training courses.
Ph: (07) 4632 5228 or (07) 4635 0991;
(07) 4663 7140 (weekends)

Cycling

Toowoomba has over 70km of bikeways
for the keen cyclist, and a gently
undulating terrain. A council guide,
Discover Toowoomba's Bikeways, is
available from local businesses and public
centres. **Dalby** also has a bikeway
adjacent to Myall Creek.

Golf

Aim for a hole in one at any of the many
golf courses in the region. These include
Toowoomba courses **City Golf Club**,
254 South St (Ph: (07) 4635 2120),
Eustondale 9 Hole Golf Course,
88 Euston Rd (Ph: (07) 4630 2220) and
Toowoomba Golf Club, Rowbotham St,
Middle Ridge (Ph: (07) 4635 1219).
Outside the city, golf enthusiasts
can try **Crow's Nest Golf Course**
(Ph: (07): 4698 1408), **Borneo Barracks
Golf Course**, Borneo Barracks, Cabarlah
(Ph: (07) 4696 6748), **Bell and District
Golf Club** (Ph: (07) 4662 2939) or
Dalby Golf Club (Ph: (07) 4662 1696).

Wagon holiday
Bottle Tree Pk, near
the town of Bell,
offers horse-drawn
wagon holidays for
the whole family.
Ph: (07) 4663 1179

Fun for the young

★ Black Forest Hill, Cabarlah (p.181)
★ Cobb & Co Museum, Toowoomba
(p.176)
★ Jondaryan Woolshed, Jondaryan
(p.175)
★ Flypast Museum of Australian Army
Flying, Oakey (p.176)
★ Highfields Pioneer Park and Museum
Highfields(p.181)
★ Lake Broadwater Conservation Park
(p.178)
★ Queens Park Craft Fair, Toowoomba
(p.183)
★ Toowoomba Bicentennial Waterbird
Habitat (p.179)
★ Valley of Diamonds, Crow's Nest
(p.178)

Darling Downs

Suggested tours – Map 35

Plains tour

Approximate distance

550km return from Brisbane CBD

About the tour

This is a drive through the rich farmlands and the history of the Darling Downs. Long roads curve through cotton fields and millet crops, with stops at sites of local industry and human drama. Visit the tiny Acland Coal Mine Museum and imagine the miners working in these cramped conditions. Take time to find the Old Station Cemetery, at Cecil Plains. Many of the headstones are made of timber. Also on the topic of the afterlife, All Saints Anglican Church, near Millmerrran, has a tiny cemetery. In the oldest grave lies an overseer who was murdered in 1864. The carpenter who murdered him was the 1st person hanged in Toowoomba.

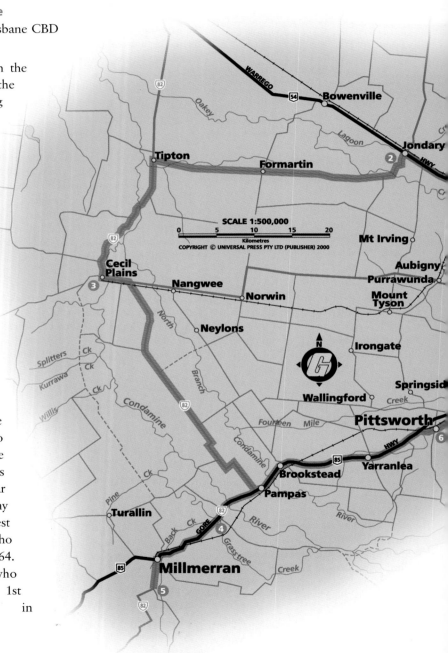

Places of interest

❶ **Acland Coal Mine Museum** (p.181)

❷ **Jondaryan Woolshed** (p.175)

❸ **Old Station Cemetery, Cecil Plains**

❹ **All Saints Anglican Church, Yandilla**

❺ **Mt Basalt Reserve** (p.178)

❻ **Pittsworth**

❼ **Drayton**

❽ **Margaret St eateries, Toowoomba**

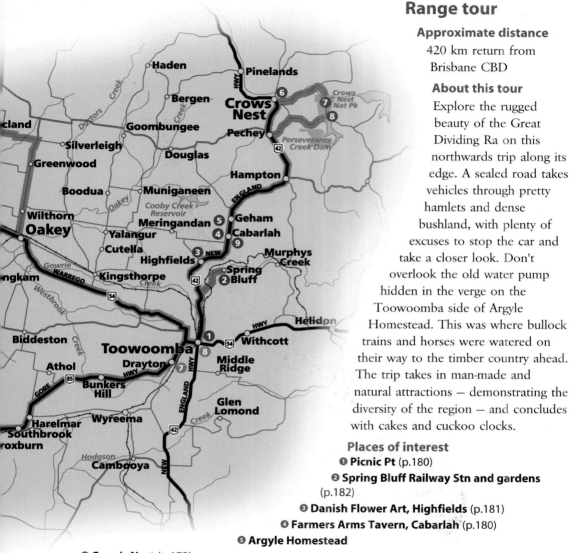

Range tour

Approximate distance

420 km return from Brisbane CBD

About this tour

Explore the rugged beauty of the Great Dividing Ra on this northwards trip along its edge. A sealed road takes vehicles through pretty hamlets and dense bushland, with plenty of excuses to stop the car and take a closer look. Don't overlook the old water pump hidden in the verge on the Toowoomba side of Argyle Homestead. This was where bullock trains and horses were watered on their way to the timber country ahead. The trip takes in man-made and natural attractions — demonstrating the diversity of the region — and concludes with cakes and cuckoo clocks.

Places of interest

❶ **Picnic Pt** (p.180)

❷ **Spring Bluff Railway Stn and gardens** (p.182)

❸ **Danish Flower Art, Highfields** (p.181)

❹ **Farmers Arms Tavern, Cabarlah** (p.180)

❺ **Argyle Homestead**

❻ **Crow's Nest** (p.173)

❼ **Valley of Diamonds, Crow's Nest NP** (p.178)

❽ **Lake Perseverance** (p.180)

❾ **Black Forest Hill, Cabarlah** (p.181)

Royal Bulls Head Inn, Drayton

Queensland's
SOUTHERN ✿ DOWNS
TOURIST • ASSOCIATION • INC

Left: **Mountain country, Southern Downs**
Right: **Queen Mary Falls**

Warwick, Stanthorpe and the Southern Downs

West of Cunningham's Gap the high, open country of the Southern Downs unfolds. The peaks of the Great Dividing Ra ease out to undulating pastures and rich farmland, skirted by ridges and dotted with small historic towns. At the city of Warwick, the sense of history is set in the sandstone of its fine old buildings.

Farther south the land rises steadily. The unsealed byroads glitter with quartz, and the coarse soil is broken by boulders of mythic size. Orchards and vineyards replace the sweep of pasture and grain. This is the famous Granite Belt. The orchard trees are loaded with apples, nectarines, peaches and plums, and the grapevines deck the trellises with arabesques of fragrant fruit. Winter brings sharp frosts, and the air is crackling-cold.

In the rugged border country is Girraween NP, famous for its spectacular granite monoliths. These are rocks on a heroic scale, dominating the scene with bands of deep shadow and planes of brilliant light. With spring come the wildflowers. Stringybark gums, grasstrees, vines and bushes all flush with blossom, softening the austere landscape with scumbles of pastel colour.

ℹ Tourist information

Allora Tourist Information Centre
Allora Cafe, 78 Herbert St,
Allora 4362
Ph: (07) 4666 3161

Naturally Queensland Information Centre (EPA)
(info on national parks)
Ground Floor, 160 Ann St,
Brisbane 4000
Ph: (07) 3227 8185
www.env.qld.gov.au

Stanthorpe Visitor Information Centre
28 Leslie Pde,
Stanthorpe 4380
Ph: (07) 4681 2057

Warwick Visitor Information Centre
49 Albion St,
Warwick 4370
Ph: (07) 4661 3122

Must see, must do

★ **Granite Belt wineries** (p.204)

★ **Heritage Trail buildings, Warwick** (p.194)

★ **The Pyramid, Girraween NP** (p.199)

★ **Queen Mary Falls** (p.201)

★ **Spicer's Gap** (p.200)

Radio stations

4GR Toowoomba: AM 864

4AK Toowoomba: AM 1242

4WK Toowoomba: AM 1359, 963

FM 88.0 Warwick: FM 88.0 (tourist info)

Country Classics: FM 88.4

4DDB FM: FM 102.7

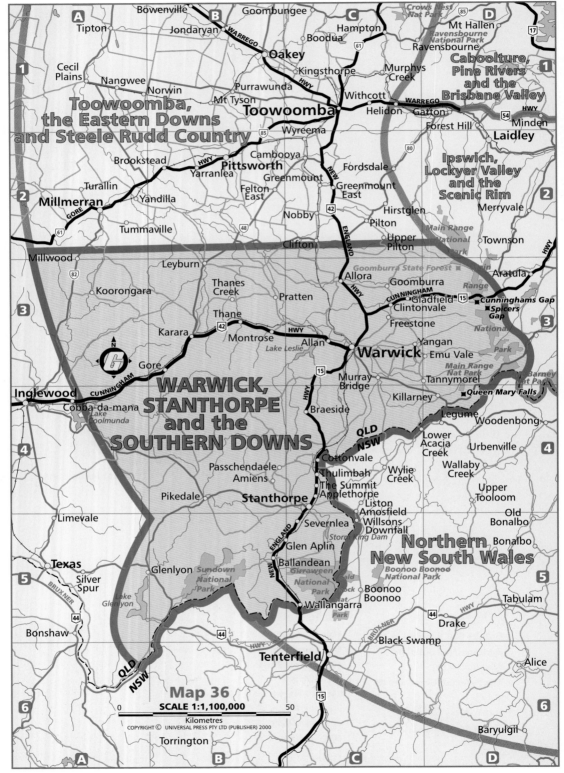

Map 36

SCALE 1:1,100,000

0   50

Kilometres

COPYRIGHT © UNIVERSAL PRESS PTY LTD (PUBLISHER) 2000

Natural features

West of Cunningham's Gap is the rich pastoral and grain-growing country of the Southern Downs. To the south, as the land rises, the deep, black earth of the Downs gives way to sandy soils, scrubby vegetation and immense granite boulders. This landscape is the result of volcanic activity that occurred here about 250 million years ago. The cool, dry mountain climate and the well-drained soils make this the temperate-fruit orchard of Qld. The air is invigoratingly crisp; in winter the temperature occasionally drops so low that snow falls.

In the rugged region south of Stanthorpe are 2 national parks — Girraween to the east and Sundown to the west. Girraween's granite terrain is the result of a complex history of volcanic activity, uplift and weathering, producing the amazing 'balancing rocks' of the region. Sundown NP, by contrast, is based on traprock, a dense rock composed of ancient marine sediments transformed under intense heat and pressure. Subsequent folding, faulting and weathering have produced a forbidding landscape of ridges and gorges.

Eastward, past Killarney, the road passes through dun-coloured hills speckled with eucalypts and hemmed in by ridges covered with a dark pelt of rainforest. Streams descend the mountains in a series of waterfalls, carving gorges through the strata of basalt and trachyte.

History

In 1827, botanist-explorer Allan Cunningham came upon 'a sumptuous pastoral country', the home of the Kambu Wal people, and called it the Darling Downs. The following year, he found the Gap that now bears his name.

The Leslie brothers took up land on the Downs in 1840, establishing the 1st free settlement in the Moreton Bay district and a thriving pastoral industry. As the wool industry burgeoned, the need to find a safe route to Moreton Bay became urgent. The route through Cunningham's Gap had proved to be too steep, and in 1857 local squatters built a track through Spicer's Gap, to the south. The road that superseded it in the 1860s was a model of the latest construction techniques.

Early in the 1870s tin was discovered at Quart Pot Creek, and the settlement of Stanthorpe was born. Later, commercial orchards were planted there. The first planting of grapes in the district occurred at Ballandean in 1859, and since the 1960s the wine industry has flourished. The Granite Belt has now established itself as Qld's premier wine district.

Cunningham's Gap
This eroded break in Main Ra was known to the local Aborigines as Cappoong.

Granite terrain, Girraween

Rough going
Allan Cunningham observed in his journal that the **Granite Belt** was 'a bold, rocky region of wild and frightful aspect'.

As well as the pastoralists and tin-miners of the early days, there were several waves of settlers in the area — German migrants in the 1890s, Italians and soldier-settlers after WWI, and Italian POWs and migrants during and after WWII.

Getting there

By road

Most travellers enter the Southern Downs via Cunningham's Gap, where the highway climbs the range through rainforest, overshadowed by the dramatic cliffs of Mt Cordeaux to the north and Mt Mitchell to the south. On the highway, 300m beyond the turnoff to Kamp Stacey (to the north), is the Main Ra NP Headquarters and Info Centre.

The New England Hwy follows the length of the Downs north–south, cross-ing the border with NSW at Wallangarra. Most of the towns, orchards and wineries of the Southern Downs are situated on or near the highway, or on scenic byroads that branch off it to the east and west.

Girraween NP can be reached by following Pyramids Rd, a 9km bitumen road that turns off the New England Hwy to the east 26km south of Stanthorpe or 11km north of Wallangarra.

To reach Sundown NP and Lake Glenlyon, take the Stanthorpe-Texas road, turning off to the east along Permanents Rd for Sundown and to the west, further south, for Lake Glenlyon.

4WDing, Sundown NP

Follow the Warwick-Killarney road SE for the Upper Condamine Valley, Killarney and the Queen Mary Falls area of the Great Dividing Ra. Alternatively, take the road east from Stanthorpe to join up with the Mt Lindesay Hwy, and then branch off to the NE just before Killarney. The Killarney-Boonah road leads past Queen Mary Falls and on through other parts of the Main Ra NP, before descending into the Fassifern Valley. Parts of this road are unsealed, steep and winding.

To explore Spicer's Gap, take Spicer's Gap Rd, which leaves the Cunningham Hwy 5km west of Aratula. The western approach, which turns off the Cunningham Hwy 1.5km west of the Main Ra NP Info Centre, passes through private property and is for 4WDs only.

Crisps Coaches, based in Warwick, services the Southern Downs and connects the region with Toowoomba and Brisbane (Transit Centre, Roma St). Ph: (07) 3236 5266

Greyhound Pioneer has a twice-daily interstate service from the Brisbane Transit Centre, stopping at several centres, including Toowoomba, Allora, Warwick, Stanthorpe and Wallangarra. Ph: 132 030

McCafferty's Express Coaches has a daily interstate service via Toowoomba, Warwick and Stanthorpe. The coaches also stop at smaller centres on request. Ph: 131 499

By rail

Passengers are no longer carried on the Brisbane-Wallangarra line, which for many years serviced the Southern Downs. (See p.191 for rail tours.)

Getting around

The Southern Downs, aside from the areas within the national parks, are best explored by car. Several scenic drives, such as the Allora-Clifton Tourist Drive and the 'Fruit Run' (Scenic Route 3) north of Stanthorpe, loop through the countryside in the vicinity of the New England Hwy. Many of these drives are unsealed, but they are generally easy going.

Australian 4WD Adventures has full-day tag-along tours in the Southern Downs through terrain not otherwise accessible to the public. Ph: (07) 4666 3668

South West Safaris, based in Stanthorpe, runs half- and full-day 4WD winery tours, and trips to the eastern and western ranges. Ph: (07) 4681 3685

Australian Fine Food Tours offers a Tastes of the Southern Downs Tour — an overnight trip from Brisbane to Granite Belt farms, sampling the fruit and vegetables of the season (stone fruits, asparagus, mushrooms, leeks and raspberries), and the local wine. Ph: (07) 3201 0258

Girraween Country Wine Tours runs half-day and full-day tours through the Granite Belt wineries daily. It also offers an Arts Tour, a Heritage Tour and other tours on request. Ph: (07) 4683 7002

Granite Highlands Maxi Tours, Stanthorpe, arranges minibus tours to the Granite Belt wineries, from Heritage Wines in the north to Bald Mountain Vineyards in the south, with Brisbane and Gold Coast departures. Ph: (07) 4681 3969

For tours to several wineries, with lunch, contact **The Grape Escape** in Stanthorpe. Ph: (07) 4681 4761

Lingalonga Tours conducts day-long tours of various wineries from Warwick and a range of other tours of the Southern Downs. Ph: (07) 4661 7504

Murray Gardens, Pancor Rd, Stanthorpe, has winery tours on request. Ph: (07) 4681 4121

For 2-day wildlife, winery and national park tours in comfortable 4WD minibuses, try **Never Never Safaris**, based at Murwillumbah. The tours leave from Brisbane and the Gold Coast. Ph: (02) 6679 1575

Panoramic Coaches, based at Warwick, runs tours of all the Southern Downs areas. It has a daily service to Killarney. Ph: (07) 4661 2816

Time Out conducts 2-day and 3-day tours of the Granite Belt, leaving from Brisbane and the Gold Coast. Ph: 1800 689 001

Red Gum Ridge Trail Rides offers half-day tours of the Granite Belt wineries in a horse-drawn carriage. Ph: (07) 4683 7169

The Australian Railway Historical Society, trading as **Sunshine Express Rail Tours**, runs Winelander Tours from Brisbane to the Granite Belt when carriages are available. The train stops at Toowoomba, Warwick and Stanthorpe, where most passengers alight for the wineries. Some continue on to Wallangarra. Ph: (07) 3371 4231 for details of scheduled tours.

Festivals and events
Allora Sunflower Festival
This festival is held on the 1st weekend in Feb, when Allora's famous sunflowers are in bloom. It is part of the Allora Show, and a Grand Parade is held in the showgrounds. Ph: (07) 4666 3394. During the festival, Scarecrow Tours are conducted by the Allora Scouts. Ph: (07) 4666 3461

Apple and Grape Harvest Festival
This festival, held in **Stanthorpe** in Feb every 2nd year, celebrates the autumn harvests. Ph: (07) 4681 2057

Annual Autumn Flower Show
This event is held in **Warwick**, 'City of Roses', in Mar. The venue is the Railway Institute Hall, Hamilton St, and the display includes fruit and vegetables as well as flowers. Ph: (07) 4661 1414

Sunflowers, Allora

National Rock Swap Festival

Anyone looking for a lively event at Easter can try this popular gem, minerals and fossils show at the **Warwick Showgrounds**. The festival also features crafts and collectibles of every kind. It is one of the biggest Easter events in the state. Ph: (07) 4661 2427

Opera in the Vineyard

This open-air, black-tie charity event is held in May at **Ballandean Estate Winery**. It features top-name singers and everyone's favourite arias from a range of operas. There is a buffet lunch, post-prandial-to-sunset concert and gala dinner dance. Ph: (07) 4684 1226

Bush Week

This 10-day 'week' is celebrated in the **Warwick district** in May. It is crammed with activities and events, including a Tall Stories night, a wheelie-bin race, several days of motorcar events, an Irish night at Allora and Goomburra, displays of arts and crafts, food and wines of the Downs, a sports day, the Killarney Horse Race, a golf day, bush poetry and a bush band. Ph: (07) 4661 5046

Gardening Extravaganza

Nurseries and other organisations connected with gardening exhibit at this expo, usually held in the **Warwick Show Pavilion** in Jun. Ph: (07) 4661 1414

The Brass Monkey Season

This is a 3-month (Jun, Jul and Aug) Granite Belt celebration of winter, season of sharp frosts, occasional snowfalls, mulled wine and open fires. It features a smorgasbord of events at various places throughout the season, such as Christmas dinner at **Happy Valley** and a traditional German dinner at **Das Helwig Haus**, Glen Aplin. Ph: (07) 4681 2057

Warwick Rose and Rodeo Festival

This month-long festival in Oct culminates in a carnival, a parade and the famous Warwick Rodeo on the last weekend. Ph: (07) 4661 9060

Granite Belt Spring Wine Festival

Each winery in the district holds its own function at this festival, held on the 1st and 2nd weekends in Oct. Ph: (07) 4681 2057

Spring Flower Show

Held in Oct during the Warwick Rose and Rodeo Festival, when Warwick's spring flowers are at their best. The show includes a floral shop-window competition and a horticultural display, usually at the **Warwick Show Pavilion**. Ph: (07) 4661 1414

Legacy Flanders Poppy Festival of Faith

This Nov event commemorates the end of WWI and honours those who died. It is held in the Remembrance Field at Das Helwig Haus, Mt Stirling Rd, **Glen Aplin**. Ph: (07) 4683 4227

Allora and District Garden Competition

The open days for this competition are in mid-Nov. Rural and township gardens are featured. Ph: (07) 4666 3161

Killarney Light Spectacular

The Christmas lights competition is a long-standing Killarney tradition, setting the town a-twinkle throughout Dec. Ph: (07) 4661 3122

Saddle bronc ride, Warwick

Main towns

For ease of reference, towns have been listed alphabetically in 2 sections: the Downs and the Granite Belt.

The Downs

Allora *Map 36 C3*

The historic township of Allora, 'best little town on the Downs', is set among fields of wheat and sunflowers and ringed by basalt ridges. It dates back to 1844, when an outstation of Patrick Leslie's Goomburra sheep property was set up at a crossing on Dalrymple Creek. It later became a bullockies' stop on the supply route to the Southern Downs station, and pubs and other services soon sprang up there. In 1859, the year of Qld's separation from NSW, the area was surveyed and the 1st town allotments were sold. The original townsfolk were a varied lot, principally Scottish, English, Irish and German.

Allora has retained much of its colonial character. Its old timber houses are in low-set, southern style, each sporting at least 1 chimney. Visitors may be startled by the sight of quaintly dressed figures lounging about front gardens, leaning on gates and perched on bicycles. These are household versions of the scarecrows that watch over the district's crops of sunflower seed. Demonstrations of scarecrow-making are held in the Community Hall. Ph: (07) 4666 3161

The town centre, too, has a 19th-century ambience, with wooden shop fronts and verandahed pubs shaded by camphor laurels. On the New England Hwy on the eastern side of the town is **St David's Anglican Church**, a classically proportioned building completed in 1888. The architect, F D G Stanley, also designed the cedar pews. Group visits by appt. Ph: (07) 4666 3786

The **Fallen Soldiers' memorial** in Warwick St, erected in 1904 after the Boer War, was the 1st war memorial in Qld. The statue is the work of Sydney sculptor William MacIntosh. Like most Australian war memorials, it is not triumphalist, but it includes some unusual details — the soldier's moustache, corduroy trousers and water bottle.

Allora Museum, 27 Drayton St, is in the original courthouse (built 1866). It houses a collection of domestic items, farm implements and photographs from the district's early days. Open Sun, 1.30pm–4pm or by appt. Ph: (07) 4666 3649

Nearby are the heritage-listed Talgai and Glengallan Homesteads. **Talgai**, dating from the 1860s, is a gracious, low-set country homestead on Dalrymple Creek Rd, 7km along South St west of Allora. Though still a family home, it has a restaurant and accommodation, and welcomes day visitors by appt (except on Sat). Ph: (07) 4666 3444. **Glengallan**, a 10min drive south on the New England

Glengallan Homestead

The 'Mary Poppins House', Allora

Mary Poppins

P L Travers, author of the children's book *Mary Poppins*, lived at 61 Herbert St, **Allora** as a child, and the town's houses were the inspiration for the story's setting

Longest journey
At **Tierny Park**, on the
Condamine River, is a
sign announcing that
Killarney stands at
'the start of the
longest river system
in Australia' (the
Murray-Darling).

Hwy and visible from the road, is a
2-storey sandstone mansion built in 1867
and presently undergoing restoration.
Open 10am–2pm on the 2nd and 4th
Suns of the month or by appt.
Ph: (07) 4666 3517

The 'Mary Poppins' houses, whimsical
scarecrows, shady creekside parks and
summer blaze of sunflowers make Allora
one of the most visitable towns on the
Southern Downs.

The Goomburra turnoff from the New
England Hwy south of Allora leads 36km
to Goomburra State Forest (p.199).

Killarney *Map 36 D4*

Killarney stands on the upper reaches of
the Condamine River in the rolling
western foothills of the Great Dividing Ra.
It is a centre for processing timber,
onions, potatoes and meat. The river
splits the town into 2 distinct parts;
North Killarney, the older part, is the
town centre. There is a tourist map in the
main street (outside the Child and Family
Health Centre), which shows points of
interest around the town. The **Killarney
Heritage Centre** in the old School of Arts
building is open Sat-Sun, 10am–2pm.

To the east of Killarney the mountains
rise steeply. Here the westward-trending
streams descend from the highland in a
series of waterfalls – **Brown's Falls, Eric's
Falls, Dagg's Falls** and **Queen Mary Falls**

(p.201). About 14km past Queen Mary
Falls is **Carrs Lookout**, facing Mt
Superbus and overlooking the source of
the Condamine River.

The **Bicentennial National Trail**
crosses the Killarney-Legume road SE of
Killarney, close to the border. This walking
and horseriding trail follows old coach and
stock routes, packhorse tracks and forest
trails from Cooktown in North Qld to
Healesville in Vic. Ph: (07) 3878 9747

Warwick *Map 36 C3*

Warwick, the 'Rose and Rodeo City',
links the rich grain-growing areas around
Allora with the orchards and vineyards of
the Granite Belt and the dairying country
further east. It is the largest town on the
Southern Downs – a place of substance
and tradition, with historic sandstone
buildings, rose gardens and wide,
unhurried streets. It stands 500m above
sea-level on the Condamine River, with a
backdrop of blue hills. European
settlement here dates from 1840.

The tourist info centre (49 Albion St)
supplies a Heritage Trail booklet and a
leaflet on Warwick's historic buildings,
including **Kerong Cottage** (1869),
St Andrew's Uniting Church (1870),
Warwick Central School (1875), the
Courthouse (1866), the **Masonic Temple**
(1886) and **Warwick Railway Stn** in
Lyons St, built of local sandstone (1880s).

Hotel, Killarney

Warwick Post Office (1898) and the Byrnes Memorial
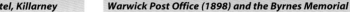

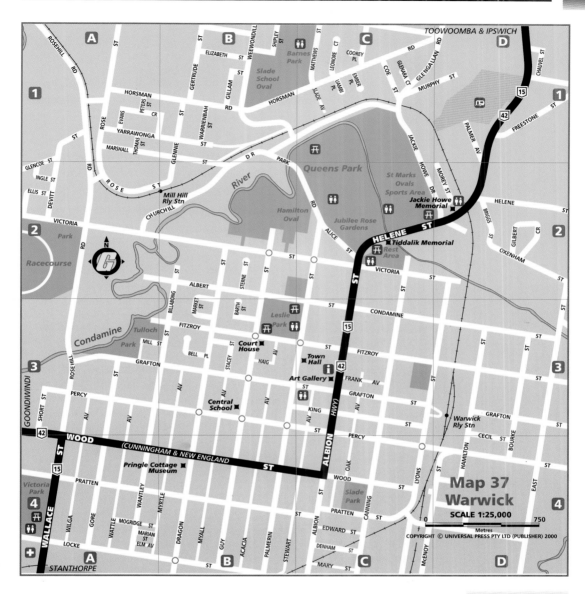

Map 37
Warwick
SCALE 1:25,000
COPYRIGHT © UNIVERSAL PRESS PTY LTD (PUBLISHER) 2000

The **Railway Goods Shed** is an example of how utility and elegance can be happily combined.

Next door to the tourist info centre is the modern and well-appointed **Warwick Regional Art Gallery**, which mounts frequent exhibitions. Open Tue-Sat, 10am-4pm; Sun, 2pm-4pm. Ph: (07) 4661 8588

In a park on the corner of Jackie Howe Dr and the Cunningham Hwy is a **memorial** to Jackie Howe, who gave his name to that symbol of sartorial comfort, the Jackie Howe singlet. A plaque relates the story of this celebrated shearer, who was born at Canning Downs in 1861 and, at a station near Blackall in 1892, established a sheep-shearing record that no blade shearer anywhere in the world was ever able to equal.

A little further south is **Queens Park** (cnr Alice and Albion Sts), with rose gardens and plaques naming the yearly winners of the rodeo awards. Across the road, on the bank of the Condamine, is the **Tiddalik monument**, carved from a granite boulder that came from the Leslie Dam (p.203).

Tiddalik the Frog
According to legend, Tiddalik swallowed all the water and caused a great drought in the land. The drought didn't break until Nabunum the Eel made Tiddalik laugh, so that all the water gushed from his mouth.

Egg-throwing at Warwick

Despite the solid respectability and prosperous tone of its public buildings, Warwick also harbours traditions from Qld's more radical past. Take, for example, the Railway Station Incident, which occurred during WWI and led to the formation of the Federal Police. When Prime Minister Billy Hughes stopped at Warwick on a campaign to win support for his conscription referendum, his reception was not as he would have hoped. An egg missile found its mark, and when the aggrieved victim called on a Qld constable to arrest the culprit, he was told that the police had 'no jurisdiction' in the matter. Less than pleased, Billy Hughes determined to found a police force that would do the prime minister's bidding.

Pringle Cottage, 81 Dragon St, is a classically proportioned sandstone building with a gracefully curved awning. It houses the **Warwick and District Historical Society Museum**. Open Wed–Fri, 10am–noon; Sat–Sun, 2pm–4pm; or by appt. Ph: (07) 4661 3234 or (07) 4661 2028

Warwick is home to Dairyfields cheese-makers' famous Warwick Classic range of cheeses, which include cheddars, cheshire, edam, and fresh brie and camembert.

Just out of town, on Glen Rd, is the **Rosenthal Lookout**, a steel tower with a platform looking back over Warwick to the Great Dividing Ra.

The Granite Belt

Apart from the large centre of Stanthorpe, Granite Belt towns are mostly tiny hamlets set among orchards, vineyards and market gardens, and linked, away from the highway, by sparkling roadways of decomposed granite. A tourist drive known as the Fruit Run (Scenic Route 3) travels parallel with the highway between Dalveen and Applethorpe, just north of Stanthorpe. West of the drive, on Amiens Rd, is an arc of old post-WWI soldier-settlements named after Western Front battlefields and towns.

Applethorpe *Map 36 C4*

This unassuming township is just north of Stanthorpe, where the Fruit Run tourist drive rejoins the highway. Though small, Applethorpe has achieved a measure of

fame by being mentioned routinely on the weather report as the centre with the lowest temperature in the state. The town shop is a good place to stock up with local fruit and vegetables.

Ballandean *Map 36 B5*

Ballandean is on the New England Hwy south of Stanthorpe, looking over a valley of farms and orchards to the Roberts Ra on the border.

The **Vineyard Cafe**, on the New England Hwy, is an award-winning restaurant in an old country church, surrounded by a large cottage garden. The restaurant's menu (which includes fresh local produce, selected local wines and breads and pastas made on the premises), its old-world atmosphere and its special musical events (such as the 'Winter Solstice Blues' and 'Baroque Goes Bush') make a visit here a nice counterpoint to the rigours of camping in the nearby Girraween and Sundown NPs. Ph: (07) 4684 1270

Ballandean is surrounded by wineries, among them **Ballandean Estate, Winewood, Golden Grove** and **Granite Ridge** along Sundown Rd, **Windermere** on Watters Rd, **Hidden Creek** along Eukey Rd, and **Robinsons** on Curtin's Rd (p.204).

Glen Aplin *Map 36 C5*

Near this town, on the highway between Stanthorpe and Ballandean, byroads lead

In memoriam
At **Glen Aplin**, south of Stanthorpe, the owners of **Das Helwig Haus** each year remember the fallen of WWI by planting a field of Flanders poppies, cornflowers and wheat.

off through the valleys to orchards and vineyards. Travellers are led along Townsend's Rd by a series of berry-shaped notices with encouraging rhymes to the **Bramble Patch** farm, perched in the hills 1000m above sea-level. Visitors can picnic under the willows and view the fare — seasonal berries, berry ice-cream, fortified berry wine and home-made jams, sauces and coulis. Open daily Oct–Apr, 8am–4pm; May–Sept, 10am–4pm. Ph: (07) 4683 4205

Wineries at or near Glen Aplin are **Kominos Wines**, on the highway; **Felsberg Winery**, an imposing establishment perched above Townsend's Rd, overlooking the Glen Aplin valley; and **Mountview Wines**, Mt Stirling Rd, 2km from Glen Aplin (p.204).

Das Helwig Haus, also on Mt Stirling Rd, is crammed with cottage-garden flowers, fruit trees, herbs and vegetables. Open daily, 10am–4.30pm. Ph: (07) 4683 4227

Fresh cherries (in season), other stonefruit, jams and liqueurs are for sale at the **Cherry Patch Fruit Stall**, north of Glen Aplin. Ph: (07) 4683 4296

Out along Thorndale Rd, west of the highway, is **Granite Gardens**, on Nicholson Rd. This 2ha garden has hundreds of roses and perennials. Ph: (07) 4681 2780 (6.30am–7.30am or 6.30pm–8.30pm) to check opening times and to make appts.

Stanthorpe *Map 36 C4*

Stanthorpe is at the heart of the Granite Belt, a prosperous town with neat gardens, low-set houses and crisp mountain air. Deciduous trees and brick chimneys give the place a traditional, south-of-the-border look. Overlooking the town are knobbly hills with rounded granite outcrops.

Quart Pot Creek, which runs through the town and was the site of the original tin mine, is bordered along much of its length by parkland. Here, just across the bridge from the town centre and to the left off the highway, is the Southern Downs Tourist Office (28 Leslie Pde). It supplies informational material and sells souvenirs in a pleasing setting overlooking the creek. Open daily, 9am–5pm. Ph: (07) 4681 2057

Orchard in blossom, Stanthorpe

The **Stanthorpe Heritage Museum**, 12 High St, is based around the original shire council chambers. Among its exhibits are a shepherd's hut from Ballandean Stn and the Willson's Downfall jail. Open Tue–Fri, 10am–4pm; Sat, 1pm–4pm; Sun, 9am–1pm. Ph: (07) 4681 1711

Stanthorpe's **Market in the Mountains**, at the Stanthorpe Civic Centre in the heart of the town, is held 9am–1pm on numerous Suns throughout the year. Ph: (07) 4681 4777

Heritage Park, on Quart Pot Creek (via Granite St), has a display shelter with info about Stanthorpe's botanical and cultural heritage.

For views over the town and the surrounding district, follow Lock St, which turns east off the highway opposite Woolworths, to the **Mt Marley Lookout**. There are picnic facilities among the boulders and cypress pines near the lookout, and a walking track that winds around the mountain, giving good views to the north. Access closed 4.30pm Fri to 8.30am Sat.

The road to the lookout passes a **war memorial** set on a hill in granite-studded gardens.

Take the Stanthorpe-Texas road and then drive 6km along Amiens Rd for Albert Verschuuren's **Handmade Stoneware Pottery**. Albert frequently uses local clay, granite and wood ash for his glazes. Open most days. Ph: (07) 4683 3205

The Summit *Map 36 C4*

This tiny township at the end of the Fruit Run (Scenic Route 3) stands at an altitude

... to end all wars
The shrine in the memorial gardens on Lock St, **Stanthorpe** bears these words:
To the memory of our gallant boys who fell in the world's war 1914–1919.

of 925m and has the distinction of possessing Qld's highest railway station. Also at the township is a well-stocked store, a church and a timber mill. A short drive away is the **Donnelly's Castle lookout** (p.203).

Wallangarra *Map 36 C5*

The historical importance of this small border town is apparent in the elegant Customs House (now a BYO cafe) and in its large railway station, which once housed a huge dining room, tea-room, ladies' lounge and wine cellar. This was where customs duties were assessed on goods passing between Qld and NSW, and where, because of the neighbouring states' 2 different rail gauges, passengers on the interstate line were obliged to change trains.

The **Customs House Cafe** serves fine food with a distinctively Australian touch, and also takes visitors on a 30min walk on the 'Federation Trail Alongside the Rail'. Open Tue–Sun, 11am–4pm (daily during holidays), and Sat nights. Bookings essential for dinner. BYO. Ph (07) 4684 3488

Nearby is a tree still showing the original surveyor's blaze that was made in 1859 to mark the new border between NSW and Qld.

At Jennings, Wallangarra's twin town on the NSW side of the border, is the old **Jennings Hotel**.

Occasionally the Australian Railway Historical Society runs **train tours** through the Granite Belt as far as Wallangarra. Ph: (07) 3371 4231

National parks and state forests

There are 3 national parks and 1 state forest in this region: the Main Ra NP (divided into the Mt Mistake, Cunningham's Gap, Mt Roberts and Queen Mary Falls sections), the Sundown and Girraween NPs on the border with NSW, and Goomburra State Forest, east of Allora. The Main Ra NP and Goomburra State Forest are characterised by rugged mountain terrain and a range of vegetation from thick rainforest to mountain heath. The Sundown and

Girraween NPs occupy drier areas, with generally poor soil. Girraween is dominated by gigantic granite monoliths and coarse, sandy soil — conditions ideal for wildflowers.

As well, in NSW, there are 2 other national parks that are easily accessible from the Granite Belt: Bald Rock NP (p.269) and Boonoo Boonoo NP.

Girraween NP *Map 36 C5*

The most famous of all the national parks in the region is Girraween, with its hallmark granite rocks. Here tracks of glittering quartz sand cross creeks and climb through heath and scrub. The park takes in about 11 700ha of turbulent terrain in the Wyberba Valley — steep ridges with rounded granite flanks, bald domes and balancing boulders of immense scale. This is an elevated landscape, the average height being 900m, and temperatures can plummet at night. In winter, temperatures well below freezing are common. Visitors are advised to take plenty of warm clothes.

Girraween means 'place of flowers', and the spring wildflower display is spectacular. The native flowering plants relish the inhospitable conditions, and are particularly at home on the scree slopes and rocky outcrops. The granite landscape is unique in Qld, and many of the wildflower species, such as the flannel flower, are here found at the most northerly extent of their range. The animals, too, are similar to those found further south. Wombats, lyrebirds and heath wrens live here, along with the rare turquoise parrot, the diamond firetail and a host of more familiar bird species.

There are picnic and camping areas on the southern bank of **Bald Rock Creek**, and the **Castle Rock camping ground** has facilities with wheelchair access. **Camping permits**, along with a wide range of brochures and other informational material, are obtainable from the info centre at Bald Rock Creek. (Particularly recommended are the *Granite Arch Discovery Walk* and *Bird Key* brochures.) Because the park is so popular, it is wise to book a campsite well in advance. Bookings are essential

Girraween NP

for school holidays and long weekends.
Ph: (07) 4684 5157

Details of the 9 walking tracks in the park are given in the Park Guide, available at the info centre. The walks range in length from 900m for the **Link Circuit** to 10.4km return for the **Mt Norman Track**. The 3km return **Pyramid Track** is an ideal introduction to Girraween for the day visitor. It takes the walker to the summit of the **Pyramid** (1080m), where the view over the park is splendid and an astonishing balancing rock can be seen at close quarters. The walk includes the ascent of a huge granite dome — hair-raising for inexperienced climbers, but not difficult for those who are fit and confident.

Though the nights at Girraween are usually cool, the days can get quite hot. Bald Rock Creek obligingly provides several swimming holes where walkers can cool off, notably at the **Bald Rock Creek picnic ground** and **The Junction**.

Goomburra State Forest *Map 36 D3*

To reach Goomburra State Forest, take the Cunningham Hwy to Gladfield, and follow the signs to the park. Alternatively, take the Goomburra turnoff from the New England Hwy 4km south of Allora. The last 6km is gravel, and may be closed after wet weather.

Goomburra State Forest

Goomburra State Forest has several roles: it protects a water catchment area, provides timber, honey and grazing land, and is an extensive natural area where people can picnic, camp and bushwalk.

The landscape ranges from the alluvial flats that border **Dalrymple Creek** to the dramatic cliffs of the escarpment of the Great Dividing Ra, providing habitats for a wide variety of native birds and animals. Blackbutt and manna gum dominate the eucalypt forests, and rainforests fill the gullies.

Balancing rocks, Girraween NP

Spotlighting
Try spotlighting at night in **Girraween NP** for the shy nocturnal animals that inhabit the bush near the camping area. Patient observers may see a feathertail or sugar glider, or even, with luck, one of the park's few wombats.

Camping is permitted at the **Manna Gum** and **Poplar Flat camping areas**, where there is a self-registering system. Both are open, grassy areas on Dalrymple Creek. Contact the Forest Service in the Dept of Natural Resources for details. Ph: (07) 3234 0205. There is a picnic area near the **Poplar Flat camping area**, with BBQs and tables.

The park has 6 walking trails, from 600m to 7km (return) in length. They give access to features such as **Araucaria Falls, Mt Castle Lookout** (with views to Mt Castle, and over the Laidley Creek valley to the Little Liverpool Ra) and **Sylvester's Lookout**, within Main Ra NP. There is vehicular access to the tracks leading to these lookouts in dry weather only.

Main Ra NP *Map 36 D3*

This is actually a series of parks protecting areas of particular beauty and interest in the western part of the Scenic Rim, which stretches to Springbrook in the east. It is part of the Central Eastern Australian Rainforest Reserves World Heritage Area, which embraces the Scenic Rim and the rainforests of northern NSW. Main Ra NP consists of 4 sections: Cunningham's Gap, Mt Mistake, Mt Roberts and Queen Mary Falls.

Cunningham's Gap

This section covers the 2 peaks that loom over Cunningham's Gap – **Mt Cordeaux** and **Mt Mitchell** – extending to **Bare Rock** and **Morgan's Lookout** in the north, and taking in **Spicer's Gap** as far south as **Spicer's Peak**.

The Cunningham Hwy ascends the range through thickening rainforest, with a striking view back over the lowlands. In open forest 3.5km west of the Gap is the Main Ra NP Headquarters and Info Centre, where the traveller can pick up brochures on all the national parks in the district. Ph: (07) 4666 1133

The section has rainforest, open forest, waterfalls and lookouts. There are walking tracks in both the Cunningham's Gap and Spicer's Gap areas. The 8 walking tracks in the Cunningham's Gap area of the section all begin at the carpark next to the highway, at the crest of the Gap, where a monument has been erected in honour of Allan Cunningham, who explored the Gap region in 1828. The tracks range from an 800m return trip to the **Fassifern Valley Lookout** to a 12.4km return hike to **Morgan's Lookout** and **Bare Rock**.

Historic **Spicer's Gap** can be approached from the east along Spicer's Gap Rd (which runs SW from the Cunningham Hwy 5km west of Aratula) or from the west, by 4WD only, along the

Expert mimic
Listen for lyrebirds if you are taking the track to **Morgan's Lookout** during winter. These birds are renowned for their mimicry and sometimes startle walkers with the hoot of a horn or the scream of a chainsaw.

Spicer's Gap

road that leaves the highway 1.5km west of the Main Ra NP Info Centre. The eastern approach ends at the Governor's Chair carpark, and the western approach ends at the Mt Matheson Trail carpark, 1.6km from the Governor's Chair.

This is a less developed area, but of great historical interest. The paved road through the Gap was built in the mid-1800s, when the Cunningham's Gap route was abandoned as too difficult, and used state-of-the-art 19th-century road-construction techniques. The sweeping curves, low gradients, metalled pavement and efficient drainage systems, parts of which can still be seen to this day, made this a relatively easy climb for coaches and drays.

Other areas of interest here are the **site of an old inn**, a **pioneer graveyard** (marked by a cairn with copper-nail inscriptions), **Moss's Well** (the only place where travellers could replenish their water) and **Governor's Chair Lookout** (a rocky ledge on the edge of a sheer cliff, where early governors were said to rest and enjoy the commanding view over the Fassifern Valley). There are 4 walks in this area, including the 3.2km return **Heritage Trail**, a self-guiding walk that follows the old road.

Camping and picnic facilities are provided 3.5km west of Cunningham's Gap on **West Gap Creek** (opposite the NP Info Centre) and on the eastern side of Spicer's Gap, near the pioneer graveyard.

Mt Mistake

Mt Mistake is the most northerly section of the park and covers 5560ha of rainforest and open forest. This is an undeveloped area: there is no road access, and the bushwalking trails here are unmarked. The approach is via the road to Goomburra State Forest, which turns off the Cunningham Hwy at Gladfield.

Anyone wishing to visit this section must first contact the ranger at the Main Ra NP Headquarters and Info Centre, on the Cunningham Hwy, 3.5km west of Cunningham's Gap. Ph: (07) 4666 1133

Mt Roberts

This is another undeveloped section of the Main Ra NP, with limited access. It is situated in rugged country in the south of the park, and includes **Mt Superbus**, at 1375m the highest peak in SE Qld. Access is via the Killarney-Boonah road, 50km SW of Boonah.

There are some bush campsites in the section, which can be reached only on foot. A list of the sites is available from the Main Ra NP Headquarters and Info Centre, on the Cunningham Hwy 3.5km west of Cunningham's Gap. Anyone intending to camp in the Mt Roberts section must book 4-6 weeks in advance. Ph: (07) 4666 1133

Queen Mary Falls

This section is west of Main Ra and 11km east of Killarney, on the Killarney-Boonah road. It is a small park of 78ha on **Spring Creek** (a tributary of the Condamine River), protecting varied forest around the 40m waterfall.

As shown in map 38, a track to the falls begins at the picnic ground, which is on the main road opposite a kiosk and private caravan park, Queen Mary Falls Tourist Park (Ph: (07) 4664 7151). It leads 500m through open eucalypt forest to a lookout balcony, giving a view of the creek as it plunges in an unbroken descent over the cliff into the rainforest-filled gorge below.

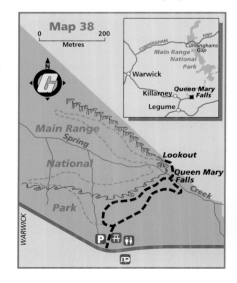

Main Range NP

Lookout, Sundown NP

Queen Mary Falls

For a longer walk, follow the track as it descends into the gorge, crosses the creek at the base of the waterfall, and climbs the southern escarpment to return to the picnic ground. The full circuit is about 2km.

Sundown NP *Map 36 B5*

Sundown NP is 16 000ha of rugged country on the Qld–NSW border, on the opposite side of the New England Hwy from Girraween NP. This is a high 'traprock' landscape, with steep ridges, rocky bluffs and peaks rising to 1000m and more. In general, Sundown's landscape is in sharp contrast with the granite terrain of nearby Girraween. There are 2 prominent peaks in the park – **Mt Lofty** in the east and **Mt Donaldson** further south.

The **Severn River** cuts a SW diagonal through the park, fed by numerous creeks that emerge from gullies and gorges on either side. The vegetation alters with the different local environments. There is a marked change in climate and soil types from north to south, and this is reflected in differences in vegetation species. Eucalypt forests, which dominate the higher, northern areas, give way in the south to woodland of silver-leaved

Farming relics, Sundown NP

ironbark, white box and cypress. The river banks are home to the river red gum, callistemon and casuarina, and vine thickets occur in the close-walled gorges.

This diversity of vegetation allows a wide variety of fauna to find a niche in the park. Ornithologists have recorded the presence of over 130 species of bird, and wallaroos, grey kangaroos, red-necked wallabies, pretty-faced wallabies, marsupial mice, gliders and possums are found there.

Once part of Glenlyon, Ballandean and Nundubbermere Stns, the park still bears relics of its farming past, such as salt troughs and cattle yards. From the 1870s, the area was also mined intermittently for tin, copper and arsenic. There are old surface diggings in the **Red Rock** area. Access to the Sundown mines is restricted to the 4WD track because of mining contamination.

To reach the **Broadwater camping area** and ranger station at the southern end of the park, travel 75km south from Stanthorpe, first on the Stanthorpe–Texas road and then on the Glenlyon Dam road, before turning off onto the gravel road that runs for 4km into the park. The road passes through a stand of striking silver-leaved ironbarks with etched-black trunks. Kangaroos graze nonchalantly beside the road and lounge in the shade. Camping alcoves are marked out among the trees on the bank of the Severn River. There is a covered display shed with info about the park and a separate self-registration point for campers.

The park can also be approached from Ballandean, in the east, although the track into the campsites is rough and a 4WD is necessary. Bushwalkers can leave their cars at the boundary and trek to their campsite.

There are no graded walking tracks in the park, but areas of interest can be reached by following the river and side creeks. A notice in the Broadwater info shed lists several suggested walks, with details about features and duration. They range from the 1hr **Permanent Waterhole Walk** to a 4–6hr walk to **Split Rock Falls** and **Double Falls**.

Be sure to fill the petrol tank and stock up with necessities before setting out for Sundown NP. The nearest place to refuel and replenish supplies is a small store at Lake Glenlyon (on the western side) or at Ballandean (to the east). For campsite bookings and info, ring Sundown NP Ranger Stn, Ph: (02) 6737 5235, or Girraween NP, Ph: (07) 4684 5157.

Other attractions

Connolly Dam *Map 39*

Connolly Dam, about 15km south of **Warwick**, stores the water for the city's needs. It is fed by Rosenthal and Fitz Creeks, and discharges via Rosenthal Creek, which joins the Condamine at Warwick. The dam is stocked with native fish, including golden perch, silver perch and Murray cod.

Donnelly's Castle

Turn off the Fruit Run (Scenic Route 3) into Amiens Rd and follow the signs through **Passchendaele State Forest** to this lookout on the top of a huge granite boulder. A track from the picnic ground leads through boulder-strewn woodland to a set of steps up the rock, which gives views over farmland to distant mountains. The area is said to have been one of the hideouts of the bushranger Thunderbolt.

Lake Glenlyon *Map 36 A5*

Also called Glenlyon Dam, this 29km-long reservoir, on Pike Creek, lies between rugged ironbark-covered hills SW of **Sundown NP**. There is a large private tourist park here (Ph: (02) 6737 5266), with sweeping lawns and a kiosk, cabins, campsites, BBQs, 2 amenity blocks, a tennis court and boat-hire service. Kangaroos graze the lawns. The lake is stocked with Murray cod, silver perch, golden perch, spangled perch and eel-tailed catfish.

A nearby **display centre** documents the natural and geological history of the dam area, and has a replica of one of the Texas Caves, which were flooded when the dam was built. Some megafauna fossils from the caves are also on display.

Lake Leslie *Map 36 C3*

Lake Leslie (also called Leslie Dam) is part of the Upper Condamine Irrigation Project. It lies off the Cunningham Hwy, 13km west of **Warwick**. The park below the scenic lookout at the dam wall has extensive lawns, large trees and protruding granite boulders. The lower face of one boulder has been carved into a Mt Rushmore-style image of the Darling Downs pioneer Patrick Leslie. Nearby is a spectacular balancing rock.

The lake has picnic areas with BBQs and is a popular venue for swimming, skiing, sailing, windsurfing and fishing. It is stocked with golden perch, Murray cod and silver perch.

Mirambeena Sheep and Emu Farm *Map 39* ④

At this family farm, about 15km east of **Warwick**, visitors can relate to a farm-full of animals (dogs, chooks, ducks, lambs and calves), watch a sheep-shearing demonstration and learn about emu-farming. Bookings essential. Ph: (07) 4667 3106

Ostrich Acres

For a guided tour of an ostrich farm, viewing various stages of the farm process, such as incubation and a chick nursery, visit Ostrich Acres on the New England Hwy at **Applethorpe**. Open daily, 10am–3pm. Ph: (07) 4683 2253

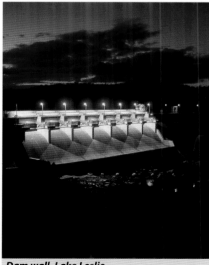

Dam wall, Lake Leslie

Granite Belt wineries

NAME	MAP 39	ADDRESS	PHONE	OPEN
Bald Mountain Vineyards	㉒	Hickling Lane, Wallangarra	(07) 4684 3186	10am–5pm Sat–Thurs; 2pm–5pm Fri
Ballandean Estate	⑲	Sundown Rd, Ballandean	(07) 4684 1226	9am–5pm daily
Bungawarra Wines	⑬	Bents Rd, Ballandean	(07) 4684 1128	10.30am–4.30pm daily
Castle Glen Vineyard	❷	Amiens Rd, The Summit	(07) 4683 2169	10am–5pm daily
Catspaw Farm Winery	❺	Texas Rd, Stanthorpe	(07) 4683 6229	10am–5pm Thurs–Sun and public and school holidays
Felsberg Winery	⑩	Townsend's Rd, Glen Aplin	(07) 4683 4332	9.30am–4.30pm daily
Golden Grove Estate	⑱	Sundown Rd, Ballandean	(07) 4684 1291	9am–5pm daily
Granite Ridge Winery	⑯	Sundown Rd, Ballandean	(07) 4684 1263	10am–5pm Fri–Tue
Heritage Wines	❶	Granite Belt Dr, Cottonvale	(07) 4685 2197	9am–5pm daily
Hidden Creek	⑮	Eukey Rd, Ballandean	(07) 4684 1383	10.30am–4pm Sat; 8am (for breakfast)–4pm Sun
Inigo	❼	New England Hwy, Glen Aplin	(07) 3397 6425	weekends or by appt
Kominos Wines	❽	New England Hwy, Severnlea	(07) 4683 4311	9am–5pm daily
Mountview Wines	❾	Mt Stirling Rd, Glen Aplin	(07) 4683 4316	9am–5pm Sat–Wed; 10am–4pm Sun
Old Caves Winery	❹	New England Hwy, Stanthorpe	(07) 4681 1494	10am–5pm Mon–Sat; 10am–4pm Sun
Preston Peak Wines	㉑	Old Wallangarra Rd, Wyberba	(07) 4684 3480	10am–4pm Sat, from Easter to end Sept; other times c/o Stanthorpe Wine Centre or by appt
Robinson's Family Vineyards	⑳	Curtin's Rd, Ballandean	(07) 4684 1216	10am–5pm daily
Rumbalara Vineyards	⑫	Fletcher Rd, Fletcher	(07) 4684 1206	9am–5pm daily
Severn Brae Estate Winery	❻	Back Creek Rd, Severnlea	(07) 4683 5292	10am–5pm Sat and Sun or by appt
Stanthorpe Wine Centre	❸	Granite Belt Dr, Thulimbah	(07) 4683 2011	10am–4pm Mon–Fri; 10am–5pm weekends, or by appt
Stone Ridge Vineyards	⑪	Limberlost Rd, Glen Aplin	(07) 4683 4211	10am–5pm daily
Windermere Wines	⑭	Watters Rd, Ballandean	(07) 4684 1353	9.30am–5pm Wed–Sun and public holidays
Winewood Vineyard and Winery	⑰	Sundown Rd, Ballandean	(07) 4684 1187	9am–5pm Sat–Sun and school holidays

Storm King Dam *Map 36 C5*

This dam, 15km SE of **Stanthorpe** on the Eukey road, caters for day-trippers with a picnic area, BBQs and a boat ramp. It also caters for large parties of overnight visitors (the lowest fee is based on 30 people). Ph: (07) 4681 1920

Sundown Observatory

Heading south from Stanthorpe on the New England Hwy, take the 1st turn right off the highway after the **Ballandean** post office, into Curr Rd, turn left at the T-intersection into Sundown Rd, and follow the signs to Sundown Observatory.

The observatory has a 46cm telescope and a display area with a satellite orbit model, moon globe and other items of astronomical interest. There are BBQ facilities and light refreshments on offer. Wheelchair accessible. Bookings advisable. Open nightly from 8pm. Ph: (07) 4684 1192

Recreational activities

Action

The ranges east of **Killarney** are popular areas for 4WDing. (Check the road conditions with someone in the know at Killarney.)

The eastern section of **Sundown NP** can be reached only by 4WD (p.202).

For dedicated 4WDing, try the **Ultimate 4WD Experience** at **Arcot Homestead**, a working sheep and cattle property west of Stanthorpe on Arcot Rd, off the Stanthorpe-Texas road. The property has over 50km of 4WD tracks, rated from 'easy' to 'extremely difficult to impossible'. Bookings essential. Ph: (07) 4653 1360

Bushwalking

The 3 national parks (**Main Ra, Girraween** and **Sundown**) and **Goomburra State Forest** present opportunities for bushwalking in extremely varied and scenic terrain (pp.198–203).

Fishing

Lakes **Leslie** and **Glenlyon**, and **Connolly** and **Storm King Dams**, are stocked with native fish and all except Connolly Dam have boat ramps. There is boat hire at Lake Leslie and Lake Glenlyon.

The **Condamine River** near Warwick is worth trying for golden perch and eel-tailed catfish.

Fossicking

Several sites in the region offer opportunities for fossicking. **Thanes Creek Fossicking Area**, where alluvial gold can be found, is reached by turning

Vines at Ballandean Estate Winery

north off the Cunningham Hwy about 37km west of Warwick, and following Thanes Creek Rd, Hart Rd and Big Hill Rd. Ph: (07) 3237 1435 or 4661 2333. Fossick for topaz, other gemstones and minerals at **Swiper's Gully, Passchendaele State Forest**, 13km NW of Stanthorpe, near Amiens. Ph: (07) 3237 1659, and (07) 4661 6600 for a **DPI permit**.

Horseriding

Red Gum Ridge on Eukey Rd, 18km SE of Stanthorpe, offers escorted trail rides of an hour or more and day rides to wineries for lunch. Visitors can also take an overnight pub ride, or camp on the trail. By appt only. Ph: (07) 4683 7169

Granite Belt wineries

The Granite Belt is dotted with wineries, from impressively appointed establishments like Heritage Wines, to simple family vineyards high in the hills. The table opposite, and map 39, show some of the region's wineries.

Weight of tradition
At **Heritage Wines**, the large fireplace, pianos, beams from the scaffolding of Sydney Harbour Bridge and table from Qld's first Parliament House make this a memorable setting for sampling Granite Belt wines.

Fun for the young

★ Allora's scarecrows (p.193)

★ Donnelly's Castle (p.203)

★ Mirambeena Sheep and Emu Farm (p.203)

★ Rosenthal Lookout tower (p.196)

★ Texas Caves display, Display Centre, Lake Glenlyon (p.203)

Trailblazers
Puglisi Cellars produced the first commercial Granite Belt vintage in 1973 and cellar-door sales began then. **Rumbalara** pioneered fortified wines in the region in 1977.

Suggested tours – Map 39

Downs towns tour

Approximate distance

460km return from Brisbane CBD

About the tour

This drive ranges between the historic city of Warwick and the 'best little town on the Downs', Allora, with its wonderfully preserved streetscapes. There are old homesteads close to the road and, for the kids, a sheep and emu farm 15km east of Warwick. Goldseekers can drive west on the Cunningham Hwy to pan at the Thanes Creek Fossicking Area and those interested in water sports can take the road into Lake Leslie. For a diversion to the picnic area and lookouts of Goomburra State Forest, take the 40km turnoff south of Allora.

Places of interest

❶ **Glengallan Homestead** (p.193)
❷ **St David's Anglican Church, Allora** (p.193)
❸ **Talgai Homestead** (p.193)
❹ **Mirambeena Sheep and Emu Farm** (p.203)
❺ **Historic buildings, Warwick** (p.194)
❻ **Lake Leslie** (p.203)
❼ **Thanes Creek Fossicking Area** (p.205)

Talgai Homestead, Allora

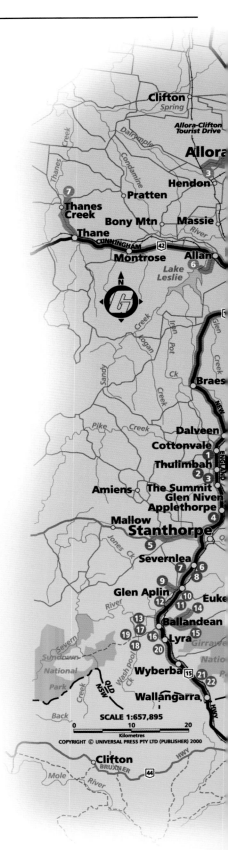

Granite Belt wineries tour

Approximate distance

150km from Brisbane CBD to Warwick; round trip tour from Warwick — 230km

About the tour

In this region there are now over 20 wineries offering tasting and cellar-door sales of red and white table wines — far too many to attempt a comprehensive survey in a 1-day tour without risk of serious impairment. Must-see wineries include the tastefully packaged Hidden Creek and the impressively sited Felsberg. The almost ubiquitous liqueur muscats should not be overlooked: they are something of a Granite Belt speciality. (See p.204 for winery addresses, phone numbers and opening hours.)

Places of interest

❶ Heritage Wines
❷ Castle Glen Vineyard
❸ Stanthorpe Wine Centre
❹ Old Caves Winery
❺ Catspaw Farm Winery
❻ Severn Brae Estate Winery
❼ Inigo
❽ Kominos Wines
❾ Mountview Wines
❿ Felsberg Winery
⓫ Stone Ridge Vineyards
⓬ Rumbalara Vineyards
⓭ Bungawarra Wines
⓮ Windermere Wines
⓯ Hidden Creek
⓰ Granite Ridge Winery
⓱ Winewood Vineyard and Winery
⓲ Golden Grove Estate
⓳ Ballandean Estate
⓴ Robinson's Family Vineyards
㉑ Preston Peak Wines
㉒ Bald Mountain Vineyards

Felsberg Winery

Brisbane ™
city of Sun Days

Left: **Numinbah
Valley,
Lamington NP**
Right: **Treetop
Walk, O'Reilly's**

Ipswich, Lockyer Valley and the Scenic Rim

High above the river valleys and coastal plain south of Brisbane are the mountain rainforests of the Scenic Rim. Travellers making the winding ascent pass through eucalypt woodland and into a rainforest world of cathedral coolness. Soaring trees press in on either side, hung with wisps of low-flying cloud. In the dim light, tracks lead off past tumbling streams, and on through gothic forests of ancient beech to top-of-the-world lookouts.

To the west are the river valleys, wild and narrow in their upper reaches, and downstream easing out to farmland. On the horizon, regal and remote, are the jagged peaks of the Mt Barney group.

The stony ridges west of Ipswich give way to the rich country of the Lockyer Valley, where the orderly arrays of crops form abstracts of gold, green and black against a backdrop of mountains.

The sheer scarps and dark forest of the Lamington Plateau, the dairy farms deep in the narrow valleys, the rolling cattle country, the country towns, the nuggety hills of Ipswich, the tourist galleries of Tamborine — all these are the moods and faces of this vast region.

Tourist information

Beaudesert Community Arts and Information Centre
Cnr Mt Lindesay Hwy and Enterprise Dr, Beaudesert 4285
Ph: (07) 5541 4495

Boonah Information Centre
Bicentennial Park,
Boonah–Fassifern Rd, Boonah 4310
Ph: (07) 5463 2233

Gatton Tourist Information Centre
Lake Apex Drive, Gatton 4343
Ph: (07) 5462 3430

Ipswich Visitors and Tourist Information
Cnr Brisbane St and d'Arcy Doyle Pl, Ipswich 4305 Ph: (07) 3281 0555

Laidley Visitor Information Centre
Das Neumann Haus, Cnr Patrick and William Sts, Laidley 4341
Ph: (07) 5465 3241

Tamborine Mountain Information Centre
Doughty Park, North Tamborine 4272 Ph: (07) 5545 3200
www.tamborinemtncc.org.au

Must see, must do

★ **Best of All Lookout** (p.228)
★ **Ipswich Heritage Tours** (p.220)
★ **Lions Road and the Border Loop** (p.231)
★ **Lockyer Valley Scenic Circuit** (p.232)
★ **Natural Bridge** (p.228)
★ **Treetop Walk, O'Reilly's** (p.226)

Radio stations

SUN FM: FM 90.5 (Beaudesert to south)
SUN FM: FM 99.5 (Beaudesert to north and Tamborine)
4CBL FM: FM 101.1
Star FM: FM 106.9 (Ipswich and Lockyer Valley)

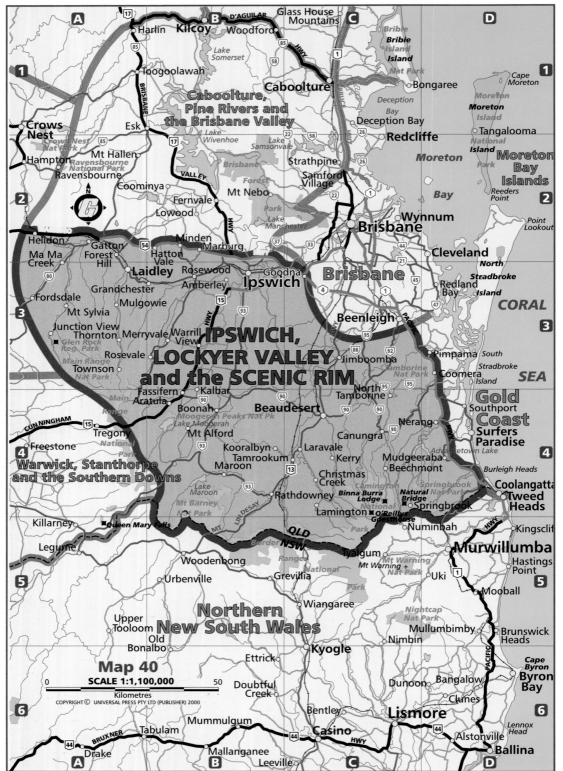

Map 40

SCALE 1:1,100,000

0   50

Kilometres

Natural features

The Scenic Rim is a series of ranges in the SE corner of Qld, sweeping in an arc around the river valleys that lie to their north. These mountains are the source of numerous streams – the Nerang, Coomera, Albert and Logan Rivers, and dozens of creeks.

There are 3 separate groups of mountains in this region: the eastern group (Springbrook, the Lamington Plateau and Tamborine), the Mt Barney group and the mountains around Lake Moogerah. (See 'Warwick, Stanthorpe and the Southern Downs' – pp.200–202 – for the continuation of the Scenic Rim through the Main Ra NP.) The mountains owe their existence to the volcanic activity that was widespread in the region tens of millions of years ago. The most dramatic of these events were the outpourings of the enormous shield volcano centred on Mt Warning; Springbrook, Lamington and Tamborine are part of its eroded basalt rim.

To the north and west the foothills subside into generally fertile river valleys interrupted by barren ridges and rugged peaks. Lockyer Creek, rising in the Great Divide near Toowoomba, flows through a broad valley of deep, black soil to join the Brisbane River north of Ipswich. The farms here are renowned for their high yields of small crops, particularly fruit and vegetables.

History

The 1st European incursion into the lands of the Wangerriburra, the Yugambeh and the other Aboriginal peoples of this region occurred in 1826, when Capt Patrick Logan, commandant of the Moreton Bay penal settlement, ventured as far south as the river that now bears his name.

In 1827, after Logan had explored the Bremer River, a convict outstation was established at Limestone Hills to quarry the abundant limestone there. Limestone Station soon became a busy river port and was re-named Ipswich in 1842. In 1865 a rail line was built between Ipswich and Grandchester (then Bigge's Camp). It was the 1st railway in Queensland, and the initial stage of a line linking Ipswich with the pastoral properties on the Darling Downs. Riverboats connected Ipswich with the port of Brisbane. By the end of the 19th century, Ipswich was a major coal-mining, rail and industrial centre.

By the early 1840s, pastoralists had spilled over from the Darling Downs into the Lockyer, Fassifern, Albert and Logan Valleys. However, the escarpments and thick rainforest of the Lamington Plateau at first deterred European settlers. In the 1860s, Surveyor Roberts entered the area to survey the border with NSW. It was not until the 1870s that others followed. These were the loggers, drawn there by the giant hardwood trees. This was the

Convict-era kiln
The ruins of an early limestone kiln can still be seen at **Cunningham's Knoll** in **Ipswich**.

Slow progress
The cliffs, waterfalls and dense rainforest in the Springbrook area made the going so difficult that in 1863 Surveyor Roberts took 6 months to survey a distance of just 5km from Springbrook to the Numinbah Valley.

View from Tamborine Mountain

View to Surfers Paradise from Tamborine Mountain

heroic age of timbergetting, when men risked their lives on flimsy springboards wedged in the mighty tree trunks high above the ground. The loggers were generally followed by dairy-farmers, who cleared large areas to plant pasture.

Getting there

By road

Three major highways lead to the Scenic Rim: the **Pacific Hwy**, which passes through Nerang and gives access to Springbrook, the Numinbah Valley, Binna Burra and Tamborine Mt; the **Mt Lindesay Hwy**, which passes through Beaudesert and on to the Mt Barney area, also giving access to Tamborine (via Canungra) and Green Mts (via Canungra or Kerry); the **Cunningham Hwy**, which runs SW through Aratula past the Moogerah peaks and on to Cunningham's Gap.

The Ipswich Mwy runs through the western suburbs of Brisbane to Ipswich. Travellers heading for the Lockyer Valley can bypass the city by taking the Warrego Hwy, which continues on the right, past the Ipswich turnoff.

Alternatively, take the Ipswich turnoff and then follow the scenic route through Walloon, Rosewood, Grandchester, Laidley and Forest Hill, before rejoining the Warrego Hwy near Gatton.

Roadrunners has a frequent weekday bus service between the Brisbane Transit Centre, Roma St, and Beaudesert, making stops along the Mt Lindesay Hwy. Ph: (07) 3352 8399

McCafferty's Express Coaches has buses running frequently from the Brisbane Transit Centre to Toowoomba, stopping at all the main towns along the Warrego Hwy. Ph: 131 499

Kooralbyn Coaches run between Coolangatta and the Kooralbyn resort Thurs–Mon. Ph: (07) 5544 6655

Southern Cross buses leave the Brisbane Transit Centre, picking up at various points in Brisbane and at Ipswich Railway Stn, and travel via Harrisville and Kalbar to Boonah. Ph: (07) 3812 2520

All State Scenic Tours has a service to O'Reilly's Guesthouse, Green Mts, every day except Sat, leaving from the Brisbane Transit Centre. Ph: (07) 3285 1777. It also has a drop-off at Canungra for people bound for Binna Burra Lodge. They are then picked up by the lodge bus, which will also pick up guests from Nerang Railway Stn by arrangement. Ph: (07) 5533 3622

By rail

The Gold Coast/Robina train runs every half-hour to Nerang. Ph: (07) 3235 5555. Binna Burra Lodge will send a bus to pick up guests from the station by arrangement. Ph: (07) 5533 3622

An electric train runs from Brisbane to Rosewood hourly, connected by a rail-bus service with many other Lockyer Valley towns. Ph: 131 230

Getting around

Araucaria Ecotours runs 3-day minibus tours from Brisbane, led by a zoologist, to explore the biodiversity of the Border Ranges from a base at Mt Barney Lodge. Ph: (07) 5544 1283, (07) 5544 3233 or (07) 3848 4318

For tours from Brisbane and the Gold Coast to Green Mts, Mt Tamborine, Springbrook and Natural Bridge in the Numinbah Valley, try **Australian Day Tours**. Ph: 1300 363 436

Coachtrans runs day tours 3 times a week from Brisbane and the Gold Coast to Mt Tamborine and Green Mts, and twice weekly to Springbrook and Natural Bridge in the Numinbah Valley. Ph: 1300 361 788

SeeMore Scenic Tours has day tours from the Gold Coast to Springbrook, Tamborine/Binna Burra and Tamborine/O'Reilly's, and also offers a Springbrook Night Sights Tour and a Tamborine Mts Sunset Tour. Wheelchair accessible. Ph: (07) 3805 5588

For a small fee, the **Ipswich Visitors Info Centre** can provide tour guides for coach groups visiting Ipswich. Bookings essential. Ph: (07) 3281 0555

Tours of the countryside around Ipswich, heritage sites, shopping centres and markets are offered by **Cassidy's Topline Tours and Guided Service** at Ipswich. Bookings essential. Ph: (07) 3201 5499

Lockyer Landcare's **Lockyer Discovery Tours** are a wide and flexible range of guided tours such as the Valley of Variety Tour (with visits to farms and historic sites, a roast lunch and entertainment from the Jackaroo Band), the Top Spots Tour (visiting Lake Dyer and the lush Laidley Valley) and the Scrubby Adventure Tour (exploring areas of natural bushland and their flora and fauna). Lockyer Landcare also has 'tag-along' tours for those who would like to take advantage of a guide's know-how but prefer to travel in their own cars. Ph: (07) 5466 1818

Sunray Tours explores the heritage sites of Ipswich. Ph: (07) 3899 2414 or 3899 9399

Backtracks 4WD Safaris takes travellers from Brisbane and the Gold Coast to the Lamington, Springbrook and Mt Tamborine NPs, and on a Glow-Worm Sundown Safari. Ph: 1800 356 693

Duncan's Off-Road 4WD Tours offers tag-along expeditions and passenger tours of the Scenic Rim. Ph: 1800 357 475

For 4WD nature tours from the Gold Coast to Lamington, Springbrook, Natural Bridge and Tamborine Mt, contact **Southern Cross 4WD Tours**. Ph: 1800 067 367

Entering Canungra

Helidon sandstone
Lockyer Landcare offers a **Hidden Treasures Tour**, which includes a trip to the Comerford Sandstone Quarry. Ph: (07) 5466 1818

The attractions of Canungra, Green Mts, Tamborine Mt and Springbrook can be uncovered with **Trailblazers Tours**. Ph: (07) 5543 4146

Sidetracks 4WD Adventure Tours offers 1-day and half-day excursions through spectacular mountain scenery near Willowbank. In Jun, during the Ipswich drag-racing carnival, Sidetracks runs a 'Winternationals special' – a 5hr scenic tour to 6 or so country pubs. Ph: (07) 3814 1166

Four organisations run steam-train rides in the Ipswich and Lockyer Valley region: **Queensland Pioneer Steam Railway** (Ph: (07) 3281 0555 or (07) 3281 8837), **Rosewood Railway Museum** (Ph: (07) 3371 4231), the **Railway Historical Centre** (Ph: (07) 3280 5440) and **SunSteam** (Ph: (07) 3807 1296). (See pp.215, 220, 223.)

Festivals and events

Ipswich Festival

This 10-day celebration of Ipswich life, held in Mar, includes a street parade on Sat. Ph: (07) 3810 6562

Rathdowney Heritage Festival

A heritage procession, country/bush band, wagon rides and food stalls are among the attractions at this festival held in Apr. Ph: (07) 5544 1222

Hang gliding, Mt Tamborine

Gatton Heritage Festival

Local community history is celebrated in this week-long festival held throughout the shire from late Apr to the Labour Day long weekend (1st weekend in May). The celebrations centre on the Historical Village (p.219). Ph: (07) 5462 3430

Gatton Heavy Horse Field Days

This event, held at the **Gatton Showgrounds** on the Labour Day long weekend in May, draws a large crowd to pay tribute to the power and patience of the great working horses of yesteryear – clydesdales, percherons, shires and Australian draughts. Ph: (07) 5546 4701

Beaudesert Bull and Bronc

A major rodeo on a night in May. Ph: (07) 5541 1893

Winternationals Drag-Racing Carnival

Held in Jun at the Willowbank Raceway, **Ipswich**. This is the largest national drag-racing event in Australia. Ph: (07) 3849 6881

Beaudesert Country and Horse Festival

Over 40 separate events are featured at this week-long festival in Jun, including a rodeo, a street parade and a country-and-western concert. Ph: (07) 5541 3233

Rathdowney Campdraft

A 3-day campdrafting event held on the Queen's Birthday weekend in Jun. Ph: (07) 5544 1297

Gatton Shire Art Awards

This week-long event held in **Gatton** in Aug features displays of local arts and crafts, and $3000 in prize money. Ph: (07) 5462 4000

Tamborine Mt Flower and Garden Festival

The Vonda Youngman Community Centre in Main St is filled with flowers and stalls, and several private gardens are open to the public when this Aug event is held. Ph: (07) 5545 1725

Bauhinia Time Festival

This arts festival, which has been held annually for over 40 years, has become a spring tradition in the Lockyer Valley. It is held in **Gatton** in Sept. Ph: (07) 5462 1252

The Queensland 500

Formerly the Sandown 500, this motor race is run at the Qld Raceway (part of the Willowbank Motorsport Precinct), **Ipswich**, in Sept. Ph: (07) 5467 3555

Laidley Spring Festival

The Laidley Spring Festival is held in Sept and features a Chelsea Flower Show, Arts Show and Orchid Show. The Chelsea Flower Show is a 30-year-old tradition, with markets, street parades, garden competition and much more. Ph: (07) 5465 1413

Canungra Hang Gliding Classic

Hang gliders gather at this Oct event, launching themselves from either **Tamborine Mt** (near the showgrounds) or **Beechmont**. Ph: (07) 5543 5631

Goodtime Brisbane Valley 100 Canoe Race, Ipswich

This canoe race, held in Oct, follows the Brisbane River from Lake Wivenhoe to Sellars Quarry, Kholo. Ph: (07) 3358 8052

Gatton Motorcycle Swap Meet

Enthusiasts travel from all round Australia and overseas to attend this 2-day event held at the Gatton Showgrounds in Oct. Ph: (07) 5462 1090

Gatton Potato Carnival

The annual harvest is celebrated in this 1-day carnival held in Gatton's main street in Oct. The carnival was first held over 30 years ago; the street parade is now its main focus. Ph: (07) 4632 7577

Jacaranda Festival

A 2-day spring festival celebrating the district's multicultural community and featuring food, art, performance, dance and music from all over the world. Held at the end of Oct at Evan Marginson Sports Ground, **Goodna**. Ph: (07) 3810 6562

Gatton Potato Festival

Oktoberfest

The German heritage of the Lockyer Valley is celebrated at the historic Marburg Hotel, **Marburg**, with German beer, cuisine and music. Ph: (07) 3281 0555

Prenzlau Bush Carnival

A carnival featuring that stalwart of bygone rural life, the clydesdale. Held in Oct at Herrmann's Heritage Farm, Prenzlau (off the Warrego Hwy between Minden and Hatton Vale). Ph: (07) 5426 8473

Kalbar Country Day

There are arts, crafts and entertainment at this Nov event in Kalbar. Ph: (07) 5463 1016

Main localities and towns

For ease of reference, towns have been listed alphabetically in 4 sections: the Fassifern Valley; the Gold Coast hinterland; Ipswich and the Lockyer Valley; the Logan River Valley.

The Fassifern Valley
Aratula Map 40 B4

The small town of Aratula, on the Cunningham Hwy, is set in dark-soil country in the shadow of Mt Edwards. The local **fruit barn**, on the highway, is piled high with fresh fruit and vegetables from the farms and orchards of the Granite Belt and the Fassifern and Lockyer Valleys. Just outside the town is the turnoff to **Lake Moogerah**, 8km away (p.231).

Petal power
SunSteam (p.214) runs a steam-train ride from Brisbane to **Laidley** for the Laidley Spring Festival.

Boonah *Map 40 B4*

On the hills above Teviot Brook, in the heart of the fertile Fassifern Valley, is the picturesque town of Boonah. The valley is a prime producer of beef, pork, vegetables and cereal crops. Boonah's town centre, still with many of the original shopfronts, has been prettily landscaped and traffic-calmed.

North of the town centre is a scenic lookout, which can be reached by walking track from the town or by driving up Mt Carmel Rd. On the Boonah-Fassifern Rd below the lookout is the visitor info centre, a replica colonial cottage in Bicentennial Park. Open daily, 9.30am–4pm. Ph: (07) 5463 2233

The **Boonah Regional Art Gallery**, in the old courthouse on Highbury St, has exhibitions of both local and visiting artists. Open Mon–Fri, 10am–2pm; Sat, 10am–noon; group visits by appt. Ph: (07) 5463 2553 or (07) 5463 2925

Country markets selling things 'home-grown', 'home-sewn' are held in Boonah, usually every 2nd Sat, 7am–1pm. Ph: (07) 5463 5708

About 4km out of Boonah on the Boonah-Fassifern Rd is **Templin Historical Village**, a museum with 12 historic buildings and thousands of exhibits. Devonshire teas are available, and guided tours can be arranged. Wheelchair accessible. Open Sun–Thurs, 9.30am–3.30pm. Ph: (07) 5463 1970

In Reckumpilla St at Mt Alford, about 10km SW of Boonah, is **Sandra's Dolls**, 'a culmination of many years of collecting'. Open daily, 10am–3pm, by appt. Ph: (07) 5463 0258

The **Lacock Mousery**, in Radcliffe Rd, 5 mins outside Boonah, welcomes visitors to the mouse farm and rattery. Open by appt. Ph: (07) 5463 2644

Kalbar *Map 40 B4*

Kalbar is situated among the gentle undulations of Fassifern farms. Many of its old buildings have been preserved. See, for example, the historic **Wiss Emporium**, built in 1909 and winner of a Qld National Trust Heritage Award.

The Gold Coast hinterland
Canungra *Map 40 C4*

The old cedargetting and sawmilling town of Canungra, strategically placed between Tamborine Mt and the Lamington Plateau, now welcomes tourists with bistros, a decorative windmill, galleries and cafes. Near the Tudor-style **Canungra Hotel** (Ph: (07) 5543 5233) is the visitors info centre, housed in the Canungra Library. The centre sells a Heritage Walk guide for the town, with a brief history of each feature. Open Sun–Fri, 9.30am–4pm; Sat, 9.30am–12.30pm. Ph: (07) 5543 5156

Boonah township

In the park opposite is a replica of the home of Canungra's 'natural artist' Edwin Bode (1859–1926). Examples of his work are on display inside.

St Luke's Church in Kidston St dates from 1936. It was built in an unusually squat Gothic style, with roofing tiles imported from Italy and a bronze-roofed steeple. Inside are walls of rosewood and furniture of red cedar.

The **Canungra Markets** are held in the School of Arts building in Christie St on the 1st Sun of the month, 8.30am–2pm. Ph: (07) 5543 7186

On the outskirts of the town is the Army's **Kokoda Barracks and training area**, where Australian and overseas soldiers are trained in close-country warfare.

On the Lamington NP road, 3km from town, is **Aussie Country Down Under**, which has resident kangaroos and koalas and specialises in tours with true-blue Aussie activities. Bookings essential. Ph: (07) 5543 5546

Canungra Hotel

Nerang *Map 40 D4*

Those who remember Nerang as a charming township on the steep western bank of the Nerang River will not recognise the confusion of housing development, light industry and massive road construction that has now spread south along the Pacific Hwy. However, for travellers seeking a picnic spot, patches of parkland still border the river, lined with stately gums.

Springbrook *Map 40 C4*

This mountain village has the dignity conferred by age. Time has allowed the forest to enfold the older lodges and tea-rooms that were built here from the 1930s on, and, despite the new development, the air is one of harmony with the environment.

At the top of the single-lane section of road that leads up to Springbrook is **Wunburra Lookout**, above a deep valley surrounded by mountains and the jewel-like Little Nerang Dam. The view is clear through the valley to the Gold Coast.

Opposite the lookout is the historic **Gleneagles Gallery and Tearooms**, a cottage with a river-stone chimney, gardens and aviaries. It sells Devonshire teas, lunches, local honey, arts and crafts and old wares. Open daily, 9.30am–5pm; closed Wed. Ph: (07) 5533 5126

A 3km **Scenic Loop** drive leads off along Springbrook Rd, returning via Lyrebird Ridge Rd.

For details of the national park areas and the lookouts, see p.227.

Tamborine Mt *Map 40 C4*

The Tamborine Mt settlement has become a large residential community and tourist centre spread out among Sydney blue gums, rainforest and a few remaining orchards and avocado groves. The 3 spurs of the mountain divide the community into the separate villages of **Mt Tamborine** in the south, **North Tamborine** in the NW, and **Eagle Heights** in the east. High on a plateau virtually surrounded by cliffs, with sweeping views in most directions and pockets of lush rainforest filled with birds, mountain streams and waterfalls, Tamborine Mt has romance enough to tempt travellers from afar. This and its proximity to Brisbane and the Gold Coast have made it a major tourist haunt.

At Eagle Heights, the concentration of galleries and other tourist shops in **Gallery Walk** rivals that of supreme mountain resorts like Montville. There is something here to tickle every fancy, from German cuckoo clocks to macadamia fudge. A walking track leads to the nearby picnic area at the entrance to the **Palm Grove section** of **Tamborine NP** (p.229).

Anyone for tea?
The **Curtis Falls Cafe**, at **North Tamborine**, has shelves laden with teapots from all over the world. It also stocks Tamborine Teapots, made on the premises.

Mt Tamborine Winery

On Forsythia Drive are the newly established **Tamborine Botanic Gardens**.

Over Wangawallan Rd from the **MacDonald Park section of Tamborine NP** (p.229) is the **Tamborine Mt Heritage Centre**; its 6 buildings include a Pioneer Hall, with dioramas of early timbergetters. Open Sun, 11am-3pm. Ph: (07) 5545 1904

St George's Church, cnr Eagle Heights Rd and Dapsang Dr, was originally a hall at St Bernard's, which was moved and rebuilt on its present site in 1938.

Memory Lane Antiques, on Long Rd, occupies a little old church with a steeply pitched roof. It was built in about 1880. Open Fri-Mon, 10.30am-4.30pm or by appt. Ph: (07) 5545 1949

At North Tamborine, the oldest part of the settlement, the **Dutch Clog Workshop**, 28 Main St, offers demonstrations of clog-making at 12.30pm and 2pm and by appt. Ph: (07) 5545 1781

Also at North Tamborine is the **Tamborine Mt Distillery**, 87-91 Beacon Rd, where liqueurs, schnapps, liqueured fruits and chocolates are made. Open Wed-Sun, 10am-4pm. Ph: (07) 5545 3452

The Tamborine Mt Tourist Info Centre at Doughty Park, North Tamborine (staffed by the local Natural History Association), distributes a *Tamborine Mt Tourist Map* with details of the area's many attractions. Open daily, 10.30am-3.30pm. Ph: (07) 5545 3200

The **Mt Tamborine Vineyard and Winery**, 32 Hartley Rd, North Tamborine, has cellar-door tastings daily, 10am-4pm. Ph: (07) 5545 3506. Its 2nd cellar door is at Flaxton Gardens on the Blackall Ra (p.117).

The finest views are from the **Main Western Rd**, which runs around the western escarpment (a favourite hang-gliding spot), from **Paradise Dr** in the residential area on the NE face, and from the **Eagle Heights Hotel** on the Tamborine-Oxenford road.

For details about the national parks on the mountain, see pp.228-30.

Ipswich and the Lockyer Valley
Amberley *Map 40 B3*
Amberley (11km west of the Ipswich CBD) is the largest operational RAAF base in Australia. It is not open to the public, but visitors are welcome at the **memorial garden**, where Australia's 1st Canberra bomber is on display.

Curtis Falls, Mt Tamborine

Gatton *Map 40 A2*

Gatton, the prosperous centre of the rich Lockyer Valley farmland, is marked by a cluster of small hills in an expanse of dark ploughed paddocks and crops of lush green. The farms around Gatton are among the most productive in Qld, with heavy yields of small crops, dairy products, pork, beef and fruit. Sawmilling is also important.

Take the Allan St turnoff north from the highway to **Pohlman's Nursery**. Groups are invited to tour the production nursery on board the 'Gum Tree Valley Express'. Open daily, 8.30am–5pm; coach and group tours Mon–Fri, 8.30am–3pm. Bookings essential. Ph: (07) 5462 1699

The **Lake Apex Fauna Sanctuary**, 2km from the town centre, brings people and wildlife together in a complex of grassy hills, lagoons and special recreation areas. The Gatton Tourist Info Centre, at the sanctuary kiosk, has a wealth of material on points of interest in the sanctuary and beyond. (Ph: (07) 5462 3430.) The lagoons are home to many bird species and attract a range of wanderers, from pelicans to pygmy geese.

Gatton Historical Village, on Freemans Rd at the southern boundary of the Lake Apex Fauna Sanctuary, consists of several historic buildings, including a slab cottage and a church built in 1892. There is also a collection of over 10 000 exhibits representing the heritage of the Lockyer Valley community. Open Sun, 1pm–4pm; other times by appt. Ph: (07) 5462 1580

There are guided tours, on request, of Win Davson's **Art Gallery and Museum**, 17 North St. Ph: (07) 5462 1252

Gatton College, to the east of the town, was established as an agricultural college in 1897. It is now part of the University of Qld and offers courses in new fields, such as tourism and food technology, along with the more traditional agri-oriented subjects.

Grandchester *Map 40 B3*

Grandchester is a tiny township 37km west of Ipswich on the banks of Western Creek and at the base of the Little Liverpool Ra. It was originally called Bigge's Camp after Frederick Bigge, a pioneer pastoralist. When the railway line was built, Governor Bowen suggested that 'Bigge's Camp' be made a more elegant name by translating it into Latin, so 'Big' became *Grand* and 'camp' became *chester*.

Grandchester's fame rests on its status as the inland terminus for the 1st railway in Qld. It was opened in 1865 – the 1st stage in a line connecting the Darling Downs with Ipswich, which was in turn linked with the port of Brisbane by riverboat. The **Grandchester Railway Stn** is the oldest station building still standing in Qld.

Just off the highway immediately to the east of the town is **Bigge's Camp Park**, set in 5ha of spotted-gum forest. It has shelter sheds, picnic facilities and monuments dedicated to the history of the area. One gives an account of the area's Aboriginal inhabitants, European exploration and settlement, and the building of the railway.

Helidon *Map 40 A2*

The town of Helidon, at the foot of the Toowoomba Ra, is famous for its sandstone and natural spas. The spa waters, which are pumped from sandstone bores and then passed through filters, are typically rich in calcium, magnesium, sodium and potassium, and are said to have curative properties for various ailments, such as arthritis and other joint problems. The **Helidon Natural Springs Spa Resort**, on the Warrego Hwy just outside the town, has a spa in every room. Ph: (07) 4697 6066

Many of the fine heritage buildings of Brisbane and Ipswich were built with Helidon sandstone. Several of the sandstone quarries in the area are open to the public, some offering tours. Inquire at the Helidon Natural Springs Spa Resort.

At **Emu Gully**, near Helidon, an **Adventure Education Centre** offers adventure-based education for all the family in a picturesque setting, with farm tours, abseiling, an animal nursery, go-karts, a giant slide, Skirmish, swimming, an artificial caving complex, 4WD motorbike tours, and much more. Bookings essential. Ph: (07) 4697 6631

Model steam train
Opposite the turnoff to **Bigge's Camp Park** is a short road leading to a scaled-down railway, where model locomotives are stoked up by the Grandchester Model Live Steam Association on the first Sun of each month.

Kids' stuff
The **Lake Apex Fauna Sanctuary** at **Gatton** copes with the boundless energy of youngsters big and small with a pedal train, BMX track, skateboard ramp and extended cycle track.

Burning interest
The **Incinerator Theatre**, built in 1936 to burn the city's rubbish, and now transformed into an intimate theatre, was designed by Walter Burley Griffin, the architect who was also responsible for designing Canberra.

Ipswich *Map 40 B3*

Superb heritage buildings grace the knobby hills of Ipswich, the oldest provincial city in Qld. There is everywhere a sense of material history, from the grittiness of the old workshops to the elegance of the hilltop homes. Care has been taken to preserve a high proportion of the early buildings — official, religious, industrial, commercial and domestic. Almost 2000 places are included on the city's Heritage Register.

The railway workshop and woollen mill no longer operate, but the city still has a core of traditional industries — coal mines, foundries, sawmills, earthenware works and abattoirs.

The Ipswich community prides itself on both its sense of history and its commitment to cutting-edge information technology. The city has switched on to the electronic age, as evidenced by its innovative Global Info-Links community-based information technology and telecommunication service, and **Global Arts Link**, in the refurbished Old Town Hall, Brisbane St, which includes a museum and an art gallery of international standard, as well as Lottie's Place, dedicated to art development for small children, with fun activities both traditional and high-tech. Wheelchair accessible. Open daily, 10am–5pm. Ph: (07) 3810 6677

Next to Global Arts Link is the Ipswich Visitors and Tourist Info Centre, cnr d'Arcy Doyle Pl and Brisbane St, which has plenty of informational material. (Ask at the centre for a free parking voucher.) A brochure of particular interest to those who are historically or architecturally inclined is *Ipswich Heritage Trails*, which maps a walking tour of the CBD and a driving tour that takes the sightseer past many of the city's grandest homes.

Queens Park, bounded on the north by Brisbane St, is a 22ha expanse of sweeping lawns relieved by stately trees and outcrops of limestone. It was set aside as a reserve in 1842. The views from the rotunda range over the knolls and valleys of the city to a backdrop of jagged mountains. The park also has a newly rebuilt fauna section (concentrating on native animals but including a farm section and exotic species such as deer and peacocks), children's playgrounds, a bush chapel, a bushhouse and a kiosk.

Denmark Hill Conservation Park, only a 10min walk from the city centre, has picnic facilities and 3 walking tracks (see map 42).

The banks of the Bremer and Brisbane Rivers are pleasant spots to picnic or launch a canoe (p.233). The Ipswich area has several **waterside parks**, such as Colleges Crossing Recreation Reserve at Chuwar and **Joseph Brady Park** at Barellan Point. **Colleges Crossing**, on the Brisbane River (Mt Crosby Rd), has been a favourite swimming spot for generations.

Qld Pioneer Steam Railway's vintage train rides leave from Swanbank, just off the Cunningham Hwy to the south of Ipswich. The trips are about 7km long and leave every 45 minutes on the 1st and 3rd Suns of the month and on 20 or so other special occasions each year. Wheelchair access is provided. Ph: (07) 3281 8837 or (07) 3281 0555

Laidley *Map 40 A3*

Laidley lies in the deep greens and sables of the surrounding farms at the entrance to the Laidley Creek valley, which narrows dramatically to the south before meeting the barrier of Mt Castle. The deep loamy soils of the Laidley farms produce an abundance of fruit and vegetables, particularly beetroot.

Belmont, a historic Ipswich home

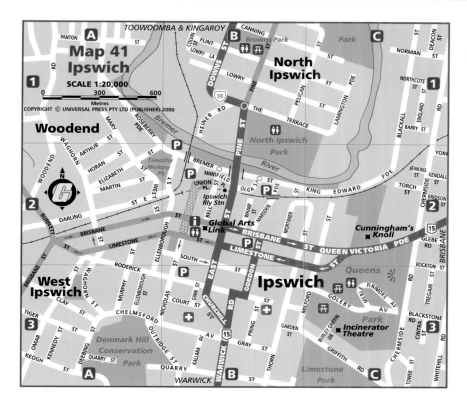

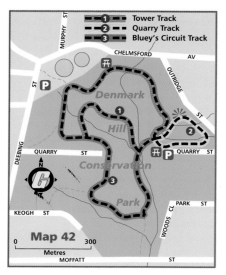

The Laidley business centre still has the air of an old country town, with wooden pubs and deeply shaded shopfronts. On the corner of William and Patrick Sts is **Das Neumann Haus**, built in 1893, testifying to the contribution made to the region by German immigrants. It is an unusual timber building combining Qld vernacular features with idiosyncratic touches. The building now houses a museum, arts and crafts shop and German cafe (Annie's Place), as well as the Laidley Visitor Info Centre: open Thurs–Sun, 9am–4pm. Ph: (07) 5465 3241

The old **Laidley Bakery**, in the main street, is a 2-storey brick building, with the decorative parapet, upper verandah and wide street awning typical of its period.

Once the 1st coach-stop past the Grandchester railhead, Laidley is now bypassed by the main route west. The town pays tribute to the old days of coaches and bullock trains with the **Pioneer Village**, cnr Drayton and Pioneer Sts. This complex includes a century-old school, pioneer cottage, stores, blacksmith's shop and police cells. Open Sun, 2pm–4pm and by appt. Ph: (07) 5465 1587

Narda Lagoon, opposite the Pioneer Village, is set in a conservation reserve designed to preserve the district's vegetation types and provide a habitat for aquatic and other wildlife. A point of

Country fare
Everyone comes to town for the **Laidley market**, held on the last Sat of each month.

Old Bakery, Laidley

engineering interest is the suspension bridge spanning the lagoon. Picnic facilities are provided.

About 5km NW of Laidley is the small township of **Forest Hill**, which has 2 historic and highly photogenic pubs.

For a panoramic view of the Laidley Creek and Lockyer valleys, drive to **Schultz's Lookout**, about 7km SW of Laidley along Blenheim Rd.

Marburg *Map 40 B2*

The small town of Marburg, just off the Warrego Hwy, was originally a centre for the sawmilling, sugar and dairy industries. It was a go-ahead town in its day, being one of the 1st provincial centres in the state to have buildings lit by electricity. Its houses are staggered down the eastern aspect of the Marburg Ra, the commercial buildings collecting at its foot to form the heart of the town.

The **Marburg Hotel** is a 2-storey wooden pub with wrought-iron verandah decoration. It was built in 1881, originally with only 1 storey.

The **Marburg Community Centre**, designed in 1918 by Ipswich architect George Brockwell Gill, is a small wooden building with a neatly ornamented porch. It was formerly a bank.

Also near the centre of town are the headquarters of the **Rosewood Scrub Historical Society**, once the Walloon Shire Council Office. It dates from 1913. A **historic shingle-roofed dairy** stands at the rear. Open 1st and 3rd Suns of each month, 1.30pm–4pm. There are picnic facilities and a drinking fountain outside.

On a hilltop on the opposite side of the Warrego Hwy is **Woodlands**, a mansion built in 1890. It is a fine example of Victorian architecture. Open by appt only. Ph: (07) 5464 4777

Rosevale *Map 40 B3*

The Bremer River, rising in the Great Divide near Cunningham's Gap, flows NE past the township of Rosevale before crossing Bainbrigge's Plain on its way to Ipswich. Rosevale is known for the **Rosevale Retreat Hotel**, a single-storey timber pub with low verandahs, shady trees and a view of Cunningham's Gap to the south.

Rosewood *Map 40 B3*

Rosewood grew up around the railway line at the turn of the century, and its streets still have the pace and spaciousness of an earlier time. The town is flanked on the north by the Bluff, part of the Little Liverpool Ra, and the

Flickering past
In the 1920s the Chauvels, pioneers of the Australian movie industry, used the **Rosevale Retreat** in some scenes of their first film, *The Moth of Moonbi*.

surrounding pastures extend south and west to a skyline of distant ranges. The road passes through open paddocks where stock have neatly trimmed the trees, crosses the railway line, and enters an old-world streetscape shaded here and there by silky oaks and casuarinas.

Rosewood is full of interesting old buildings: the **Rosewood Courthouse**, built in 1910, and the **police station** are heritage-listed.

St Brigid's Catholic Church, built in 1910, in Railway St, is the largest timber church in Qld. The interior shows a distinct German influence.

The **Rising Sun Hotel**, near the railway line, is a 2-storey timber building with striking Art Nouveau flourishes. It was designed by the Ipswich architect Will Haenke in 1908.

Glendalough, at the roundabout, is a large, showy house that grew, with the burgeoning prosperity of its owner, from a humble cottage into a grand residence.

Just outside Rosewood, near the golf course, is the eye-catching **Normanton Colliery coal-loading gantry**, a derelict timber structure of 3 storeys. The gantry was built in 1929, and was moved to its present site and enlarged in 1946-47.

Tucked into tumbling hills north of the town is the **Rosewood Railway Museum**, at Kunkala Stn, a railway siding with an operating steam train (rides on last Sun of the month from nearby Cabanda Stn), refreshment and souvenir stalls, and picnic areas. To get there, follow the Rosewood–Marburg road north out of Rosewood, turn left at Urry Rd opposite the Oakleigh Colliery, and then follow Keates Rd to Freeman Rd. Open Sun, 10am-4pm; bus groups at other times by appt. Ph: (07) 3371 4231, 10am-3pm (Tue-Fri only)

The Logan River Valley
Beaudesert Map 40 C4

Beaudesert stands at the crossroads of Mt Lindesay Hwy and the roads to Canungra to the east and Boonah to the west. It is the principal town of the prosperous farming district of the Logan River valley.

The **Beaudesert Community Arts and Info Centre**, at the northern entrance to the town, distributes useful brochures on tours of the surrounding district (such as *A Tour South of Beaudesert* and *A Beaudesert Shire Historical Church Tour*). The centre is also a gallery displaying the work of local painters, potters and craftspeople. Open daily, 9am-4pm. Ph: (07) 5541 4495

The **Beaudesert Historical Museum and Info Centre**, on Brisbane St in Jubilee Park, includes a genuine slab hut built on the Kerry selection in 1875. Open Wed and Fri, 12.30pm-4pm; Sat, Sun and public holidays, 9am-4pm (also open Tue and Thurs, 9am-4pm, in school holidays). Ph: (07) 5541 1284 or 5541 2583

St Mary's Church, off Bromelton Rd, is an imposing timber church in Gothic style, built in 1907 by G H M Addison. It features a belfry with timber decoration.

Markets are held in Westerman Park, Mt Lindesay Hwy, on the 1st Sat of each month, 7am-noon. Arts, crafts, antiques and collectables are for sale, and entertainment is provided. Ph: (07) 5544 8200

Rathdowney Map 40 B4

On the Mt Lindesay Hwy, in rolling cattle country near the dramatic peaks of the Mt Barney group of mountains, is the small town of Rathdowney, 'Gateway to the Mountains'.

At the **Historical Museum and Tourist Info Centre** on the Mt Lindesay Hwy is a hut housing a display of local plants used by the Aborigines, old photos and a range of artefacts, from a hip bath to butter pats. The centre distributes a guide to Rathdowney and its surrounds. Open Thurs-Fri, 1pm-4pm; weekends and public holidays, 9am-4pm (also open Wed, 9am-4pm, in school holidays). Ph: (07) 5544 1222

On the way into town from Beaudesert, turn left and then right into John St for the **Captain Logan Lookout** and a view over the town to the looming peaks of Mt Barney, Mt Lindesay, Mt Maroon and Mt May.

Rathdowney is within easy reach of **Mt Barney NP** (p.227), **Lake Maroon** (p.231) and scenic **Lions Rd** (p.231).

Rathdowney, 'Gateway to the Mountains'

National parks and regional parks

The Scenic Rim is the site of Qld's 1st national park, and the popularity of its splendid subtropical rainforests and extensive systems of walking tracks is still unsurpassed in the state.

The arc of mountains known as the Scenic Rim sweeps west to include the Main Ra NP, which falls within the Southern Downs region (pp.200–202). The coverage of the Scenic Rim in this chapter takes in 5 national parks: Lamington, Moogerah Peaks, Mt Barney, Springbrook and Tamborine. They are all included in the Central Eastern Australian Rainforest Reserves World Heritage Area.

Further north is Glen Rock Regional Park, a newly developed area looking down on the upper Lockyer Valley.

Glen Rock Regional Park *Map 40 A3*

Glen Rock Regional Park, an area of 6300ha, lies at the head of the Tenthill Valley 40km south of Gatton, and adjoins the Mt Mistake section of the Main Ra NP, a World Heritage Area. The park encompasses a variety of landscapes, from the fertile flats of **Blackfellow**, **Shady** and **Flaggy Creeks**, to craggy ridges, deep gorges and high plateau country.

The **Angophora Day-Use Area**, on **Blackfellow Creek**, has picnic areas in the shade of old wild apple trees. From here a walking track leads past small caves up onto the ridges, which look out over the park. Further bushwalks, horseriding trails, 4WD tracks and camping areas are planned. Ask at the Gatton Tourist Info Centre at Lake Apex for details. Ph: (07) 5462 3430

Lamington NP *Map 40 C4*

This famous national park preserves the largest remaining stand of sub-tropical rainforest in Australia. It covers 20 500ha of thickly forested ranges and valleys, where the rain comes heavily and often. Dozens of mountain torrents join the larger streams that flow through the area – the **Coomera** and **Albert Rivers** and **Christmas** and **Canungra Creeks**. The land rises southwards, reaching a height of 1100m at the **McPherson Ra**, on the Qld–NSW border.

The magnificent rainforest, with its towering, buttressed trees decked with epiphytes, its strangler figs, feathery palms and looping vines, thins here and there to open eucalypt forest and occasionally heath. In the higher regions near the border are stands of the ancient Antarctic beech.

Lamington's birdlife is rich and varied. Bellbirds, whipbirds, the astonishing catbird, and many more, fill the forest with their calls.

Rainforest, Lamington NP

The park has 2 distinct sections with well-developed walking tracks and other facilities — **Binna Burra** and **Green Mts**. The tracks here are generally graded and slope gently, but many include sets of rock steps. A night walk can be particularly thrilling, not only because of possible encounters with nocturnal animals, such as koalas and sugar gliders, but also because of the chance of seeing luminous fungi glowing in the dark, and glow-worms decorating the embankments with their tiny lights.

Further south, the terrain is wild and rugged, and is traversed by only a few rough trails.

Binna Burra

This section occupies the NE portion of the park. To reach it, drive up the escarpment from Nerang, on the Pacific Hwy, via Beechmont. There is also access from Brisbane via Canungra.

The ranger's office and info centre at the main-road entrance to the park has an array of brochures and maps, various natural-history exhibits, and interesting displays: one geological and the other showing the relative biodegradability of common items of litter. As well as the main *Walking Track Guide*, self-guides to various walks are available here. There is a picnic area with toilets nearby. Open daily, 8am–3.30pm, but staffed (by rangers and volunteers) only on weekends. Ph: (07) 5533 3584

The Binna Burra area is about 800m above sea level, and has a privileged view over the coast. It has an extensive system of walks of varying length and difficulty. There are circuit walks ranging in length from 1km to over 23km, exploring various types of forest, woodland and heath, and visiting waterfalls, lookouts and caves. One of these, the **Border Track**, is a 21.4km walk (1-way) connecting Binna Burra with Green Mts, with spectacular views into NSW from a multitude of lookouts along the volcanic rim.

There is no national park camping area at Binna Burra, but camping is available at the private camping ground run by the **Binna Burra Lodge**. There is also a picnic area, restaurant and kiosk here. Ph: 1800 074 260 for camping reservations. The lodge, which began in 1933 as a simple guesthouse, is now a resort of international standard. It includes an adventure playground with rainforest themes. Also within the lodge grounds is the **Senses Trail** (400m or 700m). A self-guiding brochure, keyed to trailside markers with Braille inscriptions, alerts the walker to the smells, sounds and textures, as well as the sights, of the rainforest. Ph: (07) 5533 3622

Green Mts

This section of Lamington NP lies to the SW of Binna Burra and is separated from it by the Coomera River valley, the Darlington Ra and the Canungra Creek valley. The main road access is via Canungra, along the Lamington NP Rd.

For one of the finest views in all the Scenic Rim, stop off on the way at the picnic area at **Kamarun Lookout**. There are views in all directions, as far as the sea in the east and SW to Mt Barney. The nearby **Rainforest Gallery and Cafe** combines views, brewed coffee, arts and crafts and alpaca products. Open by appt. Ph: (07) 5544 0106

An alternative route to Green Mts is via the unsealed Duck Creek Rd, which winds up the NW escarpment from Kerry. A 4WD is advisable for this road, especially in wet weather.

There is a national park camping ground at Green Mts, and a national park ranger station/Green Mts Orientation Centre a little further up the road, on the left. As well as brochures, maps and guides, the centre has a superb rainforest diorama with doors that open to reveal endangered species, and features keyed to a brochure entitled *If We Could Turn Back Time*. Campers should book at the centre 3–4 weeks in advance outside holiday times, and 6–8 weeks in advance for school and public holidays. Open Mon, Wed and Thurs, 9am–11am and 1pm–3.30pm; Tue and Fri, 1pm–3.30pm. Ph: (07) 5544 0634.
There is no fuel supply or store on the mountain, so buy petrol and provisions at Canungra.

Egg Rock
Egg Rock, in the **Numinbah Valley** below Binna Burra, owes its distinctive shape to its origin as a subsidiary vent of the Mt Warning volcano.

Blue cray
In pools along Green Mts tracks such as the **Toolona Creek Circuit**, it is possible to see the beautifully coloured blue Lamington spiny crayfish.

Green Mts

Opposite the ranger station is **O'Reilly's Rainforest Guesthouse**, which first received visitors in the 1920s. It has expanded to become a vibrant resort, with a range of accommodation, a souvenir shop and 'Gran O'Reilly's' cafe-restaurant, overlooking the Lost World plateau to the SW and the Albert River valley beyond. As in the Bunya Mts (p.158), visitors to O'Reilly's should resist the temptation to feed the resident fauna.

O'Reilly's has interesting week-long theme programs for guests; topics include birds, frogs, mammals, photography and stargazing. Ph: (07) 5544 0644. Part of the resort complex is **St Joseph's Church**, a tiny timber church built in 1881 at Tullamore and re-erected on its present site in 1955.

Another feature to look out for is the **Green Mts Botanical Gardens**, now under-going careful replanting to ensure that they harmonise with the rainforest environment.

There are numerous walks at Green Mts, ranging from short strolls to strenuous day-long hikes. The **Border Track**, which connects with Binna Burra (21km 1-way), passes through gloomy stands of moss-draped Antarctic beech and skirts the dramatic escarpment that forms the border with NSW. There are panoramic views over the Tweed Valley and the Mt Warning caldera.

Perhaps the most exhilarating of all is the **Treetop Walk**, which traverses a series of 9 suspension bridges slung 160m through the rainforest canopy. Along the walk there are identification keys for the 60 species of tree, the 14 species of vine and the many ferns and orchids that grow there. For a crow's-eye view south over Green Mts, the adventurous can climb steel ladders to a treetop lookout above the walkway. The best times for viewing the canopy birds are early morning and late afternoon.

Moogerah Peaks NP *Map 40 B4*

Moogerah Peaks NP encompasses 4 small national parks occupying a total area of 926ha. They are centred on the old volcanic peaks that surround Lake Moogerah, in the Fassifern Valley — **Mt French** (598m), **Mt Edwards** (632m), **Mt Greville** (770m) and **Mt Moon**

(784m). Access to all the parks is from the Cunningham Hwy or via Boonah.

There are picnic facilities and short walking tracks to clifftop lookouts at **Mt French**, with views from the East Cliff to Mt Barney and from the North Cliff over the Fassifern Valley to Cunningham's Gap. Mt French is well known in international rock-climbing circles for its cliff faces and numerous climbs of varying difficulty. Camping is also permitted here, but a **permit** must be obtained in advance. Write to the ranger, Qld Parks and Wildlife Service, 3522 Ipswich–Boonah Rd, Coulson 4310. Ph: (07) 5463 5041

The other peaks have no facilities, apart from some rough bush tracks. Visitors are advised to walk them only in the company of an experienced bushwalker, and to carry an adequate supply of food and water.

At **Mt Edwards**, there is a 1.1km track to a lookout over the Reynolds Creek gorge, between Mt Edwards and Little Mt Edwards.

The gorges that gash the SE face of **Mt Greville** are lined with scree and palm-filled rainforest. A track follows these gorges to the summit (4hr return).

Mt Moon's forbidding cliffs and scree-covered slopes discourage all but the most skilled and determined bushwalkers. Climbers must pass through private property, and permission must be sought from the owner. For further info, check with the NP ranger. Ph: (07) 5463 5041

The Stinson rescue
At **O'Reilly's**, look out for the bronze sculpture that tells the story of Bernard O'Reilly's discovery of the Stinson plane crash survivors and their rescue.

Treetop Walk, O'Reilly's

Mt Barney NP *Map 40 B4*

Mt Barney NP is relatively undeveloped, with few facilities and rugged terrain. Visitors to this park need reasonable bush skills. Access is via Rathdowney or Boonah, from the Boonah–Rathdowney road.

The park has several sections of varying size, and takes in many mountains besides the twin peaks of **Mt Barney**, including **Mt Maroon**, **Mt May**, **Mt Ballow** and **Mt Lindesay**. Their spiky peaks rising out of rolling pastures and woodland makes for spectacular scenery.

The park has significant conservation value, preserving many rare plants, particularly on the higher mountains. There are also stands of Antarctic beech on Mt Ballow, patches of rainforest on Mt Barney, montane heath on Mt Maroon and tall banksia forests on Mt Lindesay.

Mt Barney has a 3.7km (1-way) walking track leading from the carpark to the **Lower Portals**, a long pool formed within a gorge by Barney Creek. The **South Ridge route** to the summit of Mt Barney requires some stamina, but is not beyond walkers with moderate experience. Though its nickname is 'Peasants' Ridge' it is quite demanding, so take plenty of water and allow a full day for a return journey of about 18km. The other walks follow difficult trails and should be attempted only by experienced bushwalkers and climbers.

There are no camping facilities within Mt Barney NP. For bush camping within the park, it is necessary to book and obtain a **permit**. Contact the ranger, NP and Wildlife Service, MS 342, Boonah 4310. Ph: (07) 5463 5041

There are camping grounds outside the park's boundary at **Mt May Campsite** (off Newman's Rd) and **Yellow Pinch** (at the end of Upper Logan Rd). There is also a private camping ground at **Mt Barney Lodge Country Retreat**, just before Yellow Pinch. Ph: (07) 5544 3233

Springbrook NP *Map 40 C4*

The Springbrook Plateau rises 900m out of the coastal lowlands near the NSW border, a romantic backdrop to the southern Gold Coast beaches. Its rugged outline and hazy blue contours promise the sparkling air, dense rainforest, clear streams and grassy swards of mountain scenery, with far-flung vistas of coast and sea.

The 2954ha park includes the **Springbrook Plateau** and **Mt Cougal** sections in the east, and **Natural Bridge**, in the Numinbah Valley, to the west.

Springbrook Plateau

This section has magnificent stands of eucalypt, thick rainforest, rainbow-lit waterfalls and expansive vistas. Access is via the road from Mudgeeraba on the Pacific Hwy, or the Nerang-Murwillumbah road.

Light shows at Springbrook
Visit **Rainbow Falls** in the afternoon, when shimmering multiple rainbows form in the slanting light.

Springbrook NP

Purlingbrook Falls, Springbrook NP

There are 3 picnic areas: Gwongorella, Tallanbana and Goomoolahara.

Gwongorella is a landscaped area with wheelchair access and facilities at the top of Purling Brook Falls, where the stream takes a 100m free-fall into a palm-filled gorge. Several walking tracks leave from here, and there is an adjoining national park camping area.

Tallanbana, near the **Canyon Lookout**, has tracks leading down into the Canyon and to the top of **Twin Falls**.

Goomoolahara is at the end of Springbrook Rd, 100m from the **Goomoolahara Falls**.

With its high rainfall and escarpment-ringed plateau, Springbrook is the home of waterfalls. Among them is a sequence of 3 falls — **Blackfellow, Poondahra** and **Poonyahra** — which drop a total of 180m from the top of the escarpment into the rainforest.

Springbrook is famous for its lookouts, some of which — **Wunburra** and **Canyon Lookouts** and **Lyrebird Ridge Rd** — can be reached by car. Others involve a walk — 100m to **Purlingbrook Falls Lookout** and **Goomoolahara Lookout**, and 3km return to **Bilbrough's Lookout**. The **Best of All Lookout** (600m return), at the end of Repeater Station Rd, lives up to its name, with panoramic views to the coast and Mt Warning to the south. The path to the lookout passes through one of the ancient stands of Antarctic beech.

For detailed info on walking tracks, including the 15km **Warrie Circuit**, which takes in 3 waterfalls, consult the map at the ranger station and info centre located in the old schoolhouse on the eastern side of Springbrook Rd. The centre is well worth a visit for its natural-history and social-history displays. Outside, a shed houses an old local buckboard, and a path leads to a lookout. Open daily, 8am–4pm. Ph: (07) 5533 5147

Mt Cougal

The twin peaks of Mt Cougal rise out of thick rainforest on the upper reaches of **Tallebudgera** and **Currumbin Creeks**, SE of the Springbrook section. This is rugged country, and the only formal tracks and

facilities are at **Cougal's Cascades Picnic Area**, at the end of Currumbin Creek Rd. (There are no BBQs.) A short track leads through dense rainforest beside Currumbin Creek. Adventurous walkers can rock-hop to pools further upstream. Access is via Currumbin, along Currumbin Creek Rd. Ph: (07) 5576 4045

Natural Bridge

The Natural Bridge, an arch of basalt rock sculpted into architectural form by the waters of **Cave Creek**, is deep in the Numinbah Valley, under the brooding cliffs of Springbrook's western ramparts. Access is via the Nerang-Murwillumbah road.

The vault of the cavern beneath Natural Bridge is lined with thousands of glow-worms. These are the larvae of the fungus fly, and they use their tiny lights to draw insect prey into their sticky webs. It is worth taking a walk at night to see them.

There is a 1km circuit track, which continues beyond the Natural Bridge lookout and across the creek downstream of the bridge, with a side track into the cavern.

No camping is allowed in this section of Springbrook NP, but there is a well-equipped and very popular picnic area, with electric pay BBQs. The park's popularity means that it is often crowded, so it is wise to bring your own picnic equipment.

For more info, contact the ranger, Natural Bridge NP, via Nerang 4211. Ph: (07) 5533 6156

Tamborine NP *Map 40 C3*

Tamborine, the site of Qld's 1st national park, is within easy reach of both Brisbane and the Gold Coast. Like Springbrook and the Lamington Plateau, it is a remnant of the huge Mt Warning shield volcano that had such a dramatic impact on the landscape of SE Qld.

Tamborine Mt, an isolated fragment of the Darlington Ra, reaches a height of over 500m and is well placed to catch the rain-bearing winds that sweep in from the Pacific Ocean. The high rainfall and rich, red soils support rainforest and eucalypts. Magnificent views open in every direction, from the Gold Coast to Moreton Island, and around the Scenic Rim.

Tamborine NP

Tamborine is a fragmented national park, with a total of 14 sections, 7 of them developed with graded walking tracks and other facilities (see below). They are scattered over the plateau, most of which was cleared for farming late last century and is now densely settled. Each section provides habitat for a wide range of fauna, including the land mullet (a large black skink) and the Albert lyrebird. None of these areas have camping facilities, but private campsites are provided elsewhere on the mountain. Info for visitors to the park is available from the ranger. Ph: (07) 5545 1171

Cedar Creek

From a picnic area 800m in from Tamborine Mt Rd, a 3.2km circuit track leads through eucalypt forest to the waterfalls and rockpools in **Cedar Creek gorge**.

Joalah

This section, at the junction of Eagle Heights Rd and Geissmann Dr, has 3 walks: the 1.5km (return) **Curtis Falls Walk**, the 4.2km **Joalah Circuit**, and a 400m walk through rainforest to nearby Cafes. Access is from the Dapsang Dr carpark. There are no picnic facilities here.

The Knoll

The Knoll, at North Tamborine, has a grassy picnic area and a 3km circuit walk to **Cameron Falls**. Access is via Main St and Knoll Rd.

Lepidozamia Grove

In this small park on the western edge of the plateau, there is a grove of these ancient cycads. The park is beside the Main Western Rd, at the top of the 'goat track' from Canungra.

MacDonald Park

This section, on Wongawallan Rd, has picnic facilities and a 1.4km circuit walk through rainforest.

Palm Grove

Palm Grove can be approached from either Palm Grove Ave or Curtis Rd. The picnic area at the Palm Grove Ave entrance looks out over the Gold Coast. There are 3 walks here: the 2.6km **Palm Grove Circuit**, the 5.4km **Jenyn's Falls Circuit** and the 1.2km (1-way) **Curtis Rd Track**.

Witches Falls

Witches Falls, on the Main Western Rd, was the 1st national park in Qld. It was declared in 1908, with the aim of preserving an area of outstanding natural beauty.

There are 2 walks – the **Witches Falls Circuit** (3km) and the **Beacon Rd Track** (4km 1-way). The views from the lookouts in this section take in the craggy mountains of Mt Barney NP, the dramatic heights of

the Main Ra NP, and the lush Lamington plateau. Across the road are picnic facilities, set among tall eucalypts. The trees have been known to drop branches in high winds, so choose calm weather to picnic here. There are unsurpassed sunset views.

Other attractions

Advancetown Lake *Map 40 D4*

Advancetown Lake (also known as Hinze Dam), at the junction of the Nerang River and Little Nerang Creek, supplies much of the water for the Gold Coast. It is surrounded by rolling hills, and the picnic areas on the eastern banks look across the ranges of Springbrook and Binna Burra.

Sailing, canoeing and rowing are permitted, and boat ramps are provided. (Petrol-driven motorboats are not allowed on the lake.) The waters are stocked with bass, golden perch, silver perch and Murray cod. **Fishing permits** are available from the kiosk and from selected bait shops and Gold Coast Council offices. (Fishing is allowed with indigenous bait only.) There is a lookout on the eastern side of the dam wall, and a nearby kiosk, **Banjo's Inn Cafe**. Open daily, 9am–4pm. Ph: (07) 5533 2159

Barney View Uniting Church *Map 43* ◉

SW of Rathdowney, on Mt Barney Rd, is a small timber church of pleasing simplicity. It stands alone in the countryside, contemplating the rugged majesty of nearby **Mt Barney**. The church was built by community effort in 1908.

Border crossing, Numinbah Valley

After visiting Natural Bridge in the Numinbah Valley, be sure to drive on to the border with NSW for a stunning view over the Tweed Valley.

Bunny Bite Farms

Tour groups are welcome at this farm and processing plant, 'home of sweet baby carrots', at 54 Brent Rd, **Boonah**. By appt only. Ph: (07) 5463 0288

Christmas Creek

Christmas Creek rises in the rugged wilderness area south of Buchanan's Fort.

North of Hillview, travellers on Christmas Creek Rd will pass a **memorial** to the Chinese shepherds and Aborigines who lost their lives during the pastoral settlement of the district, around 1850.

Further along the road is the tiny wooden **St Mary's Sacred Heart Church**, established in 1904. Past Chinghee Creek Rd turnoff is the **Lamington Uniting Church**, which opened in 1910.

Christmas Creek Recreation Camp, further upstream, was established in 1944 and is now managed by the Qld Govt. At neighbouring **Stinson Park** picnic and camping area is a **plaque** commemorating the Stinson plane crash, which occurred in the wild country 10km to the SE in 1937. The 2 survivors found by Bernard O'Reilly were stretchered out to ambulances waiting at this site.

Lamington Glen Rd follows the creek upstream and loses itself among close, dark mountains. At the end of the road is a gate marking the border of the national park and a notice with a safety warning for bushwalkers.

Harrisville Museum *Map 43*

This museum at **Harrisville**, a small town south of Ipswich, is unusual in that its collection includes a rain gun as well as standard pioneering memorabilia. The gun was 1 of 6 bought at great cost — but to no avail — during the 1902 drought. Open 1pm–4pm 1st and 3rd Suns of the month, or by appt. Ph: (07) 5467 1325

Herrmann's Heritage Farm

The noble Australian draught horse provides the power at Herrmann's Heritage Farm, **Prenzlau**, open to bus tours and school visits by appt. The farm, which is off the Warrego Hwy between Minden and Hatton Vale, also features an animal nursery, a barn display of antiques, cow-milking and wagon rides. Ph: (07) 5426 8473

Hub o' the Rim Outdoor Centre

This centre, in the shadow of Mt Greville near **Lake Moogerah**, offers camping, hiking, canoeing, Cobb & Co coach travel and a host of educational activities. The centre is on the Bicentennial

National Trail. Caters for groups. Bookings essential. Ph: (07) 3371 4822

Ironbark Ridge Vineyard

This winery, at Middle Rd, **Purga** (off the Cunningham Hwy SW of Ipswich), offers cellar-door sales of its award-winning chardonnays and launched a shiraz and a port from its 1998 vintage. Open Wed, 1pm–4pm; Sat–Sun and public holidays, 11am–4pm; group tours by appt. Ph: (07) 5464 6787

Jimboomba church *Map 43* ❶

The age of this simple wooden church (just off the Mt Lindesay Hwy at Jimboomba) is uncertain, but services were held here as early as 1909.

Kooralbyn *Map 40 B4*

Kooralbyn is a resort in hilly country west of the Mt Lindesay Hwy south of Beaudesert. It stands on the site of the original pastoral property that was established there over 100 years ago. On the way to the main hotel building, a road to the right leads up to a scenic lookout with a view over an expanse of mountain peaks. The resort offers horseriding, golf, tennis, skydiving, bicycling, bushwalking, 4WD tours and ultra-light flights. A nearby airstrip takes light aircraft for guests who are pressed for time. Ph: 1800 073 108

Laidley Creek valley *Map 43*

The road along this valley hugs the ridges of the Little Liverpool Ra, dipping into floodways and passing within yarning distance of farmhouses. Laidley Creek slices through the deep soil, fringed by blackbean and river oaks. Opposite, the Mt Mistake Ra shoulders the creek, and at the southern end of the valley loom the battlements of **Mt Castle** (962m).

About halfway up the valley is the hamlet of Mulgowie, with its picturesque old **Mulgowie Hotel**. Deeper in the valley is **Denbigh Farm and Teahouse**, which offers light lunches Sat–Sun, 10am–3pm. Ph: (07) 5466 7190

Heading back, take the turnoff at the Mulgowie pub. The road leads across the creek to the other side of the valley and connects with the access to **Schultz's**

Lookout. This is at the top of a hill at the northern end of the Mt Mistake Ra, looking out over the Laidley and Lockyer Valleys.

Lake Maroon *Map 40 B4*

This dam, due west of **Rathdowney**, along the Rathdowney-Boonah road past **Mt Maroon** and **Mt May**, has rocky banks, picnic facilities, swings and a boat ramp. Camping is not allowed.

Lake Moogerah *Map 40 B4*

Lake Moogerah is ringed by **Mts Greville, Moon, Edwards** and **French**, a rugged group marked by bold crags, cliffs and gorges. The picnic area next to the dam wall has sweeping lawns, BBQs, shelters, lookouts, tall trees and a kiosk.

Lions Rd *Map 43*

To travel on this scenic route, which was built as a community project, leave the Mt Lindesay Hwy at Innisplain or take Running Creek Rd from Rathdowney. The road leads along one side of the Running Creek valley, with the railway threading through the flanks of the hills opposite, and passes Chinghee NP in the east. It takes the hills like a roller coaster, eventually climbing to pass through Richmond Gap in the Border Ranges NP.

Paragliding, Lake Moogerah

Singer of renown
In 1914 an Aboriginal mission was moved to **Purga** from nearby Deebing Creek. The tenor Harold Blair spent his childhood there. The mission closed in 1948.

Joy on the Lake
The Joy on the Lake kiosk at **Lake Moogerah** specialises in crayfish rolls and fresh packs of red-claws, ready for cooking on the nearby BBQs. Ph: (07) 5463 0104

Gun Alley

More than 1000 men worked on the **Spiral Loop**, and they lived in shanty towns near the railway line. One of these, Tunnel Camp, was known as Gun Alley because of the wild scenes that occurred there.

About 3km on the other side of the NSW border is a turnoff on the right to the **Border Loop Lookout**. The view down the valley between high, close mountains is lovely in itself, but the bird's-eye view of the famous **Spiral Loop**, where the railway line loops around a small peak to gain height before entering the tunnel through the Macpherson Ra, caps off this venture into NSW. The line was opened to great fanfare in 1930.

Lockyer Valley Scenic Circuit
South of **Gatton**, Tenthill Creek Rd leads past the Paradise Ranges to **Norm Goltz Park** and **Junction View**, at the confluence of Black Duck and Blackfellow Creeks.

East Haldon Rd, on the left, leads on to **Glen Rock RP** (p.224). The unsealed West Haldon Rd, which heads west from Tenthill Creek Rd, has views that make the tough travelling worthwhile. (Watch out for loose gravel.) Return to Gatton along Heifer Creek Rd, via **Ma Ma Creek** village.

The round trip is about 90km. *The Lockyer Valley Scenic Circuit*, a map with commentary, can be bought at the Gatton Tourist Info Centre at Lake Apex.

Mundoolan church *Map 43* ❷
On Mundoolan Rd, just off the Beaudesert–Beenleigh road, is St John's Church, built of local sandstone. It was erected in memory of John and Ann Collins, who settled at Mundoolan in 1844. The pews and ceiling are made of local cedar.

Tallegalla Lookout
Follow the Rosewood–Marburg road from Rosewood past the Oakleigh Colliery and the Rosewood Railway Museum to Tallegalla Lookout and cemetery. (If travelling west on the Warrego Hwy, turn left and approach from Marburg.) Away in the distance is the Great Divide.

Tamrookum church *Map 43* ❼
The lovely All Saints Memorial Church stands in the open countryside halfway between Beaudesert and Rathdowney. It was built in 1915 by the widow and children of Robert Collins, who was instrumental in creating Qld's 1st national park. The church, designed by Robin Dods, is remarkable not only for its beauty but also for the unusual curved-timber decoration on the verandah.

Recreational activities
Action
Visitors can enjoy a wide range of activities at **Yarramalong Outdoor Recreation Centre** on Lake Moogerah Rd, among them horseriding, camping, canoeing, archery, swimming, volleyball and orienteering. There are escorted trail rides on weekends and holidays, starting 10.30am–2.30pm. Ph: (07) 5463 7369

Black Duck Valley, half an hour south of Gatton, has 70 specially designed tracks for 4WDs running through 250ha of country in the foothills of the Great Dividing Ra. There also are camping areas, gymkhana runs and places to go bush-walking or swimming. Ph: (07) 5462 9116

In the air
Hot-air balloon enthusiasts can ride the breezes over the Lockyer Valley with **Balloons Above**. The meeting point is at the Lockyer Markets, on the Warrego Hwy east of Gatton. Ph: 1800 648 050

Fly Me to the Moon Hot-Air Ballooning offers flights in the Kooralbyn–Tamrookum area. Ph: (07) 3849 3185

The **Boonah Gliding Club** welcomes visitors as passengers on flights over the Fassifern Valley. Trial instructional flights are also available. Ph: (07) 3355 1920 (Mon–Fri); (07) 5463 2630 (Sat, Sun)

Tamborine Mt and Beechmont are favourite spots for hang gliders. There is a **Hang-Gliding Club** at Canungra. Ph: 190 227 6506

The **Kooralbyn Skydiving Centre** conducts tandem and solo dives. Ph: (07) 5544 6323

High-fliers can make the leap, solo or tandem, with **Ripcord Sky Divers**, cnr Warrego Hwy and Curtin Rd, Glenore Grove. Ph: (07) 5466 5521

Silent Sky Sports, Canungra, offers paragliding experiences for novices and experienced fliers alike. Tandem flights are available most weekdays and weekends by appt. Ph: (07) 5543 7237

The Gatton murders

Not far from Tenthill Creek Rd, on Boxing Day 1898, 2 sisters and their brother were murdered while returning from a dance in Gatton. The crime has never been solved.

Skyflyte Aviation offers ultralight flights over the spectacular country around Kooralbyn. Ph: (07) 5544 6406

Bushwalking

The Scenic Rim overflows with bush-walking delights, from undemanding saunters along rainforest tracks to trails up precipitous slopes (pp.224–30).

The *Ipswich Bushwalking Guide* (from the Ipswich Visitors and Tourist Info Centre) maps 7 bushwalking areas in and around Ipswich.

The grandest walk of all is along the **Bicentennial National Trail**, which takes a high-country route around the Fassifern and Lockyer Valleys. (The trail can also be travelled by trail bike or on horseback.) This section of the trail, from Blackbutt to the border, is covered by *Guidebook No. 6* (from Gatton Tourist Info Centre, Ph: (07) 5462 3430). Walkers can trek here fancy-free with a **Neranghi Pack Donkey**, trained to carry their swag. Pick-up from Gatton Tourist Info Centre or a Lockyer Landcare property. Ph: (07) 5462 6778

Horseriding

Several establishments in the region include horseriding among their attractions:

Cushavon Park, on Leach Rd, in the foothills of Tamborine Mt, offers 2-hour rides on reliable horses in quiet bushland. Ph: (07) 5543 6333 or (07) 5543 6637

Kooralbyn Resort counts horseriding among its suite of activities (p.231). Ph: 1800 073 108

Yarramalong Outdoor Education Centre at Lake Moogerah has escorted trail rides (p.232). Ph: (07) 5463 7369

Grandchester Trail Rides, at Gordons Rd, Grandchester, offers horseriding in a bushland setting, and associated attractions. Ph: (07) 5465 5346 or 015 652 378

On the water

Sailing and canoeing are popular pastimes on the 3 large dams in the area — Advancetown Lake and Lakes Maroon and Moogerah. Waterskiing is permitted on the last 2, but petrol-driven motorboats are not allowed on Advancetown Lake.

Hot-air ballooning over Advancetown Lake

Hub o' the Rim Outdoor Centre organises canoeing expeditions and instruction (p.230).

Check out the *Ipswich Canoe Trails* brochure from the Ipswich Visitors and Tourist Info Centre, Ph: (07) 3281 0555. It gives details on the **Bremer River Canoe Trail** and the **Brisbane River Canoe Trail**.

Ipswich Canoe Hire runs 1-day and 2-day fishing, camping and canoeing adventures on the Brisbane River. Canoe-borne anglers can try flicking lures around the snags for bass or Mary River cod. Ph: (07) 3201 7075

Advancetown Lake and Lakes Maroon and Moogerah are stocked with Australian native fish such as bass, golden and silver perch, saratoga and Murray cod.

Fun for the young

★ Glow-worms at Natural Bridge (p.228)

★ Herrmann's Heritage Farm (p.230)

★ Lake Apex, Gatton (p.219)

★ Lottie's Place, Global Arts Link, Ipswich (p.220)

★ Queens Park fauna section and playgrounds, Ipswich (p.220)

★ Treetop Walk, O'Reilly's (p.226)

Bushwalking

Suggested tours – Map 43

Laidley Creek valley tour

Approximate distance

250km return from Brisbane CBD

About the tour

This is a short but charming tour through a secluded valley, where the creek winds among the fertile Laidley Creek farms. The road runs along the lower slopes of the Little Liverpool Ra opposite the wild Mt Mistake Ra, with views of Mt Beau Brummel and, like a fortress guarding the end of the valley, the ramparts of the imposing Mt Castle. It returns via the western side of the valley, taking a detour to Schultz's Lookout, where the valley can be viewed from above.

Places of interest

❶ **Bigge's Camp Park, Grandchester** (p.219)

❷ **Grandchester Railway Stn** (p.219)

❸ **Das Neumann Haus, Laidley** (p.221)

❹ **Narda Lagoon, Laidley** (p.221)

❺ **Pioneer Village, Laidley** (p.221)

❻ **Mulgowie Hotel** (p.231)

❼ **Denbigh Farm and Teahouse** (p.231)

❽ **Schultz's Lookout** (p.222)

❾ **Historic pubs, Forest Hill** (p.222)

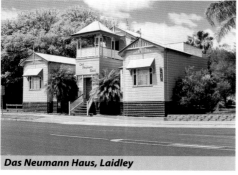

Das Neumann Haus, Laidley

Country kirk tour

Approximate distance

380km return from Brisbane CBD

About the tour

Around any bend in a quiet corner of this countryside, travellers are likely to come upon a small gem of rural ecclesiastical architecture. This route passes some well-known and less well-known churches, in farmland and township settings. They are wonderfully varied in style, from the modest but well-proportioned and magnificently situated Barney View Uniting Church, and the gaunt austerity of the old Jimboomba church, to the assertive Norman-Gothic sandstone of St John's at Mundoolan and Robin Dod's pleasing synthesis of traditions at Tamrookum.

Places of interest

❶ **Jimboomba church** (p.231)
❷ **St John's, Mundoolan** (p.232)
❸ **St George's, Tamborine Mt** (p.218)
❹ **St Luke's, Canungra** (p.217)
❺ **St Joseph's, O'Reilly's** (p.226)
❻ **St Mary's, Beaudesert** (p.223)
❼ **All Saints, Tamrookum** (p.232)
❽ **Uniting Church, Barney View** (p.230)
❾ **St Mary's Sacred Heart, Christmas Creek** (p.230)
❿ **Lamington Uniting Church** (p.230)

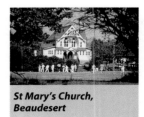

St Mary's Church, Beaudesert

GOLD COAST
TOURISM BUREAU

*Left: **Surf lifesavers**
Right: **Dolphin, SeaWorld***

Gold Coast

From a string of sleepy seaside towns to an international resort that never goes to bed ... the Gold Coast in one short history lesson. A place of high fashion, great surf and icecream sundaes, this region-turned-city styles itself as 'Australia's favourite playground' and lives up to the title with flair and pizzazz.

Whether it's a ride on the Tower of Terror at Dreamworld, sunbathing at Surfers, walking through Burleigh Heads NP or simply soaking up the scenery in one of the many cafes lining the 70km coastline, holidaying on the Gold Coast is pure pleasure. And for those who want a change of pace, slow down in the Gold Coast hinterland (p.216), a subtropical hideaway of hills and valleys, or rev up in Brisbane, only 1hr to the north.

But who can resist the glamour, the good life and, above all, the charm of this popular tourist arena where golden beaches and friendly smiles beckon all comers? Indeed, once seen, never forgotten — thousands of visitors choose to settle in the area, proving that the Gold Coast is no stopover, it's a destination.

ℹ Tourist information

Gold Coast Tourism Bureau
Level 2, 64 Ferny Ave,
Surfers Paradise 4217
Ph: (07) 5592 2699
gctb@onthenet.com.au

Gold Coast Tourism Bureau Information Centres
Cavill Ave, Surfers Paradise 4217
Ph: (07) 5538 4419
Shop 14B, Warner St,
Coolangatta 4225
Ph: (07) 5536 7765

Naturally Queensland Information Centre (EPA)
(info on national parks)
1711 Gold Coast Hwy,
Burleigh Heads 4220
Ph: (07) 5535 3032
www.env.qld.gov.au

Queensland Tourist and Travel Corporation
www.qttc.com.au
www.sunzine.net/goldcoast/
welcome.html
www.gwb.com.au/webster/travel/
gcsthome.html

Must see, must do

★ **Burleigh Heads NP** (p.246)

★ **Canal or river cruise** (p.240)

★ **Jupiters Casino** (p.244)

★ **Main Beach, Surfers Paradise** (p.244)

★ **Movie World, Sea World or Dreamworld** (p.248)

Radio stations

Beach FM: FM 88 (tourist info and Top 40)

4CRB FM: FM 89.3 (public/community radio)

SEA FM: FM 90.9 (Top 40)

ABC FM: FM 91.7 (easy listening)

Gold FM: FM 92.5 (60s and 70s music)

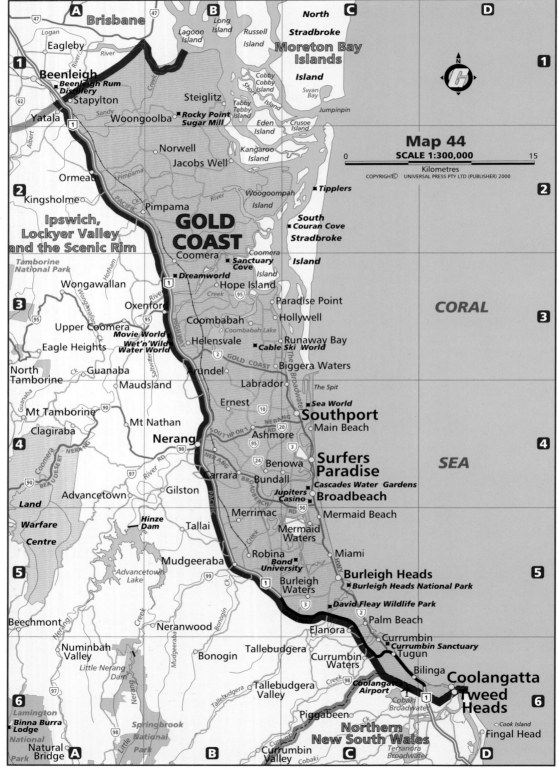

Map 44
SCALE 1:300,000
0   15
Kilometres
COPYRIGHT© UNIVERSAL PRESS PTY LTD (PUBLISHER) 2000

Natural features

The Gold Coast is a subtropical paradise in Qld's SE corner, made up of more than 1400km² of beachfront, bushland and watersystems. It has 35 beaches and 5 major waterways – the Nerang, Coomera and Tweed Rivers, and the Currumbin and Tallebudgera Creeks – as well as countless smaller creeks and constructed canals. The corridor-shaped region is bounded by Beenleigh on the outskirts of Brisbane to the north, Coolangatta to the south, the Pacific Ocean to the east and the Gold Coast hinterland to the west.

The area is situated on the edge of an ancient volcano (p.270), and the boulder-strewn beaches at its southern end are the legacy of the far-flung force of a massive eruption thousands of years ago. Within the region itself is a great diversity of vegetation and animal life, including the endangered glossy black cockatoo. The many rockpools along the beaches offer hours of pleasure to the beachcomber, and there is little chance of poor weather with 300 days of sunshine per year and an average temperature of 23°C (28°C in summer, and 21°C in winter).

History

Now the 6th-largest city in Australia, the Gold Coast was once inhabited only by members of the Yugumbir language group, in particular, the Gombemberri people. The lush terrain enabled them to hunt, fish and gather food from a variety of sources. White settlement, from the mid-1800s, altered this way of life. Curiously, the area was viewed as a holiday resort almost immediately. The construction of a railway line from Beenleigh to Southport in 1889 cemented this development, and settlement continued apace. Indigenous local people still live on the Coast but share their land with people from all over the world.

In 1933 the residents of what was then called Elston, a settlement on the banks of the Nerang River, requested that its name be changed to Surfers Paradise. Although it was some years before Surfers overtook Coolangatta as the top holiday destination of the region, this request marked another milestone in the emergence of the Gold Coast as one of Australia's best-known tourist spots. Today, over 3.9 million people visit the Coast each year (69 percent domestic and 31 percent international), and it is home to a permanent population of almost 400 000 people.

Getting there

By air

Domestic flights from most Australian cities and regional centres include a stop at Coolangatta Airport, located at the southern tip of the Gold Coast and only 20min from Surfers Paradise. Some international and charter flights also touch down here.

By road

The easiest way to travel by car to the Gold Coast, whether from the north or the south, is via the Pacific Hwy (Hwy 1). There are several turnoffs from this onto the Gold Coast Hwy, which passes through all the townships along the length of the coast.

Bus companies, such as **Pacific West Coachtrans, Kirklands, McCafferty's** and **Greyhound/Pioneer**, provide regular services from Brisbane to the Surfers Paradise bus station on Cavill Ave. Buses depart from the Brisbane Transit Centre, Roma St, CBD.

City status
The townships of the Gold Coast officially became the **Gold Coast City** in 1959.

David on the coast
The replica of Michelangelo's *David* in the Raptis Plaza, Surfers Paradise, is carved from a block of marble from the same quarry used for the original around 500 years ago.

Local history
The Gold Coast City Council Local Studies Library (Australia Fair, Southport) is a useful reference library for those interested in the history of the Coast. Open Tue–Fri, 10am–4.40pm.
Ph: (07) 5571 2099

Gold Coast vista

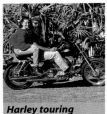

Harley touring

Pacific West Coachtrans offers the most extensive bus services, and its coaches travel as far as Tweed Heads (p.264). Door-to-door pickups from most CBD hotels can be arranged. Coachtrans also offers Airporter, a return trip to Brisbane Airport (domestic and international). Contact Trans Info, Ph: 131 230, or Pacific West, Ph: (07) 5588 8777.

Surfside Bus Lines offers regular services between Gold Coast townships. Contact Trans Info, Ph: 131 230.

Interstate coach services arrive daily at the Surfers Paradise bus station.

For those wishing to visit northern NSW, Kirklands Bus and Coach runs regular services into the Northern Rivers hinterland from the Gold Coast. Ph: (02) 6622 1499 or 1300 367 077

All Brisbane taxi companies take passengers to the Gold Coast (p.13). A local service, Regent Taxis, also travels between towns and, in addition, offers personalised tours. Ph: (07) 5588 1234

By rail

The Citytrain travels daily from Brisbane to the Gold Coast hinterland town of Robina. From there, Surfside Bus Lines takes passengers to coastal towns. There are also stops at the townships of Coomera, Helensvale and Nerang. Contact Qld Rail, Ph: (07) 3235 5555, or Trans Info, Ph: 131 230.

Overnight train services are available from Sydney to Murwillumbah (p.259). Buses connect passengers with all the Gold Coast centres. For info on long-distance rail travel, Ph: (07) 132 235.

Disabled access

Many transport providers have facilities and services catering for disabled travellers. Qld Government Travel Centre has a directory of such providers. Ph: 131 801

Getting around

Transport services cater for the region's growing permanent population and its many visitors with a range of options. Call Trans Info (Ph: 131 230) for public transport info or, for specialist services, ask at a tourist info centre.

Gold Coast canal

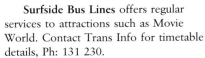

Surfside Bus Lines offers regular services to attractions such as Movie World. Contact Trans Info for timetable details, Ph: 131 230.

Pacific West Coachtrans offers a range of services including Theme Park transfers, a door-to-door tour of the 3 theme parks (p.248), Jupiters Casino (p.244) and Currumbin Wildlife Sanctuary (p.247). Contact Trans Info, Ph: 131 230, or Pacific West, Ph: (07) 5588 8777, or, for Theme Park transfers, (07) 3236 1000

With over 450km of canalways, 5 water systems with tributaries, and the ocean itself, boat cruises are a natural choice for the Gold Coast sightseer. There is an amazing variety from which to choose.

Island Queen cruises take in canal and harbour sights, travelling to Sanctuary Cove, Sea World, Surfers and South Stradbroke Island. Cruises – ranging from 1hr to a full day – depart daily at 9am and 10am from Cavill Ave, Surfers Paradise or Marina Mirage, Sea World Dr, The Spit, Main Beach. Ph: (07) 5557 8800. www.islandqueen.com.au

Jetaway Cruises offers a similar range of trips. Ph: (07) 5538 3400. Shangri-la Cruises, established in 1952, runs day trips, as well as night cruises with floor shows. Ph: (07) 5557 8888. Both companies depart from the same locations as the *Island Queen*.

For a fish *and* fowl experience, try the Amphibious Aquabus, a bus that drives into the water and floats like a boat. It travels through Surfers and into the Broadwater for a scenic splash before returning to dry land. Ph: (07) 5539 0222. Or take a trip back in time on the Tall Ship Sailing Cruises, a journey aboard a square-rigger sailing ship. The service offers cruises to Sanctuary Cove and, overnight, to Stradbroke and Moreton Islands. Ph: (07) 5532 2444

The adventurous can try skippering their own boat on the Captain Barb-e Pontoons. These pontoons include a toilet, BBQ, ice box and catering (on request). Wheelchair accessible. Also available are jet skis, wave runners and 2-seater and 3-seater mini boats. Ph: (07) 5531 6176

Cruising on a tall ship

Try **Caddy Chauffeured Limousines** (Ph: 1800 639 878) for a stretch in a Cadillac, a mini-coach or a Luxury LTD. Or become a pillion passenger on the **Eagle Harley Tours** bikes (Ph: (07) 5592 3722), taking in tours of the Gold Coast and surrounds.

Festivals and events

Magic Millions Racing Carnival

This prestigious summer racing carnival is held every Jan at the Gold Coast Turf Club, Racecourse Dr, **Bundall**. It takes place over a 10-day period of parties, punting and seaside fun. Ph: (07) 5538 1599

Australian Surf Lifesaving Championships

The Gold Coast beaches are renowned for their surf, and lifesaving clubs are liberally sprinkled along the coastline. In Mar-Apr, local lifesavers get the chance to show their prowess in a 4-day world-class contest of skill, stamina and team effort. Most events take place at **Kurrawa Beach**. Ph: (07) 5527 5660

Wintersun Festival

Held in the mild winter month of Jun, the Wintersun Festival celebrates the passing of the year's shortest day with a rock'n'roll celebration. Dance competitions, hot-rod displays and plenty of fun are offered at **Coolangatta's** Queen Elizabeth Park and nearby locations in the **Tweed region**. Ph: (07) 5536 9509

A La Carte in the Park

This family-friendly event showcases local restaurants and wine companies. It is held in Jun at Anzac Pde, **Southport**, and in Sept on the beach near Queen Elizabeth Park, **Coolangatta**. Ph: (07) 5538 4419 or (07) 5536 7765

Gold Coast Marathon Week

In Jul, diehards and tryhards lace up their running shoes to test themselves in the various events making up the Gold Coast Marathon Week. There were around 12 000 participants in 1998. Ph: (07) 5527 1363

Sydney to Gold Coast Classic

Australia's 2nd-largest ocean race begins in Sydney on 1 Aug, as a flotilla of yachts unfurl their sails and prepare to battle it out. The race ends on the ocean side of the **Southport Broadwater**. Ph: (07) 5591 3500

Gold Coast Show

The 1st day of the Gold Coast Show, held at the **Parklands Showgrounds** in late Aug, is a public holiday. Over this and the following 2 days, circus acts, fashion parades and driving demonstrations rub shoulders in a crowded schedule culminating in fireworks every night. Ph: (07) 5591 3422

Surf lifesaver on duty

City Garden Awards

This is an opportunity for keen Gold Coast gardeners to show off their efforts in subtropical springtime. The Sept event includes awards for the best gardens and gives visitors the chance to stroll through some beautiful vistas. Ph: (07) 5582 8217

Sanctuary Cove Classic Yacht and Car Concours

This event features European and American classic cars and timber yachts. It is held in early Oct at **Sanctuary Cove**, made famous in the 1980s by the then high-flying businessman Christopher Skase who built the Sheraton Mirage there. Ph: (07) 5577 8691

Honda Indy 300

For a week in mid-Oct, the streets of **Surfers Paradise** are transformed into a racing-car circuit for one of the biggest races in the country. This event, begun in 1991, is on the international Grand Prix calendar. The region jump-starts into one long party, including an air show and street parties. Ph: (07) 5588 6800

Tropicarnival

Overlapping with the Indy, the Tropicarnival is a celebration of life on the coast. The event began in 1981 as a small street festival, and is now a 16-day extravaganza. It includes nightly fireworks, an all-nations parade and display of traditional arts, skills and cuisine, comedy acts and free concerts. Many of the activities take place in the Evendale Festival Park, Bundall Rd, **Surfers Paradise**. Free festival programs are available from tourist info centres and selected retail outlets.

Asia Pacific Masters Games

1998 was the inaugural year for the Asia Pacific Masters, a 12-day, 12-sport event in which most of the contestants are over 30. The Nov games, including such sports as basketball and sprinting, take place every 2nd year on the **Gold Coast**. Ph: (07) 5564 0480

Carols by Candlelight

With locals celebrating Christmas Australian-style, many Carols by Candlelight festivities take place in the open air. Contact the Public Relations section of the Gold Coast City Council for details. Ph: (07) 5582 8211. The Mayor's Christmas Concert, a free event in early Dec, takes place at the **Southport Broadwater**.

Honda Indy 300

The Spit

Take a hike on the Spit, one of the few natural coastal habitats in the region and the perfect place for sunset-watching. Located close to Surfers Paradise it marks the beginning of the Southport Broadwater. At the southern end of the Spit, Sea World (p.248) and the Marina Mirage (p.251) abut the road. Further north, large areas of grassland, coastal shrubs and the Gold Coast seaway offer anglers, surfers, picnickers and walkers a change of pace and scenery. The seaway itself gives a view of South Stradbroke Island (p.54), and a ferry provides daily transport there (Ph: 018 758 136). The seaway was opened in 1986 as part of an effort to prevent a northwards sand drift from creating a sand bar in the Nerang River entrance. The Spit has sealed roads and a cafe — and plenty of nooks and crannies for those in search of solitude. The 6km walk from Surfers to Sea World takes about 1hr (see map 45).

> **A friendly reminder**
>
> Signs on the **Spit**'s tip remind surfers of the need to take care when crossing the Seaway. The Gold Coast experiences unpredictable seas, and 35 beaches are patrolled daily.

Main localities and towns

For ease of reference, towns have been listed alphabetically in 2 sections: north Gold Coast and south Gold Coast.

North Gold Coast
Sanctuary Cove *Map 44 B3*

Driving down an avenue lined with palms suggests opulence, and arrival clinches it. Made up of resorts, a village and 2 golf courses, this locale is home to the Sanctuary Cove Classic Yacht and Car Concours (p.242). Sanctuary Cove offers boat entry to the Coomera River and the Pacific Ocean,

and cruises visit daily from Surfers, with coach connections to nearby Dreamworld and Movie World. BBQs, picnic tables, swings and toilets are available on the tiny public foreshore. There is road access to Paradise Pt and Runaway Bay.

The **Gold Coast Brewery** (No. 1, Main Wharf) is a boutique operation with tours, beer tastings and entertainment in the beer garden. Wheelchair accessible. Ph: (07) 5577 8528. www.emugigs.com/gcbrew

Southport *Map 44 C4*

Just to the north of Surfers Paradise lies Southport. The **Southport Broadwater**, Australia's largest expanse of calm water, stretches northwards from the township as far as Moreton Bay and is popular with sailors of all descriptions. Indeed the Sydney–Gold Coast Classic (p.243) finishes here. Fishing is also a frequent activity in this idyllic spot.

Southport was once a little town with bathing boxes dotted along the foreshore. It was named by an early hotel proprietor, Thomas Hanlon, after his birthplace in England. On the site of the Hanlon's Family Hotel is now the **Hotel Pacific**, with magnificent sea views. Adjoining this is **Australia Fair** (p.250), a huge shopping complex. Both venues are wheelchair accessible.

Map 45

0 — 2 Kilometres

Labrador · The Spit · SEAWORLD · Heydon Heights · Sea World · The · GOLD COAST · Broadwater · NORTH ST · HIGH ST · SMITH ST · Southport · QUEEN ST · NERANG · FERRY ST · PR · Fishermans Wharf · CORAL · SEA · Main Beach · HWY · Paradise Waters · RD · Surfers Paradise

N · G

Southport Broadwater

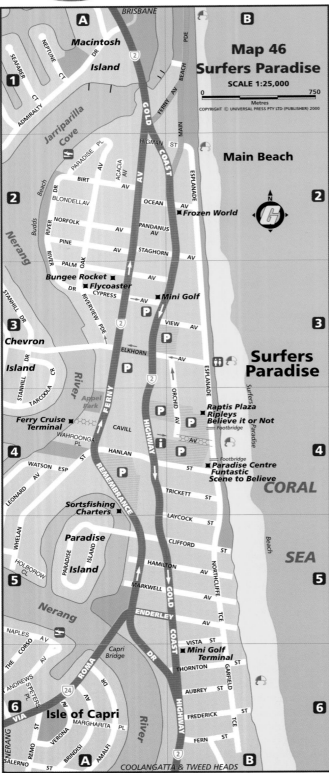

Surfers Paradise *Map 46 B3*

Stepping onto the sand at **Surfers Paradise Beach** is the dream of a million holiday-makers. Once a quiet seaside town, Surfers is now the jewel in the crown of the Gold Coast – a tourist hotspot catering for all tastes and fancies.

The hub of the action, **Cavill Ave**, stretches down towards the beach in a colourful parade of cafes, retail outlets, amusements and street entertainment. At the ocean end, the avenue becomes **Cavill Mall**. Surfers Paradise Beach itself has a promenade and some lawn areas. It is a place to see and be seen, or simply to get down to some serious sunbathing.

Main Beach, 2min to the north, is regarded as one of the best places on the coast for windsurfing. As with most Gold Coast beaches, it is well supplied with open-air showers, taps and drinking fountains. It also has a surf lifesaving club.

For those wanting to cool off, **Frozen World** (cnr Gold Coast Hwy and Ocean Ave) is a winter wonderland. This snow and ice 'fantasy' includes a rock-climbing wall, laser combat on ice and ice-carvers at work. The ice displays were originally created, in over 5000hrs, by 15 Chinese carvers brought to Australia for this purpose. Wheelchair accessible. Open daily, 10am–5pm. Ph: (07) 5570 3922 (info line) or (07) 5570 3633 (group bookings)

Tall tales, spooky stories, lots of laughs ... **Ripley's Believe It or Not! Museum** (Raptis Plaza, Cavill Mall) displays a potpourri of oddities, human and otherwise, for true believers and the merely curious. See the fattest man in the world, dinosaur eggs, a piece of coal from the ill-fated *Titanic* and lots more. Open daily, 9am–11pm. Ph: (07) 5592 0040. www.fan.net.au/ripleys

South Gold Coast
Broadbeach *Map 44 C4*

Broadbeach, immediately south of Surfers, is best known for the **Pacific Fair** shopping complex (p.251), and the adjacent **Conrad Jupiters Casino**. For those who want to live it up, the casino is a 24hr extravaganza of floor shows, bars, restaurants and facilities for gambling.

Cavill Mall, Surfers Paradise

'Big Man of the Ocean'

A statue on Surfers Paradise Beach's promenade commemorates **Peter Lacey**, named Kamarun Tumgum ('Big Man of the Ocean') by the Gombemberri tribe. He was a medal winner at 22 consecutive Australian Surf Lifesaving Championships and won 4 world championships.

Banks of gaming machines are matched by over 90 table games. The casino is set in a landscaped garden traversed by waterways, while overhead a giant neon waterfall draws the eye at night. Wheelchair accessible. Ph: (07) 5592 1133

On Sun the **Broadbeach Mall**, connected to Jupiters by monorail, has free face-painting, amusement rides for little children and lots of options for hearty brunches. **Broadbeach Market** (p.249) offers trash and treasures on the beachfront. Or combine the 2 at the **Kurrawa Surf Lifesaving Club**, on the beach, where modestly priced continental and cooked breakfasts are served on the balcony overlooking the ocean.

Coolangatta *Map 47 B2*

The name 'Coolangatta' comes from a ship which was wrecked offshore during a storm in 1846. The ship in turn was named after a NSW property, the name coming from the local Aboriginal word for 'good outlook' — more fitting, perhaps, for the Qld town than the ill-fated ship. The town itself lies on the Qld side of the Qld–NSW border, and shares the appellation 'Twin Towns' with its NSW neighbour, Tweed Heads (p.264).

War memories

On 14 May 1943, the hospital ship AHS *Centaur* was making its way from Sydney to New Guinea. On board the ship were 332 service personnel. Australia was at war. As the ship passed Stradbroke Island, it was torpedoed by a Japanese submarine. Within 3min the ship sank and 268 people lost their lives. The few survivors clung to rafts and debris in the rough waters for 34hrs before being rescued. Among them was the sole survivor of the female nursing team, Sr Savage, who kept up other survivors' spirits with songs, prayers and encouraging words. The Centaur Memorial, a stone monument at Point Danger, at the southernmost tip of the Gold Coast, commemorates the *Centaur*'s victims and survivors.

A watery memory

The **Snapper Rocks Sea Baths**, now demolished, were built in Coolangatta in 1956. They were one of the Gold Coast's first tourist attractions, and featured sea baths, a shark pool and a dolphin show.

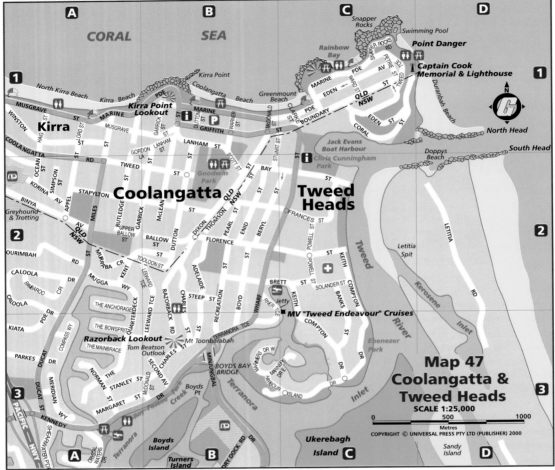

Map 47
Coolangatta &
Tweed Heads
SCALE 1:25,000

0   500   1000
Metres
COPYRIGHT © UNIVERSAL PRESS PTY LTD (PUBLISHER) 2000

Greenmount Beach

Coolangatta was once the best-known holiday destination on the Coast. Over the last few decades it has assumed a quieter though still popular status. **Greenmount Beach**, on the foreshore (Marine Pde), is a great place for little children with its shallow water and lack of surf. High above is **Greenmount Hill**, with electric BBQs, seating and stairs to the beach. Wheelchair accessible. Nearby is the town itself, its centre, **Griffith St**, a busy strip of cafes and other businesses with something for every budget.

Queen Elizabeth Park, at Kirra Pt, has free community entertainment on the 2nd Sun of every month (11am-2pm). The park was named in honour of Queen Elizabeth II who attended a Royal Surf Carnival there in 1963. The park includes relics, BBQs and seating. Wheelchair accessible.

National parks

Burleigh Heads NP *Map 48* ❸

This area of native forest is set on Burleigh Heads with magnificent 180° views of the ocean and adjacent beaches. The local indigenous population has a long association with the park, and many of the volcanic rock formations hold strong spiritual significance for them. The terrain is made up of pandanus palms and tussock grassland, open forest and littoral rainforest. There are several walks, including a circuit, and all have easy tracks for children and adults alike. The park was declared a protected area in 1947. Wheelchair accessible in some places.
Ph: (07) 5576 0271

Parks and gardens

Cascades Water Gardens *Map 48* ⑤

The Cascades Water Gardens are an oasis in the heart of the Gold Coast. Entry is from the Gold Coast Hwy, at **Broadbeach**. There is a large grassed area for ball games, a playground, toilets and covered picnic tables, as well as marked walks around the ponds. Free entertainment on the 1st Sun of every month. Wheelchair accessible. Open to vehicles daily, 6am–6pm; pedestrians all hours.

MacIntosh Park *Map 46 A1*

Ducks are a popular attraction for children at MacIntosh Park (Gold Coast Hwy, **Surfers Paradise**). As well as a pond, this pretty park has swings, covered picnic tables, BBQs and plenty of room for play. There is free entertainment on a seasonal basis. Entry to the park is by car or via a suspension bridge. MacIntosh Park is close to **Main Beach** and is wheelchair accessible. Open all hours.

Other attractions

Captain Cook Memorial and Lighthouse *Map 48* ⑥

High above Coolangatta-Tweed Heads is windswept **Point Danger**, looking out over Rainbow Bay. Here stands the **Captain Cook Memorial and Lighthouse**, erected in 1970 in commemoration of Cook's naming of the point in 1770. The memorial is on the border of Qld and NSW, with its 4 columns in alignment with the points of the compass. A replica of Cook's capstan, forming part of the memorial, has been cast from ballast retrieved from the waters 200 years after it was jettisoned by Cook.

Point Danger is also home to the Air Sea Rescue patrol, a reminder of the turbulent currents and dangerous rocks that fringe this part of the coastline. The patrol maintains a 24hr radio watch and marine rescue service from the lighthouse. Drop a coin in the **wishing well** nearby and help raise funds for the service. From the picnic benches, in a sheltered grass area immediately below the lighthouse, there is a wonderful view of the ocean. BBQs and toilets are available. Wheelchair accessible.

Currumbin Sanctuary *Map 48* ⑥

Celebrating 50 years in 1997, Currumbin Sanctuary (Gold Coast Hwy, **Currumbin**) features 27ha of bushland, native animals and related attractions. Come and feed the lorikeets, share a photo opportunity with a koala, ride the mini train, or visit the animal nursery. Protected by the National Trust, the sanctuary is dedicated to the conservation of Australian wildlife and includes an animal hospital. It is 18km south of Surfers Paradise and about 1hr from Brisbane. Wheelchair accessible. Open

Fish and chips
Charis Bros Seafoods, on the Broadwater at Labrador, is said to have the best fish and chips on the Coast. Sit in the park overlooking the water and watch the pelicans as you eat.

Beautiful butterflies
Butterflies are everywhere in SE Qld. Species around the Gold Coast include the yellow and black tailed emperor, the brilliant-green Richmond birdwing (one of Australia's largest butterflies), and the orange and black painted lady.

Burleigh Heads NP

Currumbin Sanctuary

daily, 8am–5pm. Ph: (07) 5598 1645 (info line) or (07) 5534 1266. www.currumbin-sanctuary.org.au

David Fleay Wildlife Park *Map 44 C5*

David Fleay Wildlife Park (West Burleigh Rd, **Burleigh Heads**) was founded more than 40 years ago by Dr David Fleay, the 'Father of Conservation' on the Gold Coast. There are 4 flora communities, including mangrove swamps, eucalyptus bushland, rainforest and wetlands, and many native animals, including brolgas, bilbies (of Easter fame) and tree kangaroos. A 2km boardwalk allows pushers, prams and wheelchairs easy passage around the animal enclosures. Open daily, 9am–5pm. Ph: (07) 5576 2411

Theme parks

Among the biggest attractions on the Gold Coast are its 4 theme parks: Dreamworld, Movie World, Sea World and Wet'n'Wild Water World.

Dreamworld *Map 44 B3*

Test out blood-pressure levels on the Tower of Terror or the Giant Drop at Dreamworld (Pacific Hwy, **Coomera**), 40min from Brisbane and 20min from Surfers. These rides, plunging punters 38 storeys downwards at speeds of up to 160km, are just 2 of the many experiences at this fantasy adventure park. Dreamworld offers amusements, a wildlife sanctuary, giant cinema screen

and 12 themed 'worlds'. Open daily, 10am–5pm (with some attractions opening at 9am). Wheelchair accessible. For info on the park and transport options, Ph: (07) 5588 1122 or 1800 073 300 (toll free). www.dreamworld.com.au

Sea World *Map 44 C4*

Sea World is the largest marine park in the southern hemisphere. Located on the ocean's edge 3km from Surfers Paradise (Sea World Dr, **Main Beach**), it hosts a dolphin show, water-ski displays, rides, a monorail, underwater views and much more. Wheelchair accessible. Open daily, 9.30am–5pm. Ph: (07) 5588 2205 (24hr). www.village.com.au

Warner Bros Movie World *Map 48* ❶

Meet Bugs Bunny and Batman at the theme park also known as 'Hollywood on the Gold Coast'. Here, film and TV production continues apace with magic shows, Wild West rides and an assortment of characters known and loved by generations of movie-goers. Movie World also offers studio tours and a peek into how special effects are created. Wheelchair accessible. Located on the Pacific Hwy, **Oxenford**, 40min south of Brisbane and 20min north of Surfers, the park is open daily, 9.30am–5.30pm, with rides operating 10am–5pm. Ph: (07) 5573 8485. www.holidays.village.com.au

Ripley's Believe It or Not! Museum

Warner Bros Movie World

Main Beach, Surfers Paradise

Wet'n'Wild Water World *Map 44 A3*
Wet'n'Wild Water World (Pacific Hwy, **Oxenford**) provides water-filled fun for all age groups — the Giant Wave Pool, an 8-lane waterslide, flying fox, stunt show, the Terror Canyon (for those who still haven't had enough), a picnic area and Movie World just next door. Wheelchair accessible. Open daily, 10am; seasonal closing times. Ph: (07) 5573 2277. www.holidays.village.com.au

Recreational activities
Action
Take a dive from the 150m **Bungee Downunder** (Sea World Dr, The Spit) into the Broadwater. Just 500m from Sea World, this floating jump site offers dives into the water below or a hair-raising skim of the surface. Open daily, 10am–5pm. Ph: (07) 5531 1103

Cable Ski World (Oxley Dr, Runaway Bay), at the northern end of the Gold Coast, is Australia's largest ski park. It offers a range of attractions such as waterskiing, jet-skiing, paddleboats, mini ski boats and bungee-jumping, as well as a bistro and bar, in a bushland setting. Lessons available. Wheelchair accessible. Open daily, 10am–5pm (until 9pm on Fri). Ph: (07) 5537 6300

Those with a head for heights can shoot into space on the **Bungee Rocket** (cnr Palm Ave and Gold Coast Hwy,

Markets on the beach
For those who want something a little different, beachfront markets are held in **Surfers Paradise** every Fri night, at **Broadbeach** on the 1st and 3rd Sun of the month, every 2nd Sun in **Coolangatta**, and on the last Sun of the month at **Burleigh Heads**. Here, local arts and crafts are on display for browsers and bargain-hunters. A special 'summertime' opportunity (Sept-Jun) is the Fri night Lantern Market in the **Broadbeach Mall**. Artists and craftspeople demonstrate their skills as well as sell their wares. The biggest market of all is the **Carrara Markets** (Market St, Carrara). Over 500 stalls of trash, treasure, entertainment and fresh produce are laid out every Sat and Sun. A tourist courtesy bus is available for buyers and browsers staying in local hotels and motels. All markets are wheelchair accessible. Ph: (07) 5533 8202, (07) 5533 8208 or (Carrara) (07) 5579 9388

Budds Beach
Budds Beach, tucked away at the back of Surfers, has paddleboats and canoes for hire as well as swings and a boat ramp.

Sunset stroll
Currumbin Beach at twilight is a very pretty spot for a stroll.

● ● ● ● ● ● ● ●

Bullseye
Try pistol shooting at the **Southport Indoor Pistol Club**. No licence is required and qualified instructors give advice on handling and safety at the 20-lane range. Ph: (07) 3865 4595

Poodle-spotting
The **Pink Poodle Motel**, Surfers Paradise, with its pink walls and giant neon poodle, is one of the several larger-than-life places that add character to the Coast. It was a central motif in a recent novel by Qld writer Matt Condon, *A Night at the Pink Poodle*.

Surfers Paradise), a 50m ride. Open daily, 10am–10pm. Ph: (07) 5570 2700

Taking the Pimpama Tourist Area exit from the Pacific Hwy, motorists may hear the revs before they come across **Le Mans Kart Racing Complex**. This 700m go-kart circuit is open daily, 10am–5pm, and offers a variety of karts for hire. No licence is required. Ph: (07) 5546 6566

Skates are available for hire or BYO at **Skaters Paradise Roller Rink** (Bay St, Southport). Ph: (07) 5532 7999

Surfers Paradise Tenpin Bowling Centre (Level 1, Paradise Centre, Cavill Ave, Surfers Paradise) is open daily, 9am–midnight. Ph: (07) 5538 5222

Full motorcycle licence holders can take off solo, as can moped riders at **Moped City**, Shop 5, Surfers International, Hanlan St, Surfers Paradise (Ph: (07) 5538 1511) or 102 Ferny Ave, Surfers Paradise (Ph: (07) 5592 5878). Motorbikes and bicycles are also available for hire.

In the air

Tiger Moth Joy Rides offers a passenger seat in the open cockpit of a DH82 Tiger Moth. Ph: (07) 5538 9083. Joyflights in **Air Waves** planes are a little less challenging and include stops for picnics, walks and a swim on South Stradbroke Island. Ph: (07) 5564 0444

Freefall parachuting with an instructor is available from **Tandem Skydive**. Ph: (07) 5599 1920

Sea World Helicopters promise customised travel and a choice of 5 tours. These include South Stradbroke Island and Sea World, Jupiters Casino, Burleigh Heads, Currumbin Valley and Tweed Heads. A minimum of 2 people is required; tours by appt. Ph: (07) 5588 2224/5588 2222 or book at the Sea World Helicopter Ticket Office.

Balloon Aloft (Ph: (07) 5593 3291) and **Balloon Down Under** (Ph: (07) 5530 3631) give an old-fashioned experience with absolutely modern safety. A champagne breakfast adds to the pleasure.

The arts

The **Gold Coast Arts Centre** (135 Bundall Ave, Surfers Paradise) includes a regional gallery and theatre, and holds many arts events within its spacious environs. The regional gallery is one of the foremost in the country, and houses a significant collection of contemporary art as well as works documenting the history of the Coast. Many national theatre tours have a season here. Wheelchair accessible. Open Mon–Fri, 10am–5pm; Sat, Sun and public holidays, 11am–5pm. Ph: (07) 5581 6567

The Gold Coast also has several amateur theatres and many smaller galleries. Contact a tourist info centre for details.

Cycling

The *Gold Coast Cycling Guide*, available from tourist info centres or the City Council, outlines the routes set up for or conducive to cycling. Ph: (07) 5581 6000

Golf

There are around 40 golf courses (including putting courses and driving ranges) on the Gold Coast. Course designs include woodland, Australian bush, landscaped lawn and traditional links. For details, contact a tourist info centre. Alternatively, try a small-scale version at **Lilliput Mini Golf** (cnr Vista St and Gold Coast Hwy, Surfers Paradise, and cnr Cypress Ave and Gold Coast Hwy, Surfers Paradise), with 18 holes for miniature putting. Open daily, 9am–8pm. Ph: (07) 5592 2281 or (07) 5531 5515

Shopping

Versace or Vegemite, Gucci or Guerlain ... the Gold Coast turns it on and puts it out in everything from gold lamé to 100% cotton. The city has department stores, designer boutiques, markets and miscellaneous businesses. Outside Brisbane, it has the widest range of goods anywhere in Qld.

There are 6 major retail centres on the Coast. **Australia Fair** (Gold Coast Hwy, Southport) is a place for the family shopper. A central attraction is Fig Tree Garden, where a Moreton Bay fig over 200 years old stands amid the shops. The tree was a great favourite of the children who attended the Gold Coast

Marina Mirage, The Spit

Kindergarten, formerly on this site. Open Mon–Wed and Fri, 9am–5.30pm; Thur, 9am–9pm; Sat, 8.30am–5.30pm; Sun 10.30am–4pm. Ph: (07) 5532 8811

The **Marina Mirage** (Sea World Dr, The Spit) consists of exclusive boutiques and speciality shops – and an aviary of native birds. Its waterfront position and spectacular architecture, including a line of rooftop sails, make it an experience for the sightseer as well as the serious shopper. Open daily, 10am–6pm.

In Surfers Paradise the **Paradise Centre** (Cavill Ave) offers an assortment of retail outlets and includes a supermarket. Open Mon–Wed and Fri, 9am–6pm; Thur, 9am–9pm; Sat, 9am–5.30pm; Sun, 10.30am–4pm. Ph: (07) 5577 0088

Pacific Fair (Hooker Ave, Broadbeach) is probably the best known of the Coast's retail centres. Set beside Jupiters Casino (p.244) and the Nerang River, it bends the distinction between shopping centre, recreational area and tourist attraction by including bars, restaurants and playgrounds. Open Mon–Fri, 9am–5.30pm; Thur, 9am–9pm; Sat, 8.30am–5.30pm; Sun, 10.30am–4pm. Ph: (07) 5539 8766

Robina Town Centre (Robina Town Centre Dr, Robina) is modelled on a European hill town. Built in 1996, this addition to the Coast's retailing community suggests village life even as it offers cinemas, markets, cafes, more than 200 speciality shops and a lake. Its elegant bell tower stands out from a distance, as does the flamboyantly yellow balloon of the Balloon Walk. Open Mon–Wed and Fri, 9am–6pm; Thurs, 9am–9pm; Sat, 8.30am–5.30pm; Sun, 10.30am–4pm. Ph: (07) 5575 0400

In and on the water

Lessons and gear are available from the many diving companies operating on the Coast, including **Gold Coast Dive Centre** (Ph: (07) 5532 8830), **Kirra Dive Centre** (Ph: (07) 5536 6622) and **Auscuba Diving** (Ph: 0412 189 198).

Fun for the young

★ Cable Ski World, Runaway Bay (p.249)
★ Le Mans Kart Racing Complex, Pimpama (p.250)
★ Main Beach, Surfers Paradise (p.244)
★ Skaters Paradise Roller Rink, Southport (p.250)
★ Spending a day at a theme park (p.248)
★ Surfers Paradise Tenpin Bowling Centre, Surfers Paradise (p.250)
★ Wet'n'Wild Water World, Oxenford (p.249)

Fun and games
Beach volleyball — the ideal game in a perfect setting — is open to beginners and veterans alike. Ph: (07) 4638 7235 for serious fun or look out for casual competitions on the beaches.

Suggested tours – Map 48

Amusements tour

Approximate distance
167km return from Brisbane CBD

About the tour
No child can resist the excitement offered by one of the many amusements of Gold Coast life. This tour tackles the hotspots with the same level of energy as an 10-year-old. It includes a mixture of fun and education in a rapidfire race through a few of the most well-known attractions at the Coast such as Movie World, Australia Fair and Ripley's Believe It or Not! Museum. There is room to stretch the legs and feed the ducks inbetween times, and a cooling dip at the end of the day.

Places of interest
❶ **Movie World** (p.248)
❷ **Australia Fair, Southport** (p.250)
❸ **Frozen World, Surfers Paradise** (p.244)
❹ **Ripley's Believe It or Not! Museum, Surfers Paradise** (p.244)
❺ **Cascades Water Gardens** (p.247)
❻ **Kurrawa Beach** (p.245)

Warner Bros Movie World

Beachside tour

Approximate distance
235km return from Brisbane CBD

About the tour
Take a drive along the famous Gold Coast shoreline, with the sparkling waters of the Pacific Ocean as a navigational guide. This tour traces a route that reveals some of the natural delights — and a glimpse of the high life — that make the Gold Coast Australia's ultimate beach holiday destination. Build sandcastles at Main Beach. Hike along a forested track at Burleigh Heads NP. Visit the native animals at Currumbin Sanctuary. Or simply gaze out to sea at the Captain Cook Lookout before sipping on a martini at Jupiters Casino. There is as much or as little activity as travellers desire — and all at a DIY pace.

Places of interest
❶ **Main Beach, Surfers Paradise** (p.244)
❷ **Cavill Mall, Surfers Paradise** (p.244)
❸ **Burleigh Heads NP** (p.246)
❹ **Elephant Rock, Currumbin Beach** (p.247)
❺ **Currumbin Sanctuary** (p.247)
❻ **Captain Cook Memorial and Lighthouse** (p.247)
❼ **Jupiters Casino** (p.244)

Burleigh Heads

Map labels:

South Stradbroke Island

Paradise Point
Hollywell
ombabah
Runaway Bay
Biggera Waters
rador
The Spit
Sea World
Southport
Main Beach ❶
Frozen World
Ripleys Believe It or Not
Surfers Paradise ❷
Bundall
Cascades Water Gardens
Broadbeach
❺ ❻ Kurrawa Beach
❽ Jupiters Casino
Mermaid Beach
CORAL
Mermaid Waters
bina
Bond University
Miami
SEA
Burleigh Heads
❸ Burleigh Heads National Park
Burleigh Waters
eedy eek
PACIFIC
Palm Beach
Elanora
Currumbin
allebudgera
❹ Elephant Rock
❺ Currumbin Sanctuary
Currumbin Waters
Tugun
Bilinga
Coolangatta
llebudgera Valley
Coolangatta Airport
Captain Cook Memorial & Lookout ❻
Tweed Heads
Razorback Lookout
Piggabeen
Cobaki
Cobaki Broadwater
Cook Island
Terranora Broadwater

SCALE 1:215,000
0 2 4 6
Kilometres
COPYRIGHT © UNIVERSAL PRESS PTY LTD (PUBLISHER) 2000

Big Sky
COUNTRY

NEW ENGLAND
NORTH WEST
NEW SOUTH WALES

Northern Rivers
tropicalnsw

Left: **Byron Bay,
Beach vista**
Right:
Mt Warning NP

Northern New South Wales

The popular image of Australia is of 'a land of sunburnt plains'. For residents of northern New South Wales (NNSW), the reality is a lush paradise tucked away on the continent's eastern seaboard where rainforests stretch to the ocean, the high sweep of sugarcane is set against vivid skies, and the shrieks of cockatoos can be heard rising in the morning air. Encompassing sections of 2 Tourism NSW areas within its ambit (Northern Rivers, Tropical NSW and Big Sky Country), this is 'God's own country' — a place where people stop awhile ... and stay.

Famous for its sunny climate, abundant greenery and majestic ranges, the upper reaches of NSW attract people from all walks of life. Farmers rub shoulders with dreadlocked hippies and blues aficionados with old bushies. The diverse populace means that, as well as a plethora of natural attractions, NNSW contains a rich cultural life. This is a region in which nature and culture coexist in a landscape of breathtaking beauty.

ℹ Tourist information

Ballina Information Centre
Cnr River St and La Balsa Plaza,
Ballina 2478 Ph: (02) 6686 3484

Byron Bay Visitor Centre
80 Jonson St, Byron Bay 2481
Ph: (02) 6685 8050

Lismore Visitor and Heritage Centre
Cnr Ballina and Molesworth Sts,
Lismore 2480 Ph: (02) 6622 0122
tourism@liscity.nsw.gov.au
www.liscity.nsw.gov.au

Murwillumbah Visitors Centre (incl. World Heritage Rainforest Centre)
Alma St and Pacific Hwy,
Murwillumbah 2484
Ph: (02) 6672 1340
info@tactic.nsw.gov.au

Tenterfield Visitors Centre
157 Rouse St, Tenterfield 2372
Ph: (02) 6736 1082
www.northnet.com.au~tenterf

Tweed Heads Visitors Centre
4 Wharf St, Tweed Heads 2485
Ph: (07) 5536 4244 or 1800 674 414
info@tactic.nsw.gov.au

Must see, must do

★ **Bald Rock, Bald Rock NP** (p.269)

★ **Byron Bay** (p263)

★ **Mt Warning summit, Mt Warning NP** (p.270)

★ **Nimbin** (p.268)

★ **Tweed River houseboat** (p.274)

Radio stations

2NR ABC: AM 94.5/720/738 (NNSW)

Radio 97: AM 97.2 (Tweed Heads and surrounds)

2LM: AM 900 (NNSW)

2NCRL: FM 92.9 (NNSW)

COW-FM: FM 107.9 (Casino and surrounds)

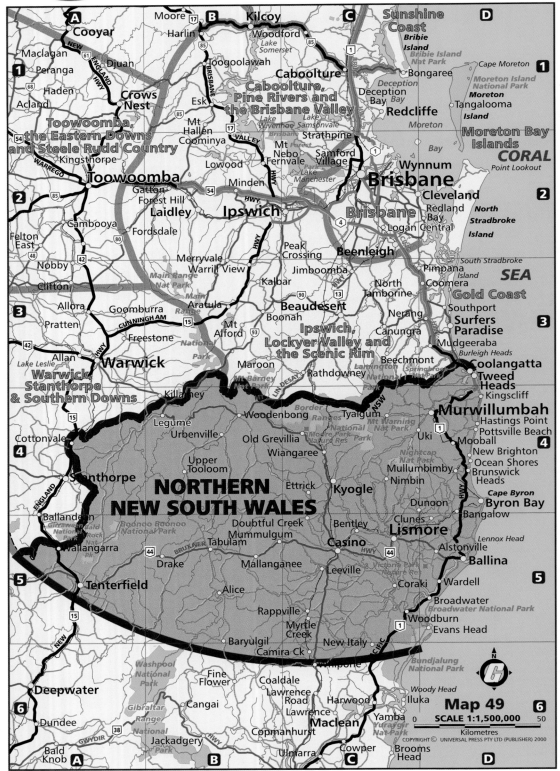

Map 49

SCALE 1:1,500,000

Kilometres

COPYRIGHT © UNIVERSAL PRESS PTY LTD (PUBLISHER) 2000

Natural features

Dominating NNSW are its waterways and ranges — and the caldera of the long-extinct Mt Warning volcano (p.270). The major rivers of the region are the Tweed, Wilson, Richmond and Clarence. Mightiest of all is the Richmond, which stretches for 260km from the Border Ranges (p.269) to the coastal town of Ballina (p.261). The rivers, and their many tributaries, give the area the alternative moniker of the Northern Rivers region.

NNSW covers a vast tract of land, the perimeters of which are marked, to the north, by the Nightcap and Border Ranges NPs dividing NSW and Qld (pp.269-70), in the south by Broadwater NP (p.269), and, westwards, by Bald Rock NP (p.269). Scattered between these ancient forests are other, smaller national parks, grasslands, rainforest remnants, wetlands and granite tablelands in an undulating landscape. The region comprises the easternmost extremity of the continent, with almost 300km of coastline, and is a mixture of subtropical and temperate climes. Temperatures range from just above zero on the tablelands during the winter months to the mid-30s on the coast in the summertime. Generally, the climate is pleasantly sunny although visitors are advised to dress warmly between Apr and Sept.

History

Several indigenous language groups lived in the NNSW region before white settlement, the descendants of whom still live here today. In the Tweed district, for example, were the Ngandowal people, while the coastal strip extending to Evans Head supported members of the Bundjalung group. Originally, the latter name was recorded as Minjyungbal and the place names 'Minyon' and 'Minyon Falls' are still in use. Due to the many ranges covering the region, different languages or dialects, customs and diets developed according to terrain. However, some tribes would travel from as far inland as present-day Casino to the coast in order to trade and find food in winter.

John Oxley, Surveyor-General of the Colony of NSW, is reported to have been the 1st white man to venture into the hinterland. In 1823 he sailed about 7km upstream on the Tweed River. After him came a succession of farmers, timbergetters and goldminers. The Richmond River, in the southern part of the region, similarly served as the principal route into the hinterland — and farming — until tracks and, later, roads were constructed. Even now, many areas remain inaccessible due to the rugged and heavily wooded terrain.

Today, NNSW is home to people from all parts of the world. Its large population — at last count, over 200 000 people —

Nightcap NP

View of Mt Warning from the Tweed River

The road to Tenterfield

resides in picturesque hamlets, townships and villages, as well as on the land. Dairy and cattle farming co-exist with crops such as sugarcane, avocado, macadamia and tea tree. A large fishing industry supplies prawns, oysters and other aquatic delights to Brisbane, Sydney and beyond. Tourism is the biggest business of the area; its many natural and man-made attractions make this region a veritable cornucopia of delights.

Getting there
By air
Coolangatta (p.000) is the main airfield for the region despite being situated on the other side of the Qld–NSW border.

A number of small airfields also serve NNSW. Ballina, Lismore, Casino and Grafton all operate regular services, with the bulk of the flights coming from Sydney. **Ansett Airlines** schedules daily flights from Sydney to Lismore and Ballina (Ph: (02) 6686 4384 or 131 344). **Qantas**, via its subsidiary **Sunstate**, has flights from Brisbane on weekends and Tue (Ph: 131 330). **Eastern Australian Airlines** flies from Sydney to Grafton several times a day, Mon–Fri, and has a daily flight on weekends (Ph: 131 313). **Hazelton Airlines** has flights to both Casino and Lismore from Sydney several times a week (Ph: (02) 6622 3113 or 131 713). Contact Ballina Airport (Ph: (02) 6686 4384) or Lismore Airport (Ph: (02) 6621 9558) for general inquiries.

Air North Coast (Ph: (02) 6622 3223) and **Northern Rivers Aero Club** (Ph: (02) 6621 4844) both offer charter services to and from Lismore.

By road
The main route into the region is via Hwy 1 (known as the Pacific Hwy in the stretch between Brisbane and Sydney). The highway travels along the NNSW coast and gives motorists an opportunity to take in the stunning ocean views. Other principal highways in the NNSW region include the inland New England and Newell Hwys, and, from the west, the Bruxner Hwy, and, NW, Summerland Way.

Interstate bus companies make daily runs through the main centres of NNSW. These companies include **Greyhound/ Pioneer, McCafferty's** and **Kirklands. Kirklands Bus and Coach** (Ph: (02) 6622 1499 or 1300 367 077) runs regular services in the hinterland as well as to the Gold Coast and Brisbane. **Blanch's** (Ph: (02) 6686 2144) runs services in the Ballina area while further up the coast the **Brunswick Bus Services** (Ph: (02) 6685 1385) takes in the Byron Bay-Brunswick Heads strip. Further north again, **Surfside Bus Lines** (Ph: 131 230) includes Tweed Heads in its Gold Coast run. Nearby, the **Murwillumbah Bus Company** (Ph: (02) 6672 6222) runs through the Tweed Valley. On the

Bush safaris
Never Never Safaris include 1–6 day trips around the Border Ranges NP, Bald Rock NP and further afield.
Ph: (02) 6679 1575

western boundary of the region the charming town of Tenterfield is serviced by the **Tablelands Bus Service** (Ph: (02) 6736 1864) and **Jarrett's** (Ph: (02) 6736 2052), while Casino is serviced by **Blunt Bus and Coach** (Ph: (02) 6662 2917).

Several regional centres have taxi companies. Among these are **Ballina Taxis** Ph: (02) 6686 9999, **Byron Bay Taxis** Ph: (02) 6685 5008, **Casino Taxis** Ph: (02) 6662 1110, **Kyogle Taxi Services** Ph: (02) 6632 1555, **Lismore Taxis** Ph: (02) 6621 2618, **Region Taxis** Ph: (07) 5536 1144, **Tenterfield Taxis** Ph: 018 669 449 and **Tweed Valley Taxis** Ph: (02) 6672 1344.

By rail

Countrylink has daily services between Brisbane and Sydney. Buses connect trains with regional centres not on the line, including a daily service from Lennox Head, Ballina and Alstonville connecting to Lismore, and from the Gold Coast, the Tweed Coast, Murwillumbah, Bangalow and Lismore connecting to Casino. Ph: 132 232 or (02) 6622 1959

Getting around

There are several bus tours on offer for those in search of something off the beaten track. **Byron Bay to Bush Tours** takes in Nimbin, Minyon Falls, Mt Warning and a cooling dip in a rainforest pool on its Rainbow Trip (Ph: (02) 6685 6889). **Jim's Alternative Tours** travels much of the same terrain, with the added feature of a visit to the Fruit Spirit Alternative Retreat. There is also an 'alternative market' tour. Ph: (02) 6685 7720

Forgotten Country Ecotours includes 1–2day trips to Bald Rock, Tenterfield, Nimbin and Mt Warning, with an emphasis on bush skills (Ph: (02) 6687 7845). Or learn more about local indigenous culture on **Feel the Dreamtime** full-day Aboriginal tours. These begin and end in Byron Bay, and take in the Tweed Valley area. Ph: (02) 6680 8505

The **Nimbin–Byron Bay Shuttle Bus**, as well as providing a link between the 2 towns, also offers tours of North Coast

markets, Nimbin Rocks and Minyon Falls, and Cape Byron Lighthouse (Ph: (02) 6687 2007). For exploration further north, **Tweed Discovery Half Day Tours** offers quick trips to a variety of sights, such as Tropical Fruit World (p.272), Pioneer Plantation (p.272), Mt Warning (p.270), Murwillumbah (p.267) and the Tweed Coast (p.264). Ph: (07) 5536 9604 or 1800 674 414

With so many waterways in the Northern Rivers region, boating is an obvious attraction. Inquire at a local visitors centre for info about the following and other trips.

Cruise the Richmond River by day or night on the **MV** *Richmond Princess*, located at Ballina. Wheelchair accessible by arrangement (Ph: 018 664 786 or (02) 6687 1216).

The **MV** *Bennelong* offers a trip from Ballina to Lismore, travelling along both the Richmond and Wilson Rivers. These rivers once provided the main access to the hinterland and are rich in the history of white settlement of the region. Wheelchair accessible. Ph: (02) 6688 8266 or 0414 664 552

Alternatively, try **Tweed Rainforest and River Cruises**, which traverses the Tweed River and the nearby Terranora Lakes, passing through rainforest, tilled ground, cane fields and the river terrain itself. A variety of cruises are available. Wheelchair accessible. Ph: (07) 5536 8800 or 1800 674 414

Festivals and events
Caldera First Light Festival

On New Year's Eve people gather at **Murwillumbah** in readiness for the 1st light of the new year. Mt Warning, which catches the 1st rays of sun on the Australian continent, is the focus of all eyes in this magical festival. Numbers are strictly limited. Ph: (02) 6672 6360 or (02) 6672 1340

Byron Bay Blues Festival

The internationally famous **Byron Bay** Blues Festival in late Mar has a mixture of the famous and the unknown as acts. Trumpets sound and saxes wail as everyone 'gets down and boogies'. Ph: (02) 6680 3600

Arts and crafts
The *Northern Rivers Antique Art and Craft Tours* pamphlet (available at visitors centres) outlines some of the many antique shops, art galleries, craft shops and studios within NNSW and groups them according to location.

From Murwillumbah to Mullumbimby

Tenterfield Oracles of the Bush

Discover the next Banjo Paterson at Oracles of the Bush, a festival celebrating bush literature and music in the pretty SW town of **Tenterfield**. The event, which attracts the crowds from near and far, is held over 3 days in mid-Apr. Ph: (02) 6736 1082

Richmond River Cane Festival

In early May the town of **Wardell** holds the Richmond River Cane Festival. As well as cane sampling and exhibiting, there are horse races, bands and poets, and tableloads of tucker. Ph: (02) 6686 3484

Mardi Grass Festival

Also in May, but with a very different flavour, is the Mardi Grass Festival in **Nimbin**. Organised by the Help End Marijuana Prohibition Embassy, this is a celebration of all things hemp. Music, food, activities for children and the odd bit of politicising combine to make the festival a heady affair. Ph: (02) 6622 0122

Beef Week

Twelve days don't make a week unless it's Beef Week, held in the last week of May in the beef capital of the Northern Rivers region, **Casino**. The town is the centre of the local cattle industry and turns on a treat with competitions, dances, rodeo, ball and Beef Queen contest. Ph: (02) 6662 1936

Casino Orchid Show

The **Casino** Orchid Show coincides with Beef Week and is a lovely display of blooms for amateur green fingers and professional gardeners alike. Ph: (02) 6662 3566

Wintersun Rock and Roll Nostalgia Festival

This is the largest rock and roll festival in Australia. Over 10 days in Jun, non-stop dancing leads the way in a fun-filled celebration of rock music. The festival is staged by the 'Twin Towns', **Tweed Heads** and **Coolangatta**. Ph: (07) 5536 1181

Evans Head Fishing Classic

Serious anglers head for **Evans Head** in Jun. This week-long competition offers prizes amounting to more than $30 000 and entertainment is provided at the Recreation Reserve (adjacent to the Silver Sands Caravan Park). There are different categories of competition, with prizes every night. In 1998 more than 1000 fishing enthusiasts participated in the event. Ph: (02) 6682 4611

Bentley Art Show

The many artists of the region gather together for this competition, held in late Jul at the Bentley Hall, **Bentley**, north of Casino. Works are for sale as well as viewing. Details are available at local visitors centres.

Seafood Bowling Carnival

Well-groomed bowling greens are everywhere in NNSW, revealing the sport's popularity among locals. In Aug the Evans Head Bowling Club, **Evans Head**, hosts a competition. A special feature is the seafood menu, caught in local waters. Ph: (02) 6682 4611

Casino Gold Cup

In mid-Aug the Gold Cup, **Casino**'s main racing event, is held at the Casino Showground. The event is the culmination of a year-long calendar of horse and greyhound events. Ph: (02) 6662 3566

Wintersun Rock and Roll Nostalgia Festival

Breakfast with the butchers

During **Casino's Beef Week** hundreds of people flock to eat a hearty breakfast of — what else? — beef, tended, prepared and served by the region's farmers.

Tweed Valley Banana Festival

Tweed Valley Banana Festival and Harvest Week

Murwillumbah goes bananas in late Aug during the Tweed Valley Banana Festival, a 12-day event including a street parade and carnival, 'State of Origin' dog trials, a billy cart 'Grand Prix', a spring orchid show and advice on 1001 ways to eat a banana. Ph: (02) 6672 6186

Northern Rivers Folk Festival

Take a drive down to **Lismore** in early Oct for the Northern Rivers Folk Festival. Ph: (02) 6621 7537

Spring Wine Festival

Tenterfield, on the edge of the Granite Belt (p.268), celebrates the ripening of the vine in a springtime festival of wine and song. This event also takes place in early Oct. Ph: (02) 6736 1082

Longboard Invitational

Evans Head lies between 2 beaches stretching to more than 20km of unbroken coastline. This position is ideal for the Longboard Invitational, heralding the start of the surfing season over a long weekend in Oct. Ph: (02) 6682 4611

Coraki Tea Tree Festival

Tea-tree oil production is the region's fastest growing agricultural industry, and over 2 days in late Oct locals gather on the banks of the Richmond River at **Coraki** to celebrate this native plant. Water sports, boat races, a street parade, stalls and entertainment are just some of the many activities — as well as the sampling of tea-tree oil products. Ph: (02) 6683 2622

Great Eastern Fly-in

Come Christmas and New Year, the skies above **Evans Head** are filled with light and ultralight planes. Aircraft come from all over Australia to participate in 3 days of flying, soaring and daredevil adventure. Ph: (02) 6682 4611

Doug Moran National Portrait Prize

The self-proclaimed richest portrait prize in the world, with an award of $100 000 for the winner and $1000 for each of the 30 finalists, finds its home at the Tweed River Regional Art Gallery (p.267), **Murwillumbah**. Finalist entries are hung from late Dec to the end of Jan, with the winning painting becoming part of the permanent collection. The competition began in 1988, the year in which the gallery opened. Ph: (02) 6672 0409

Main localities and towns

For ease of reference, towns have been listed alphabetically in 2 sections: on the coast and the hinterland.

On the coast
Ballina Map 50

Ballina sits at the mouth of the Richmond River on the Pacific Coast, 35km east of Lismore and 45km to Byron Bay's south. Ballina is a fishing town, but is also popular with family holiday-makers. **Shaws Bay** (Compton Dr) and **Shelly Beach** (Shelly Beach Rd) are both good spots for children. The latter even has a wading pool. Other attractions include river cruises (p.259), whale-spotting — especially in Jun–Jul — and the **Big Prawn** complex (Pacific Hwy), a seafood eatery with an enormous mock prawn on its roof.

Pioneer memorial
At the **Pioneer Memorial Park**, next to the Missingham Bridge, between Ballina and Lennox Head, the gravestones of early settlers have been set in bluestone, making a Pioneer Memorial Wall.

Post-it note
The **Empire Vale Post Office**, near Ballina, is one of the tiniest post offices in NSW. Built in 1946, it is still operating as a business.

Ballina Marina

Big Prawn, Ballina

visitors centre, which houses a restored raft from the La Balsa Expedition, a journey from Ecuador, South America to Australia in 1973. Wheelchair accessible. Open daily, 9am-4pm. Ph: (02) 6681 1002. Nearby is the **Memorial Pool**, with a giant slide. Hours vary according to season. Ph: (02) 6686 3771

Champion athletes come from all walks of life and Ballina takes this one step further with the **Kerry Saxby Walkway**, named in honour of local Olympic, Commonwealth and World walking champion Kerry Saxby. The walkway runs along the riverbank from the visitors centre to the ocean. Wheelchair accessible. Visible from the path is **South Ballina**, on the far side of the river and only accessible from the centre of Ballina by car ferry. Take a drive along River Dr and out towards the ocean to get a taste of the wild beauty and solitude of the area.

The **Ballina Opal and Gem Museum**, displaying a range of gemstones, opals, diamonds and crystals (which are also for sale), is housed in the same building. Wheelchair accessible. Open daily, 9am–5pm. Ph: (02) 6686 2559

Also of interest is the **Ballina Naval and Maritime Museum**, next to the

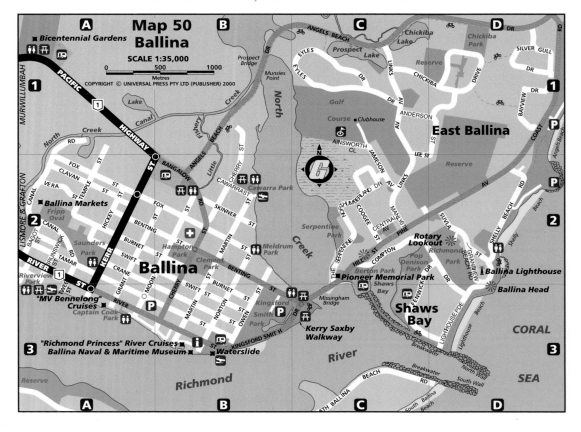

Byron Bay *Map 55*

At the easternmost point of the Australian continent is this popular tourist spot and mecca for surfers. White beaches fringe rolling green hills, with the 22m **Cape Byron Lighthouse** as landmark and beacon for both. Only 2.5hr from Brisbane, Byron Bay offers cosmopolitan dining, all manner of accommodation and non-stop street entertainment. The population is a mix of farmers, alternative lifestylers, backpackers and weekenders, who together contribute to making this one of the busiest places on the northern coast.

Beyond the beauty of the bay itself is an abundance of things to do. A must-see is the **Pighouse Flicks Cinema** (Skinners Shoot Rd), a casual spot with canvas-backed seats and a tropical garden. Open daily; varying sessions (Ph: (02) 6685 5828). The **Great Northern Hotel** (Jonson St) is a classic colonial hotel which also provides a venue for touring national and international bands in its famous 'Backroom' (Ph: (02) 6685 6454). **Wategos Beach**, just south of Byron, draws the serious surfer while families can safely swim or paddle at **Main Beach** before strolling up to the town centre (**Jonson** and **Lawson Sts**) for afternoon tea or a spot of shopping in one of the many stores lining the streets. Crystals, fine linen, tofu burgers and the very latest fashions are just some of the wonderfully eclectic range of goods on offer.

Evans Head *Map 49 D5*

This tiny village is the Dreamtime birthplace of the Bundjalung nation. Located 30km south of Ballina, the town is perched between the Broadwater (p.269) and Bundjalung NPs. Entry from the Pacific Hwy is via one of 2 sealed roads which wind their way through native heathland and forest.

Evans Head has a population of 2400 which swells to half as much again for the Evans Head Fishing Classic (p.262), which draws a crowd at the Longboard Invitational (p.263), and multiplies during the Christmas vacation. **Main Beach** and the **Shark Bay Picnic Area** are 2 favourite spots for holiday-makers. 'The Heads' has clubs, pubs, a market and plenty of eating places for after-hours revelry. For daytime adventure there are long clean beaches, the nearby **Evans River** (known locally as Little River) and the national parks.

As well as being a popular family holiday destination, the town's location offers keen sailors the chance to try their skill at sea or on the river. The **Evans Head Boat Harbour** has plenty of moorage, and is also the home of the local fishing fleet. The 1st Australian prawning fleet was established here, as was the 1st scientific cultivation of oysters in Australia. These days, Evans Head opens its doors to hikers, surfers, sunbathers and nature-lovers as well as retaining its working heart.

Byron Bay life
On the front of the **Byron Bay Community Centre** is a mural which depicts the pot pourri of people who make up the township.

Minjungbal Cultural Centre
The Minjungbal Aboriginal Cultural Centre, on Kirkland Rd, South Tweed Heads, is run by indigenous locals and provides info and entertainment about the Tweed Aboriginals and the natural environment. Open Mon–Fri, 9am–4pm; Sat, 9am–2pm. Ph: (07) 5524 2109

Cape Byron Lighthouse

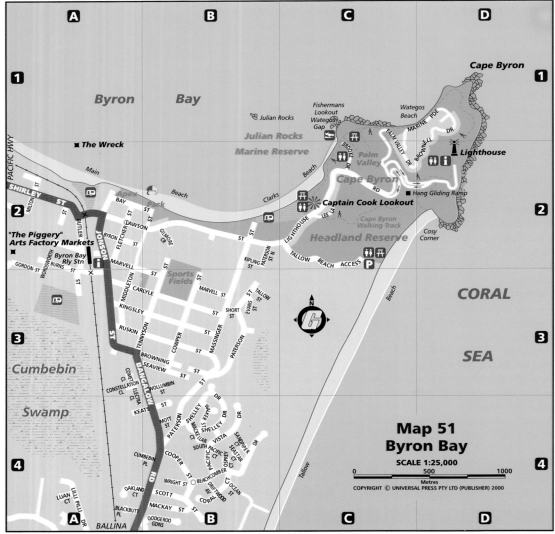

Map 51
Byron Bay

SCALE 1:25,000

0   500   1000
Metres

COPYRIGHT © UNIVERSAL PRESS PTY LTD (PUBLISHER) 2000

Tweed Heads *Map 49 D3*

There is no sense of hustle or bustle when entering Tweed Heads. The town has a leisurely approach to life and is best known for its fishing opportunities, gaming clubs and holiday facilities as well as being a home for retirees from more southern climes. Situated on the Qld–NSW border and at the mouth of the Tweed River, Tweed Heads shares the name 'Twin Towns' with its northern neighbour, Coolangatta (p.245).

The main shopping precinct, on the Pacific Hwy, faces **McMahons Beach**, a sheltered inland beach with picnic tables,

BBQs, playground, lawn area and a splendid **war memorial**. It is a perfect spot for toddlers, and the local visitors centre adjoins the parkland. Just down the road is one of the largest clubs in the area, the pink-and-purple **Twin Towns Services Club** (Pacific Hwy). National and international acts such as Kate Ceberano and Neil Sedaka feature here in a year-long calendar of events. The club offers free transport from regional towns and childcare. Wheelchair accessible. Open daily from 9am; closing times vary. Ph: (07) 5536 2277 or, for show bookings, (07) 5536 1977 or 1800 014 014. www.twintowns.com.au

The hinterland
Casino Map 49 C5

'Beef Capital of Australia' proclaims the sign as vehicles enter Casino, a regional centre with a population of 12 000. The town is located in the SW of NNSW and forms part of Richmond River Shire. Indeed, the Richmond River borders the town as it sweeps its way northwards towards Qld. Casino itself is host to the famous Beef Week (p.260) and is the main commercial and business centre for the Northern Rivers region. Colonial buildings such as the gorgeously pink **post office** hint at past wealth, and the town still exhibits a robust energy.

Abutting the town is the **Jabiru-Geneebeinga Wetlands** (Qld Rd). This seemingly quiet nook is teeming with insects, birds and small animals. Sit at one of the picnic tables and watch black swans and plovers make their way through the foliaged water. Toilets and a mini train (limited hrs) make this a good stop for small children. Also of interest is the **Platypus Pool** (Irving Bridge), home to one of the world's most unusual mammals. The platypus is a notoriously shy animal so visitors need to be patient, an easy task in this beautiful bushland setting.

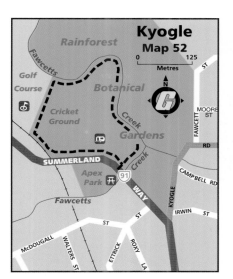

Lismore Map 53

Tucked away in the NE of the NNSW hinterland is the Rainbow Region's 'capital', the town of Lismore. With a population of 45 500, a university and 2 major shopping centres, this is a thriving place. Lismore is also rich in history, with several particularly fine examples of colonial architecture grouped together on Molesworth St. These include the **Lismore Municipal Building**, which houses a museum (open Mon-Fri, 10am–4pm), the **Commonwealth Bank** with its huge columns framing a stately

Kyogle bat colony
Take a stroll through the Botanical Gardens on the banks of Fawcetts Creek, Kyogle and discover the large fruit bat colony in residence here.
Distance: 1km
Duration: 15min.

South of the border

The Tweed Coast is one of the many attractions of NNSW. This 35km coastal stretch begins at Fingal, just below Tweed Heads, and has its southernmost point at the hamlet of Wooyung. Along the way are a series of tiny seaside towns, wetlands and coastal flora. Its northern end is marked by the **Tweed River**, a favourite fishing spot for generations of anglers. The river's estuaries are famous for Australia's largest mangrove jack but there are plenty of other species, including whiting, mulloway and mudcrab, to be found. Various drives are suggested by NSW Tourism but alternative routes are easily accessible. Not to be missed is the **coastal road** itself, a magical tour between forested terrain and pristine beaches. Along the way, sightseers can discover the region's first **lighthouse** at Fingal, try out the surf at **Cabarita**, or paddle at **Cudgera Creek** (p.271). Most townships are well provided with facilities, including boat ramps.

Play the pokies
For info on the many clubs in the Tweed area, contact **The Tweed Clubs**, PO Box 167, Tweed Heads, NSW 2485.

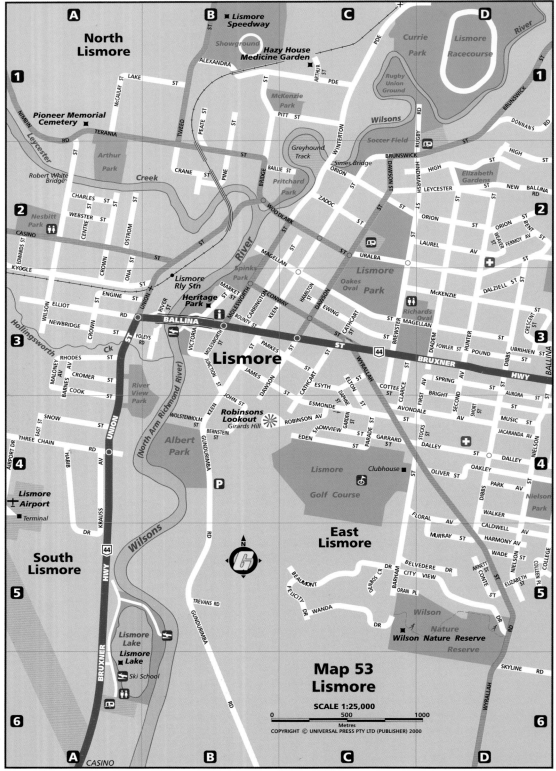

A **B** **C** **D**

North Lismore

■ *Lismore Speedway*

Showground

Hazy House
Medicine Garden ■

Currie Park *Lismore Racecourse*

River

1

LAKE ST ALEXANDRA ST

McKenzie Park

Rugby Union Ground

1

Pioneer Memorial
Cemetery ■

NIMBIN RD TERANIA ST
Leycester

Arthur Park

Creek

Robert White Bridge

CRANE ST PINE ST

PITT ST BAILLIE ST

BRIDGE ST

Greyhound Track

Simes Bridge

ORION ST

WINTERTON ST

Wilsons

Soccer Field

BRUNSWICK

RUGBY ST

HARSHM ST

DAWSON ST

HIGH ST

LEYCESTER ST

HIGH ST

Elizabeth Gardens

NEW ST BALLINA RD

DONNANS RD

BRUNSWICK ST

2

Nesbitt Park

CHARLES ST
WEBSTER ST
CENTRE ST
OSTROM ST

CASINO ST
EDWARDS ST
KYOGLE ST

CROWN ST ONA ST

ENGINE ST

ST

River

Spinks Park

WOODLARK ST

ZADOC ST

MAGELLAN ST

URALBA ST

Lismore Park

Oakes Oval

ORION ST

LAUREL AV

McKENZIE ST

ORION ST

WEAVER ST

FERMOY AV

BENT ST

DALZIELL ST

2

3

Hollingsworth Ck

RHODES ST
MALONEY AV
BARNES ST
CROMER ST
COOK ST

WILSON ST ELLIOT ST
NEWBRIDGE ST
CROWN ST

ENGINE ST

UNION ST

FOLEYS RD

RIVER ST

BALLINA ST

VICTORIA ST

MOLESWORTH ST

Lismore Rly Stn

Heritage Park ■

MARKET ST

MOLESWORTH ST

BOUNTY ST

CARRINGTON ST

KEEN ST

CONWAY ST

HAMILTON ST

DAWSON ST

EWING ST

CATHCART ST

Richards Oval

BREWSTER ST

MAGELLAN ST

FOWLER ST

HUNTER ST

POUND ST

DIADEM ST

UBRIHIEN ST

CRESCENT ST

BALLINA ST

3

Lismore

BRUXNER **44** **HWY**

4

AIRPORT DR

SNOW ST

THREE CHAIN RD

BABIH ST

KRAUSS AV

UNION ST

(North Arm Richmond River)

River View Park

Albert Park

JUNCTION ST

JAMES ST

DAWSON ST

JOHN ST

WOLSTENHOLM ST

BERNSTEIN ST

KEEN ST

Robinsons Lookout

Girards Hill ✳

CATHCART ST

ESYTH ST

ESMONDE ST

ROBINSON AV

EDEN ST

SHOWVIEW ST

DAPHNE ST

GARDEN ST

PARADE ST

ELTON ST

COTTEE ST

CLARICE ST

AVONDALE AV

GARRARD ST

STOCKS ST

SPRING AV

FIRST AV

BRIGHT ST

SECOND AV

SHORT ST

DALLEY ST

AURORA ST

MUSIC ST

JACARANDA AV

NIELSON ST

DALLEY ST

4

Lismore Airport ✈

■ Terminal

WYRALLAH ST

Lismore Golf Course

♿

Clubhouse ■

OLIVER ST

OAKLEY ST

DIBBS ST

PARK AV

Nielson Park

WALKER ST

5

South Lismore

44

BRUXNER HWY

Wilsons

RD

GUNDURIMBA RD

TREVANS RD

East Lismore

BEAUMONT DR

FELICITY DR

WANDA DR

DEMBOS CR

BARHAM DR

CITY VIEW DR

ORAN PL

BELVEDERE DR

ARNETT ST

CONTE ST

ELIZABETH ST

COLLEGE RD

Wilson Nature Reserve

FLORAL AV

CALDWELL AV

MURRAY ST

HARMONY AV

WADE ST

5

6

Lismore Lake

■ *Lismore Lake*

Ski School

GUNDURIMBA RD

Wilson Nature Reserve

Reserve

WYRALLAH RD

SKYLINE RD

Map 53
Lismore

SCALE 1:25,000

0 ——— 500 ——— 1000
Metres

COPYRIGHT © UNIVERSAL PRESS PTY LTD (PUBLISHER) 2000

6

A CASINO **B** **C** **D**

entrance, and the quaint former **Post and Telegraph office**, complete with lattice-worked cupola.

The **Lismore Regional Gallery**, 131 Molesworth St (Ph: (02) 6622 2209), is the 3rd oldest regional gallery in NSW and one of several galleries in the Northern Rivers region. It was opened in 1954 and houses a collection of significant Australian artists such as Margaret Olley, a native of the region, as well as work by contemporary local artists. Open Tue-Sat, 10am-4pm; Sun, 11am-3pm. Another sizeable gallery is the **Southern Cross University Art Museum**, Military Rd (Ph: (02) 6620 3883). Open Mon-Fri, 9am-5pm.

A highlight of Lismore for families is the **Tiny Tots Playground**, adjoining the Visitors and Heritage Centre. This inspired creation is designed for toddlers, and contains such delights as tiny swings and bridges, a mini railway (which operates Sat and Sun, 10am-4pm; Thur and holiday weekdays, 10am-2pm) and slides. The playground forms part of **Heritage Park**, which has picnic, BBQ and toilet facilities. Wheelchair accessible.

Alternatively, visitors can waterski on **Lismore Lake**, south of the town, or cruise the nearby **Richmond** and **Wilson Rivers**, both teeming with birdlife.

Murwillumbah *Map 54*

Murwillumbah is a treasure trove of colonial history as well as being the business and civic centre of the Tweed Valley. Situated only 30km SW of Tweed Heads, the town's horizon is dominated by Mt Warning. The town itself is hilly, giving excellent views over the valley where, among other crops, sugarcane, tropical fruits, tea and coffee are grown.

There are displays featuring the local flora and fauna at the **World Heritage Centre** (cnr Pacific Hwy and Alma St), which is attached to the visitors centre, and art works in the **Tweed River Regional Art Gallery** (Tumbulgum Rd), home of the famous Doug Moran National Portrait Prize (p.261). Open Wed-Sat, 10am-5pm. Ph: (02) 6672 0409

A stroll around the town centre will give a glimpse of its past lives, as exemplified by the 19th-century architecture of the **Mt Saint Patrick College** and the 1930s-style **Regent Cinema**. If looking for a quiet moment, seating and tables are located on the banks of the **Tweed River**, which borders the town. Here, small boats and keen anglers add to the view.

For those interested in the story of how the town developed, the **Murwillumbah Museum**, cnr Qld Rd and Bent St

Murwillumbah

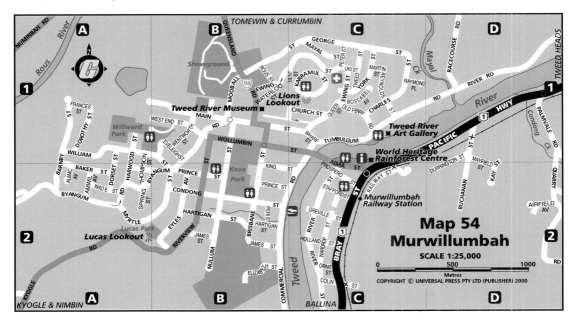

Cullen St, Nimbin

(Ph: (02) 6672 1865), has volunteers to help with queries as well as to show the mementoes on display. Open Wed and Fri, 11am–4pm; 4th Sun of the month, 11am–3pm. Other remnants of the past may be found at the **markets** held in Main St (1st Sat of the month), Knox Park (2nd and 4th Suns of the month) and the Showgrounds (every Sun).

Murwillumbah is also a central point for journeys to other attractions such as **Tree Tops Environment Centre**, between Condong and Cabarita Beach, (Ph: (02) 6672 3068), **Tropical Fruit World** (p.272), the **Pioneer Plantation** (p.272) and the **Tweed Coast** (p.265).

Nimbin *Map 55* ⑤

In 1973 Gough Whitlam was prime minister, the country was on the brink of change and the Aquarius Festival was held in the NNSW town of Nimbin. Previously a sleepy hamlet, the town has since become famous as the counter-cultural capital of Australia. Driving into its main roadway, **Cullen St**, Nimbin's alternative identity is immediately evident in the vividly painted shopfronts and the passing parade of hippies. The shops and cafes add to the flavour, offering hemp clothing and sunflower juice along with more traditional fare. Place names such as Alternative Way and **Protestor Falls** are common. The town is only 30km north of Lismore but feels like another world.

Nimbin Museum has a quirky overview of the history of hippy culture, while at the **Triple Blah Theatrette** short and unusual films are screened. The local pub, **Freemasons Hotel**, has a shaded back deck overlooking a valley, and is a pleasant place to while away an afternoon. All these sites are in Cullen St.

Just east of town is **Nightcap NP** (p.270) and, amid sprawling hills to the west, the majestic **Nimbin Rocks**, the result of volcanic activity millions of years ago. A drive around **Lillian Rock**, north of Nimbin, on an unsealed road offers chance views of the notoriously scarce lyrebird. This backroad travels all the way to Kyogle, past virgin forest and agricultural land. Birdsong and insect calls fill the air.

Tenterfield *Map 49 A5*

Not every country town can claim international fame, but Tenterfield is up there with the best of them thanks to its most famous son, singer-songwriter Peter Allen. The entertainer, who was born here, wrote the song 'Tenterfield Saddler' about his grandfather, who worked for some 50yrs as a saddler in the heritage-protected **Saddler's Shop** (High St). A little place made of blue granite, a sign on the shop's wall reminds customers, *In God we trust. All others cash.*

Tenterfield has another claim to fame – as the 'birthplace of the nation'. It was in this town, tucked away in the SW corner of NNSW, that Sir Henry Parkes, known as the 'Father of Federation', gave a speech in 1889 that set in motion the push towards federation of the Australian colonies.

Tenterfield is a pretty town that suggests prosperity. An avenue of maple trees lines its southern entrance and verandahs shade the main street, lined by an imposing array of buildings. These include a **masonic temple**, **courthouse** and the **Cameo Cafe**. The cafe is a step back into the 1950s, with its lolly counter, juke box, booths and all the trappings of the time. Highly recommended, especially for the chocolate malted milkshakes.

From Tenterfield there are day trips to nearby attractions such as **Bald Rock** (p.269). The town has an excellent *Visitor's Guide*, available from the local visitors centre.

National parks and nature reserves

NNSW has 6 World Heritage-listed wilderness areas, at least 14 state forests, countless parks and nature reserves, rainforest remnants and a series of mountain ranges. Terrains range from the brutal beauty of Mt Warning NP's crags and cliffs, to the coffee-coloured rocks of Broadwater NP, to the granite landscape of Bald Rock NP. Advice, maps and brochures are available from the NSW NPWS Info Centre.

Bald Rock NP *Map 49 A5*

Tucked away in the western corner of NNSW is this national park, once home to 2 groups of the Bundjalung people and at least 1 group from the Kamilaroi. These original inhabitants regarded Bald Rock itself — the largest granite rock in the southern hemisphere — as a sacred place, and indigenous guides are available to explain some of its significance (which persists today). **Bald Rock** is the largest of a series of granite domes, or inselbergs, that characterise this park, creating caves, canyons, archways and echo points. There are 2 walks to its summit: one is a steep 1.2km climb (with the 1st 300m on a sealed level path that is wheelchair accessible) and the other a 2.5km trek. Entry to Bald Rock NP is from the Mt Lindesay Hwy, 29km NE of Tenterfield. Picnic and camping facilities are available.

Border Ranges NP *Map 49 C4*

Looming over Nimbin and Kyogle is the Border Ranges NP, a thickly forested area including part of the largest subtropical rainforest in Australia. The 30 712ha park, as its name suggests, borders NSW and Qld. As well as eucalypts, gums, grasslands and 4 types of rainforest, the park includes an ancient Antarctic beech forest. About 25 percent of the bird species found in Australia live here, and birdwatchers can spend hours observing such species as the eastern yellow robin, white-throated warbler and regent bowerbird. Different species populate the different types of terrain. Entry to the park is from the Barkers Vale turnoff on the Murwillumbah-Kyogle road or at Wiangaree on Summerland Way. Roads are unsealed but negotiable in most weather conditions. Camping and picnicking are allowed at specified spots, and there are walking tracks of varying lengths.

Broadwater NP *Map 49 D5*

Broadwater NP is in southernmost NNSW, adjacent to the town of Evans Head. Until 1922, traditional lifestyles and initiation ceremonies took place in the area; nowadays, the local Bundjalung people mostly live on Cabbage Tree Island and Box Ridge, to the north and the west of the park respectively. Broadwater consists of 3800ha, including 8km of beach frontage, and its vegetation is predominantly heath and wetlands. Golden bush pea and swamp lilies are just 2 of the many wildflowers that bloom here in springtime, creating a ribbon of colour against the blue sea. A dirt road off the Broadwater-Evans Head road gives access to **Broadwater Beach** as well as a small picnic area with tables, toilets and BBQs. Much of the park is inaccessible to trekker or vehicle, but there is a lookout on the **Broadwater Headland** (wheelchair accessible) and a walking track to **Salty Lagoon** as well as a lookout on the beach.

Big rock

Bald Rock measures 750m in length, 500m in width, 260m in height and is 1227m high at its summit. The local people gave the name Boonoo Boonoo ('Big Rock') to the area before the arrival of white settlers.

Twilight, Byron Bay

Mt Warning NP

Cape Byron Headland Reserve
Map 51 C2

3km east of Byron Bay is Cape Byron Headland, a craggy reserve of coastal heath, littoral rainforest and banksia forest. Walking tracks wind around the cape, with goats grazing on the steep slopes. The 1901 **lighthouse** sits on the crest and is still in use today, its beam marking the night hours. Cape Byron is rich in Aboriginal and European history and holds great significance to the local Arakwal clan. There is some wheelchair accessibility.

Moore Park Nature Reserve *Map 49 C4*

This tiny reserve is perched on the NW edge of the Border Ranges. It includes the only viable remnant of gallery rainforest in NSW. The Richmond River runs along its edge. Only 20mins due north from **Kyogle**, Moore Park has been a popular picnic spot for locals since the 19th century, and picnic tables and wood-fuelled BBQs are situated at its entrance. The dominant plant species is the black bean, silky oak, prickly tea tree, flooded gum and the Moreton Bay fig are also found here. The picnic ground is wheelchair accessible.

Mt Warning NP *Map 49 C4*

To get to the summit of **Mt Warning** it is necessary to haul oneself up an incline with the help of a fixed chain. Once on top, there is a 360° view of the countryside from any one of 4 lookouts. The trek takes 4.4km. Mt Warning sits within 2210ha of rainforest, scrubland and wet forest, including giant stinging trees, brush box and booyangs. Over 100 species of birdlife have been recorded in the park, and there are many mammals and reptiles (watch out for snakes). Entry to the park is from the Murwillumbah-Kyogle road, 12km from Murwillumbah. BBQs and picnic areas are available, as are a variety of walking tracks.

Nightcap NP *Map 55* ⊙

This 4277ha national park is situated on the southern rim of the Mt Warning caldera. The park is of deep spiritual significance to the Bundjalung people and it is believed that burials and initiations once took place here. Nightcap NP is rich in rainforest because of its volcanic soil and high rainfall. It also includes brush box, eucalypts and palm forests. The park is located 30km SW of Murwillumbah, and there are 3 entry points to it: from a sealed road 12km out of Nimbin, from Terania Creek Rd at The Channon, or via the Lismore-Mullumbimby road near Dorroughby (dry weather only). There are some picnic areas in the park.

Mt Warning

NNSW is dominated by Mt Warning and the effects of its eruption millions of years ago. A cone-shaped mountain with two 'shoulders', Mt Warning is now situated within a 2210ha national park. Once, however, it was the central point of the largest shield volcano of the region. It stood at 2000m, now 1157m, and its lava flows covered some 5000km². The mountain remains highly significant to the local indigenous people, who call it 'Wollumbin' (fighting chief of the mountains). Mt Warning received its English name from Captain Cook, who sailed past in 1770. He intended the name to serve as a warning of the treacherous reefs off the coast. One of the features of the mountain is its caldera, or bowl-shaped cavity, carved out over aeons by wind and rain. This gives Mt Warning a distinctive landform of rugged beauty.

Rocky Creek
Rocky Creek Dam, next to **Nightcap NP**, is a beautiful spot for picnickers and bushlovers. Facilities, including a boardwalk, are provided.

Terania Creek, Nightcap NP

Victoria Park Nature Reserve
Map 49 C5

In the 19th century a vast lowland rainforest, known as the 'Big Scrub', covered 75 000ha of NNSW (roughly the same size as present-day Sydney). It stretched from Mullumbimby to Lismore to Ballina. White settlers destroyed most of the forest and today there are only remnants, one of which is Victoria Park. Located 16km SE of Lismore, the park is made up of 17.5ha, including 8ha of rainforest. A sheltered clearing, including picnic tables and BBQs, is an ideal place to stop for lunch and ballgames. Victoria Park Reserve has several walks, one of which is a **100m boardwalk** (wheelchair accessible).

Parks and gardens
Bicentennial Leisure Gardens
Map 55 ❹

This 54ha environmental park was created in 1988 as one of Australia's many Bicentennial Year projects. It adjoins **Pottsville**, and is set between 2 arms of **Cudgera Creek**. The park includes coastal eucalypt forest, heath and rainforest remnants, and fresh and saltwater wetlands. There are walking tracks, picnic amenities, BBQs, fresh drinking water and a large grassed area.

Cudgen Lake *Map 49 D4*
At Cudgen Lake, **Cudgen**, absolute solitude can be found amid the trees and the reeds. The preservation of the natural setting comes before anything else, so the only access point is from an unsealed road. The area also includes the **Cudgen Nature Reserve** and a boat ramp.

Cudgera Creek *Map 55* ❸
Not far away from Cudgen Lake is Cudgera Creek, at **Hastings Pt.** The mouth of the creek forms a shallow-water spot for fishing, swimming, sunbathing and canoeing. Picnic tables, BBQs and some play equipment are provided. This is a great place for families with toddlers.

Knox Park *Map 55* ❺
A pleasant stroll along the Peace Walk at Knox Park, **Murwillumbah**, can be followed by a quiet rest beside the park's pond. Here, a statue entitled 'The Cedar Cutter' commemorates the timbergetters who opened up the Tweed Valley to white settlement in the 1840s. For younger travellers, a skate ramp and playground are available.

Lumley Park *Map 49 D5*
Hidden away at the Lismore entrance to **Alstonville** lies Lumley Park, a tiny area of untouched bushland with a track winding through its rambling foliage. Next to the park is a large camomile lawn and a quaint disused croquet clubhouse dated 1931. Across the road are toilets and picnic tables.

Fingal memory
At the **Fingal Lighthouse** is a plaque embedded in the ground which reads: *Pip Masters, 1904–1992. Born on this site to Alf and Mary Masters (nee Arnold). Grandson of William Arnold, first keeper of Fingal Lighthouse.*

**Crystal Castle,
Montecollum**

Other attractions

Crystal Castle *Map 55* ❼

The Crystal Castle (Monet Dr, **Montecollum**) is in the beautiful surrounds of the hinterland close to Byron Bay, via Coolamon Scenic Dr. An array of natural crystals and gems are on show. Open daily, 10am–4.30pm. Ph: (02) 6684 3111

Melaleuca Stn *Map 49 D4*

The recently constructed Melaleuca Stn (Pacific Hwy, **Chinderah**) recreates the architecture and atmosphere of a 1920s railway station. The property is located between Tweed Heads and Murwillumbah, and is visible from the hwy. Its grandiose facade emerges from the green landscape like some strange dream of glories past. On entering the grounds, visitors are offered damper with billy tea, before boarding a coal-fired steam train and riding through a tea-tree plantation. There is an animal nursery to visit, and a chance to paddle in the lake and watch bush entertainment. (Remember to wear a hat.) Wheelchair accessible. Open daily, 10am–5pm. Ph: (02) 6674 3777

New Italy Museum *Map 49 C6*

Italian immigrants settled in the NNSW region in the 19th century, and their descendants live here still.

Commemorating the Italian contribution to the local culture is the New Italy Museum, located **SW of Woodburn**. The complex includes an old school and there is the opportunity to taste Italian cuisine. Open daily, 10am–5pm. Ph: (02) 6682 2622

Open-air Cathedral *Map 55* ❸

Drive through forested hills and nut plantations to the hamlet of **Bexhill** and visit the Open-air Cathedral. A simple cross and altar made out of stone sit before logs marking 'pews' on **Inspiration Pt**, overlooking the Corndale Valley and the Nightcap NP. Occasional church services such as the Easter ceremonies are celebrated here. At any time this is a place for quiet reflection. Wheelchair accessible (except in wet weather).

Pioneer Plantation *Map 49 D4*

The leaves of the banana plant provide a canopy for explorers at the Pioneer Plantation (Pottsville Rd, **Mooball**), located 25km SE of Murwillumbah. Owned and run by the descendants of early settlers of the district, this is an operating banana plantation. Other attractions include native gardens, indigenous and exotic animals, guided walks and picnic facilities. Wheelchair accessible. Open daily, 10am–5pm. Ph: (02) 6677 1215

**Mountaintop
prayer**

*Enter the temple
   beautiful,
the house not made of
   hands,
rainwashed and green,
windswept and clean,
beneath the blue it
   stands
and no cathedral
   anywhere
seemeth so lovely and
   so fair.*

Inscription at the Open-
air Cathedral, **Bexhill**

Melaleuca Stn, Chinderah

Pioneer Plantation, Mooball

Thursday Plantation *Map 49 D5*

At Thursday Plantation (Pacific Hwy, **Ballina**), all things teatree are on offer. Visitors can learn about the tea tree from seed to retail product, or wander through the 10 000 teatree maze. There is a cafe, aromatic gardens, guided tours and an annual sculpture show, as well a natural amphitheatre where musical performances often take place. Wheelchair accessible. Open daily, 9am–5pm. Ph: (02) 6686 7273

Tropical Fruit World *Map 49 D4*

There are many treats on offer at Tropical Fruit World (Duranbah Rd, **Duranbah**), set in 65ha of subtropical bushland. These include native animals, a mini train, a 'magic garden' with such delights as 'Chewing Gum' trees and 'Chocolate Pudding' fruit, and a ride through the plantations of bananas, pineapples and guava. Wheelchair accessible. Open daily, 10am–5pm. Ph: (02) 6677 7222

Tweed Maritime Museum *Map 49 D3*

The sometimes treacherous NNSW coastline has occasioned many tales of heartbreak and heroism. At the Tweed Maritime Museum (Pioneer Park, Kennedy Dr, **Tweed Heads West**), some of this history is outlined in

exhibits, including an electronic display of Captain Cook's voyages and a special room given over to the *Centaur* tragedy. In a nearby building is a **photographic gallery** of the Tweed and Twin Towns area. Wheelchair accessible. Open Tue, Fri and the 3rd Sun of the month, 11am–4pm. Ph: (07) 5536 8625

Recreational activities

Action

When the sky is overcast or it's time for a break from the sunbathing, go tenpin bowling at **Ballina Bowl**, 16 Clark St (Ph: (02) 6686 5342), or try out the

Whale-watching

rollerskating at the **Ballina Indoor Sports and Skate Centre**, Barlows Rd (Ph: (02) 6686 2806).

Practise climbing at **Wave Rock Byron Bay Indoor Rockclimbing Centre**, 1/91 Centennial Circuit (Ph: (02) 6680 8777). No experience is necessary on any of the 50 or so climbs. Then try it out for real with **Pioneering Spirit**, a guided climb of Mt Warning. The journey begins at 9.30am and ends at 5.30pm. Ph: (02) 6685 7721

In the air

The terrain of NNSW is even more striking from the air. Try **Byron Air Charter** (Ph: (02) 6684 1416) or **Barnstormers Australia** (Ph: 0412 078 869) for joyflights. **Ballina Flying School** also offers casual rides, including whale-watching trips. Ph: (02) 6686 8588

For those who want to feel the wind against their faces, **Skydive** (Ph: (02) 6685 7755), **Skylimit** (Ph: (02) 6684 3711) and **Byron Airwaves** (Ph: (02) 6629 0354) offer hang gliding, skydiving and microlight flights. All 3 companies are based at Byron Bay.

Cycling

Cycling is a popular activity in the coastal areas of NNSW. Evans Head, Ballina and Lennox Head have developed a cycleway network, and brochures showing paths and sights are available from the local visitors centre. For info on other cycling opportunities or bike hire, inquire at any visitors centre.

Golf

Teven Golf Course (Elthan Rd, Teven) is one of the many courses in NNSW. Located at Teven, 10km NW of Ballina, the privately owned 9-hole course is set in manicured greens amid the lush hinterland. A full listing of NNSW courses is available from visitors centres. Ph: (02) 6687 8386

Horseriding

Ride along a deserted beach with **Byron Beach Rides** (Ph: (02) 6684 7499). **Chillingham Trailrides** offer mountain treks. Ph: (02) 6679 1369

House boat, Tweed River

On and in the water

Byron Bay Sea Kayaks offers 2 sessions per day, with breakfast or afternoon tea included. Ph: (02) 6685 5830

At **Canoe Tours** the day's adventure begins at 9.30am and ends at 4pm, with a pickup from any Byron Bay accommodation. The canoe journey is from Mullumbimby to Brunswick Heads. Lunch is supplied. Canoe Tours also offers a 2–3day trip on the Upper Clarence River. Ph: (02) 6687 1092

As well as providing surfers with the largest unbroken sea line on the northern coast, Lennox Head gives sailors and windsurfers a chance on Lake Ainsworth. **Lennox Head Sailing** offers lessons and sailboard, catamaran and ski hire. There are picnic tables and BBQs for those who simply want to watch. Ph: (02) 6687 6010

'Do it yourself' on a houseboat. **Tweed River House Boats** offers wheelchair accessible vessels for a lazy holiday in beautiful surrounds. Ph: (07) 6672 3525 or 1800 674 414

Charter a vessel at **Ballina Charters** (Ph: (02) 6681 1833) or **Cape Byron Marine Charter Services** (Ph: (066) 856 858) for sightseeing, fishing (bait and tackle supplied) and whale- and dolphin-spotting. Other houseboat and charter companies operate in the region; contact a visitors centre for local details.

The Northern Rivers region, with its network of waterways and the Pacific Ocean to the east, provides some of the best fishing spots in Australia. For info on fishing spots and regulations, ask at visitors centres or call local **Fishwatch** offices. Ph: 1800 043 536 for regional numbers. The ABC-Radio North Coast Fishing Report is presented every Fri and Sat at 6.20am.

Feel the rush of adrenalin with whitewater rafting, offered by **Wildwater Adventures** (Ph: (02) 6653 4469), with pick-ups from Byron Bay. Trips range from 1–4 days, on creeks and rivers. No previous experience is necessary.

Scuba-diving is available at **Sundive** (Ph: (02) 6685 7755). The company has a

Surfing off the Tweed Coast

dive training pool at Byron Bay as well as offering daily dive and snorkelling trips. **Buddyline Dive Tours** also offers scuba-diving at Byron Bay, Pottsville and Tweed Heads. Ph: 1800 814 222

Learn to Surf at Byron Bay (Ph: 1800 707 274) offers professional instruction, free equipment (including wetsuits) and the chance to share a wave with a dolphin. Former US surf champion **Rusty Miller** also offers instruction with all equipment provided, along the coast. Ph: (02) 6684 7390

For a really special experience, try **Surfaris**. The company organises fantastic trips which travel between Sydney and Byron Bay offering surfing lessons, camping, a wilderness experience and great company along the way. Qualified instructors guide travellers along the coastal route taken by surfers in the 1960s with the advent of the Malibu surfboard. Surfaris include free return trips to Sydney every Sun. Ph: 1800 634 951

Tropical Fruit World, Duranbah

Fun for the young

★ Bald Rock NP (p.269)

★ Bat colony, Kyogle (p.265)

★ Knox Park, Murwillumbah (p.271)

★ Main Beach, Byron Bay (p.263)

★ Melaleuca Station, Chinderah (p.272)

★ Protestor Falls, Nimbin (p.268)

★ Tiny Tots Playground, Lismore (p.267)

★ Tropical Fruit World, Duranbah (p.273)

A nutty feast
Macadamia nuts are one of the primary crops in the region, and **Christmas All Year Round** (cnr Alphadale Rd and Bruxner Hwy, Alphadale) boasts that it has the largest range of macadamia products in the southern hemisphere.

Suggested tours – Map 55

Mountain tour

Approximate distance
567km return from Brisbane CBD

About the tour
Explore the magnificent heritage-protected inland scenery of NNSW on this trip around the mountains. Starting the trip with a stroll down Lismore's historical precinct, Molesworth St, it's only a short drive from there to the Open-air Cathedral, Bexhill, and a view of clouds and treetops. Venturing further north, the rugged Nightcap NP offers hiking opportunities and nearby attractions such as Protester Falls. The hippie town of Nimbin gives the opportunity to observe some counter-culture before, turning southwards again, travellers pass the needle-like Nimbin Rocks and more picturesque scenery. A cup of tea and a hot scone at The Channon will give weary travellers a new lease of life on the way home.

Places of interest
❶ **Tiny Tots Playground, Lismore** (p.267)
❷ **Molesworth St, Lismore** (p.265)
❸ **Open-air Cathedral, Bexhill** (p.272)
❹ **Protester Falls, Nimbin** (p.268)
❺ **Nimbin** (p.268)
❻ **Nightcap NP** (p.270)
❼ **Nimbin Rocks** (p.268)
❽ **The Channon** (p.270)

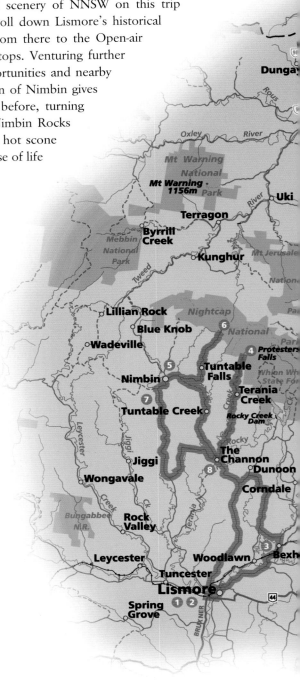

Kingscliff

Beachcombing tour

Approximate distance

375km return from Brisbane CBD

About the tour

This tour takes in some of the most stunning coastline in eastern Australia. From the mouth of the Tweed River to the white sands of Byron Bay, a winding route passes through spectacular scenery and a variety of terrain. Bustling townships sit side by side with untouched bushland, with the lagoon-like Cudgera Creek and the Bicentennial Leisure Gardens, Pottsville, lying within a short distance of one another. Climb a track to historic Cape Byron Lighthouse or stop for lunch on the esplanade at Kingscliff; each stop will give a different view. Homeward-bound, call in at the pretty town of Murwillumbah.

Places of interest

❶ **Tweed Heads clubs** (p.265)

❷ **Kingscliff Esplanade**

❸ **Cudgera Creek, Hastings Pt** (p.271)

❹ **Bicentennial Leisure Gardens, Pottsville** (p.271)

❺ **Byron Bay** (p.263)

❻ **Cape Byron Lighthouse** (p.263)

❼ **Crystal Castle, Montecollum** (p.272)

❽ **Knox Park, Murwillumbah** (p.271)

❾ **Tweed River Regional Art Gallery** (p.267)

Index and Gazetteer

Brisbane Digital Coverage Map

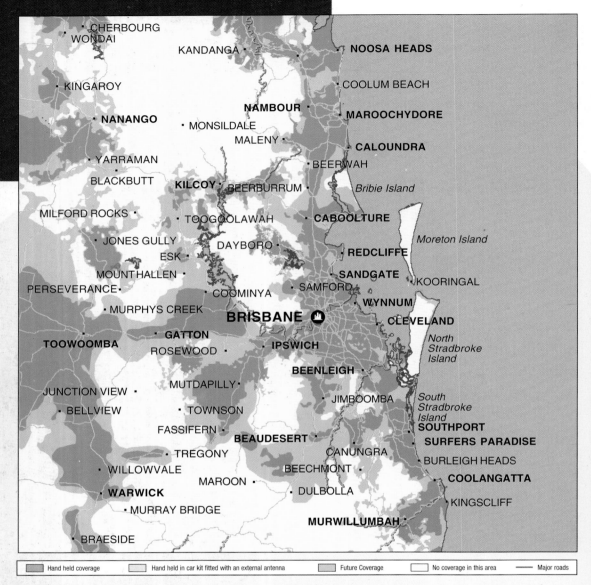

Hand held coverage	Hand held in car kit fitted with an external antenna	Future Coverage	No coverage in this area	—— Major roads

This coverage map shows the extent of the Telstra MobileNet® Digital service generally at the time of publication. It also shows the planned coverage expansion of Telstra MobileNet Digital service based on the targeted rollout schedule at the time of publication. As it may be necessary to change or modify the rollout schedule, Telstra reserves the right to do this without notice. The percentage of total land areas of Australia covered by Telstra MobileNet Digital service is about 5% and the percentage of the total population of Australia within this coverage is about 94%. As with any radio system there are places inside the marked coverage area where a mobile phone may not work due to a variety of factors. For example, radio reception can be degraded or non-existent in certain places, particularly basements, lifts, underground car parks and large buildings. However, MobileNet Digital is endeavouring to provide the best depth of radio reception practicable into such areas. Reception can also be affected by mountains, tunnels and road cuttings.

If you have any questions as to the Telstra MobileNet® service coverage please ring the Telstra MobileNet coverage information line on **018 018 888** (no call charge †), or contact your local Telstra MobileNet Dealer.

http://www.telstra.com.au

For other information call Telstra MobileNet Customer Service on **018 018 111** (no call charge †)

Telstra Corporation Limited A.C.N. 051 775 556
®Registered trade mark of Telstra Corporation Limited
†No call charge when call is made from a Telstra service